DEFINING NEIGHBORS

JEWS, CHRISTIANS, AND MUSLIMS
FROM THE ANCIENT TO THE MODERN WORLD

Edited by Michael Cook, William Chester Jordan, and Peter Schäfer

A list of titles in this series appears at the back of the book.

DEFINING NEIGHBORS

Religion, Race, and the Early Zionist-Arab Encounter

Jonathan Marc Gribetz

PRINCETON UNIVERSITY PRESS
PRINCETON AND OXFORD

Published by Princeton University Press, 41 William Street,
Princeton, New Jersey 08540
In the United Kingdom: Princeton University Press, 6 Oxford Street,
Woodstock, Oxfordshire OX20 1TW
press.princeton.edu
Detail of map: Hans Fischer, Palästina, 1890. Eran Laor
Cartographic Collection, The National Library of Israel.

Library of Congress Cataloging-in-Publication Data
Gribetz, Jonathan Marc, 1980– author.
Defining neighbors : religion, race, and the early Zionist-Arab
encounter / Jonathan Marc Gribetz.
pages cm. — (Jews, Christians, and Muslims from the ancient
to the modern world)
Includes bibliographical references and index.
ISBN 978-0-691-15950-8 (hardcover)
1. Zionism—History—20th century. 2. Palestinian Arabs—History—
20th century. 3. Jewish-Arab relations. 4. Khalidi, Ruhi, 1864–1913.
5. Ben-Yehuda, Eliezer, 1858–1922. 6. Palestine—History—1799–1917.
7. Palestine—History—1917–1948. I. Title.
DS149.G738 2014
320.54095694—dc23
2013040012
British Library Cataloging-in-Publication Data is available
This book has been composed in Charis
Printed on acid-free paper. ∞
Printed in the United States of America
1 3 5 7 9 10 8 6 4 2

To Sarit, Sophie, Daniela, and Max

Contents

Acknowledgments ix

Note on Transliterations xiii

Introduction 1

CHAPTER 1
Locating the Zionist-Arab Encounter: Local, Regional, Imperial, and Global Spheres 15

CHAPTER 2
Muhammad Ruhi al-Khalidi's "as-Sayūnīzm": An Islamic Theory of Jewish History in Late Ottoman Palestine 39

CHAPTER 3
"Concerning Our *Arab* Question"? Competing Zionist Conceptions of Palestine's Natives 93

CHAPTER 4
Imagining the "Israelites": Fin de Siècle Arab Intellectuals and the Jews 131

CHAPTER 5
Translation and Conquest: Transforming Perceptions through the Press and Apologetics 185

Conclusion 235

Bibliography 249

Index 269

Acknowledgments

I am indebted to many for their assistance and support as I wrote this book, and it is a pleasure to have this opportunity to express my appreciation.

I began this project as a doctoral candidate at Columbia University, where I came to study Jewish history with Yosef Hayim Yerushalmi, of blessed memory, and Michael Stanislawski. In seminars with Yerushalmi and Stanislawski, I observed how great historians read and analyze texts; I hope that their influences are recognizable here. As my graduate studies progressed, my research interest in Zionism led me to Middle Eastern history. Rashid Khalidi, through his research, mentorship, and generosity, sent me on a journey into the fascinating world of Late Ottoman Palestine from which I have yet to emerge. Khalidi also kindly shared with me Muhammad Ruhi al-Khalidi's unpublished manuscript, a text that sparked many of the questions that drive this book. My committee also included two scholars from other universities, Derek Penslar and Ronald Zweig, who treated me—and have continued to treat me—as their own.

As I was completing my dissertation, I had the privilege of spending a year at the Center for Advanced Judaic Studies at the University of Pennsylvania, where I was welcomed by the center's director David Ruderman. My conversations there with other scholars interested in secularism and modern Jewish history—including Annette Aronowicz, Ari Joskowicz, David Myers, Amnon Raz-Krakotzkin, Daniel Schwartz, Scott Ury, and Yael Zerubavel—were most helpful as I considered some of the implications of my work. At the CAJS I also gained a dear colleague and friend, Ethan Katz, who has read and critiqued many parts of this book multiple times.

After I finished my doctorate, the indefatigable Hindy Najman graciously invited me to the University of Toronto. I had the opportunity there to work more closely with my mentor Derek Penslar, who took me under his wings and has wisely and selflessly guided me intellectually and professionally ever since. In Toronto, I also benefited greatly from the intellectual friendships of Doris Bergen, Sol Goldberg, Jens Hanssen, Jeffrey Kopstein, Alejandro Paz, Robin Penslar, Natalie Rothman, and Harold Troper.

I continued working on the manuscript of this book as an assistant professor at Rutgers, where I was blessed with wonderful colleagues in the Jewish Studies and History departments. Toby Jones, Hilit Surowitz-Israel, Paola Tartakoff, Azzan Yadin-Israel, and Yael Zerubavel read key portions of the manuscript and provided critical advice. Other Rutgers colleagues, including Debra Ballentine, Douglas Greenberg, Paul Hanebrink, Jennifer Jones, James Masschaele, Sara Milstein, Eddy Portnoy, Gary Rendsburg, Jeffrey Shandler, Nancy Sinkoff, Camilla Townsend, and Eviatar Zerubavel, helped make my time at Rutgers exciting and productive. I am grateful as well to Arlene Goldstein and Sherry Endick for their exceptional administrative support.

While revising the manuscript, I benefited from the vast knowledge and abundant generosity of Israel Bartal and Israel Gershoni, two scholars who, to my great fortune, were spending the academic year in New Jersey.

Other friends and colleagues who have read and commented on parts of this manuscript at various stages include Leora Batnitzky, Julia Phillips Cohen, Chaim Cutler, Alan Dowty, Jessica Fechtor, Benjamin Fisher, Jackie Gram, David Horowitz, Abigail Jacobson, David Koffman, Steven Lipstein, Jessica Marglin, Eli Osheroff, Elias Sacks, Daniel Stolz, and Joseph Witztum. Omid Ghaemmaghami meticulously reviewed my Arabic transliterations; Rachel Feder painstakingly proofread the entire book; and Menachem Butler provided electronic bibliographical support.

Jeremy Dauber, Martha Himmelfarb, Jeffrey Prager, Peter Schäfer, Debora Silverman, and Moulie Vidas have offered sage counsel at every turn.

I received valuable feedback when I presented parts of this project at workshops and symposiums at Brown, Harvard, Princeton, and Yale, and at the annual conferences of the Associations of Jewish Studies, Israel Studies, and Middle Eastern Studies.

I also obtained important suggestions from the anonymous reviewers of two articles I have published that emerged from this project: "An Arabic-Zionist Talmud: Shimon Moyal's *At-Talmud*," *Jewish Social Studies* 17, no. 1 (Indiana University Press, 2010), and " 'Their Blood Is Eastern': Shahin Makaryus and *Fin de Siècle* Arab Pride in the Jewish 'Race,' " *Middle Eastern Studies* 49, no. 2 (Taylor & Francis, 2013). I thank the editors and publishers of these journals for allowing me to include some of this material here.

I gathered most of the sources on which this book is based during a year of research in Jerusalem. I am grateful to the staffs of the Central Zionist Archives, Israel State Archives, al-Aqsa Library, Haifa Municipal Archive, Jerusalem Municipal Archive, Lavon Labor Archive, Rishon Lezion Archive, and Central Archives for the History of the Jewish People. I am especially thankful to Haifaʾ al-Khalidi, who not only opened the renowned Khalidiyya Library to me for weeks on end but also welcomed my wife and me into her historic Jerusalem home. My months at the Central Zionist Archives were made particularly pleasant by the friendship of, and frequent coffee breaks with, Noah Haiduc-Dale.

I could not have undertaken my research without the support of foundations and fellowships that had faith in me and my project. These include the Wexner Graduate Fellowship, Schusterman Israel Scholarship, U.S. Department of Education's Foreign Language and Area Studies fellowship, Kathryn Wasserman Davis Critical Language Fellowship for Peace at Middlebury College, Memorial Foundation for Jewish Culture, and Foundation for Jewish Culture. To assist in the preparation of the manuscript, I received generous grants from Columbia's Institute for Israel and Jewish Studies and from the Israel Institute.

As my work on this book comes to a close, I have been fortunate to return to two old-new intellectual homes. I spent a year at Harvard's Center for Jewish Studies, where I was graciously welcomed back by Shaye Cohen, Peter Gordon, Rachel Greenblatt, Jay Harris, and Ruth Wisse. And I embark on a new position at Princeton in Near Eastern Studies and Judaic Studies, joining the extraordinary faculty and intellectual community that inspired me as I was writing my dissertation years earlier in Firestone Library.

Fred Appel of Princeton University Press has been enthusiastic about this project from our first meeting in Toronto and has, with the assistance of Sarah David, Juliana Fidler, and Ali Parrington, shepherded it along with great care. Anita O'Brien copyedited the book and Tom Broughton-Willett compiled the index.

My parents, Rhonda and Michael Gribetz, have generously supported and lovingly encouraged me as I pursued a career in academia. My father insisted on reading every paper I wrote along the way, and my mother, who proofread key portions of the manuscript, made sure I took care of myself and always looked like a *mensch*. I am also grateful to my mother-in-law, Esther Dreifuss-Kattan, my father-in-law, Shlomo Kattan, and Miriam Lewensztain, who, from across the country, took great interest in this project; to my brothers Eric and Seth, sisters-in-law Carin, Orit, and Gabriela, and brother-in-law Pavel for their advice, generosity, and good cheer; and to my grandmother Florence Gribetz, who has inspiringly modeled open-mindedness and endless learning.

Finally, I express my boundless love and gratitude to my wife, Sarit Kattan Gribetz, whose sharp, critical mind made a mark on every page of this book. From our sweet daughters, Daniela and Sophie, identical-but-different twins, I have learned much about self and other and the porous boundary in between, while our son, Max, born just as I was completing this manuscript, reminds me that seemingly fixed groups and categories such as "our family" can expand, with love.

Note on Transliterations

In transliterating Arabic and Ottoman Turkish, I have generally followed the *International Journal of Middle East Studies* transliteration guide. In transliterating Hebrew and Yiddish, I have generally followed the *Encyclopaedia Judaica* transliteration guide. For ease of reading, in the body of the book personal names and foreign words that have entered the English lexicon are written without diacritical marks. For the benefit of those interested in locating referenced texts, the transliterations in the bibliographical information provided are more precise. For the sake of consistency in transliteration between Hebrew and Arabic text titles, I have capitalized only the first letter of the first word (unless the title begins with a definite article, in which case I have capitalized the letter immediately following the article) and personal names found within the title. For Hebrew, I have generally followed the rule that a sheva under the first letter of a word is a sheva naʿ (a rule Ben-Yehuda followed in transliterating the name of his newspaper in the masthead as *Hazewi*), except in the body of the book when noting proper names that have a conventional English spelling (such as in the last name of Israel's second president, Ben-Zvi).

DEFINING NEIGHBORS

Introduction

On the final Saturday of October 1909, two members of Palestine's intellectual elite met for an interview in Jerusalem. Eliezer (Perelman) Ben-Yehuda, fifty-one at the time, had immigrated to Palestine from Russian Lithuania nearly thirty years earlier. Muhammad Ruhi al-Khalidi, eight years Ben-Yehuda's junior, was born in Jerusalem, though he spent much of his adult life outside of Palestine, in France and Istanbul. These men had much in common, aside from their shared city. Both had received traditional religious educations—Ben-Yehuda in the Hasidic Jewish world of Eastern Europe, al-Khalidi in the Sunni Muslim environment of Ottoman Palestine—and, like many of their intellectual contemporaries, both had also tenaciously pursued modern, secular studies. Ben-Yehuda made his career in journalism in Jerusalem, while al-Khalidi first became involved in academia in France and finally found his place in Ottoman imperial politics. Each believing that the fates of the Zionists and Arabs in Palestine were linked, Ben-Yehuda and al-Khalidi, friends for some time, met that Saturday, just before al-Khalidi was to return to Istanbul as one of Jerusalem's three representatives to the newly reconstituted Ottoman Parliament (see figures 1 and 2).

I began my research for this book in an attempt to discern how Zionists like Ben-Yehuda and Arabs like al-Khalidi thought about one another in the earliest years of their encounter, in the Late Ottoman period.[1] In the late twentieth and early twenty-first centuries—after about a hundred years of violent conflict—mutual hatred and delegitimization between Zionists and Arabs have dominated much of each side's discourse about its counterpart. Many versions of such discourse circulate: *there is no such thing as a "Palestinian"; contemporary Jews are merely Europeans with no connection to the Holy Land; there were hardly any Arabs in*

[1] The classic work on Zionist-Arab relations during the Late Ottoman period remains Mandel, *The Arabs and Zionism before World War I.* See also Roʾi, "The Zionist Attitude to the Arabs 1908–1914"; Roʾi, "Yeḥasei yehudim-ʿarvim be-moshavot ha-ʿaliyah ha-rishonah"; Roʾi, "The Relationship of the Yishuv to the Arabs"; Beʾeri, *Reshit ha-sikhsukh yisraʾel-ʿarav, 1882–1911*; Shafir, *Land, Labor, and the Origins of the Israeli-Palestinian Conflict, 1882–1914*; Marcus, *Jerusalem 1913*; Campos, *Ottoman Brothers*; Jacobson, *From Empire to Empire.*

FIGURE 1. Muhammad Ruhi al-Khalidi (1864–1913). From Walid Khalidi, *Before Their Diaspora: A Photographic History of the Palestinians, 1876–1948* (Washington, DC: Institute for Palestine Studies, 1984), 74. Courtesy of the Institute for Palestine Studies.

Palestine before the Zionists came; *Zionism is racism*; *Palestinian nationalism is nothing more than antisemitism*; and so on. Notwithstanding sporadic strides toward peace, these are the terms through which many who are engaged in today's Arab-Israeli conflict perceive one another.

Was this always so? The short answer is, of course, no; the mutual perceptions of Zionists and Arabs (and their latter-day descendants, Israelis, Palestinians, and others in the region) have not been static but rather have evolved over decades of political struggle and violence. How, then, did these communities view one another at the start of their encounter, before the century of violence that ensued? This book sets out to answer this question.

Exploring texts written by Zionists and Arabs about or for each other in the years before the Great War,[2] before the political stakes of the encounter were quite so stark, I will argue that the intellectuals of this

[2] The book draws on texts written beginning in the mid-1890s through the years of the Great War; the bulk of the sources examined were produced during the final decade of Ottoman rule. The same period, in Zionist-centered historiography, would be denoted as the age of the first two *aliyot* (waves of Zionist immigration). In identifying the period studied in this book, I will also refer to it as pre–World War I or, conscious of its connections to contemporary trends in Europe, as the fin de siècle. On the use of fin de siècle in the Ottoman Middle East, see Hanssen, *Fin de siècle Beirut*.

FIGURE 2. Eliezer Ben-Yehuda (1858–1922).

period often thought of one another and interpreted one another's actions in terms of two central categories: *religion* and *race*. The historical actors, that is, tended to view their neighbors as members of particular religions—as Jews, Christians, or Muslims—or of genealogically, "scientifically" defined races ("Semitic" or otherwise). While the Arab-Israeli conflict is generally viewed as a prototypical case of a *nationalist* feud—and thus the Late Ottoman period is imagined as the first stage of that nationalist dispute—when we look carefully at the early years of the encounter, we see that the language and concept of "the nation" were not yet the dominant—and certainly not the only—terms through which the communities defined one another. This book explores in detail the implications of the religious and racial categories employed in the encounter's first decades.

What I am proposing here is not that the ideas of nationalism (broadly, that humanity is naturally divided into nations, and that those nations should strive for cultural and political independence in their historic homelands) did not yet motivate many Arabs and Jews in the years before the Great War. On the contrary, this was precisely the age of the birth of modern Jewish and Arab nationalisms, and these years also witnessed the earliest stages of a uniquely Palestinian Arab nationalism.[3] Nor am

[3] For differing views on the rise of a uniquely Palestinian Arab nationalism, see Khalidi, *Palestinian Identity*; Muslih, *The Origins of Palestinian Nationalism*; and Kimmerling and Migdal, *The Palestinian People*.

I suggesting that Arabs and Jews never saw one another as nationalist groups. Each side was certainly aware of the developing nationalism of the other. This book shows, however, that when we set aside presupposed categories and let our analysis of mutual perceptions in Late Ottoman Palestine be guided by the terms that emerge from the sources themselves, we find that the categories and interpretations were more expansive than a single-minded focus on nationalism would permit. Indeed, we begin to glimpse a new portrait of the early years of the Zionist-Arab encounter—one that is much richer, more nuanced, and in many respects more interesting than that of conventional accounts of the encounter between the communities represented by Ben-Yehuda and al-Khalidi; that is, between those whom we now commonly regard as simply "Zionists" and "Arabs."[4]

Moreover, as a study of reciprocal attitudes that examines the preconceptions and modes of interpretation employed by the various parties in this encounter,[5] this book does not suggest that the various communities in Late Ottoman Palestine are most accurately defined—by those of us looking back a century later—as "religious" or "racial" communities. Modern theorists of religion, race, and the nation have compellingly demonstrated that these categories are historically con-

[4] By referring to elites such as Ben-Yehuda and al-Khalidi as "representatives" of Palestine's Zionist (or Jewish) and Arab (or Muslim) communities, I do not mean to suggest that they shared the qualities, life conditions, or experiences of the nonelites. Rather, they represented the various communities in the sense that each saw himself, and was seen by others within and beyond his own community, as speaking on behalf of the community. This was literally so in the case of al-Khalidi, as he was elected to represent the Jerusalem region in the Ottoman Parliament, and more figuratively so for Ben-Yehuda, who was recognized as a leader of the early Zionist community, even as he differed from other Zionists more focused on land and labor (rather than language and culture). On Ben-Yehuda, see the recent biography by Yoseph Lang, *Daber ʿIvrit!*. On al-Khalidi, see Khalidi, *Palestinian Identity*; Kasmieh, "Ruhi Al-Khalidi 1864–1913"; al-Khateeb, "Ruhi Al-Khalidi."

[5] I borrow the phrase "a study of reciprocal attitudes" from Israel Yuval's work on "Perceptions of Jews and Christians in Late Antiquity and the Middle Ages," the subtitle of his *Two Nations in Your Womb*. Yuval explains that his book is "intended to be a study of reciprocal attitudes of Jews and Christians toward one another, not a history of the relations between them." Rather than presenting "a systematic and comprehensive description of the dialogue and conflicts between Jews and Christians, with their various historical metamorphoses," Yuval aims "to reveal fragmented images of repressed and internalized ideas that lie beneath the surface of the official, overt religious ideology, which are not always explicitly expressed." His objective, in other words, "is to engage in a rational and open discussion of the roles played by irrationality, disinformation, and misinformation in shaping both the self-definition and the definition of the 'other' among Jews and Christians in the Middle Ages" (1). While I, too, am interested in the place of "irrationality, disinformation, and misinformation," I am as interested in the place of rationality and "accurate" information in the ways in which the communities I study understood one another.

tingent and socially constructed. As one scholar of race recently put it, it is at this stage "almost unnecessary to point out that ideas of race, in whatever form, are constructions of human culture and not an objective reality." If this is true of race—the category that, among the three, claims the most "objective," "scientific" authority—how much more so does this apply to religion and nation.[6] By employing these terms throughout this book, I do not intend to reify them but rather to understand what they meant for the historical actors. Furthermore, especially at the very historical moment studied in this book—the late nineteenth and early twentieth centuries—these categories were particularly undefined and fluid, and the distinctions between them had not yet hardened.[7] Part of the aim and the challenge of this book is to explore how these categories were employed in a period and place in which each was used inconsistently.

Paying more careful attention to religion and race as categories of mutual perception significantly alters our understanding of the early Zionist-Arab encounter in several respects. After so many decades of intensive local, regional, and global focus on the questions of whether and how to slice the pie of Palestine,[8] it is common to presume, as one

[6] Hall, *A History of Race in Muslim West Africa*, 13. On the modernity of the notion of religion, see most recently Nongbri, *Before Religion*. As Nongbri writes, "it has become clear that the isolation of something called 'religion' as a sphere of life separated from politics, economics, and science is not a universal feature of human history. In fact, in the broad view of human cultures, it is a strikingly odd way of conceiving the world" (2–3). On the complexity of the Arabic term generally translated as "religion" (*dīn*), as well as *milla* and *umma*, see Nongbri's discussion (39–45). While the view of nations as "imagined communities," as Benedict Anderson famously named them, has dominated recent scholarship on nationalism, there are theorists, such as A. D. Smith, who see certain essential features as defining the nation. See Smith, *The Ethnic Origins of Nations*; Anderson, *Imagined Communities*.

[7] On the connections between conceptions of race and nation, see the chapter "Race and Nation: An Intellectual History" in Weitz, *A Century of Genocide*, 16–52. Michael Banton has aptly noted that "imprecision in the nineteenth-century use of the word race was assisted by the upsurge in European nationalism and the readiness to see that sentiment as an expression of race, so that race was often equated with nation as well as type." Banton, *Racial Theories*, xiv. The challenge of distinguishing between these categories is, of course, not merely terminological but conceptual as well. Some, for instance, have seen nationalism as a modern form of religion. As Carlton Hayes has argued, "since its advent in western Europe, modern nationalism has partaken of the nature of a religion." Identifying the role of a national state, writes Hayes, "it is primarily spiritual, even otherworldly, and its driving force is its collective *faith*, a faith in its mission and destiny, a faith in things unseen, a faith that would move mountains." Hayes, *Nationalism*, 164–65.

[8] The 1937 Peel proposal, the 1947 United Nations partition plan, and the variety of post-1948 peace plans are well-known. There were, however, other lesser-known such suggestions. For a discussion of a proposal in 1924 and mention of others, see Gribetz, "The Question of Palestine before the International Community, 1924," 66, 76n.54.

prominent historian of the Israeli-Palestinian conflict has claimed, that "the problem is, simply put, a dispute over real estate."[9] While Zionists and Arabs in the years before the Great War were surely becoming competitors for Palestine's real estate, by expanding our view and becoming aware of the place of race and religion, we find that the Arab-Israeli conflict is "a dispute over real estate" as much as an inheritance fight between siblings is "a dispute over jewelry and china." Yes, the inheritance might be jewelry and china, but these objects are laden with meaning and significance for the senses of identity and legitimacy of the inheritors. The Arab-Zionist or Palestinian-Israeli conflict has not merely been a dispute over the dunams of a land that can hardly be named without caveat or controversy. It has been a struggle over history and identity between people who regard themselves as acutely connected to each other—religiously and genealogically.[10]

In other words, these communities understood one another not as complete strangers, engaging with each other for the first time in a modern nationalist struggle over a contested piece of land, but rather as peoples encountering deeply familiar, if at times mythologized or distorted, others. Regarding both religious and racial modes of categorization, the sense of commonality was as salient as the extent of difference. The fact that the "Zionist-Arab" encounter was one between Jews, on the one hand, and Christians and Muslims, on the other, such that the individuals involved were members of religious civilizations with long and complex histories of engagement, was not incidental but in fact crucial to how all parties experienced the encounter.[11] Similarly, the fact that this was an encounter between Jews and Arabs, peoples who were imagined by race theorists to be members of a single ancient race or, at any rate, close racial (Semitic) relatives was not inconsequential to either Jews' or Arabs' experience of this encounter but rather, for many, central to it.[12] Whereas a focus on nationalism and territory raises issues of possession and sovereignty that imply conflict,

[9] Gelvin, *The Israel-Palestine Conflict*, 2nd ed., 2–3. Gelvin, of course, recognizes the conflict's greater complexity. I cite his succinct formulation here to stand in for the territorial approach to the conflict.

[10] On the social implications of genealogical thinking, see Zerubavel, *Ancestors and Relatives*.

[11] In the historiography of this period, religion typically features in two limited arguments: first, whether the Christian Arabs of Palestine were more politically or nationalistically conscious and more anti-Zionist than their Muslim counterparts; and second, widening the geographical scope, whether Christian-edited Arabic newspapers in the Levant were more anti-Zionist than those edited by Muslims. See, e.g., Mandel, *The Arabs and Zionism before World War I*, 130; Khalidi, *Palestinian Identity*, 134; Bickerton and Klausner, *A Concise History of the Arab-Israeli Conflict*, 30.

[12] On the concept of Semites, see, e.g., Anidjar, *Semites*; Gabriel Bergounioux, "Semitism."

expanding and enriching our focus to include the parties' ideas of religion and race permit a more nuanced and historically accurate story to be told. A number of thinkers regarded religion or race as elements of unity even as others understood them as grounds for hostility.

Furthermore, by excavating the religious and racial elements of the early encounter, we are able to see more clearly just how complicated the eventual bifurcation in Palestine was between Zionist and Arab, Israeli and Palestinian. For a time, some perceived three groups—Jews, Christians, and Muslims—while others actually saw just one group—Semites. From multiplicity or singularity, a hardened binary emerged. Dividing the communities into two discrete nations, along the particular demographic lines that were ultimately drawn, was, however, neither obvious nor inevitable. Consideration of the place of race and religion helps expose not only the contingency of the eventual bisection but also its complexities.

A Journey of Intellectual Encounter

This book makes the case for the prominence of religious and racial modes of classification and explores the implications of these categories in Late Ottoman Palestine, by means of a journey through texts and among the individuals and communities that produced them. The journey begins in Jerusalem, the scene of the encounter between Ben-Yehuda and al-Khalidi (chapter 1). I situate the city in its multiple political, social, cultural, and intellectual contexts. By properly placing Jerusalem within these contexts—Palestine, the Ottoman Empire, the crossroads of Syria and Egypt, the target of European interest and influence—we are better able to understand why, in the late nineteenth and early twentieth centuries, Palestine's communities would have perceived one another in religious and racial terms, and what they might have meant by these terms. After offering this historical contextualization, chapter 1 provides a survey of the communities present in Palestine in the final years before the start of the Great War and a discussion of some of the challenges in identifying and categorizing these communities.

The journey continues with a focused study of an unpublished manuscript and its intriguing author, Muhammad Ruhi al-Khalidi (chapter 2). Al-Khalidi's 120-page Arabic work, *Zionism or the Zionist Question*, was written in the final years of Ottoman rule. Through his composition, al-Khalidi sought to explain Zionism to his intended Arabic-reading audience. What is striking about this manuscript is that, though its subject is ostensibly Zionism—a phenomenon generally regarded by observers and practitioners alike as a modern and, especially in its early years, secular (even *secularist*), nationalist movement[13]—the author devoted much of his manuscript to describing details of the Jewish religion and Jewish history. For al-Khalidi, to understand Zionism, both its origin and, in his mind, its folly, his readers would have to understand Judaism. Religion was, at least for this prominent figure, central to the way in which he perceived Zionism in Palestine. These Zionists were, after all, *Jews*, and this author, trained in traditional Islamic studies as well as European scholarship, interpreted the Jewish nationalist movement through a distinctly religious lens.

If al-Khalidi looked at Zionists and saw Jews, defined religiously, whom did Zionists see when they looked at their Arab neighbors? To address this question, I turn in chapter 3 to the Hebrew Zionist press published in Palestine in the years preceding the Great War. The Zionists in Palestine maintained a vibrant press with numerous newspapers, each of which represented a different political-ideological demographic of Palestine's small Zionist population. Paying careful attention to the terminology used to describe the non-Jewish natives of Palestine in a sampling of Hebrew newspapers from three of the main Zionist groups, we will find that, though Zionist nomenclature frequently employed the term "Arab," religious labels—"Christian Arabs," "Muslim Arabs," and terms such as "Christians" and "Muslims" that made no mention of the subjects' "Arabness" at all—were also used regularly. I argue that the use of religious labels reflected what appears to have been a widespread belief that the way in which Palestine's natives related to the Zionists not only correlated with, but was actually determined by, the natives' respective religions. Muslims, members of a faith imagined to be inherently tolerant and decent, would welcome Zionists into Palestine, so it was argued, were it not for the instigation of Christians, whose religion is essentially intolerant, violent, and anti-Jewish. In the minds of Palestine's Zionists in the Late Ottoman period, I contend, they were engaged in an encounter with Christians and Muslims as much as with a group they regarded as Arabs.

In my study of the Hebrew newspapers, I focus particularly on the use of religious labels and the Zionists' varying views regarding Christianity and Islam. However, in the course of this analysis, I show that

[13] In this sense, Zionism is not unique, of course, as the phenomenon of nationalism is broadly regarded as secular in nature. Describing a view he challenges as overly simplistic, A. D. Smith writes that "it is usual to see in nationalism a modern, secular ideology that replaces the religious systems found in premodern, traditional societies. In this view, 'religion' and 'nationalism' figure as two terms in the conventional distinction between tradition and modernity, and in an evolutionary framework that sees an inevitable movement—whether liberating or destructive—from the one to the other." Smith, *Chosen Peoples*, 9.

race-language also appeared in unexpected ways. In one particularly curious passage, Zionist editors described an Arabic newspaper that opposed Zionism as the work of "the Christian Arab enemies, who hate us religiously and racially." These "Christian Arab enemies" were distinguished from "our Muslim neighbors" who had always viewed the Jews "like brothers to the Arabs and members of the same race." This is but one instance of the slippage between religious and racial categories employed by some Zionists as they perceived their non-Jewish neighbors in Palestine. Religion was just *one* category through which Zionists imagined Palestine's Arabs; race, too, was considered by some to be a critical component of the nature and identity of their neighbors.

Recognizing the utility of the press in exploring Zionist perceptions of the Arabs, I then turn back to the other side of the encounter. Here, though, I broaden the study beyond the geographic confines of Palestine, through an analysis of three of the wider region's most influential Arabic intellectual journals (chapter 4). Because Palestine's intellectual elite read and contributed to these journals—indeed, I conducted my research with copies of the journals that were present in Palestine during the Ottoman period—the journals are an essential source for discerning the ways in which Arab intellectuals in Palestine and beyond perceived the Jews and Zionism. In these journals—*al-Hilāl*, *al-Muqtaṭaf*, and *al-Manār*—and in other works by their editors, perhaps even more than in the Zionist newspapers, ideas concerning race, and particularly the Jews' racial relationship with Arabs, were central to the way in which the Jews and Zionists were perceived. The focus on race, however, was certainly not to the exclusion of other means of categorization and interpretation of the Jews and Zionism; conceptions of the Jewish religion were crucial as well.

Through my reading of the Zionist press as well as my research in Zionist archives, I found that I was far from the first to take an interest in the ways in which the Arabic press portrayed the Zionists. Rather, Zionists of the Late Ottoman period, especially in the final half-decade before the First World War, were *themselves* already deeply concerned by Arab perceptions of Zionism and the Jews. In chapter 5, then, I move from a study of perceptions to a study of perceptions-of-perceptions. I begin by investigating Zionist programs aimed at understanding and influencing Arab perceptions of the Zionists, including efforts to translate Arabic newspaper articles about the Jews, to write articles sympathetic to Zionism for the Arabic press, and to fund Arabic papers that were supportive of Jewish efforts in Palestine. Through studying these efforts, we will discover the crucial role played by Arabic-literate Sephardic Zionists because of their linguistic capabilities. This will lead us, finally, to two Arabic books about Judaism and the Jews written by members of the Palestine-born Sephardic Zionist community: Shimon Moyal's *at-Talmūd* and Nissim Malul's *Asrār al-yahūd*. The authors, Moyal and Malul, were also involved in the Zionist projects to translate and influence the Arabic press; these works of apologetics were another weapon in the battle against Arab opposition to Zionism. The books were written for non-Jewish Arabic readers with the explicit goal of diminishing "misunderstanding." We will study these texts, then, to discern how certain Zionists, anxious about their native neighbors' perceptions of Zionism, defended the Jewish religion and their community in the Arabic idiom of the fin de siècle. Through these works, the authors negotiated the complex terrain of bifrontal religious apologetics, directed at members of two religions, Christianity and Islam. Analyzing these texts permits us to understand how those raised in the Middle East, at home in Arab culture, and fluent and literate in Arabic, conceived of their neighbors and imagined how they might most effectively be persuaded to embrace Zionism. Tellingly, they chose to focus largely on religion.

As I have noted, this book's emphasis on the religious and racial categories of perception should not be taken to imply that these were the *only* categories employed in the fateful intercommunal encounter that occurred in Late Ottoman Palestine. Rather, what this book seeks to demonstrate is that, though often overlooked, religious and racial categories were prominent in the perceptions of this period, and that these categories prove essential for understanding the early encounter. Though for reasons that I will suggest relate to the new political discourse that emerged from the Great War (and was enshrined in the treaties signed at the war's conclusion) these categories were often unspoken or even explicitly denied political relevance, they are also crucial, I argue, for making sense of later developments in Zionist-Arab and Israeli-Palestinian relations. I return to these more recent matters in the conclusion.

Textual Encounters

This book sets out to study the intellectual encounter between Zionists and Arabs in the Late Ottoman period in Palestine and beyond. Though I began with an instance of this encounter, namely, Eliezer Ben-Yehuda's 1909 interview of Muhammad Ruhi al-Khalidi, records of face-to-face intellectual conversations (that is, discussions of ideas) between Zionists and Arabs in this period are scant. This lack of evidence, one suspects, is more a comment on the nature of the sources than on the frequency of such encounters historically, even if the latter were uncommon. Nevertheless, to discern how Zionists and Arabs perceived and understood one another, it is necessary to look beyond texts that specifically document or narrate personal encounters. Instead, we are led to texts that reveal—whether explicitly or through close, critical analysis—the ways members of the various communities in Palestine and beyond conceived of this encounter. Through these texts, we are able to shed light both on the encounter and on the way participants perceived it.

While evidence of face-to-face intellectual encounters is elusive, through analyzing texts that reveal perceptions this book also studies what might be regarded as *textual encounters*, and of these there is ample evidence. In fact, most of the texts I analyze here were written with explicit reference to another text or set of texts. Consider the many points of contact. Al-Khalidi's manuscript relies heavily on, and at times responds to and revises, both Shimon Moyal's *at-Talmūd* and the *Jewish Encyclopedia*'s entry on "Zionism" by the American Zionist Richard Gottheil. Gottheil himself presumably read *Tārīkh al-isrāʾīliyyīn*, a book on the history of the Jews written by *al-Muqtaṭaf*'s editor Shahin Makaryus (the copy I located bears the stamp of Gottheil's private library).[14] Rashid Rida, editor of *al-Manār*, reviewed Makaryus's *Tārīkh al-isrāʾīliyyīn* in his journal. *At-Talmūd*, though written by Moyal, was a project envisioned by the Arabic journal *al-Hilāl*'s editor Jurji Zaydan and was written to counter the antitalmudic claims of European books that had recently been translated into Arabic and disseminated in the Middle East. The publication of Nissim Malul's *Asrār al-yahūd* was announced in *al-Hilāl*.[15] Hebrew newspapers in Palestine, and soon the Zionists' Palestine Office in Jaffa, translated and tried to influence the Arabic press. And Moyal wished to translate the Haifa-based editor Najib Nassar's pamphlet on Zionism, which was itself a translation of Gottheil's "Zionism." In other words, the *texts*, if not always their authors, were in conversation.

While they often addressed or were informed by one another, the texts on which this book focuses vary widely in numerous respects. They range from the most private (e.g., an unpublished and uncirculated manuscript) to the most public (e.g., newspapers, journals, speeches, and published books) and many others in between (e.g., archival material reserved for internal Zionist Organization consumption). Some of

[14] Gottheil's name is handwritten on the first page of the copy available in Columbia University's collection.

[15] The book is described in a brief notice as "a book in defense of the Jews and their religion, written by Nissim Effendi Malul. The first part has been published and is available from the author in Egypt." *al-Hilāl* 19 (October 1910–July 1911), 448.

the sources are descriptive (e.g., accounts of day-to-day incidents in Palestine), while others are prescriptive and even polemical (e.g., religious apologetic literature). Finally, the texts were written in a variety of languages (Arabic, Hebrew, Yiddish, Judeo-Arabic, German, and French).

My aim in this selection is not to claim that these texts constitute a "representative sample," a futile goal for an intellectual history project of this type, but rather to offer a wide variety of kinds of sources, each of which sheds light on another aspect of the mutual perceptions under review. For instance, through mining Zionist newspapers for references to the Zionists' non-Jewish neighbors, I show how Zionist writers thought of their counterparts in Palestine when they were simply (that is, presumably reflexively and unselfconsciously) naming them. This is a type of observation that could not be obtained through the study of, for example, more philosophical or apologetic texts, such as those of Moyal or Malul. These latter—*at-Talmūd* and *Asrār al-yahūd*—allow us to understand how Judaism, Jewish history, and Zionism might be presented to non-Jewish Arabic-readers in a way that the Hebrew newspapers obviously could not. At the same time, though al-Khalidi's manuscript provides a unique perspective on one influential Arab leader's perceptions of the Jews and Zionism, fin de siècle Arabic journal articles offer insights into the way a far broader range of Arab intellectuals imagined the Jews and conceived of their relationship to them. Moreover, these articles were not generally concerned specifically with Zionism or even Palestine, so they permit us to view Arab perceptions differently from those proffered in a text explicitly focused on Zionism. The range of sources examined in this book, in other words, permits us to analyze perceptions in this encounter on both micro and macro levels.[16]

Blended History and the Scholarly Taboos of Religion and Race

Two final points are in order about the significance of this book, both historically and historiographically. First, it is worth highlighting one broader way in which this project attempts to contribute to the study

[16] Because of the radical transformations that occurred in Palestine with the fall of the Ottoman Empire and the establishment of the British Mandate—not least the significant increase in intercommunal tensions—retrospective accounts of the Late Ottoman period are exceedingly problematic for a study of mutual perceptions. Therefore, though I appreciate the considerable utility of autobiographical memoirs and oral histories in certain historiographical projects, I have consciously avoided these sources here. For the potential benefits of such material, see Doumani, *Rediscovering Palestine*, 11–12. On the need for cautious skepticism, see Stanislawski, *Autobiographical Jews*.

of Palestine. For political and linguistic reasons, the histories of the communities of Palestine have generally been studied as just that: separate *histories*. This exclusivity of focus and narrowness of vision have left a more blended history as a clear desideratum. Joining other recent historians,[17] I have tried to explore the interconnectedness of these histories and to argue that there is much one can learn about this society when we view it as a whole, however complex and fragmented. This book, then, is meant to serve as a bridge in overcoming the false dichotomy between the "Jewish history of Palestine" and its "Middle Eastern history," revealing Palestine's central place in the nexus between Europe and the Middle East and that between Jews and Arabs—Christians and Muslims.

Second, religion and race have, in different ways, been taboo subjects in the scholarship on the Arab-Zionist encounter, where nationalism is generally viewed as the critical category. Reasons for this include the blinding effects of secularization theory; the secularist nature of much nationalist historiography; the post-Holocaust Jewish inclination to obscure or ignore the pervasiveness of racial discourse among prewar Jews;[18] the polemics surrounding the identification of Zionism with racism; and the reluctance to associate Arabs with race-thinking given this ideology's prominent place in colonial discourses of oppression.[19] Owing to these factors, scholars have generally shied away from exploring religion and race in the history of Jews and Arabs in Palestine. In defying these inclinations, this book joins a new wave of scholarship that has begun to examine the interplay of race and religion in the broader rise of nationalisms. Increasingly, in the words of one observer, scholars have contended that these categories must be viewed not merely as "interacting" or "intersecting" but as "inextricably linked" and "co-constituted."[20] While this scholarship has largely focused on the *self*-perceptions of groups, this book suggests that we can understand the nexus of race, religion, and nation only as part of a wider worldview, one in which the definitions and perceptions

[17] An early effort in this regard was undertaken in Ben-Arieh and Bartal, *Shilhei ha-tekufah ha-ʿot'omanit (1799–1917)*. See also Lockman, *Comrades and Enemies*; LeBor, *City of Oranges*; Jacobson, *From Empire to Empire*; Campos, *Ottoman Brothers*.

[18] This inclination has been challenged by scholars such as John Efron and Eric Goldstein. See Efron, *Defenders of the Race*; Goldstein, "The Unstable Other"; Goldstein, *The Price of Whiteness*. For a recent, important collection of primary sources on this subject, see Hart, ed., *Jews and Race*. See also Falk, "Zionism and the Biology of the Jews."

[19] On the "culture of silence—the refusal to engage in discussions on slavery and racial attitudes" in the Maghrib, see el Hamel, " 'Race,' Slavery and Islam in Maghribi Mediterranean Thought."

[20] See Goldschmidt and McAlister, *Race, Nation, and Religion in the Americas*, 6–7.

of others—neighboring and often competing groups—played an absolutely pivotal role. By reexamining the sources in which Zionists and Arabs of the Late Ottoman period depicted or addressed one another, the book not only reinflects their history of identity formation with the categories of religion and race; it also illuminates the often counterintuitive role of each of these categories in blurring perceived differences between members of the two groups.

CHAPTER 1

Locating the Zionist-Arab Encounter: Local, Regional, Imperial, and Global Spheres

When Muhammad Ruhi al-Khalidi and Eliezer Ben-Yehuda sat together that Saturday in October 1909, they met in Jerusalem. *Where*, though, was Jerusalem in the autumn of 1909? Attempting to answer this seemingly simple question is in fact a complicated task, and the challenge highlights the numerous geographical, social, cultural, political, and intellectual levels of encounter that are studied in this book. The following pages place Jerusalem in its local setting in Palestine, and Palestine more broadly in its Ottoman, Middle Eastern, and European contexts. As we shall see, the categories of religion and race employed by the communities of Palestine in their mutual perceptions are best understood within these multiple contexts.

Jerusalem, Palestine, and the Holy Land

When late nineteenth-century Jewish nationalists began to immigrate to the land they viewed as their biblical and/or historic patrimony (they generally called it the Land of Israel or Palestine interchangeably), the region was governed by the Ottoman Empire, which, but for a decade earlier that same century (1831–1840), had ruled the area since 1517. Under the Ottoman regime, there was no official, administrative unit called Palestine (nor, for that matter, the Land of Israel).[1] The region had officially been named Palaestina under the Romans in antiquity and Jund Filasṭīn after the Arab conquest until the Mongolian invasion,[2] and there was a land legally called Palestine after the demise

[1] On the so-called invention of the Land of Israel, see Sand, *The Invention of the Land of Israel*. See also Bartal, "Me-ʿereẓ kodesh' le-ereẓ historit—'Otonomizm' ẓiyoni be-reshit ha-meʾah ha-ʿesrim."

[2] Porath, *The Emergence of the Palestinian-Arab National Movement 1918–1929*, 4–5.

of the Ottoman Empire in the Great War, when the country was under British Mandate. Between the thirteenth and the twentieth centuries, however, the region's rulers did not treat it as a separate political or administrative entity, and it was not formally called Palestine.[3] In other words, notwithstanding the increasingly common scholarly preference for the term "Late Ottoman Palestine"[4] (a term I also use in this book), al-Khalidi's native and Ben-Yehuda's adoptive city of Jerusalem was, more precisely, in the larger territory the Ottomans named—forgive the confusion—Jerusalem, or in Ottoman and Arabic, al-Quds.

Jerusalem had not always been the name of an independent Ottoman administrative unit. Though the idea had been proposed earlier, this was an innovation fully enacted by the Ottomans only in the final quarter of the nineteenth century.[5] Earlier in the century, the region we know of as Palestine (today's Israel, West Bank, and Gaza Strip) was part of the Ottoman *vilayet* (province) of Syria, three *sanjaks* (districts) of which were Acre (in the north), Nablus (in the center), and Jerusalem (in the south).[6] Due in part to their recognition of the growing

[3] See Thomas Philipp's discussion of the anachronistic use of "Palestine" in *Acre*, 1–8, 233n.1.

[4] Consider, for instance, Agmon, *Family & Court*; Saposnik, *Becoming Hebrew*; Ben-Bassat and Ginio, *Late Ottoman Palestine*; Perry and Lev, *Modern Medicine in the Holy Land*; Campos, "A 'Shared Homeland' and Its Boundaries"; Schidorsky, "Libraries in Late Ottoman Palestine between the Orient and the Occident"; McCarthy, *The Population of Palestine*; Kushner, ed., *Palestine in the Late Ottoman Period*. On debates in the historiography of the Late Ottoman period in Palestine, particularly concerning the attitude of the Ottomans toward Zionist immigration, see Reinkowski, "Late Ottoman Rule over Palestine."

[5] There had been two earlier, short-lived moves (in 1841 and 1854) to separate Jerusalem from Damascus and to make it an independent *sanjak*. The final, lasting separation, however, took place in 1874. Abu-Manneh, "The Rise of the Sanjak of Jerusalem in the Late Nineteenth Century," 42–43; Schölch, *Palestine in Transformation, 1856–1882*, 12–13; Gerber, *Ottoman Rule in Jerusalem, 1890–1914*, 6; Khalidi, *Palestinian Identity*, 35, 218n.37. The same had been done to Mount Lebanon in 1861 after intercommunal violence erupted the previous year. See Cleveland, *A History of the Modern Middle East*, 91. Benny Morris renders the year of the transformation of Jerusalem into an independent mutasarriflik as 1887. Morris, *Righteous Victims*, 7.

[6] As of the Ottoman reforms of 1864, the empire was divided into a number of different levels of administrative units. The first level was that of the *vilayet*, or province, which was ruled by a governor (*vali*). Vilayets were divided in turn into a number of *sanjaks*, or districts, which were themselves composed of subdistricts that were governed by *kaymakams* (subgovernors). An exceptional status was that of the *mutasarriflik* or independent sanjak, which, though much smaller than a typical vilayet, was under the direct authority of the sultan rather than through the intermediary of a *vali*; as we shall see, mutasarrifliks were typically created to bypass the standard Ottoman administrative hierarchy to satisfy particular political interests, whether domestic or foreign. See Davison, *Reform in the Ottoman Empire, 1856–1876*, 136ff; Gerber, *Ottoman Rule in Jerusalem, 1890–1914*; Gerber, *State and Society in the Ottoman Empire*, 9:33–76. On eighteenth- and early nineteenth-century Acre, see Philipp, *Acre*.

international (especially European) significance of Jerusalem and the interests of powers beyond the empire in the Holy Land, the Ottoman central authorities in Istanbul, seeking to maintain a closer grip on the region, finally separated the sanjak of Jerusalem from the vilayet of Syria in 1874.[7] The Jerusalem region was given the special status of a *mutasarriflik*, a district whose administrators answered directly to the Ottoman sultan in Istanbul rather than to the governor of a province. In 1887 the remaining two sanjaks of Palestine—Acre and Nablus—were also separated from the vilayet of Syria, though they were joined not to the mutasarriflik of Jerusalem but rather to the newly established vilayet of Beirut.[8]

Thus when we think of al-Khalidi and Ben-Yehuda's Jerusalem as having been located in Late Ottoman Palestine, in Ottoman administrative terms we mean the mutasarriflik of Jerusalem as well as the sanjaks of Nablus and Acre. That Palestine was not a single administrative unit is important for our purposes because recognizing that it was part of several provinces and the way in which it was integrated into a vast empire highlights the extent to which this region must be understood in its broader Ottoman context. Considering wider events and changes in the Ottoman Empire is critical for fully comprehending phenomena in these three small Ottoman districts.

"Late Ottoman Palestine," though, is more than a convenient but inaccurate shorthand for the distinct regions of Jerusalem, Nablus, and Acre. For the primary subjects of this book, namely, the residents of these Ottoman regions and their contemporaries in the Middle East and Europe, Palestine (or the Land of Israel) as such was indeed a meaningful unit. In other words, to acknowledge the lack of political boundaries around a land called Palestine is not to imply that such boundaries, however imprecise and flexible, did not exist in people's minds. Moreover, noting the absence of official borders should not be

[7] Scholars differ on what motivated the Ottomans to make this change. Haim Gerber argues that the change was due to external factors, particularly "the impact of the West." Gerber, *Ottoman Rule in Jerusalem, 1890–1914*, 6–7. Cf. Abu-Manneh, "The Rise of the Sanjak of Jerusalem in the Late Nineteenth Century," 41–42. Abu-Manneh highlights the internal Ottoman factors that, he argues, were at least as important as the European in accounting for Jerusalem's rise in status in the nineteenth century. Porath points to "the internal interest in Jerusalem and the dispute between various Christian sects over the rights to the Holy Places." See Porath, *The Emergence of the Palestinian-Arab National Movement 1918–1929*, 15–16. David Kushner highlights the importance of Egypt's "record of expansionism in the nineteenth century," which "made Palestine a vulnerable border region and enhanced the importance of its internal and external security." Kushner, *To Be Governor of Jerusalem*, 23.

[8] Schölch, *Palestine in Transformation, 1856–1882*, 12. See also Hanssen, *Fin de siècle Beirut.*

taken to suggest that an "imagined" territory is any less significant historically than one that was politically, legally, or sovereignly bound. This was, after all, the "Holy Land" as understood by Jews, Christians, and Muslims alike, those within the land and, no less, those far beyond its imagined borders. Its general territorial contours were known to Jews and Christians from the Bible and to Muslims from the Qurʾan and later Islamic commentary.[9]

In fact, the notion of a place called Palestine, as a single entity, was especially meaningful precisely in the fin de siècle period. Three phenomena sparking renewed interest in the Holy Land during this period are worth highlighting here: the dramatic increase of European Christian missionary activity (especially in the wake of European intervention in response to Muhammad Ali's conquest of the Levant);[10] the rise of Zionism, a Jewish nationalism that focused its ambitions on Ereẓ Yisraʾel (typically translated into European languages by Zionists themselves as Palestine);[11] and the beginning of a distinctly Palestinian identity among the land's Arab majority.[12] The primary location of the encounter analyzed in this book, then, may indeed be called Palestine.

Jerusalem, the Ottoman Empire, and Intercommunal Difference

Ben-Yehuda and al-Khalidi's Jerusalem was not only the central city of the district that shared the city's name, or of an imagined place called Palestine; it was also part of the Ottoman Empire. That this encounter

[9] On the variety of ways the borders have been imagined, beginning in the Hebrew Bible, see Havrelock, *River Jordan.* For different post-Ottoman Zionist versions of the imagined borders, see Shelef, *Evolving Nationalism*, 25–106. On Islamic views, see, e.g., Porath, *The Emergence of the Palestinian-Arab National Movement 1918–1929*, 1–16. The Qurʾan refers to the "Holy Land" in Q. 5:20–21, in which Moses says, "O my People! Enter the Holy Land which God has assigned unto you, and turn not back ignominiously, for then will you be overthrown, to your own ruin." Cited in Abu Sway, "The Holy Land, Jerusalem and al-Aqsa Mosque in the Qurʾan, Sunnah and Other Islamic Literary Sources," 88. See also Q. 17:1–4, which refers to al-masjid al-aqṣā, "whose precincts we have blessed."

[10] The presence of missionaries in Jerusalem is discussed further below. See also Perry, "ha-Naẓrut ha-maʿaravit: Protastantim"; Perry, *British Mission to the Jews in Nineteenth-Century Palestine.*

[11] A classic study of Zionist ideology is Shimoni, *The Zionist Ideology*. For a recent introduction to the history of Zionism, see Engel, *Zionism.* Zionists in the pre-1948 period often translated *Ereẓ Yisraʾel* as "Palestine." After the creation of the State of Israel, and especially since the 1960s, there has been a marked ambivalence among Zionists toward the use of the term Palestine, associated as it is with a competing nationalist movement.

[12] On the complex phenomenon of Palestinian identity, see Khalidi, *Palestinian Identity.*

took place within this vast, if shrinking, empire is hardly incidental to this story.[13] Ben-Yehuda wished to interview al-Khalidi, after all, precisely because of the latter's political role in the Ottoman Empire. But to understand how the encounter between al-Khalidi and Ben-Yehuda, and the communities they represented, was conceived, the Ottoman imperial context is critical far beyond the particulars of al-Khalidi's parliamentary position. The way in which people relate to one another is informed (though of course not wholly determined) by the systemic, structural categories offered by the societies in which they live. Put somewhat differently, how a state formally defines its subjects necessarily affects how the people themselves define and relate to one another, even as the influence may not be unidirectional. Moreover, it is in periods when the formal definitions are challenged or in flux that one may expect to see the relationship between legal definitions and informal perceptions most acutely, and the era surrounding the period of study in this book was perhaps the most significant such moment of flux in Ottoman history.

For most of its history, the Ottoman Empire formally defined its diverse subjects by their religions. Through an arrangement that eventually came to be known as the "*millet* system,"[14] the Ottoman government related to its various religious minority populations via their religious leadership. It was once imagined that each millet's religious leader in Istanbul had always been the representative of the community throughout the empire, such that, for instance, the Istanbul *hahambaşi* (chief rabbi) represented all the empire's Jews from the earliest years of Ottoman Jewish history. More recently scholars have discovered that the system was, until the nineteenth century, much more localized and ad hoc, in contrast to the later claims of centralization and

[13] As Yuval Ben-Bassat writes, "in order to embed the discussion on proto-Zionist-Arab encounters in Palestine at the end of the nineteenth century into a broader historical context, it is important to examine the Ottoman framework in which Jewish-Arab relations unfolded." Ben-Bassat, "Beyond National Historiographies," 112. While my study focuses on texts found in Jerusalem and elsewhere in Israel, I have learned much from several recent scholars who have begun mining the Ottoman archives for Ottoman-Turkish language materials concerning the Arab-Zionist encounter. See, for instance, Ben-Bassat, "Rural Reactions to Zionist Activity in Palestine before and after the Young Turk Revolution of 1908 as Reflected in Petitions to Istanbul"; Fishman, "Palestine Revisited."

[14] The Turkish word *millet* comes from the Arabic *millah*, a Qur'anic term of Aramaic origin. The term, according to Bernard Lewis, originally meant "a word" and came to represent a group that accepts a particular word or revealed book. In the Ottoman Empire, explains Lewis, "it became a technical term, and was used for the organized, recognized, religio-political communities enjoying certain rights of autonomy under their own chiefs." See Lewis, *The Political Language of Islam*, 38–39. See also Ayalon, *Language and Change in the Arab Middle East*, 19–21.

stability.[15] This important historiographical revision notwithstanding, the fact remains that imperial authorities defined Jews, Greek Orthodox, Armenians, and of course Muslims in *religious* terms. In a society in which the state formally distinguishes[16] between its communities based on religion, we might not be surprised to find that the communities themselves perceived their neighbors in religious terms as well.[17]

In the mid-nineteenth century, however, under external pressure from Europe, the Ottoman government, led by the bureaucrats of the Sublime Porte, took a number of steps to equalize the rights and duties of the empire's population; the new legal reforms passed in this regard were known as the Tanzimat ("Reorganizations," 1839–1876).[18] The Ottoman Law of Nationality of 1869, for instance, formally changed the legal categories used by the Ottoman government. No longer would the government define those within its boundaries as Muslim, *dhimmī* (i.e., Christian and Jew), and non-Muslim foreigner. Now the official categories were *ecnebī* (foreign national without regard to religious affiliation) and Ottoman (including "non-Muslim Ottomans"). For these

[15] Scholars have questioned to what extent the millet system was indeed a "system" (rather than an ad hoc set of practices) when it actually was instituted (in the early years of the empire or in the nineteenth century) and when it was dissolved (during the Tanzimat or at the end of the empire). See Braude and Lewis, *Christians and Jews in the Ottoman Empire*. One direction for future scholarship in this area is to use these revisions to understand how this imperial system informed and affected intercommunal relations. One wonders whether Jews and Arabs in the Late Ottoman period viewed each other in different ways from their predecessors given the evolving ways in which religious communities related to the empire. The case of Jews, Christians, and Muslims in Palestine suggests that Jews and Arabs in the Late Ottoman period may have come to view each other in terms that at least in part mimicked the religious basis of the communal structures imposed by the Ottoman state. At the same time, it also reveals how extra-Ottoman influences, such as European race-thinking, could simultaneously penetrate communal consciousness in this era.

[16] "Distinction" is not necessarily equivalent to negative "discrimination." Notwithstanding the Tanzimat reforms of the mid-nineteenth century, though, there were certainly areas of discrimination as well. For a discussion of intercommunal relations in the Ottoman Empire and the forces of distinction, see Quataert, *The Ottoman Empire, 1700–1922*, 174–79.

[17] Further complicating this study is the fact that, as Quataert puts it, "ethnic terms confusingly often described what actually were religious differences." In the Balkan and Anatolian lands, for instance, "Ottoman Christians informally spoke of 'Turks' when in fact they meant Muslims. 'Turk' was a kind of shorthand referring to Muslims of every sort, whether Kurds, Turks, or Albanians (but not Arabs)." Ibid., 175. As I will demonstrate in my analysis of Hebrew newspapers, Late Ottoman Zionists sometimes appeared to use the term Arab when they actually meant Muslim.

[18] See "The Tanzimat Era" in Hanioğlu, *A Brief History of the Late Ottoman Empire*. For a variety of theories explaining the Ottoman motivations for the Tanzimat, see Quataert, *The Ottoman Empire, 1700–1922*, 65–68.

reasons, the Tanzimat are often regarded as a major effort to secularize the empire by undermining certain legal distinctions based on religion.

Though the Tanzimat exemplified "a general inclination toward a more secular conception of the state," according to historian Hanioğlu, this inclination was realized only partially. Among the notable exceptions to the secularist reorientation, the *sharīʿa* (Islamic religious) courts were maintained; indeed, they outlasted the empire itself.[19] This meant that people distinguished themselves, and were distinguished by others, according to their religions when they were engaged in certain legal matters.[20] Moreover, in the late nineteenth century those groups that wished to gain a greater degree of autonomy within the Ottoman system, on Ottoman terms, did so on the basis of religion. In 1870, for instance, the Bulgarians appealed to the Ottoman authorities for recognition not as *ethnic* Bulgars, explains Hanioğlu, "but as a distinct religious community in the traditional mode," headed by an ethnarch in Istanbul.[21] Religious categories thus remained central to the way the empire related to its subjects even in the Tanzimat era.

In fact, in certain respects, religion became even more central to the empire's relationship with its diverse populations, and these populations' relationships with one another, beginning in the nineteenth century. It was during this period that the various European states, increasingly eager to seize parts of what they believed to be a crumbling empire (or at least to keep their European rivals from doing so), began more aggressively to claim to represent particular non-Muslim elements among the population of the Ottoman lands. The French claimed the right to protect the empire's Catholics; the Russians to protect the Greek Orthodox; the British to protect (at various times) Russian Jews, Druze, and Copts.[22] Outside governments, that is, established their influence in the Ottoman Empire through their focus on or exploitation of religious difference, notwithstanding any Ottoman imperial desires to minimize the importance of such difference since the age of the Tanzimat.

At times, non-Muslims were not only protected but also granted certain economic advantages owing to their association with Europeans. By the terms of the so-called Capitulations, a set of ad hoc agreements

[19] Hanioğlu, *A Brief History of the Late Ottoman Empire*, 74.

[20] There were also "secular" courts, which were formally recognized in 1847. As Glidewell Nadolski explains, "these were independent of the Shariʿa and Christian courts in that they dealt with international commercial relations, an area that had traditionally been outside the jurisdiction of the Shariʿa." Nadolski, "Ottoman and Secular Civil Law," 522–23. See also "Ḳanūn," in EI³.

[21] Quataert, *The Ottoman Empire, 1700–1922*, 75–76.

[22] Kushner, *To Be Governor of Jerusalem*, 35–36.

between the Ottoman Empire and various European powers, Europeans in Ottoman territory were generally exempted from Ottoman taxation, a privilege that was sometimes passed on to elements of the Ottoman religious minority with which the European power associated.[23] This economic inequality—effectively favoring non-Muslims over Muslims—bred resentment and, along with other factors, intercommunal tensions. As historian Ussama Makdisi puts it, "just as the Ottomans were moving away from a vaguely defined *millet* system, in which the Sunni Muslims were treated as socially and culturally superior to other communities of the Empire, and were moving toward a more integrative form of government, the Europeans favored and intervened on behalf of the Christians."[24] When violence ultimately arose between local Christians and Muslims, as it did, for instance, in Mount Lebanon in the mid-nineteenth century, Europeans interpreted the events as "sectarian" conflict and evidence of the need further to intervene and protect the empire's Christians. As Makdisi argues, "the beginning of sectarianism did not imply a reversion." Rather, "it marked a rupture, a birth of a new culture that singled out religious affiliation as the defining public and political characteristic of a modern subject and citizen."[25]

The net effect of the Tanzimat period on the empire's focus on religion and religious difference is thus ambiguous: in certain respects the Tanzimat diminished this focus while in other regards the reforms and the response to them actually heightened it.[26] This ambiguity is well illustrated in the issue of Ottoman military conscription for non-Muslims. Among the Tanzimat reforms, for the first time non-Muslims technically became subject to the Ottoman military draft. Including Christians and Jews in the army was meant to remove an important

[23] The term Capitulations refers to a set of agreements between the Ottoman Empire and various European powers, beginning as early as the sixteenth century, with Selim II's agreement with France in 1569. The agreements would permit the foreign subjects to travel in the Ottoman Empire under the rule of their home country's laws, exempting them from Ottoman "legal and fiscal jurisdiction." Initially temporary measures, by the eighteenth century new agreements came to be regarded as permanent. A non-Muslim Ottoman subject was able to receive from a European representative a certificate, known in Ottoman as a *berat* (title of privilege), which would grant the person the equivalent status of a European subject, thereby also exempting the person from Ottoman taxes. See Quataert, *The Ottoman Empire, 1700–1922*, 79.

[24] Makdisi, *The Culture of Sectarianism*, 11.

[25] Ibid., 174.

[26] On "the complex and contradictory nature of the Tanzimat" with regard to their impact on non-Muslims in the empire, see Nadolski, "Ottoman and Secular Civil Law," 521–25. James Gelvin has noted the irony that a "policy of promising equality to all inhabitants of the empire regardless of religious affiliation hardened communal boundaries and precipitated instances of intercommunal violence." Gelvin, "Secularism and Religion in the Arab Middle East," 121.

area of separation and distinction between Muslims and non-Muslims in the empire. There was not, however, an immediate influx of non-Muslims into the Ottoman army, as non-Muslims were offered a legal escape from the military: they were permitted to pay an exemption fee, the *bedel-i askeri*. As the exemption fee option was widely exercised (indeed, it effectively replaced the repealed poll tax on non-Muslims),[27] with only rare exceptions, the change had few practical implications, and thus the legal, military distinctions between Muslims and non-Muslims persisted.[28] Moreover, as we shall see, when, after the Young Turk Revolution of 1908, Ottoman authorities sought in greater earnest to draft non-Muslims into the imperial military,[29] the men were called on to appear at separate drafting stations on different days, according to their *religiously defined* community: Christian young men to gather in this location on Tuesday, draft-age Jews to assemble in that building the following Thursday, and so on. In other words, even in an act aimed explicitly at eliminating distinction based on religious difference in the empire, that distinction could effectively be magnified.[30]

Intercommunal difference was certainly on the minds of the Ottoman governors of Jerusalem in particular during the Late Ottoman period. Whereas Jews were generally permitted to immigrate to the Ottoman Empire, since the first years of Jewish nationalist immigration to Palestine in the 1880s the Ottomans attempted to limit the influx of Jews into the Holy Land. These efforts, including legal restrictions both on the length of Jewish visitors' stays in Palestine (the so-called

[27] "The traditional poll tax, or *jizya*," explains Stillman, "which had symbolized the dhimmī's humble, subject status since the early days of Islam was now [through the Tanzimat] rescinded. The fiscal change was, however, cosmetic, in a sense, since the *jizya* was replaced with a new levy, the *bedel-i askeri* . . . which exempted non-Muslims from military service, for which they had become technically liable with the granting of civil equality. This destigmatized tax was entirely suitable to most non-Muslims, who had no desire to enter the army." Stillman, *The Jews of Arab Lands in Modern Times*, 9. Zürcher points out that the *bedel*, just like the *jizya* before it, "was paid collectively by Christian and Jewish communities to tax-farmers and, later, salaried treasury officials." For a detailed analysis of the Ottoman military conscription system, see Zürcher, "The Ottoman Conscription System, 1844–1914."

[28] See Lewis, *Semites and Anti-Semites*, 123.

[29] On the decision to impose universal conscription, see Campos, *Ottoman Brothers*, 150–53. On the persistence of the Ottoman *bedel-i askeri* even during the First World War, despite its high cost (ranging from thirty to fifty gold Turkish pounds), see Penslar, *Jews and the Military*, 68.

[30] According to Hanioğlu, the Young Turk Weltanschauung, "as it developed between 1889 and 1902, was vehemently antireligious, viewing religion as the greatest obstacle to human progress." Despite this perspective, the Young Turks "attempted to use religion as a device for modernization." Hanioğlu, *Preparation for a Revolution*, 305–6.

Red Slip policy)[31] and on land purchases by Jews, were haltingly enforced and largely ineffective whether due to Jewish evasion, Ottoman corruption, or, as Ali Ekrem Bey (Jerusalem's Ottoman governor from 1906 to 1908) saw it, European consular interference and deception.[32] Ali Ekrem wrote to his imperial superiors in June 1906 that "because of the particular importance which Jerusalem holds for the Christians, it is natural that each one of the foreign countries ardently attempts to increase the number of its citizens in the place, even if they might be Jews."[33] Other egalitarian imperial trends notwithstanding, the Ottomans rulers of Palestine were legally bound to discriminate against Jews in terms of immigration and land purchase and thus necessarily were concerned with intercommunal difference in Palestine.[34]

The world in which al-Khalidi and Ben-Yehuda met, and the terms of their encounter, were informed not only by the Ottoman Tanzimat of the previous century, but as important and more immediately, by the intellectual and political transformations that led to the end of Sultan Abdul Hamid II's reign the year before the two Jerusalem leaders sat together for their interview. In these transformations, we find important evidence of the rise of race-thinking in the empire. Though it is referred to as the Young Turk *Revolution*, the overthrow of Sultan

[31] For discussion of this policy, see chapter 2.

[32] On the Ottoman government's ineffectual attempts to limit Jewish immigration and land purchasing in Palestine, see Mandel, "Ottoman Policy and Restrictions on Jewish Settlement in Palestine," 328; Mandel, "Ottoman Practice as Regards Jewish Settlement in Palestine." According to Mandel, Ottoman resistance to Jewish immigration to Palestine was motivated by the Sublime Porte's fear of "the possibility of nurturing another national problem in the Empire" and by its desire not "increase the number of foreign subjects, particularly Europeans," and even more specifically Russians, "in its domains." Mandel, "Ottoman Policy and Restrictions on Jewish Settlement in Palestine," 314. Mandel summarizes the development of the policies as follows: "the Government placed restrictions on Jews entering Palestine from 1882 onwards, which were designed to prevent Jewish settlement in the country. One decade later, it also imposed restrictions against Jewish land purchase in Palestine. Its opposition to Jewish settlement was heightened in 1897 when the Zionist Movement . . . was founded; and in 1901 the restrictions were against Jewish entry and land purchase in Palestine were revised in the form of consolidated regulations." Mandel, "Ottoman Practice as Regards Jewish Settlement in Palestine," 34. On the various methods Jews used to bypass this policy, including departing from Jaffa and reentering in Haifa or Beirut, see Kushner, *To Be Governor of Jerusalem*, 68–69.

[33] This line is found in the the fascinating 1906 report written by Ali Ekrem Bey about Jewish immigration in Kushner, *To Be Governor of Jerusalem*, 184.

[34] For Ali Ekrem (similar, as we shall see, to Muhammad Ruhi al-Khalidi), the primary motivation for Jews to come to Palestine in particular was their religious "fervor" (*taʿaṣṣub*). Jerusalem, he wrote, "is the Jews' precious paradise." Ibid., 182. He understood this population, which he surely recognized was not uniformly religiously observant, to be defined and driven nonetheless by their religion.

Abdul Hamid II in 1908 was designed rather to *reinstate* the Ottoman Constitution and parliamentary system that had been created more than three decades earlier, at the end of the Tanzimat period in 1876 just before they were suspended when Abdul Hamid II ascended as the new sultan. The precise aims and true effects of the revolution are sources of sustained scholarly debate.[35] During the period itself, however, many perceived a Turkist ethno-national particularism among the revolution's leaders and ideologues, even as the revolution promised "Liberty, Equality, Fraternity, and Justice."[36]

When, for instance, the Young Turk intellectual Yusuf Akçura identified the ideological options he saw available to the Ottoman administration in 1904 (namely, Pan-Ottomanism, Pan-Islamism, and Pan-Turkism), he insisted that it would be best "to pursue a Turkish nationalism based on race."[37] Between 1904 and 1907, the Young Turk journal *Türk* published a plethora of articles on race theory and the Turkish race, and its editors used the language of race in arguing for the Turkishness of various Turkic groups.[38] In 1907, for instance, the journal noted that "currently some learned Azerbaijanis comprehend that they are racially Turkish, and that sectarian differences, such as those between the Sunni and Shiite sects" had been exaggerated by opportunistic Muslim rulers.[39] Though the platform of the Young Turk political party, the Committee of Union and Progress (CUP), guaranteed "complete liberty and equality irrespective of race and sect,"[40] Muslims not of Turkish origin, let alone Christians and Jews, were disturbed by what they saw as the CUP's true agenda of "Turkification." Regardless of whether these suspicions were warranted, race-thinking was part of the Ottoman discourse, especially in the years surrounding the Young

[35] For a clear, concise narrative of the revolution, see Masters, *The Arabs of the Ottoman Empire*, 211–13. For a study of the effects of the revolution on the Jewish, Armenian, and Greek Orthodox leaderships and communities of Jerusalem, see Der Matossian, "Administrating the Non-Muslims and the 'Question of Jerusalem' after the Young Turk Revolution."

[36] Hanioğlu, *A Brief History of the Late Ottoman Empire*, 150; Campos, *Ottoman Brothers*, 82. On the hopes of certain Arab proponents of Ottomanism (including Ruhi al-Khalidi) in the immediate wake of the Young Turk Revolution, see Abu-Manneh, "Arab-Ottomanists' Reactions to the Young Turk Revolution."

[37] Hanioğlu, *A Brief History of the Late Ottoman Empire*, 147. On the "national and racial outlooks" associated with the rise of Turkish nationalism, see Kushner, *The Rise of Turkish Nationalism, 1876–1908*, 41–49.

[38] Hanioğlu, *Preparation for a Revolution*, 297. According to Hanioğlu, after the revolution the Young Turks ceased discussing race in public as they shifted their rhetoric to Ottomanism, but in private correspondence race remained central to their thinking.

[39] *Türk*, no. 158 (March 14, 1907), 1. Cited in ibid., 68.

[40] Cited in Campos, *Ottoman Brothers*, 82.

Turk Revolution. To understand how al-Khalidi and Ben-Yehuda conceived of one another, then, it is critical to appreciate the religious elements of the Ottoman system as well as the rise of racial discussions in the period of their encounter.

Jerusalem between Beirut and Cairo

Even as al-Khalidi and Ben-Yehuda's city was by the late nineteenth century technically, politically separated from Greater Syria and instead designated as part of the independent Ottoman mutassariflik al-Quds, Jerusalem remained within the intellectual and cultural orbit of the northern Syrian centers of Beirut and Damascus. This integration was especially pronounced in the period of the fin de siècle, when the Syrian cultural sphere expanded and became linked with that of Egypt, particularly with intellectual circles in the cities of Cairo and Alexandria. In this period, known in Arab and Middle Eastern intellectual history as the Nahḍa (the renaissance or reawakening), many important journalists, authors, scholars, and activists from Syria moved south to Egypt. In Egypt, a society ruled since 1882 by the British, these (mostly Christian) Syrian transplants escaped Ottoman censorship and joined forces with local Egyptian intellectuals to produce, among other things, widely read and highly influential scientific and literary Arabic journals, some of which were first created while the editors were still in Syria. Though fin de siècle Jerusalem was hardly an intellectual capital on the order of Beirut or Cairo, Palestine's geographic centrality between Syria and Egypt meant both that intellectuals from north and south passed through Jerusalem and that the literary and cultural elite of Arabic-reading Palestine were necessarily engaged with the ideas generated and published in the centers—including al-Khalidi, who wrote on occasion in the Nahḍa journals.

Locating Jerusalem within the Syria-Egypt cultural orbit highlights other ways in which race was on the minds of intellectuals in al-Khalidi and Ben-Yehuda's city. Perhaps the most formative experience for one circle of Nahḍa figures—the editors of the journal *al-Muqtaṭaf*—was the controversy over Darwinism at the Syrian Protestant College (SPC) in 1882. This crisis, known alternatively as the "Darwin Controversy" or the "Lewis Affair,"[41] began when Edwin Lewis, a young American physics instructor at the SPC, delivered a speech at the college's

[41] This affair has been the subject of several scholarly studies, including Elshakry, "Darwin's Legacy in the Arab East"; Jeha, *Darwin and the Crisis of 1882 in the Medical Department.*

commencement that the college administration deemed to be overly sympathetic to Darwinian theory. In fact, Lewis's speech, given just over two decades after the publication of Darwin's *On the Origin of Species* (1859), did not unequivocally advocate for the scientific merits of Darwinism. "As for the adequacy of this doctrine," Lewis said, "we cannot at the moment make a final judgment, since many aspects still need investigation, evidence, and thorough examination before arriving at any judgment."[42] Notwithstanding such caveats, Lewis's speech was summarily condemned by the more conservative forces in the missionary school and ultimately led to Lewis's ouster from the faculty.

Only inflaming matters from the perspective of the college administration, *al-Muqtaṭaf*—a journal based at SPC and edited by two of the college's instructors—published Lewis's speech, thereby providing it with a far larger audience than that which had originally heard it at the commencement ceremony.[43] An extended discussion ensued in the pages of *al-Muqtaṭaf* about the speech and about Darwinism, a theory the editors (if not Lewis) found compelling. In 1884, in the wake of this affair, the editors were dismissed from their positions at the college. Within months they migrated and transplanted their journal to Cairo, where during an earlier visit in 1880 they had been warmly received and discovered the popularity of *al-Muqtaṭaf* among intellectuals in Egypt.[44]

Upon reestablishing itself in Cairo, *al-Muqtaṭaf* continued defending Darwin's theory and some of the social implications that were drawn from it.[45] While notions of race predated Darwin, many understood Darwin's theory scientifically to explain human variation and the existence of human races. Darwin used the term "race" in *The Origin of Species* (the extended title of which includes "the Preservation of Favoured Races in the Struggle for Life"), though he did so, as scholars Robert Bernasconi and Tommy Lott explain, "only in the broad biological use of the word," not in the sense of races of humanity. Later, though, in his *The Descent of Man* (1871), Darwin more carefully considered the implications of his theory in a chapter "On the Races of Man."[46] While even in *The Descent of Man* Darwin expressed uncertainty about how to account for races among humans, Social Darwinists perceived a

[42] An English translation of Lewis's speech, which Jeha argues was originally written in Arabic, is found in Jeha, *Darwin and the Crisis of 1882 in the Medical Department*, 160–70.

[43] See Farag, "The Lewis Affair and the Fortunes of al-Muqtataf."

[44] Elshakry, "Darwin's Legacy in the Arab East," 28.

[45] Ibid.; Elshakry, "Global Darwin."

[46] See Bernasconi and Lott, *The Idea of Race*, 54–83.

clear link between "natural selection" and human racial hierarchies.[47] Given its role in the traumatic transplantation of *al-Muqtaṭaf* to Egypt, Darwinism and ideas associated with it took on a central place in the thought and identity of the journal, its editors, and ultimately its many readers.

Moreover, as Omnia El Shakry has shown, among the intellectual, scientific fin de siècle Arabic journals, *al-Muqtaṭaf* was not alone in its interest in race-thinking. Jurji Zaydan published articles about race in his contemporaneous journal *al-Hilāl*,[48] and in 1912 he also wrote an entire book on the subject of race, *Ṭabaqāt al-umam aw as-salāʾil al-bashariyya* (Classes of the Nations, or Races of Man).[49] Zaydan's study explores the origins of human races and analyzes the various qualities (physical and spiritual) purportedly associated with each.[50] Race, then, was part of the intellectual, cultural, and philosophical worldview of turn-of-the-century Arabic journals, both reflecting and informing their broader readership's interests in this means of conceiving of humanity and human difference.

Questions of race were not merely of academic or theoretical interest in fin de siècle Egypt. Rather, as Eve Troutt Powell has demonstrated, racial thinking was pervasive in nineteenth- and early twentieth-century Egypt as Egyptians conceived of their role in dominating the Sudan (ruled by Egypt from 1821 until 1885 and again, under the British, beginning in 1899).[51] Even before the British conquest of Egypt in 1882 and certainly during the British occupation as well, the discourse concerning Egypt's role in the Sudan—its "civilizing mission"[52]—was articulated in racial terms. "In late-nineteenth-century Egypt," Powell contends, "writers and nationalists were acutely aware of the discourse on race being conducted in western Europe, and they used it to frame their various perspectives about the Sudan and its people."[53]

[47] On Social Darwinism, see Hofstadter's classic, *Social Darwinism in American Thought.*

[48] E.g., the 1900 *al-Hilāl* article "*Aṣnāf al-bashar.*"

[49] Zaydān, *Ṭabaqāt al-umam aw as-salāʾil al-bashariyya.* The book draws on the work of the Irish scholar Augustus Henry Keane. On Keane, see "Dr. A. H. Keane," *Nature* 88 (February 8, 1912), 488. Keane's work on race is important in this context given his views on Jewish and Arab racial qualities. "Expansion and progress are the dominant characteristics of the Aryan, concentration and immutability of the Semitic intellect, a special reservation having always to be made in favour of the Jews, most versatile perhaps of all peoples." Keane, *The World's Peoples*, 328.

[50] On Zaydan's work on race and its use of Keane, see El Shakry, *The Great Social Laboratory*, 58–60.

[51] Troutt Powell highlights the writings of, among others, Muhammad at-Tunisi, Selim Qapudan, Rifaʿa Rafiʿ at-Tahtawi, ʿAli Mubarak, Yaʿqub Sanuʿa, and ʿAbdallah Nadim.

[52] Powell, *A Different Shade of Colonialism*, 5.

[53] Ibid., 17.

Racial thinking was a central part of the ways in which intellectuals and others to Palestine's north, in Syria, and south, in Egypt, categorized and conceived of themselves and of others. When the Jerusalem of al-Khalidi and Ben-Yehuda is understood in this Nahḍa nexus, it is unsurprising to discover that these men's communities also employed racial modes as they perceived one another.

Jerusalem and Europe

Finally, in numerous ways both real and imagined, Ben-Yehuda and al-Khalidi's Jerusalem was linked to Europe. In a personal sense, these two individuals were partly European: Ben-Yehuda and many of his fellow Zionists in Jerusalem were born in Eastern Europe, while al-Khalidi had studied in Paris and served as the Ottoman consul general in the south of France. Intellectually, culturally, even linguistically (the conversation was likely conducted in French),[54] their encounter in Jerusalem was one critically informed by, even inseparable from, Europe.

Jerusalem, and Palestine more broadly, were the focus of immense European attention in the fin de siècle. This attention is evident, of course, in Zionism, the European-born Jewish nationalist movement directed at Zion (the mountain that serves as a synecdoche for both Jerusalem and the entire Land of Israel). European interest is also apparent, though, in the communities of European Christian missionaries, educators, and consuls that settled in Palestine in this period. Beginning in the mid-nineteenth century, numerous European countries, including Britain, Prussia, France, Austria, Russia, Italy, Greece, Spain, Holland, Belgium, Norway, Denmark, and Sweden, established new consulates in Jerusalem.[55] Also beginning in the 1830s and continuing through the end of the Ottoman period in Palestine, European Protestant missionary communities established themselves in Jerusalem.[56] These missionaries founded and staffed schools, hospitals, and other institutions that served the needs of the often impoverished communities of Palestine. By Ottoman law, Christian missionaries were prohibited from proselytizing Muslims. Instead, they focused their missionizing efforts on the Jews (through, for example, the London Society for Promoting

[54] An irony, of course, as Ben-Yehuda is best known for his efforts to revive Hebrew as a quotidian, spoken language and for his stubborn refusal to speak to his son in any language other than Hebrew.

[55] Ben-Arieh, *Jerusalem in the 19th Century—the Old City*, 185–86.

[56] Perry, "ha-Naẓrut ha-maʿaravit," 141–45.

Christianity amongst the Jews) and on local members of other Christian denominations (such as Greek Orthodox and Catholics).[57]

The presence of these missionary groups in Late Ottoman Jerusalem has a number of important implications for this book. First, given the intensive and sustained missionary activities in Jerusalem in the nineteenth century, Palestine during this period cannot be seen in isolation from Europe. That European powers exercised political influence through these Christian missions is widely acknowledged, as is the fact that the missions themselves reflected this political influence. More important for our purposes, though, because the missionaries were technically limited in their permitted targets of proselytization, they were by necessity conscious of and invested in religious difference among Palestine's population. This institutionalized sensitivity to religious distinctions for a powerful group in Palestine was clearly recognized by Palestine's various religious communities and, as a result, played its own role in sustaining, or even magnifying, such distinctions. Moreover, owing to the threat (and also the promised educational, cultural, economic, and of course religious rewards) of proselytization by European Christians, religion in Late Ottoman Palestine was a highly sensitive subject. This, too, suggests that for all communities in Palestine, far beyond the missionaries themselves, religion was a central concern.

We must also keep in mind that these foreigners, whether diplomats or missionaries, brought with them contemporary European ideas about how to define and categorize people, including the developing notions of race. These were, after all, part and parcel of the ideology of the civilizing (i.e., Christianizing) duty that drove the missionaries out into the distant frontiers of the Ottoman Empire.[58] The European presence in Palestine, then, only accentuated concerns with both religion and race that were already prominent there from other more "indigenous" sources.

Finally, many European Jewish intellectuals and scientists were influenced by and even involved in the development of race-thinking in European science and anthropology. In fact, there was a strong element of race-thinking among certain European Zionists, including some who

[57] Ben-Arieh, *Jerusalem in the 19th Century—the Old City*, 250–64; Perry, *British Mission to the Jews in Nineteenth-Century Palestine.*

[58] On the issue of race in the ideology of *American* Christian missionaries in the Middle East, see Makdisi, *Artillery of Heaven*, 262. Of the Syrian Protestant College in Beirut, Makdisi writes, "The college's Christian idealism and missionary character were nevertheless refracted through a mid-century American racialist reading of the world. As its first president, Daniel Bliss, put it so succinctly: 'We open its doors to the members of the most advanced and most backward of races. As for me, I would admit the Pigmies of Central Africa in the hope that after a lapse of a few thousand years some of them might become leaders of Church and State.' " Ibid., 209.

immigrated to Palestine. As John Efron and others have shown, identifying the Jews as a race was useful for the purposes of establishing the Jews as a distinct nation (at a time when the terms and concepts of "nation" and "race" were often used interchangeably). In the course of this book, we will see the implications of European race-thinking not only on Jewish self-perception but also on Zionists' perceptions of others, especially the Arabs of Palestine.[59]

Palestine's Population

Having placed al-Khalidi and Ben-Yehuda's Jerusalem in its Palestinian, Middle Eastern, Ottoman, and transnational contexts, we must now turn to the question of who was living in Palestine during this Late Ottoman period. For a variety of reasons both methodological and political, Palestine's historical demographics are hotly contested.[60] First, though the Ottomans registered their populations, primarily for the purposes of taxation and conscription, non-Ottoman subjects were excluded as they provided neither taxes nor conscripts.[61] Because the large majority of immigrant Jews from Europe chose to retain their European citizenship or subject status, so as to benefit from the legal and tax advantages of the Capitulations[62] and to avoid the Ottoman military draft, Ottoman records are not terribly useful for gauging the size of the Jewish immigrant population. Second, the Ottoman registers did not count Bedouin as they too were considered irrelevant for taxation and conscription. These records are thus imprecise for ascertaining the number not only of Jews but also of Arabs in Palestine. Third, given the problems associated with the sources and thus the necessity for estimation, the numbers scholars offer often indicate as much about the scholar's political inclinations vis-à-vis the Israeli-Palestinian conflict as they do about the number of residents of Palestine at any given

[59] Efron, *Defenders of the Race*; Hart, *Jews and Race*; Falk, "Zionism and the Biology of the Jews," 587–607.

[60] For a discussion of the problems associated with demographic analysis in Ottoman Palestine, as well as an impressive attempt at engaging in such an analysis, see McCarthy, *The Population of Palestine*, especially 2–5. The work that generated perhaps the most controversy and debate on this question is Peters, *From Time Immemorial*. See also Said and Hitchens, eds., *Blaming the Victims*, 296. For an insightful discussion of the demographic ambiguities of Late Ottoman Palestine, see Jacobson, *From Empire to Empire*, 3.

[61] McCarthy notes one exception: "Official statistics of resident noncitizens," he explains, "were published only in 1895 (for the year 1893)." McCarthy, *The Population of Palestine*, 23.

[62] On the Capitulations and the Jews, see Friedman, "The System of Capitulations and Its Effects on Turco-Jewish Relations in Palestine, 1856–1897."

moment. Zionists and their supporters tend to prefer higher estimates of the Jewish population and lower estimates of the Arab population, while Palestinians and their advocates have the opposite preferences.

For the purposes of this study of intellectual history, it will suffice to provide rough population estimates intended solely to offer the reader a general, if admittedly imprecise, sense of the size of the populations of Late Ottoman Palestine.[63] In 1881, before the first large Jewish nationalist immigration, Palestine's population was likely about 462,000, consisting of 400,000 Muslims, 42,000 Christians, and 20,000 Jews (including perhaps 5,000 Jews without Ottoman citizenship). By the start of the Great War, the population had increased to about 740,000, including 600,000 Muslims, 80,000 Christians, and somewhere between 60,000 and 85,000 Jews (of whom fewer than 40,000 were Ottoman citizens).

In other words, the vast majority of the population throughout the Late Ottoman period consisted of Arabic-speaking Muslims. Of these, most were Sunnis, though there were also small pockets of Shiites and Druze, especially in the northern regions bordering on present-day Lebanon.[64] Though the majority of Palestine's Sunnis belonged to the Shāfiʿī *madhhab* (jurisprudential school), the most influential mufti (expounder of Islamic law) was that of the Ḥanafī *madhhab*, as this was the school followed by the Ottoman rulers and applied in the Islamic courts. The various muftis, as well as the *naqīb al-ashrāf* (the representative of the local descendants of the prophet Muhammad, plural *nuqabāʾ*), were selected from the families of Palestine's *ʿulamāʾ*, the religious-scholarly (and usually also economic) elite. Whereas the muftis and nuqabāʾ al-ashrāf were generally drawn from the local Muslim population, the *quḍāh* (Islamic court judges, sing. *qāḍī*) were usually foreigners (though there were some exceptions in the early nineteenth century). The qāḍī of the Ḥanafī court in Jerusalem was a much respected position, appointed by the highest religious official in Istanbul, the *shaykh al-islām*.[65] The leaders of Palestine's rural population, which constituted the majority of the Muslim community, were village and regional shaykhs and, in the late nineteenth and early twentieth centuries, a new Ottoman position called the *mukhtār*.[66]

[63] For our purposes, if the actual numbers were somewhat higher or lower, this book's argument would not be much affected. I base my estimates primarily on McCarthy, *The Population of Palestine*.

[64] Abassi, "Temurot ba-ukhlusiyah ha-muslimit bi-rushalayim 1840–1914."

[65] Mannāʿ, "ha-Ukhlusiyah ha-ʿarvit: Ḥevrah, kalkalah ve-irgun," 8:164–65.

[66] The Ottomans created this position to replace the prominence of the shaykhs and thereby gain a stronger hold on the rural population. Ultimately the shaykhs maintained much of their power. Ibid., 173.

Among the Christian population, about half were Arabic-speaking members of the Greek Orthodox faith, an Eastern Orthodox church led by a patriarch (who was, by ecclesiastical law, always Greek in origin) in Jerusalem. The remaining half of the Christians in Palestine consisted of members of a variety of denominations, including Greek Catholics (especially in the Galilee), Latin Catholics (led by a patriarch in Jerusalem under the Vatican's jurisdiction), Maronites, Armenian Orthodox, Syrian Orthodox, Syrian Catholics, and Copts, in addition to a small but growing (due to conversion by British missionaries) population of Protestants, particularly Arab Episcopalians.[67] While the Muslim population was overwhelmingly rural, about three-quarters of the land's Christians lived in urban environments.[68]

Like the Christians of Palestine, the Jews both before and after the Zionist immigrations were primarily urban. The pre-Zionist Jewish communities were concentrated in the so-called Four Holy Cities—Jerusalem, Hebron, Tiberias, and Safed.[69] Though Zionists founded a number of agricultural *moshavot* (colonies such as Petah Tikva,[70] Rishon Le-Zion, Rosh Pina, and Zikhron Yaʿakov) and *kevuẓot* (collective settlements, the first of which was Deganiah, established in 1909), the Jewish residents of these rural communities constituted no more than 20 percent of the total Jewish population at the end of the Ottoman period.[71] Most Jewish immigrants, in other words, moved to Palestine's towns, especially Jerusalem and, increasingly as the years progressed, Jaffa.

Critical scholarship over the past several decades has contested certain received assumptions about the "Zionists" of pre–World War I Palestine. In earlier historiography, which followed the dominant nomenclature of the period itself, Palestine's Jewish community was seen as composed of two broad units: the "old *yishuv*" and the "new *yishuv*." The old yishuv was imagined to be the Jewish religious

[67] Robson, *Colonialism and Christianity in Mandate Palestine*, 5; Harani, "ha-ʿEdot ha-noẓriyot"; Ervine, "Yerushalayim ha-armanit"; McCarthy, *The Population of Palestine*, 8–13.

[68] On village life in the region around Jerusalem, see Oren-Nordheim, "ha-Merkhav ha-kafri bi-svivot yerushalayim be-shilhei ha-tekufah ha-ʿot'manit." On the urban nature of the Christian community, see Robson, *Colonialism and Christianity in Mandate Palestine*, 3.

[69] On the pre-Zionist Jewish community of Palestine, see, inter alia, Bartal, *Galut ba-areẓ*; Eliav, *Ereẓ yisraʾel vi-shuvah ba-meʾah ha-19*.

[70] Petah Tikva was actually first founded in 1878 by Jews from Jerusalem—not new Zionist immigrants—but it was soon abandoned and then resettled by First Aliyah immigrants in 1882.

[71] Gelvin renders these 12,000 Jews as 15 percent, but he is working with a total number of 85,000, which is generally regarded as an inflated figure for the Jewish community before the First World War. See Gelvin, *The Israel-Palestine Conflict*, 69.

population of Palestine—Ashkenazim and Sephardim—some whose ancestors had resided in the Holy Land for generations, others recent immigrants who wished to study the Torah and be buried in sacred soil. These individuals lived in Palestine because of the perceived holiness of the place but lacked any Jewish nationalist motivations and even forcefully opposed Zionism when it appeared. The new yishuv of Ottoman Palestine, on the other hand, was portrayed as composed of mostly secular, ideological Jewish nationalists who had immigrated to Palestine after 1881 in the course of the first two *aliyot* (waves of Jewish nationalist immigration to Palestine) out of the conviction that the Jews should—without waiting for the advent of the messiah or any other divine act—create a modern Jewish society in Palestine and even a state of their own.

Recent scholarship has challenged this conventional distinction between the old and new *yeshuvim* on two main fronts. First, scholars have recognized that Jewish nationalist sympathies and tendencies were exhibited by members of the so-called old yishuv, among both Sephardim and Ashkenazim. Second, historians have noted that many of the Eastern European Jewish immigrants who arrived between 1881 and 1914 chose to immigrate to Palestine rather than the United States not out of ideological commitment but because of more pragmatic concerns, such as the price of a ticket. In addition, many of these new immigrants were themselves religiously observant Jews.[72]

Moreover, the traditional distinction between the First *Aliyah* and the Second *Aliyah*, the Jewish immigration waves to Palestine between 1881 and 1904 and between 1904 and 1914, respectively, has also been compellingly problematized. The earlier view held that Second Aliyah immigrants arrived with much more ideological zeal—Zionist, socialist, agriculturalist—than their First Aliyah predecessors. Once more, scholars have since demonstrated that this perception of the Second Aliyah is rooted in generalizations from the experiences of this immigration wave's outspoken, prolific, and influential minority, which ultimately came to dominate the politics of the yishuv and then, for decades, those of the State of Israel. The majority, however, were, like most immigrants at any time and place, motivated by the desire to improve their socioeconomic position rather than to participate in any ideological revolution.[73]

[72] An interesting popular, nonacademic work on the religious nature of early Zionist immigration is Finkel, *Rebels in the Holy Land*.

[73] See Bartal, " 'Old Yishuv' and 'New Yishuv' "; Kaniel, "The Terms 'Old Yishuv' and 'New Yishuv.' " For a more recent revision, see Alroey, *Imigrantim*. See also Alroey, "Journey to Early-Twentieth-Century Palestine as a Jewish Immigrant Experience."

I focus on the ideas of Palestine's Zionists[74] (rather than those of all yishuv residents) in my analysis of Jews' perceptions of their non-Jewish neighbors in order to look particularly at those individuals and communities who we would imagine employed primarily nationalist modes of categorization. After all, we might not be surprised were we to find that antinationalist Jews did not conceive of their Arab neighbors in exclusively national terms—why would they think of others as members of nations when they did not even consider themselves as such? Ideological Zionists who believed that they were first and foremost members of a Jewish nation, on the other hand, would perhaps see not only themselves but also the world around them primarily in national terms. Thus it is especially interesting to discover the religious and racial aspects of committed Zionists' perceptions of their neighbors in Palestine.

The issue of national identity among Palestine's Arabs is more complicated still. The loyalties and national identities of Palestine's Arabs—that is, native Muslim and Christian Arabic-speakers—were at this stage multifarious and in flux. As Rashid Khalidi has shown, Arabs of Late Ottoman Palestine could simultaneously imagine themselves as loyal Ottomans, Muslims or Christians, Arabs, Palestinians, while also associating strongly with their hometown or village and extended family.[75] While recent scholarship has argued that distinctly Palestinian national identity existed even before the First World War, because of the extent of the variety of Palestinian Arab identities at this early stage in the development and articulation of these notions, it would not be possible to write this book only about individuals who affiliated exclusively or even primarily as Palestinians. I therefore have chosen the category of Arabs of Palestine or Palestinian Arabs, which I use interchangeably, though of course I remain cognizant of the particular national identities of the subjects of this study, to the extent that they may be discerned.[76]

[74] I include in this study individuals such as Eliezer Ben-Yehuda, who, motivated by Jewish nationalist ideology, immigrated to Palestine in 1881. Technically Zionism as an official organization was founded only in 1897, with Theodor Herzl's establishment of the Zionist Congress; while acknowledging the somewhat anachronistic terminology, I include in this study Jewish Palestinocentric nationalists in Palestine (e.g., those associated with the Hibbat Zion or Bilu movements) even before 1897.

[75] See especially the chapter "Competing and Overlapping Loyalties in Ottoman Jerusalem" in Khalidi, *Palestinian Identity*, 63–88.

[76] In my use of the term Palestinian Arab, I follow Lockman, who writes: "Adding the term 'Arab' when referring to the people whom we would today simply call 'the Palestinians' may seem redundant, but in fact it avoids an anachronism, for it was really only after 1948 that the Palestinian Arab people came to call themselves, and be called by others, simply Palestinians. During the mandate period most Palestinian organizations

Another segment of the population of Late Ottoman Palestine that has received substantial scholarly and popular interest in recent years is the community of Sephardim. The label *sefaradi* literally means Spanish and technically refers to Jews who emigrated from the Iberian Peninsula, especially in the aftermath of the expulsion of 1492. For a variety of reasons, however, the term came to be used as a catch-all for non-European, non-Ashkenazic Jews, that is, for "Easterners" (Hebrew: *mizraḥim*), whether or not they had any family history in Spain. Though the use of this term as an all-inclusive "Jewish other" category is partly attributable to Ashkenazic ignorance of or disinterest in the details of non-Ashkenazic difference, there is much more to the story. When the Spanish Jewish exiles came to the Ottoman Middle East, they found diverse Jewish communities, some of which had been in existence for centuries. These pre-Sephardic Middle Eastern Jews included Greek-speaking Romaniot, Ashkenazim, Italians, and Arabic-speaking *musta*ʿ*ribūn*.[77] Over time the Sephardim came to dominate many of these communities, including in Palestine, both politically and culturally.[78] In Palestine the Ottoman sultan regarded the Sephardic leadership as the central authority among local Ottoman Jews. By the mid-nineteenth century, these Jews came to be represented by an imperially appointed chief rabbi, always of the Sephardic rite, known in Ottoman Turkish as the *hahambaşi* and in Hebrew as the *rishon le-ẓiyon*.[79] In other words, regardless of their place of origin, most Middle Eastern Jews in Palestine were officially affiliated with the Sephardic community.

That there was a significant population of native Arabic-speakers among the Jewish community—even among the ideologically Zionist community—of Late Ottoman Palestine further highlights the intriguing complexities of identity in this historical setting. Focusing on this community, a number of scholars have recently raised the question of whether we might regard these Jewish Arabic-speakers as "Arab Jews." Just as we speak of American Jews, German Jews, European Jews, and

---

and institutions (in today's sense) officially called themselves 'Arab,' sometimes with 'Palestinian' as a modifier; hence the Arab Executive, the Arab Higher Committee, the Arab Workers' Congress, the Palestinian Arab Workers' Society, and so forth. Moreover, I want to be sure to distinguish between the Arab and Jewish communities in Palestine, and use of the term 'Palestinian' with reference to a period in which Palestine was still undivided might cause confusion." Lockman, *Comrades and Enemies*, 18.

[77] Levy, *The Sephardim in the Ottoman Empire*, 3–4. See also my entry on "*musta*ʿ*ribūn*" in the *Encyclopedia of Jews in the Islamic World*, 2nd ed.

[78] On the waves of Sephardic immigration to Palestine, see Eliav, *Ereẓ yisra*ʾ*el vi-shuvah ba-me*ʾ*ah ha-19*, 92–95.

[79] Elmaleh , *ha-Rishonim le-Ẓiyon*; Haim and Eliachar, *Te*ʿ*udot min ha-osef shel Eliyahu Elyashar*, 17–18.

so on, should we not speak of Arab Jews? While the phrase Arab Jew might strike the early twenty-first-century ear as awkward if not oxymoronic, perhaps discomfort with the term is a result of the subsequent Arab-Israeli conflict, when Arab and Jew were presumed enemies, not qualifiers of single individuals or communities. Before the intensification of this conflict, could these not have been terms of potential hybridity rather than hostility? Determined to resist this political anachronism—the view that Arabs and Jews necessarily meet on opposite ends of a battlefield, not a hyphen—a number of recent scholars have taken to referring to this population as Arab-Jews.[80]

In fact, appellations similar to "Arab Jews" were not unheard of in the Late Ottoman period. The phrase *yahūd awlād al-ʿarab* (Jews children of Arabs) appeared in certain Late Ottoman Arabic writing in reference to native Jews of Palestine, according to scholar Salim Tamari.[81] Ashkenazic Zionists would, on occasion, criticize Middle Eastern Jews viewed as overly enmeshed in Arab culture as "Arabs of the Mosaic faith."[82] In late 1908 someone even signed a notice in Ben-Yehuda's Hebrew newspaper with the name "*ha-ʿivriyah ha-ʿarviyah*" (the Arab Hebrew woman).[83]

Yet what I have found is that the response to that notice seems to represent a more typical view from the period: "To the Arab Hebrew woman! If you are a Hebrew, you are not an Arab. If an Arab, not a Hebrew. So, you are neither a Hebrew nor an Arab. C.Q.F.D."[84] Though hardly a cogent logical proof, this statement, read in the context of the variety of writing extant from the period, suggests that a blanket embrace of "Arab Jew" to describe Arabic-speaking Jews would represent a terminological anachronism. Because I share the desire to rethink

[80] In the Iraqi context, Orit Bashkin has proposed using the term Arab Jew to refer not only to those who explicitly regarded themselves as such, but also to Jews who "practiced . . . Arab Jewishness, in that they wrote in Arabic, read Arabic texts, interacted with fellow Muslim and Christian Arabs, and enjoyed Arab cinema, music, and theater." Bashkin, *New Babylonians*, 2. For a discussion of the concept of Arab Jews in different historical settings, see Levy, "Historicizing the Concept of Arab Jews in the Mashriq"; Gottreich, "Historicizing the Concept of Arab Jews in the Maghrib." On Palestine, see Jacobson, "The Sephardi Community in Pre–World War I Palestine"; Jacobson, "From Empire to Empire."

[81] Tamari cites "the autobiographies of Khalil Sakakini and Wasif Jawhariyyeh," but he does not note particular pages in these texts. Tamari also mentions the title *abnāʾ al-balad* (sons of the country), also used in these texts to refer to "native Jews of Palestine." Tamari, *Mountain against the Sea*, 164.

[82] See Kaniel, "Anshei ha-ʿaliyah ha-sheniyah u-venei ha-ʿedah ha-sefaradit," 309n.17. Cf. Schreier, *Arabs of the Jewish Faith*.

[83] *ha-Ẓevi* 25:42 (November 27, 1908), Supplement, 2.

[84] Ibid.

complex identities and challenge oversimplified, presentist labels, the guiding principle I try to follow throughout the book in my choice of labels (when the choice is indeed mine) is to use appellations that I believe would have made sense to either the subject or the subject's neighbors, and ideally both.[85]

Beyond the way in which my study bears on the historicity of the Arab Jew concept, I raise it here for another important reason as well. The recent debate regarding the Arab Jew has served as a welcome call for greater self-consciousness in how we employ labels. As I argue in this book, the ways in which people labeled others tell us something about how they viewed and understood these individuals and groups. This contention can be no more correct for the subjects of our scholarship than it is for the scholars who write about them. I thus proceed with caution but also with the conviction that so long as we are aware of the challenge, we need not be paralyzed by it. As I hope this book demonstrates, a new and fascinating view of this early encounter emerges from a critical, self-aware reading of the sources.

[85] Compare this discussion to the recent scholarship on the origins of the term Christian and the problematic distinction between Christian and Jew. See, e.g., Townsend, "Who Were the First Christians?"

CHAPTER 2

Muhammad Ruhi al-Khalidi's "as-Sayūnīzm": An Islamic Theory of Jewish History in Late Ottoman Palestine

Eliezer Ben-Yehuda published his interview of Muhammad Ruhi al-Khalidi for the readers of Ben-Yehuda's Hebrew daily newspaper *ha-Ẓevi.*[1] In the interview, al-Khalidi rejected the creation of Jewish colonies in Palestine and, while he would support the rights of individual Jews to immigrate if they were to accept Ottoman citizenship and assimilate into the Arab environment, he vigorously denounced mass Jewish nationalist immigration to Palestine.[2] While the exchange recorded in *ha-Ẓevi* certainly reveals al-Khalidi's hostility toward Zionism, it also offers other insights into how these two men understood one another, and the peoples they represented.

For Ben-Yehuda, al-Khalidi was a respected intellectual colleague, "an author who had written articles in Arabic periodicals on Islamic and Arab issues, and who participated in academic conferences of Orientalists." Moreover, Ben-Yehuda considered al-Khalidi "an acquaintance and friend from the bad days, when we needed to close the door behind us and whisper out of fear that the spies of [Sultan] Abd al-Hamid were secretly listening to our words." Ben-Yehuda had held sensitive discussions with al-Khalidi in the past, conversations, we might imagine, in which these two individuals sought to understand each other and the various groups of which they were leaders. After seeking al-Khalidi's view on the present Ottoman grand vizier, Ben-Yehuda's interview then broached "the difficult point," namely, Ottoman policy on Jewish immigration to Palestine. While emphasizing that Jewish-Arab

[1] *ha-Ẓevi*, November 2, 1909.

[2] As a result, al-Khalidi's position is often cited in the scholarship on the early Palestinian Arab opposition to Zionism. See Mandel, *The Arabs and Zionism before World War I*, 77; Beʾeri, *Reshit ha-sikhsukh yisraʾel-ʿarav, 1882–1911*, 146. On Ben-Yehuda's motivations for the interview, see Lang, *Daber ʿivrit!*, 623.

fraternity is "most natural and most desirable," al-Khalidi expressed his disapproval of separatist Jewish nationalism in Palestine. "We conquered this land," he insists, "not from you [i.e., the Jews]." Rather, "we conquered it from the Byzantines who ruled it at the time," and thus "we owe nothing to the Jews," who, he emphasizes again, "were not here when we conquered the land." Justifiably, these words are generally taken to demonstrate al-Khalidi's fierce rejection of the contemporary Jewish claim to Palestine.[3] Yet, when read closely, they implicitly acknowledge that, though the Jews "were not here when we [Arabs] conquered the land," they *had been* in Palestine beforehand.

For al-Khalidi, history, even that of remote times, was of real importance in the modern period. The Arab conquest of Palestine occurred over one thousand years earlier (638 CE), and yet al-Khalidi does not discount the contemporary relevance of the details of this historic conquest. If it had been the Jews (rather than the Byzantines) from whom the Arabs had conquered Palestine, one infers from al-Khalidi's logic, the situation and the considerations of justice more than a millennium later would be quite different. But what, then, was the meaning of the Jews' history in Palestine? Al-Khalidi, later dubbed a "pioneer of modern historical research in Palestine,"[4] did not disregard the potential significance of the Jews' ancient kingdoms in Palestine, and indeed, until his death, he struggled with this question through his still-unpublished manuscript on Judaism, Jewish history, and Zionism. It is to this manuscript that we now turn our attention.[5]

Reading the *Jewish Encyclopedia* in the Shadow of al-Aqsa

When Richard James Horatio Gottheil set out to write the new *Jewish Encyclopedia*'s entry on "Zionism" in the very first years of the twentieth century, he undoubtedly had a wide variety of potential readers in mind: Jews and non-Jews, native English-speakers, European intellectuals, and individuals who supported the nascent Jewish nationalist movement along with the many more who were indifferent or opposed to it.[6] Gottheil, professor of Semitic languages at Columbia University,

[3] On Ben-Yehuda's disillusion with al-Khalidi by 1912, see Lang, *Daber ʿivrit!*, 615–16.

[4] Asad, *Muḥammad Rūḥī al-Khālidī.*

[5] I thank Rashid Khalidi for generously granting me access to this invaluable document.

[6] The *Jewish Encyclopedia* (JE) was published by Funk and Wagnalls between 1901 and 1906. For a study of the encyclopedia and its significance in American Jewish history, see Schwartz, *The Emergence of Jewish Scholarship in America.*

together with his coeditors on the encyclopedia board, believed that this broad range of readers would warmly embrace the landmark encyclopedia project, the first to synthesize the knowledge about Judaism and the Jews, from the Bible to the present day, that had been amassed over the previous century and a half of "scientific" study.[7] One reader Gottheil might not have anticipated, however, was Muhammad Ruhi al-Khalidi.

Al-Khalidi (1864–1913), though only two years younger than Gottheil (1862–1936), was born in Jerusalem, thousands of miles from Gottheil's native Manchester, England, and across the world from the Jewish Orientalist's adoptive New York. Al-Khalidi was the scion of one of the wealthy, elite Muslim Arab families (along with the Husseynis and Nashashibis) of Ottoman Palestine. He grew up in the Bāb as-Silsila neighborhood of the Old City of Jerusalem, steps away from the Dome of the Rock.[8] Despite the geographical and cultural distance between al-Khalidi's Jerusalem and Gottheil's New York, Gottheil's extended entry on Zionism in the *Jewish Encyclopedia* did indeed reach al-Khalidi's eye. Al-Khalidi appears to have come across Gottheil's article at some point during his own years shuttling between Jerusalem and Istanbul when he served, between 1908 and 1913, as one of Jerusalem's representatives in the newly reconstituted Ottoman Parliament.[9] As a native of Palestine and as a leader of its Arab population, al-Khalidi was deeply concerned and troubled by the increasing immigration of foreign Jews into his country, by the associated ideology that claimed his homeland as the Jews' own, and by the political program that, as he saw it, was actively seeking to transform the land into a Jewish state. Al-Khalidi—whose intellectual curiosity and broad range of interests led him to write such varied scholarly treatises as *al-Kīmiyāʾ ʿind al-ʿarab* (Chemistry among the Arabs), *Tārīkh ʿilm al-adab ʿind al-ifranj wa-l-ʿarab wa-Fīktūr Hūgū* (The History of Literature among the Europeans, the Arabs, and Victor

[7] See the preface to the JE.

[8] These biographical data are gleaned from al-Khālidī, "Kitāb as-sayūnīzm aw al-masʾala aṣ-ṣahyūniyya li-Muḥammad Rūḥī al-Khālidī al-mutawaffā sanat 1913"; Khalidi, *Palestinian Identity*; Mannāʿ, *Aʿlām filasṭīn fī awākhir al-ʿahd al-ʿuthmānī (1800–1918)*; al-Khateeb, "Ruhi Al-Khalidi."

[9] The first Ottoman Parliament lasted for less than one year (March 1877 through February 1878) during the Ottoman Empire's "first constitutional era" (1876–1878). The constitution was then suspended by the sultan and only restored three decades later, after the Young Turk Revolution of 1908. Shortly thereafter, elections were held for the new Ottoman Parliament. See Hanioğlu, *A Brief History of the Late Ottoman Empire*, 118–23, 150–67. Al-Khalidi successfully ran for a parliamentary position in the election of November–December 1908 and then again in the election of February–April 1912.

Hugo),[10] and *al-Muqaddima fī al-masʾala ash-sharqiyya* (Introduction to the Eastern Question)—wished to understand more deeply the phenomenon of Zionism.[11]

Gottheil's twenty-one-page encyclopedia entry offered al-Khalidi a unique window into the world of this movement. It was at once the work of a man deeply involved in and therefore familiar with the history of Zionism and, at the same time, an ostensibly nonpolemical account of the movement's historical, religious, and political underpinnings.[12] Having read Gottheil's article and numerous other works on Judaism and Jewish history, al-Khalidi set out to write his own book—in Arabic—on Zionism, and Gottheil's encyclopedia entry would serve as one of his central sources. Taking seriously Gottheil's claim that "the idea of a return of the Jews to Palestine has its roots in many passages of Holy Writ," al-Khalidi looked to the ancient history and texts of the Jews as he worked to understand and analyze Zionism. During the final years before his untimely death in 1913 at the age of forty-nine, al-Khalidi crafted a book manuscript that, while titled "as-Sayūnīzm ay al-masʾala aṣ-ṣahyūniyya" (Zionism or the Zionist Question), is actually an extended account of and commentary on the history of "the Israelites" from the Bible until al-Khalidi's own day.[13]

Al-Khalidi's manuscript provides the historian with a veritable treasure trove of insights into the ways in which a native Muslim Arab of

[10] First published in 1904; republished in 1912. This book is actually a collection of articles al-Khalidi wrote in the journal *al-Hilāl* between 1902 and 1904. As Brugman notes, "despite its pretentious title, the work chiefly dealt with Victor Hugo, apart from some passages about the Arabic *balāgha* and about the literary connections between Arabic literature and the French and English literatures." Brugman, *An Introduction to the History of Modern Arabic Literature in Egypt*, 331. See also Kasmieh, "Ruhi Al-Khalidi 1864–1913," 135–36.

[11] Despite its hagiographic tone, Kasmieh's article offers useful insights on al-Khalidi's varied interests. See "Ruhi Al-Khalidi 1864–1913," 132.

[12] Though Shuly Rubin Schwartz is correct in pointing to Gottheil's reference to Herzl as "a martyr to the Jewish cause" as evidence of Gottheil's "decided slant in favor of the modern political movement [Zionism] to which he was devoted," the bulk of Gottheil's article on the history of Zionism is written more dispassionately. See Schwartz, *The Emergence of Jewish Scholarship in America*.

[13] In the scholarship on the Arabs and Zionism, al-Khalidi is best known for his public broadside against Zionism in the Ottoman Parliament in May 1911. In response to an earlier speaker's demand that the national and religious beliefs of all groups within the empire must be respected, al-Khalidi began by asserting that he was not an antisemite but simply an opponent of Zionism. He proceeded by offering a brief history of Ottoman Jewry since the Jews' expulsion from Spain and then continued with an exposition on the intellectual roots of Zionism from the Bible onward. Al-Khalidi's speech, the few others that supported it, and the general resistance his views encountered among the other Ottoman parliamentarians, were widely publicized in the contemporary Arabic press. See Mandel, *The Arabs and Zionism before World War I*, 112.

Late Ottoman Palestine perceived and comprehended Jews, Jewish history, and the emerging Zionist movement. In over 120 pages of handwritten text, al-Khalidi offers the reader a glimpse into his world and worldview—social, cultural, intellectual, religious, political—at this critical moment in the history of relations between Zionists and Arabs, between Jews, Christians, and Muslims in Palestine.

In this chapter I closely analyze al-Khalidi's manuscript, mining its pages for evidence of the ways in which al-Khalidi conceived of the Jews and Judaism, Jewish identity and Zionism, and the Jews' historic and contemporary relationship to Palestine. I investigate the sources, in addition to Gottheil's encyclopedia entry, that al-Khalidi employed to learn and write about the Jews. The author, we find, went to great lengths to gain an internal understanding of the Jews and Zionism, using their own sources, ranging from the Hebrew Bible to *at-Talmūd* (a 1909 Arabic book by a Sephardic Jew on the Jewish oral law), to learn how the Jews view themselves. At the same time, I argue that even in his sensitive, internal analysis of Jewish history, al-Khalidi read through a lens colored by his own particular fin de siècle Muslim upbringing, by the long tradition of Islamic-Jewish religious polemics, and by the more recent introduction by Europeans in the Levant and by Arab visitors to Europe of European Christian antisemitic stereotypes and discourse into the Middle East. More generally, al-Khalidi's manuscript represents a case study that reinforces a broader claim of this book, namely, that in the early encounters between Zionists and Arabs in Palestine, religion played a prominent, and generally underappreciated, role as a category and tool of understanding and interpretation.

An Education from al-Aqsa to the Sorbonne

Considering his personal background and upbringing, it comes as no surprise that religion played a part in informing al-Khalidi's understanding of Zionism. Al-Khalidi spent his childhood years in Jerusalem obtaining a traditional Islamic education in religious schools and at the al-Aqsa Mosque.[14] The Shāfiʿī mufti of Jerusalem certified that al-Khalidi had completed training in all the classical subjects of the Islamic curriculum. His religious studies continued in Jerusalem as well as in Nablus, Tripoli, and Beirut, where his father Yasin took up Ottoman-appointed religious positions at various times during the son's youth. By age fifteen, al-Khalidi had already been granted a scholarly

[14] For a succinct review of the development of schools in Ottoman Palestine, and al-Khalidi's own education, see Kasmieh, "Ruhi Al-Khalidi 1864–1913," 123–31.

title in the Ottoman Islamic religious hierarchy by none other than the shaykh al-islām in Istanbul.[15] Al-Khalidi was well educated in Islam and steeped in Islamic tradition.

At the same time, as al-Khalidi became a young man, he acquired those elements of a Western education that began to be offered in the new Ottoman state schools,[16] and even at the Jewish Alliance Israélite Universelle (AIU) school in Palestine, where he apparently studied briefly.[17] Al-Khalidi's secular education began in Palestine but continued, with much greater intensity, when he left the Levant. In 1887, at age twenty-three, al-Khalidi went to the Ottoman capital, Istanbul, where he studied at the Mekteb-i Mülkiye (School of Civil Service). Following more than six years in Istanbul, al-Khalidi, now nearly thirty, traveled to Paris, where he undertook a three-year course in political science and then enrolled in the École des Hautes Études of the Sorbonne. Under some of the most distinguished French Orientalists of the day, including the Jewish Arabist Hartwig Derenbourg, he studied the philosophy of Islam and Eastern literature.[18] Al-Khalidi even went on to a brief career as an academic in France. He taught Arabic to students and scholars of Oriental studies and presented a scholarly paper at the 1897 International Congress of Orientalists in Paris on "Statistics from the Islamic World," which he published in both French and Arabic.[19]

[15] Khalidi, *Palestinian Identity*, 76–77.

[16] Al-Khalidi studied at the *ruşdiyye* schools in Jerusalem and Tripoli and at the *Sultaniyye* schools in Beirut. See ibid., 76–77. For a concise overview of the development of various forms of education in Palestine, see Ayalon, *Reading Palestine*, 19–39. See also Khalidi, "Intellectual Life in Late Ottoman Jerusalem," 225.

[17] Khalidi, *Palestinian Identity*, 77. For an example of the schedule of subjects taught in the AIU Jerusalem school in the late nineteenth century, see the 1892 "*Ecole de l'Alliance Israélite à Jérusalem: Programme des Classes*," bk. 2, p. 316, in CAHJP AIU Jerusalem archival file. The languages included in the academic program were Arabic, French, Hebrew, and Turkish. According to Ben-Arieh, "the first to recognize the importance of the [Alliance] school were not Jews but gentiles, among them the district governor and the Khalidi and al-Husseini families." Ben-Arieh, *Jerusalem in the Nineteenth Century: Emergence of the New City*, 269. Of the Alliance school's early history, Jeff Halper notes that, with one exception (David Yellin), "all the pupils attending were non-Europeans—Jews of Sephardi of Middle Eastern background and a number of Arabs." Halper, *Between Redemption and Revival*, 174.

[18] In 1885 Hartwig Derenbourg (1844–1908), son of Orientalist scholar Joseph Derenbourg, was appointed to the chair in Arabic and to the first chair in Islam at the École des Hautes Études. He studied, inter alia, the Arabic writings of the medieval Jewish scholar Saadiah and compiled a catalog of Arabic manuscripts in Spain. See "Derenburg," EJ[2].

[19] The French version, "Statistique de l'Univers Musulman," was published under "Rouhi el Khalidy." For the Arabic version, see Khalidi, *Palestinian Identity*, 237n.76.

It would clearly be wrong to reduce al-Khalidi to an essentialized image of "a traditional Muslim" or a *homo islamicus*[20]—not only because such an essentialized image could never be an accurate depiction of anyone but also because, as we have seen, he received an advanced Western education. It would be equally inappropriate, however, to disregard al-Khalidi's religious identity and background altogether, especially when our concern is a religiously educated individual's understanding of a people distinguished by, perhaps most prominently, a different religion, and all the more so when that other religion (Judaism) is one for which there is an inherited discourse. Al-Khalidi's diverse backgrounds must all be considered, then, in analyzing his manuscript and his perceptions of the Jews and Zionism.

The Manuscript and Its Structure

When al-Khalidi died in 1913, his manuscript was in the process of being transcribed by a professional copyist, presumably in preparation for publication. With the author's passing and the traumatic world war that began several months later, however, the manuscript was placed aside and, it would seem, forgotten. Within only a few years, anyone who came across it in the Khalidi family's Jerusalem library would likely have deemed it hopelessly outdated, a victim of the Balfour Declaration and the terms of the Mandate for Palestine that the new League of Nations had granted to Great Britain.[21] It would regain readers' interest only as a relic of the past. The manuscript was discovered decades later by the scholar Walid Khalidi among his family's papers, and he has written the only academic article, in Arabic, exclusively devoted to the text, offering a detailed summary of its content.[22]

[20] See Lockman, *Contending Visions of the Middle East*, 73–78. Lockman employs the characterization of the *homo islamicus*—especially the nineteenth-century European Orientalist perception of the "Islamic man" as "something quite separate, sealed off in his own specificity"—set forth in Rodinson, *Europe and the Mystique of Islam*, 60.

[21] The Khalidi Library was formally founded at the end of the nineteenth century with manuscripts and books collected by members of the family over centuries. Today the library exists in two separate locations, both just outide of Bab as-Silsala in the Old City of Jerusalem. One location contains an extensive collection of Islamic manuscripts; the other, known as "the annex," holds printed books, journals, and newspapers in Arabic, Turkish, and European languages. See Conrad, "The Khalidi Library."

[22] See al-Khālidī, "Kitāb as-sayūnīzm aw al-mas'ala aṣ-ṣahyūniyya li-Muḥammad Rūḥī al-Khālidī al-mutawaffā sanat 1913." In this article, Walid Khalidi offers a biography of Muhammad Ruhi al-Khalidi and outlines the structure and content of the text. See also Kasmieh, "Ruhi Al-Khalidi 1864–1913," 136–40, which relies entirely on Walid al-Khalidi's article.

Fortunately, Walid Khalidi located both Ruhi al-Khalidi's original—a set of small notebooks containing somewhat scrawled, antiquated Arabic script[23]—as well as the copyist's 123 numbered pages of neatly written text in more modern handwriting, thereby permitting scholars to analyze both.[24]

Al-Khalidi's composition may be divided into six chapters.[25] The first offers an introduction to Zionism and lays out the general narrative to be explored in greater detail in the course of the book. The second chapter deals with the religious roots of Zionism in the Bible and the Talmud. Next, al-Khalidi offers a survey of the history of the Jews from the death of King Solomon through the destruction of the Second Temple. This is followed by a chapter on the dispersion of the Jews and the places in which they took refuge and settled over the ensuing centuries. The fifth chapter returns to the subject of Zionism, outlining the history of the modern movement. The final chapter looks at the major Jewish organizations of al-Khalidi's time, explaining the various religious and ideological positions found among them.

In constructing large portions of his book, al-Khalidi followed the basic outline of Gottheil's twenty-one-page entry on "Zionism." At points, al-Khalidi's text is simply an Arabic translation of Gottheil's words. That a Muslim Arab notable from Late Ottoman Palestine was familiar with the new *Jewish Encyclopedia* points to the often overlooked intellectual interchange between Jews and Arabs during this period. While it is not known where al-Khalidi found the copy of the *Jewish Encyclopedia* that he used (it is not currently present in the Khalidi Library, but it was presumably available in the nearby Jewish National Library[26] in Jerusalem), it is possible that Gottheil himself shared

[23] Comparing writing known to be from al-Khalidi's own hand to the text of these smaller notebooks, Walid Khalidi has concluded that these are Ruhi al-Khalidi's original composition.

[24] The variations between the two versions are generally only minor, and, according to Rashid Khalidi, the copyist's version was probably created during Ruhi al-Khalidi's lifetime and supervised by al-Khalidi himself, permitting the scholar to use the more legible and organized version with reasonable confidence that it represents al-Khalidi's work.

[25] Here I follow Walid Khalidi's chapter divisions, in "Kitāb as-sayūnīzm aw al-masʾala aṣ-ṣahyūniyya li-Muḥammad Rūḥī al-Khālidī al-mutawaffā sanat 1913," 42–43.

[26] The first Jewish public library in Jerusalem (Midrash Abravanel) was founded in 1892 by the B'nai Brith organization. The Jewish National Library in Jerusalem was founded in 1894; this latter institution united the B'nai Brith library as well as the then-defunct library of Eliezer Ben-Yehuda (beit ha-sfarim li-vnei yisraʾel). On these Jewish libraries of Late Ottoman Jerusalem, see Salmon, "ha-Yishuv ha-ashkenazi ha-ʿironi be-ereẓ yisraʾel (1880–1903)," 590–92.

his article with al-Khalidi.[27] Between 1909 and 1910 Gottheil lived in Jerusalem, where he headed the American School of Archaeology;[28] it is likely, given their shared Orientalist interests, that Gottheil and al-Khalidi came to know one another during that period.[29] It is also possible that the two were known to one another—or had even met in person—more than a decade earlier. When al-Khalidi presented his academic paper on Muslim demographics to the 1897 International Congress of Orientalists, Gottheil was already professor of Semitic languages at Columbia University, an active member of the American Oriental Society, and head of the Oriental Department of the New York Public Library.[30] Moreover, the editors and writers of the *Jewish Encyclopedia* were familiar with al-Khalidi's scholarly work; the encyclopedia's entry on "Islam," for instance, notes that al-Khalidi's article on the demographics of the contemporary Muslim world "should especially be mentioned."[31] Al-Khalidi, in other words, was an acknowledged colleague of Jewish scholars such as Gottheil, Kohler, Goldziher, and others in the international fin de siècle scholarly effort toward under-

[27] Al-Khalidi, to be sure, was not the only Arab in Palestine to make use of this *Jewish Encyclopedia* article for his presentation and analysis of Zionism. See my discussion below of Najib Nassar's articles and pamphlet on Zionism.

[28] For a contemporary mention of Gottheil in Palestine, describing him as "the famous Orientalist . . . head of the School of Archaeology in our city," see *ha-Ḥerut* 2:86 (April 20, 1910). The American School of Archaeology at Jerusalem (later renamed the American School of Oriental Research) was founded in 1900 by the American semiticist Charles Cutler Torrey.

[29] According to Rashid Khalidi, Gottheil is listed among the Khalidi Library's visitors in the library's guestbook. The guestbook that was kindly shown to me by Haifa al-Khalidi appears to have been first used in the late 1920s, so there is no clear evidence that Gottheil visited the library during his 1910–1911 stay in Palestine. An intellectual biography of Richard James Horatio Gottheil, an American Zionist expert in Arabic and Muslim-Jewish relations in the medieval period, has yet to be written.

[30] See *Journal of American Oriental Society* 18 (April 1897), 387. Unable to locate a list of participants at the 1897 International Congress of Orientalists in Paris, I am uncertain whether Gottheil attended that meeting.

[31] This article was jointly written by Kaufmann Kohler and Ignaz Goldziher. Kohler (1843–1926) was born in Bavaria before immigrating to the United States where he became a leading Reform rabbi and president (1903–1921) of the Reform movement's Hebrew Union College. In 1885, Kohler convened the so-called Pittsburg Conference, which will be discussed below. This *Jewish Encyclopedia* article provides evidence that Kohler was familiar with al-Khalidi's scholarship; it is not clear, however, whether the two figures knew one another personally. If they were acquaintances, we might better understand al-Khalidi's conception of Jewish history—and particularly the revolution of modern Jewish history—as laid out below. Goldziher (1850–1921), a Hungarian Jewish scholar, was an expert on, inter alia, the history of Islamic hadith and was among the initiators and contributors to the *Enzyklopedie des Islam*. See Conrad, "Ignaz Goldziher on Ernest Renan."

standing Islam and the Arab world. They were reading his work and he was reading theirs.

Al-Khalidi's decision to use an article written by an American Zionist (indeed, the first president of the Federation of American Zionists[32]) as a primary source for the history of the Jewish relationship to the Holy Land offers a number of clues about his purpose in writing this book. First of all, in constructing his "as-Sayūnīzm," al-Khalidi did not aim to offer his readers a polemical screed against Zionism. Rather, his text was meant to provide his audience with a sophisticated, informed narrative of Jewish history and Zionism. For this reason, out of the many possible articles and books about Zionism, one that was meant to be encyclopedic, but still written by a sympathetic insider, was an ideal match.[33] At the same time, al-Khalidi's manuscript has its biases, and, as we shall see, they are not always subtle. Using the Jews' own encyclopedia, and an avowed Zionist's article, might be seen as part of an effort to establish legitimacy and credibility for al-Khalidi's own critique of Zionism.

While al-Khalidi's Arabic translation of Gottheil's article serves as one structural core of his text, the manuscript is more than a simple translation of a single encyclopedia entry. It draws on many varied sources, several of which will be discussed in detail in this chapter. Notwithstanding al-Khalidi's reliance on these various sources and the manuscript's self-presentation as an objective historical treatise, a close reading of the text permits us to discern al-Khalidi's own philosophy and perspective.

Assessing Audience

For whom would al-Khalidi have written such a book? Lacking any explicit statement in the text concerning the particular type of reader he expected, we are left simply to conjecture to whom the work was

[32] This was the umbrella organization of local American Zionist societies and the predecessor to the Zionist Organization of America.

[33] Encyclopedic, but not necessarily pretending to complete objectivity. In his 1912 forward to his book called *Zionism*, Gottheil questioned the necessity and even the value of objectivity in historical writing: "It is sometimes held that an historian must be unbiased, and must stand vis-à-vis to his subject much as a physician does to his patient. Such detachment may be valuable for a mere chronicler, to whom dry dates and lifeless facts are all-important. But a people has a soul, just as individual human beings have. To understand that soul, something more is needed than mere dates and facts. If evolution is creative, as Monsieur Bergson holds, the attempt must be made to understand in what that creative spirit consists, and this can be attained only by active sympathy with the peculiar phase of the soul-life the historian has to depict. This need not prevent him from taking a broad view of the opinion of others who do not see the light in exactly the same fashion." See Gottheil, *Zionism*, 14.

directed based on internal textual evidence. Given the manuscript's language, of course, the intended audience would have been readers of Arabic. In the Late Ottoman period in the Middle East, including in Palestine, the qualification of literacy characterized but a small minority of the Arabic-speaking population.[34] Al-Khalidi's intended readers, by definition then, would have been among the intellectual (and, by extension, economic) upper class. But al-Khalidi did not assume that his readers would necessarily be as highly educated as himself, nor as familiar with European society and languages as he was. Consider, for instance, the opening lines of the manuscript. Al-Khalidi explains:

> Zionism, in the European[35] languages, is derived from the word "Zion," i.e., *Ṣahyūn*, with the addition of the particle "ism," which denotes a political view or a religious-philosophical idea. Zion is the name of the mountain upon which are located the fortress of Jerusalem and the tomb of David the son of Solomon, peace upon them, and is used as a general term for all of the holy city of Jerusalem and its surroundings.[36]

In defining Zionism, al-Khalidi betrays certain of his presumptions about his audience. The reader was not expected to know any European language, requiring an explanation of the suffix "ism"[37] that would be superfluous for anyone who had studied in Europe or had been educated in European missionary schools in the Middle East. The text, in other words, does not aim toward the very highest level of Arab society's educational elite. At the same time, the reader was assumed to recognize place names within Jerusalem as well as the biblical and Qurʾanic figures of David and Solomon—whose patrilineage is (accidentally?) reversed.[38] The readers for whom al-Khalidi wrote his

[34] For an excellent study of Arabic literacy in Palestine, see Ayalon, *Reading Palestine*.

[35] The word used here is *ifranj*, literally "French." According to Ayalon, "*ifranj*, the Arabicization of 'Franks,' was originally attributed to that particular people as distinct from other European ethnic groups; by the eve of the nineteenth century, however, it had come to denote Christian Europe at large." See Ayalon, *Language and Change in the Arab Middle East*, 16.

[36] al-Khālidī, "as-Sayūnīzm, ay al-masʾala aṣ-ṣahyūniyya" [copyist version], 1.

[37] The suffix "-ism," or a close equivalent, such as "-ismus," is found in English, German, Russian, and the various Romance languages.

[38] The reversal appears in both the original version and that of the copyist. David and Solomon are mentioned frequently in the Qurʾan, but there does not appear to be any ambiguity that Solomon is the son of David, and not vice versa. Sura 27 says that "Solomon succeeded David," and Sura 38 claims that "We gave Solomon to David." I assume that this was simply an accidental error (perhaps al-Khalidi intended to write *abū* rather than *bin*) that was not caught by the copyist.

work, then, were basically educated Arabic-readers, especially those familiar with Palestine, though not necessarily themselves residents of Palestine.

Did al-Khalidi envisage Christian Arab readers, or only Muslims like himself? Would he have considered Arabic-reading Jews as a potential audience? As we will see, al-Khalidi generally writes respectfully of Christianity and emphasizes its commonalities with Islam; Judaism, on the other hand, is set in opposition to both religions, and not in Judaism's favor. Because the text portrays Judaism as the outsider religion, and because a large portion of the manuscript consists of a retelling of the history of the Jews and their faith, it is unlikely that Jews were among the intended readership. Christian Arabs, on the other hand, might well have been desired readers; indeed, al-Khalidi, while crafting his text, had surely read the 1911 translation of and commentary on the *Jewish Encyclopedia*'s "Zionism" article by Najib Nassar, a Palestinian Orthodox Christian.[39] Nassar and his fellow Christian Arabs in Palestine and the Levant were participants in al-Khalidi's intellectual, social, and political milieu.

The Ancient Jewish Link to Palestine

Al-Khalidi accepts the historical link of the Jews to Jerusalem, whether he calls it Ūrshalīm or al-Quds, and to the Holy Land, whether he denotes it as Ṣahyūn (Zion) or Filasṭīn (Palestine).[40] This acceptance is in keeping with the precedent of al-Khalidi's uncle and intellectual mentor, Yusuf Diyaʾ al-Khalidi (1842–1906).[41] As mayor of Jerusalem, Yusuf Diyaʾ al-Khalidi sent a letter on March 1, 1899, to the chief rabbi of France, Zadoc Kahn,[42] asking that the note be passed along to Theodor Herzl. Even as he opposed Zionism, Yusuf Diyaʾ al-Khalidi, writing in French, conceded: "The idea in itself is only natural, beautiful, and

[39] Naṣṣār, *aṣ-Ṣahyūniyya*. This text will be discussed later in this chapter.

[40] Though late twentieth- and early twenty-first-century Arab anti-Zionist polemics have developed a discourse of denial of Jewish historical claims to Palestine (represented by Yasser Arafat's famous, if apocryphal, "What Temple?" rhetorical quip), this denial, like all ideas, also has a history. Future research might seek to trace the historical development of the position, which has been informed by a complex array of political, religious, archeological, and, recently, genetic arguments.

[41] On Yusuf Diyaʾ al-Khalidi, see Khalidi, *Palestinian Identity*, 67ff.

[42] The last governmentally-recognized Chief Rabbi of France, Kahn (1839–1905) was an early member of Hibbat Zion who sympathized with Herzl. See "Kahn, Zadoc," in *EJ*^{2}, 11:724.

just. Who can contest the rights of the Jews on Palestine? My God, historically it is your country!"[43]

Like his uncle, Ruhi al-Khalidi never questions the basic historical claims of the Hebrew Bible concerning the Israelite kingdoms in the Holy Land, nor does he cast doubt on the direct link between his Jewish contemporaries and the biblical Israelites. On the contrary, consider these lines, in which al-Khalidi writes of the exiles to Babylonia: "The captives in Babylonia demonstrated their abundant yearning for Zion and Jerusalem. No nation among the nations reached their height of grieving over their homelands and the degree of their longing for it. They wandered along the banks of the Euphrates crying over Jerusalem and bewailing her in poems and psalms."[44] Al-Khalidi has read these "poems and psalms"; he cites their "style," "allegories," and "metaphors" as having served as models for such literary talents as Victor Hugo, the French writer about whom he was writing another book at the same time.[45] Al-Khalidi proceeds to quote fifteen poetic lines of Psalm 137, "By the rivers of Babylon," followed by a "rhetorically superior" passage from Lamentations, 2:11–13. Next, in demonstrating that "the hope to return to Jerusalem and for the restoration of the ancient Davidic kingdom remained alive in the hearts of the exiles," al-Khalidi quotes several verses from Ezekiel 37, including 21–22:

> then say to them, Thus says the Lord GOD: I will take the people of Israel from the nations among which they have gone, and will gather them from every quarter, and bring them to their own land. I will make them one nation in the land, on the mountains of Israel; and one king shall be king over them all.[46]

Al-Khalidi continues for pages with this discussion, citing verse after biblical verse exhibiting the ancient aspiration of the Israelite return to Palestine. While the passages he cites sometimes overlap with those listed by Gottheil in his *Jewish Encyclopedia* article, as often as not they appear to be of al-Khalidi's own choosing, or perhaps drawn on

[43] The original seven-page letter is held in the Central Zionist Archives (CZA H197). For references to it, see, e.g., Khalidi, *Palestinian Identity*, 74–75; Dowty, *Israel/Palestine*, 63; Marcus, *Jerusalem 1913*, 46–47; La Guardia, *War without End*, 205.

[44] al-Khālidī, "as-Sayūnīzm, ay al-mas'ala aṣ-ṣahyūniyya" [copyist version], 15.

[45] The book on Hugo was published the year before al-Khalidi's death. al-Khālidī, *Tārīkh ʿilm al-adab ʿind al-ifranj wa-l-ʿarab wa-Fīktūr Hūgū.*

[46] al-Khālidī, "as-Sayūnīzm, ay al-mas'ala aṣ-ṣahyūniyya" [copyist version], 15. Unless otherwise noted, I use the *New Revised Standard Version* for translations of biblical texts into English.

another source; this Ezekiel passage, for example, is not mentioned in Gottheil's "Zionism" entry.[47]

Not only does al-Khalidi unreservedly offer biblical passages that stress the Israelites' yearning to return to their land, but he sees this same desire continuing into postbiblical Jewish history as well. "The mystical part of the Talmud," al-Khalidi explains, elaborating on Gottheil's article,

> is loaded with Zionist aspirations on the model of that which appears in the books of the Old Testament. It is pointed out in it [the Talmud] and in the midrashic writings[48] that the *messiah*[49]. . . will assemble the dispersed, and with them they will gain mastery over Jerusalem [al-Quds]. Among the rabbis [*aḥbār*][50] of the Jews, there are those who believe that the Messiah the son Joseph will collect the Children of Israel around him and march with them to Jerusalem, and he will gain mastery over the power of enemies and will restore the religious worship in the Temple [al-haykal], that is, al-masjid al-aqṣā [the al-Aqsa Mosque], and establish his dominion.[51]

Here al-Khalidi faithfully renders an uncensored translation of the material Gottheil presents in his article, while adding further specificity that leaves no room for doubt as to the precise locations in question. The Temple to which these Jewish authors wish to restore the religious worship is, al-Khalidi explains, the al-Aqsa Mosque, or at least it would stand on the same site.[52] And then al-Khalidi adds an explanation, not found in Gottheil's entry, about what this "religious service" is. It is "the slaughtering of sacrifices," he clarifies, "and burning them on the altar above the rock." This term for "the rock," *aṣ-ṣakhra*, refers to the

[47] Nor, for that matter, are they found in Nassar's *aṣ-Ṣahyūniyya*, which appears to list only those passages mentioned in Gottheil's "Zionism" article.

[48] Al-Khalidi uses the phrase *al-kitābāt al-midārjiyya* in translating/transliterating Gottheil's phrase "midrashic writings."

[49] Al-Khalidi first transliterates "messiah" into Arabic script and then translates it: *al-massayā ay al-masīḥ*.

[50] Gottheil uses the term "philosophers."

[51] al-Khālidī, "as-Sayūnīzm, ay al-masʾala aṣ-ṣahyūniyya" [copyist version], 23.

[52] This passage is found as well in Naṣṣār, *aṣ-Ṣahyūniyya*. Nassar, however, inserts al-Ḥaram ash-Sharīf (the Noble Sanctuary), i.e, the Temple Mount, as opposed to al-Khalidi's al-masjid al-aqṣā, in identifying this location. This difference may be connected to the different religious affiliations of Nassar and al-Khalidi, the latter preferring the unambiguously Qurʾanic term while the former offers a more general name relating to the area's holiness. Given the common presumption that the ancient Jewish temple stood at the center of Herod's Temple Mount, approximately where the Dome of the Rock now stands, it is curious that al-Khalidi identified the Temple with al-Aqsa rather than with the Dome.

one beneath the Dome of the Rock (qubbat aṣ-ṣakhra). Again, not only does al-Khalidi present postbiblical Jewish longing to return to Palestine in accordance with Gottheil's text, but he also expands on Gottheil to emphasize that the places to which the Jews have sought to return are among the very holiest of places for contemporary Muslims, the Dome of the Rock and the al-Aqsa Mosque (shrines al-Khalidi could see from his window on Bāb as-Silsila Street).[53]

Al-Khalidi provides abundant examples as he portrays the enduring Jewish hope of the return to Zion through the course of history. He discusses, inter alia, the case of the second-century Jewish rebel leader Bar Kokhba; rabbinic predictions of the date when the Jews will be restored to their former glory; the medieval Andalusian poetic longing for Zion in the work of Ibn Gabirol, Solomon Halevi, and Judah Halevi; and the seventeenth-century Sabbatean immigration to Palestine.

On the other hand, al-Khalidi recognizes that this declared desire to return to Palestine was just part of the story of the Jewish Diaspora. In narrating the events of the expulsion of the Jews from Spain in 1492, for instance, al-Khalidi notes that of the 185,000 refugees, 90,000 immigrated to the sympathetic and welcoming Ottoman Empire. "Of these," al-Khalidi continues, "1,500 families settled in Jerusalem, 1,700 families in Safed and 500 families in Damascus." The number of émigrés who "settled in Syria and Palestine did not exceed 15,000 individuals," he estimates, emphasizing that this number represented only "one-sixth of the immigrants to the Ottoman kingdom. The rest spread out in Constantinople, Salonika, Edirne [Adrianople], Izmir, and so on." This is not to mention the 75,000 Jews, in al-Khalidi's approximation, who immigrated to various European lands, or the 65,000 who converted to Christianity. Al-Khalidi takes this opportunity further to expound on the condition of "justice and equality" as existed for the Jews under Islam, in contrast to the Jewish condition under Christendom.[54] But what underlies these statistics is the relatively minuscule proportion of fifteenth-century Jews who actually chose to immigrate to Palestine and fulfill their purported longing when forced to choose a new

[53] In chapter 4 we will find that al-Khalidi was not the only one of his Arab intellectual contemporaries to equate the Temple and al-Aqsa. See *al-Manār* 13:10 (November 1910), 726.

[54] Tracing the history of this idea, Mark Cohen explains that "already at the end of the Middle Ages one encounters among Jews the belief that medieval Islam provided a peaceful haven for Jews, whereas Christendom relentlessly pursued them." Later, in the nineteenth century, "the fathers of modern, scientific study of Jewish history transformed this perception into a historical postulate." Cohen describes the way in which both Christian and Muslim Arabs used this notion in the twentieth century, especially in their opposition to Zionism. See Cohen, *Under Crescent and Cross*, 3–8.

home. Nonetheless, if al-Khalidi was wondering, given the small scale of actual Jewish immigration to Palestine over the centuries, just how meaningful were those frequent expressions of the dream of returning to Zion, he did not explicitly express this doubt in his manuscript.

"Mendelssohn's Theory"

To the extent that we may discern al-Khalidi's position on Zionism from this ostensibly objective, academic text, however, it is not any insincerity in the historic wish of the Jews to return to Palestine that ultimately delegitimizes the modern Zionist movement. Nor, for that matter, does al-Khalidi even mention objections along the lines of those that his uncle, Yusuf Diyaʾ, had sent to Zadoc Kahn and Herzl more than a decade earlier. In the same letter discussed above, Yusuf Diyaʾ had concluded that "the reality is that Palestine now is an integral part of the Turkish Empire, and, what is more important, it is inhabited by others than the Jews." Yusuf Diyaʾ, we see, articulated his argument against Zionism in pragmatic, political, and demographic terms.

For Ruhi al-Khalidi, the argument seems to be on another plane entirely—one internal to Judaism, Jewish discourse, and Jewish history. While the vast majority of Jews may not have chosen to return to Palestine in the many centuries following the Roman conquest and exile (just as was the case, al-Khalidi does not fail to observe, with the meager return from the Babylonian exile),[55] al-Khalidi still does not impute any illegitimacy to the Jewish *will* to return. Rather, he respectfully presents the history of this ancient and long-lasting hope.

The Jewish relationship to Palestine changed, however, in the modern period, according to al-Khalidi, and the transition is linked to one man: the eighteenth-century German Jewish political and religious philosopher Moses Mendelssohn (1729–1786). In al-Khalidi's rendering, with the advent of what he calls "Mendelssohn's theory" (*naẓariyyat Māndilsūn*), Jewish identity underwent a radical transformation that indicted any manifestation of Jewish nationalism thereafter as a clear violation of its principles. Mendelssohn is a key figure in al-Khalidi's narrative of Jewish history, and one finds various formulations of "Mendelssohn's theory" at several points within the text, beginning on the second page of the manuscript. "Mendelssohn's theory," writes al-Khalidi,

[55] al-Khālidī, "as-Sayūnizm, ay al-masʾala aṣ-ṣahyūniyya" [copyist version], 28.

> separated the Mosaic religion from Jewish nationalism [*al-qawmiyya al-yahūdiyya*][56] and abolished this nationalism. It obliged the Jews to acquire the citizenship of the countries [*jinsiyyat al-bilād*] in which they were born, such as Germany, Austria, France, and England, to imitate[57] the rest of the Christian peoples of these countries, and to enter with them [the Christians] into European civilization. It [Mendelssohn's theory] made them forget the land of Palestine from which they left and the Hebrew language, which they stopped speaking two thousand years earlier.[58]

For al-Khalidi, what he called Mendelssohn's theory was the bold disentangling of Jewish religion and Jewish nationality. This theory, according to al-Khalidi, embraced "the Mosaic religion" while it decisively and irrevocably disposed of the nationality and all its concomitant marks of distinction: Jewish language, land, and customs. Al-Khalidi asserts that "whoever looked upon" western European Jews—who, in al-Khalidi's view, accepted and modeled Mendelssohn's theory—"saw nothing other than Frenchmen or Englishmen, for example, without regard to their being Jewish or Christian, whether Catholic or Protestant, due to the great degree of similarity between them."[59]

Al-Khalidi mixes a sociological observation—that the Jews (at least in western Europe) did in fact acculturate among their Christian neighbors—with the doctrinal statement he names "Mendelssohn's theory." Strikingly, it is the latter, the *theory*, that is critical for al-Khalidi. Mendelssohn's theory, in al-Khalidi's conception of modern Jewish history, is not merely the translation of sociological reality into ideological terms. Rather, it has prescriptive, even binding, force. In a restatement of this theory, al-Khalidi writes, "it is *not permitted* for a Jew who was born in Prussia or Austria or France, for example, to consider himself anything but a Prussian or Austrian or Frenchman." Moreover, "he does not have the right to call for Jewish nationalism. . . . It is not permissible to consider his nationality to be Jewish nationalism, nor his homeland Palestine."[60] The language al-Khalidi uses in describing Mendelssohn's theory is strikingly legal in nature. This theory has the power to "abolish" nationalism; to "oblige" the acquisition of

[56] Al-Khalidi uses the term *qawmiyya*, which, in the early twentieth century, could mean either nationalism or nationality. See P. J. Vatikiotis, M. Brett, A.K.S. Lambton, C. H. Dodd, G. E. Wheeler, F. Robinson, "Kawmiyya," in *Encyclopaedia of Islam.*

[57] Al-Khalidi uses the term *at-tashabbuh*, literally "imitation," though perhaps "acculturate among" would more accurately match the sense implied here.

[58] al-Khālidī, "as-Sayūnīzm, ay al-masʾala aṣ-ṣahyūniyya" [copyist version], 2

[59] Ibid.

[60] Ibid.

citizenship; to "not permit" Jews to think of themselves in particular ways; to deny Jews "the right" to make certain political or ideological proclamations.

Mendelssohn's Theory versus al-Khalidi's "Mendelssohn's Theory"

Before attempting to account for the immense power al-Khalidi ascribes to "Mendelssohn's theory," it is worth considering the extent to which al-Khalidi's presentation of the theory corresponds to the views Moses Mendelssohn actually articulated in his philosophical, political, and polemical writings. In reality, Mendelssohn never claimed that the Jews were no longer a "nation" and that they were henceforth merely a "religion,"[61] even if, as Leora Batnitzky has argued, he "invent[ed] the modern idea that Judaism is a religion."[62] In this sense, al-Khalidi's rendering of Mendelssohn's theory is not an accurate representation of the Jewish philosopher's position. But this is not to say that al-Khalidi (or his source on this matter) was wholly unjustified in linking the distinction between Jewish religion and Jewish nationhood to Mendelssohn.[63]

A primary assumption of what al-Khalidi labels "Mendelssohn's theory" is the contention that there is a meaningful distinction between "religion," on the one hand, and "nation," on the other. For Mendelssohn, especially in his classic treatise *Jerusalem, Or, on Religious Power and Judaism* (1783), the relevant dichotomous categories were not religion and *nation* but rather religion and *state*. Mendelssohn argued for a distinction between these latter spheres and insisted that "religion" as such had no place in affairs of the "state." He did not see this distinction as novel to his own day. Rather, he projected it into the biblical past: once the ancient Israelites accepted a monarch, "state and religion were no longer the same, and a collision of [civic and religious]

[61] On the absence from Mendelssohn's oeuvre of a "direct explicit statement . . . that the Jews are not a nation, but only a religion," see Barzilay, "Smolenskin's Polemic against Mendelssohn in Historical Perspective," 18.

[62] See Batnitzky, *How Judaism Became a Religion*, 13–28.

[63] Nor is this to say that al-Khalidi was the first to make this claim. The early Zionist thinker Peretz Smolenskin (d. 1885) understood Mendelssohn very similarly. Isaac Barzilay has described the ways in which Smolenskin, who wrote a generation before al-Khalidi, misunderstands or misrepresents Mendelssohn's belief in Jewish nationhood. Though Mendelssohn "can be defended as a believer in Jewish nationhood, it is not a strong defense," Barzilay contends, as the claim "is only formally correct, but not substantially, especially not in the framework of Judaism of Mendelssohn's own time." Barzilay, "Smolenskin's Polemic against Mendelssohn in Historical Perspective," 18–28.

duties was no longer impossible."[64] In this vein, Mendelssohn approvingly cites Jesus's "cautious advice," which he repeats numerous times in *Jerusalem*, that one must "render unto Caesar that which is Caesar's and unto God what is God's."[65] For Mendelssohn, following the New Testament language, there were two realms: that of Caesar (the state) and that of God (religion).

Though the conceptual distinction between state and religion is obviously not identical to that between nation and religion, it is nonetheless important for our assessment of al-Khalidi's reading of Mendelssohn insofar as it demonstrates Mendelssohn's insistence on a separate sphere called "religion." While Mendelssohn grants this sphere biblical vintage, scholars and theorists in the field of secularization have argued that it is rather a modern construction and, according to some, the hallmark of secularization. In his review of the various theories of secularization, José Casanova asserts that "secularization as differentiation" is "the valid core of the theory of secularization." As Casanova writes in *Public Religions in the Modern World*:

> The differentiation and emancipation of the secular spheres from religious institutions and norms remains a general modern structural trend. . . . Each of the two major modern societal systems, the state and the economy, as well as other major cultural and institutional spheres of society—science, education, law, art—develops its own institutional autonomy, as well as its intrinsic functional dynamics. Religion itself is constrained not only to accept the modern principle of structural differentiation of the secular spheres but also to follow the same dynamic and to develop an autonomous differentiated sphere of its own.[66]

Mendelssohn's claim that religion, as such, may be differentiated from other spheres of life—be they the state, the nation, or something else—is in large part what makes Mendelssohn a useful figure for al-Khalidi. Even if al-Khalidi was not quite correct in attributing the separation of nation and religion to Mendelssohn, he was correct to note Mendelssohn's assumption of and insistence on "differentiation." If, as Charles Taylor puts it, in ancient societies, "religion was 'everywhere,' was interwoven with everything else, and in no sense constituted a separate 'sphere' of its own,"[67] al-Khalidi recognized that Mendelssohn asserted both the conceptual distinction between religion and other

[64] Mendelssohn, *Jerusalem, Or, on Religious Power and Judaism*, 132.
[65] Ibid.
[66] Casanova, *Public Religions in the Modern World*, 212.
[67] Taylor, *A Secular Age*, 2.

spheres and the imperative to make this distinction. For al-Khalidi, concerned as he was with matters of nationalism and the nation in the very different environment of the early twentieth century (rather than Mendelssohn's eighteenth-century Europe), the critical sphere from which to separate religion was the nation (as opposed to Mendelssohn's state).

Differentiation, however, is only one way in which al-Khalidi's version of Mendelssohn's theory represents a fair reading of Mendelssohn (regardless of whether al-Khalidi actually *read* Mendelssohn). Al-Khalidi, as we have seen, highlighted the degree of acculturation effected by Jews, particularly those of western Europe, in the period following Mendelssohn. Though al-Khalidi perceived a direct, causal link between Mendelssohn and this acculturation, the latter was a social phenomenon that began before Mendelssohn and had numerous, complex causes (not merely a Mendelssohnian dictum). Nonetheless, Mendelssohn was a vocal and important advocate of certain aspects of acculturation.[68] In the final pages of *Jerusalem*, he contended that there was "no wiser advice" that might be offered his fellow Jews than to "adapt yourselves to the morals and the constitution of the land to which you have been removed," even while "hold[ing] fast to the religion of your fathers too."[69] Al-Khalidi would seem justified in reading these lines as a call to acculturation in all spheres of life aside from those explicitly deemed "religious."

Finally, along with differentiation and acculturation, Mendelssohn's theory, as articulated by al-Khalidi, severed the Jews from Palestine, renouncing the historic links between the people and the land that had been preserved over the previous centuries. Again, though Mendelssohn did not express this view exactly, this claim, too, has a basis in his writings, especially in his polemical exchange with Johann David Michaelis. In the early 1780s Michaelis, a Christian opponent of the emancipation of the Jews in the German lands, contended that the "messianic expectation of a return to Palestine" casts "doubt on the full and steadfast loyalty of the Jews to the state and the possibility of their full integration." The Jews, Michaelis had written, "will always see the state as a temporary home, which they will leave in the hour of their greatest happiness to return to Palestine."[70] In his effort to counter Michaelis's argument against Jewish emancipation, Mendelssohn claimed

[68] Mendelssohn advocated elements of acculturation even as he attempted to combat acculturation in other respects (e.g., by reintroducing Jews to their linguistic and religious heritage and by arguing against the rejection of Jewish law).

[69] Mendelssohn, *Jerusalem, Or, on Religious Power and Judaism*, 133.

[70] "Johann David Michaelis' Arguments against Dohm (1782)," in Mendes-Flohr and Reinharz, eds., *The Jew in the Modern World*, 43.

that Michaelis had misunderstood or misconstrued the impact of the Jews' messianic expectation. Mendelssohn wrote that "the hoped-for return to Palestine" has "no influence on our conduct as citizens." He continued:

> This is confirmed by experience wherever Jews are tolerated. In part, human nature accounts for it—only the enthusiast would not love the soil on which he thrives. And he who holds contradictory opinions reserves them for church and prayer. In part, also, the precaution of our sages forbids us even to think of a return by force.[71] Without the miracles and signs mentioned in the Scripture, we must not take the smallest step in the direction of forcing a return and a restoration of our nation.[72]

Mendelssohn explained that the Jewish hope for a return to Palestine could have no impact on the loyalty of the Jews toward states that tolerate them. In making his case, Mendelssohn appealed first to a psychological observation that people tend to love a place where they are able to live and flourish, and second to a rabbinic prohibition that, in his view, expressly forbade the Jews from restoring their nation in Palestine on their own, without the miraculous, divinely ordained redemption.[73]

Though Mendelssohn minimized the significance of the wish to return to Palestine (an attempt that must be understood in the context of the eighteenth-century political debate over Jewish emancipation), he never proposed severing the Jews' link to Palestine or ceasing to pray for their return to the Holy Land. He argued, rather, that this link and hope had no practical influence on the way the Jews related to the states in which they lived. Al-Khalidi, or whatever textual or oral source he was using for his presentation of Mendelssohn's theory, misunderstood (or interpreted liberally) the actual argument Mendelssohn made concerning Palestine. At the same time, it should be noted that in the subsequent debates over the "assimilation" of the Jews within European Christian society, both supporters and opponents pointed to the earlier figure of Mendelssohn as having heralded the "assimilation" they either desired or dreaded.[74]

[71] That is, to attempt to bring about redemption through human effort.

[72] See "Moses Mendelssohn: Remarks Concerning Michaelis' Response to Dohm (1783)" in ibid., 48–49.

[73] Mendelssohn was presumably referring to the passage in the Babylonian Talmud Tractate *Ketubot* 110b–111a in which the people of Israel are said to forswear "going up by a wall" and "rebelling against the nations of the world."

[74] In the *Jewish Encyclopedia* article on Mendelssohn, for instance, the authors write that Mendelssohn's "translation of the Pentateuch had an important effect in bringing the

THE POWER OF "MENDELSSOHN'S THEORY"

For our purposes, though, it is al-Khalidi's understanding of Mendelssohn's theory, not Moses Mendelssohn's actual philosophy, that is most important. What is it that endows *naẓariyyat Māndilsūn* with such considerable power? The answer, I propose, lies in what al-Khalidi understands to have been broad rabbinic consensus on Mendelssohn's principles. Again, beginning on the first page of his manuscript, al-Khalidi explains that the Torah, the Talmud, and Jewish medieval literature all foresee a Jewish return to Palestine, though the Jews were "not sufficiently powerful to realize" this aspiration. This ambition nonetheless remained until "the last centuries," writes al-Khalidi, when with the advent of freedom, Mendelssohn "created a modern theory whose correctness was certified by the community[75] of rabbis, '*asqāmah*.' " At this early stage in al-Khalidi's manuscript, we encounter a somewhat vague idea of rabbinic certification of Mendelssohn's theory, an *asqāmah*, a term al-Khalidi initially leaves undefined.[76] Later in his manuscript, al-Khalidi mentions the word again, in explaining why some rabbis religiously forbid Zionism. He notes that these rabbis rejected Zionism because of its violation of "Mendelssohn's theory" and its "infringement of the rules of the religious assembly, '*asqāmah*.' " The text proceeds to cite the 1908 proclamations of opposition to Zionism issued by various Ottoman Jewish religious and communal leaders, published in the Ottoman Turkish press. "We, your Mosaic citizens," asserts one such

---

Jews to share in the progress of the age. It aroused their interest in the study of Hebrew grammar, which they had so long despised, made them eager for German nationality and culture, and inaugurated a new era in the education of the young and in the Jewish school system." Similarly, fin-de-siècle Zionists also associated Moses Mendelssohn with anti-Zionism (via the Jewish Reform movement, of which Zionists considered Mendelssohn to be the founder). See, e.g., Nordau, *Zionism*. In this pamphlet Nordau insists that Jews' prayers to return to Palestine were always meant literally until "towards the middle of the eighteenth century the so-called 'movement of enlightenment,' of which the popular philosopher Moses Mendelssohn, is recognized as the first herald, began to penetrate Judaism." The followers of this movement, according to Nordau, saw "the dispersion of the Jewish people" as "an immutable fact of Destiny," and they "emptied the concept of the Messiah and Zion of all concrete import." The "Mendelssohnian enlightenment consistently developed during the first half of the nineteenth century into 'Reform' Judaism, which definitely broke with Zionism."

[75] Al-Khalidi uses the term *jumhūr*. This might also be translated as "the majority of rabbis" or even "all the rabbis."

[76] This term and its relationship to the Hebrew *haskamah* will be dealt with at length later in this chapter.

Jewish leader from Izmir, "are the greatest opponents of Zionism."[77] Such, al-Khalidi infers, is the power of Mendelssohn's theory.

The reader finally encounters al-Khalidi's clearest explanation of this asqāmah halfway through the manuscript in yet another discussion of *naẓariyyat Māndilsūn.* "Mendelssohn's theory," al-Khalidi writes, "means that there is never again to be Jewish nationalism."[78] Al-Khalidi emphasizes that "Mendelssohn was not alone in this view." Rather, all the Jews of western Europe agreed with his theory, and thus "it was certified by the community of rabbis.[79] Their people resolved to accept it and they named this consensus with the term of their religious law[80] '*asqāmah,*' which means the consensus of the people. Their acceptance of this theory was not political only, but rather religious and religious-legal."[81] With this final explication of Mendelssohn's theory and its binding "religious and religious-legal" authority over contemporary Jewry,[82] we might finally decipher al-Khalidi's theory of modern Jewish history and identity. Al-Khalidi notes a dramatic change in the ways in which Jews in the modern world conceived of themselves—and particularly of their national identity—and he is quite correct to do so. Though, as we have seen, he may have been mistaken historically, or at least overly simplistic, in linking this transformation directly to Moses Mendelssohn, al-Khalidi was hardly exceptional in associating Mendelssohn with an opposition to Zionism; Jewish Zionists and anti-Zionists of al-Khalidi's time did the same.[83]

What, though, did al-Khalidi have in mind when he wrote of this so-called asqāmah? While the term is presumably a corruption resulting from the Arabic transliteration of a European-language transliteration of the Hebrew term *haskamah,* or "agreement," the particular historical

[77] See al-Khālidī, "as-Sayūnizm, ay al-masʾala aṣ-ṣahyūniyya" [copyist version], 6; al-Khālidī, "as-Sayūnizm, ay al-masʾala aṣ-ṣahyūniyya" [author's version].

[78] Al-Khalidi uses the phrase *al-qawmiyya al-yahūdiyya.*

[79] *jumhūr al-ḥākhāmīn wa-r-rabānīn.* This phrase might also be understood as "most of the rabbis" or even "all the rabbis."

[80] Al-Khalidi uses the Islamic legal term *sharīʿa.*

[81] The final words are "*dīniyyan wa-sharʿiyyan.*" al-Khālidī, "as-Sayūnizm, ay al-masʾala aṣ-ṣahyūniyya" [copyist version], 55.

[82] Or at least those in western Europe. There is an ambiguity in al-Khalidi's presentation of this consensus: at times he portrays it as the agreement of *all* the Jews and their rabbis, whereas at other times he limits the claim to western European Jewry.

[83] Even al-Khalidi's Zionist neighbor Ben-Yehuda linked the claim that the Jews are "not a people" to Mendelssohn. "Even in countries where the Jews never heard of the name Moses Mendelssohn or his teachings," Ben-Yehuda wrote in 1880, "Jewish youth is repeating the pattern of the Jews in Germany by turning away from its people and the language of its forefathers. The Maskilim of Berlin wrote many books and created elaborate theories to prove that we are not a people." See Hertzberg, *The Zionist Idea,* 163.

agreement al-Khalidi had in mind is less certain.[84] Given al-Khalidi's many years in France, one possibility is that the broad rabbinic consensus to which al-Khalidi refers here is Napoleon's 1806 Assembly of Notables, which declared that "in the eyes of Jews, Frenchmen are their brethren,"[85] and the subsequent 1807 Paris Sanhedrin, which claimed that "the learned of the age shall possess the inalienable right to legislate according to the needs of the situation" and thus demanded of Jews "obedience to the State in all matters civil and political."[86] Beginning in 1898, al-Khalidi served as Ottoman consul general in Bordeaux, where he surely met Jews from the region's highly acculturated Sephardic community that, a century earlier, had eagerly embraced Napoleon's conditions for French citizenship.[87] It is possible that al-Khalidi's Jewish acquaintances in the French port city told him of this watershed event, which Herzl's newly founded Zionist movement seemed to undermine.

Alternatively, al-Khalidi may have been thinking of the resolutions of the various Reform rabbinical conferences of the mid- to late nineteenth century that Gottheil mentioned in his encyclopedia article on "Zionism."[88] Gottheil had pointed to the 1845 "Conference of Rabbis" in Frankfurt-am-Main, the Philadelphia Conference of 1869, and the 1885 Pittsburgh Conference. The rabbis of the Frankfurt Conference, Gottheil writes, "decided to eliminate from the ritual 'the prayers for the return to the land of our forefathers and for the restoration of the Jewish state.' " The language Gottheil cites from the Pittsburgh Conference's resolutions even more closely matches al-Khalidi's version of Mendelssohn's theory: "We consider ourselves no longer a nation, but a religious community," proclaimed these Reform rabbis, "and we therefore expect neither a return to Palestine . . . nor any of the laws concerning a Jewish state."[89] To al-Khalidi, these rabbinical

[84] I refer to this as a "corruption" not only because of the loss of the initial *h* but also because of the use of a *q* in place of a *k*.

[85] See Mendes-Flohr and Reinharz, *The Jew in the Modern World*, 128–32.

[86] See ibid., 135–36.

[87] See Hyman, *The Jews of Modern France*, 2–15, 41ff.

[88] The first of these conferences, the 1844 Brunswick Conference, considered ratifying the Parisian Sanhedrin rulings. See Meyer, *Response to Modernity*, 134–35.

[89] Interestingly, the Pittsburgh Conference was convened by the German-born American Reform rabbi Kaufmann Kohler. Kohler, who strongly opposed Zionism, was coauthor of the *Jewish Encyclopedia*'s entry on "Islam" that, as noted above, referenced al-Khalidi's article on Muslim demographics. I am not aware of any evidence that suggests that Kohler and al-Khalidi knew one another personally, but each was certainly familiar with the other's work. For a comparison of the definition of Jewishness articulated in the "Pittsburgh Platform," on the one hand, and in the Palestine Liberation Organization's charter of the 1960s, on the other, see Gribetz, " 'Their Blood Is Eastern,' " 143.

assemblies—articulating what came to be known in modern Jewish historiography as "classical" Reform ideology[90] and what al-Khalidi names with the shorthand "Mendelssohn's theory"—irrevocably altered the nature of Judaism.

Translating Consensus

Al-Khalidi's theory of the illegitimacy of modern manifestations of Jewish nationalism, as I have thus far portrayed it, is remarkable for its concern with the internal dynamics and reasoning of Judaism. Yet his theory of the rabbinic consensus on "Mendelssohn's theory" is curious, indeed, and may, at least in part, reflect the *Islamic* influences on al-Khalidi's understanding of the way in which religious law is established.[91] Consider once more the language al-Khalidi uses in defining the asqāmah:

> *wa-ajmaᶜat ummatuhum ᶜalā qubūlihā wa-sammū hādhā al-ijmāᶜ bi-iṣṭilāḥ sharīᶜatihim (asqāmah) wa-maᶜnāhu ijmāᶜ al-umma.*
>
> And their people [*umma*][92] agreed to accept it[93] [i.e., Mendelssohn's theory] and they named the consensus [*ijmāᶜ*] [which they had reached] "*asqāmah*"—a term from their religious law—which means the consensus [*ijmāᶜ*] of the people.

I highlight the Arabic terminology here because the word *ijmāᶜ*, which al-Khalidi equates with asqāmah, is of utmost importance. Ijmāᶜ is the term used for the Islamic theory of "consensus," one of the four recognized sources for determining law in Sunni Islam. As Wael Hallaq explains, ijmāᶜ

> functions both as a sanctioning instrument and as a material source of law. Once agreement has been reached on an issue, usually a question of law, that issue becomes epistemologically certain and thus insusceptible to further interpretation. . . . The epistemological value attached to consensus renders this instrument so powerful in the realm of doctrine and practice in the

[90] See Meyer's chapter on "classical" Reform in *Response to Modernity*, 264–95.

[91] As we shall see, though, the Islamic principle that al-Khalidi projects onto Judaism was actually integrated into Judaism by way of Islam in the medieval period.

[92] The term *umma* could also mean 'nation' as well as 'religious community.' On the use of this term, see Lewis, *The Political Language of Islam*, 32; Ayalon, *Language and Change in the Arab Middle East*, 21–22.

[93] *wa-ajmaᶜat* could also be rendered: "decided unanimously." See below on *ijmāᶜ*.

> community that it can override established practice as well as clear statements of the Qurʾan.[94]

This is precisely the function and power al-Khalidi imputes to the rabbis' so-called asqāmah concerning Mendelssohn's theory. In their consensus, their ijmāʿ, the rabbis have overridden the established national nature of pre-Mendelssohnian Judaism and have thereby delegitimized any subsequent expression of Jewish nationality. "Mendelssohn's theory" has become, to use using Hallaq's words, "epistemologically certain and thus insusceptible to further interpretation." Zionism, then, is not merely a violation of the opinion of a group of rabbis; it is a blatant contravention of now-unquestionable law.

This is not to say that al-Khalidi merely projected an Islamic concept onto Judaism without precedent or reason. Though it is not clear that al-Khalidi was familiar with this phenomenon, Jews especially of the medieval Islamic world (Maimonides, most famously) were apparently influenced by the Islamic notion of ijmāʿ.[95] Moreover, as we shall see in chapter 5, one of al-Khalidi's textual sources, an Arabic work on the Talmud written by a Jewish contemporary, appeals to the tool of and the term ijmāʿ in its explanation of the composition of the mishnah. What is interesting, then, is not *that* al-Khalidi uses this concept but rather *how* he uses it: the stress he places on it, the term he claims it translates, and the contention that what happened with what he calls Mendelssohn's theory represented just such an ijmāʿ.

If, in al-Khalidi's mind, the consensus, formal or otherwise, of the Jews in premodern Jewish history was that they were not merely a religion but a nation[96] and that their nation retained historic links to Palestine, to which it wished to return, how could this *new* consensus adopting "Mendelssohn's theory" overturn the earlier belief? To attempt to answer this question, we must consider in greater detail al-Khalidi's particular religious milieu. While al-Khalidi was trained, as we have seen, in traditional Sunni Islamic studies, he and his family were intimately involved with a new religious modernist, reformist tendency within late nineteenth-century and early twentieth-century Islam that

[94] "Consensus," OEMIW. On *ijmāʿ*, see also Hallaq, *A History of Islamic Legal Theories*, 75–81; Coulson, *A History of Islamic Law*, 77–80.

[95] See Libson, *Jewish and Islamic Law*, 9, 24, 198n.65. Judith Romney Wegner contends that *ijmāʿ* has a Jewish precedent as it is "conceptually equivalent to that expressed in the Talmud by the word *ha-kol*." Wegner, "Islamic and Talmudic Jurisprudence," 42–43.

[96] To understand al-Khalidi's theory, we must overlook the anachronism he employs in imagining the antiquity of this dichotomy.

would become known as the Salafi movement.[97] These modernists sought to reform Islam by looking to the model of the earliest followers of Muhammad (known as *as-salaf aṣ-ṣāliḥ*, "the worthy ancestors"). The fin de siècle Salafis contended that much of contemporary Islam did not conform to the practices of the original Muslim community and was burdened with habits and practices that had no justification in the religion. Islam thus could and should be creatively transformed to accommodate the new social and intellectual realities of the modern world, just as those original Muslims exercised judicious creativity in interpreting the Qurʾan and the Sunna for their own time.[98]

One of the most prominent and influential figures in the late nineteenth-century modernist reform movement was the Egyptian mufti Muhammad ʿAbduh (1849–1905).[99] ʿAbduh, according to George Hourani, "denied that priority in time necessarily meant superior wisdom, except in the case of the Companions and Successors" of Muhammad, that is, *as-salaf aṣ-ṣāliḥ*. As a result, ʿAbduh was open to the possibility of modifying the legal rulings of earlier generations, whether because they can now be judged to have been mistaken or because, given new historical circumstances, the older views are obsolete or even harmful.[100] In ʿAbduh's words, a generation's "obligation to obey consensus is due to the public interest, not to infallibility . . . and interest appears and disappears, and varies with different times and conditions."[101]

Al-Khalidi—whose family library in Jerusalem contains many of ʿAbduh's works, including one autographed by ʿAbduh himself—seems to have been influenced by this Salafi conception of *evolving*

[97] The standard narrative of the birth of the Salafi movement has been provocatively challenged by Henri Lauzière, "The Construction of *Salafiyya*." Muhammad Qasim Zaman, however, contends that Rida and his associates employed the term Salafi as a self-designation. Zaman, *Modern Islamic Thought in a Radical Age*, 7. In highlighting the close relationship between the Khalidi family and the key figures of the Salafi movement, Rashid Khalidi points to a photograph of the formal opening of the Khalidi Library, in which the prominent Salafi Shaykh Tahir al-Jaza'iri appears. Al-Jaza'iri collaborated with Hajj Raghib al-Khalidi in the creation of the Khalidi Library. "Several of al-Jaza'iri's books, some in multiple copies," adds Khalidi, "are found in the [Khalidi] Library, together with many examples of the writings of other *salafis* such as al-Sayyid Rashid Rida." See Khalidi, *Palestinian Identity*, 43–45; Khalidi, "Intellectual Life in Late Ottoman Jerusalem," 224.

[98] Commins, *Islamic Reform*.

[99] On ʿAbduh, see, e.g., Sedgwick, *Muhammad Abduh*; Hourani, *Arabic Thought in the Liberal Age, 1798–1939*, 130–60; Haim, ed., *Arab Nationalism*, 16–22; Adams, *Islam and Modernism in Egypt*.

[100] Hourani, "The Basis of Authority of Consensus in Sunnite Islam," 39.

[101] Muhammad ʿAbduh, *Tafsīr al-qurʾān al-ḥakīm*, ed. M. Rashid Rida (Cairo, 1927–1936), cited in ibid., 40.

ijmāᶜ.[102] If there had been an ijmāᶜ among premodern Jews that held that the Jews were a nation, al-Khalidi might have explained, the consensus had evolved, given the "different times and conditions" in which post-Mendelssohnian Jewry lived. A new consensus declared that the Jews are now no longer a nation but rather purely a religion. That is to say, not only did al-Khalidi read an Islamic notion into Jewish history, he employed a particular theory thereof that Muslim thinkers were developing in his specific intellectual, religious, and social context.

In al-Khalidi's own terms, though, might not Herzl's Zionist congresses have represented the latest ijmāᶜ, now asserting that the Jews still are, or are once again, a nation wishing to return to Palestine, thereby overturning the imagined asqāmah concerning "Mendelssohn's theory"? While, of course, it would have been inconvenient for al-Khalidi's anti-Zionist case to concede that a new Jewish generation's asqāmah had restored the Jews' nationhood and their claim to Palestine, this political inconvenience is not necessarily what drove al-Khalidi's interpretation. Notwithstanding the Zionist movement's claim to speak on behalf of world Jewry, when al-Khalidi penned his manuscript in the years preceding the war, the Balfour Declaration, the fall of the Ottoman Empire, and the establishment of the British Mandate in Palestine, there was no Jewish asqāmah on Zionism to speak of. Many Jews, and particularly Jewish religious leaders of varied stripes including Reform and Orthodoxy, had rejected Zionism; al-Khalidi had no reason to imagine that Zionism constituted a new Jewish asqāmah.[103]

How, though, did al-Khalidi arrive at the term "asqāmah" in his rendering of ijmāᶜ? As noted, Jews in the medieval Islamic world, especially the later Geonim and even Maimonides, appear to have been influenced by the Islamic principle of ijmāᶜ.[104] The term, however, was not typically translated into Jewish discourse as *haskamah*. While the

[102] On Rida's interpretation of *ijmāᶜ*, see also Zaman, *Modern Islamic Thought in a Radical Age*, 47–53.

[103] After al-Khalidi's death, the situation obviously changed dramatically, and there gradually developed among Jews something resembling a consensus, though still not unanimity, on Zionism. As far as I am aware, though, no subsequent Palestinian or Muslim thinker has taken up al-Khalidi's ijmāᶜ-asqāmah theory. Its time, too, has passed. On the persistence of anti-Zionism on the fringes of the American Jewish Reform movement in the mid-twentieth century, see Kolsky, *Jews against Zionism*.

[104] As Libson writes, "the appeal to consensus as a legal source is in effect Gaonic innovation . . . the Geonim accord it, in practice, quasi-formal status as a legal source and a major element in deciding the law." Libson, "Halakhah and Reality in the Gaonic Period," 94. See also Neusner and Sonn, *Comparing Religions through Law*; Neusner, Sonn, and Brockopp, *Judaism and Islam in Practice*.

specific source for al-Khalidi's use of this term has proved elusive, certain possibilities present themselves. The Hebrew term *haskamah*, (pl. *haskamot*), literally "agreement," has had various technical usages over the centuries. For instance, printed Hebrew books beginning in the early modern period would often have a letter from a well-known and respected rabbi at the end of the volume; with the advent of title pages in the sixteenth century, such letters began to appear at opening of books. This letter, known as a *haskamah*, would serve as an imprimatur, offering praise for the book and its author and assuring, if not the highest quality of scholarship, at least a religiously inoffensive work. *Haskamot* would often also operate as copyrights, threatening with excommunication those who might, within a certain period of time after publication, reproduce the work without permission.[105]

A second technical usage of *haskamah*, or more precisely, of *ascama*, with the initial 'h' unpronounced, was current among Sephardim, Jews of Spanish origin for whom an "h," as in Spanish, would generally be silent. In Sephardic parlance, an ascama was the set of laws governing a Jewish community's internal administration, essentially the by-laws of a semiautonomous religious community or, later, of a particular synagogue.[106] Having encountered Sephardic Jews not only in Jerusalem but also in France and Istanbul, perhaps al-Khalidi had heard this term. Or he might well have seen the *Jewish Encyclopedia*'s entry entitled "Ascama," which mentions these two variant usages of the term. But neither variant precisely matches the sense that al-Khalidi attaches to the term.[107]

Perhaps al-Khalidi learned the term from his Hebrew-speaking acquaintance in Palestine, Eliezer Ben-Yehuda, the renowned enthusiast for the revival of Hebrew as a modern spoken language for the Jews of Palestine. While the possibility is surely tantalizing—after all, we know from Ben-Yehuda's interview with al-Khalidi that they knew each other fairly well—it is problematic. The particular

[105] According to Moshe Carmilly-Weinberger, the first *haskamah* of this sort appeared in the fifteenth century, in the *Agur* by Jacob Landau. Moshe Carmilly-Weinberger, "Haskamah," *EJ*^{2}. I thank Elisheva Carlebach and Malachi Beit-Arié for sharing with me their knowledge about such *haskamot*.

[106] The ascamot were a close parallel to the *taqanot* in the Ashkenazic communities of Europe. On the Sephardic usage, see Levy, *The Sephardim in the Ottoman Empire*, 51–52; Angel, "The Responsa Literature in the Ottoman Empire as a Source for the Study of Ottoman Jewry," 656–76.

[107] Moshe Carmilly-Weinberger offers yet another definition of *haskamah*, as "rabbinic approval and approbation of the legal decisions of colleagues, usually attached to the original legal decision and circulated with it." This, too, does not fit al-Khalidi's image of a mass, unanimous agreement of rabbis to a particular position. See Carmilly-Weinberger, "Haskamah," 444–45.

meaning al-Khalidi attributes to the term appears to have been unknown to Ben-Yehuda (whose personal lexicon is discernible to an extent unique to the compilers of dictionaries). In his comprehensive Hebrew dictionary, Ben-Yehuda identified five senses of the word *haskamah*,[108] none of which precisely corresponds to al-Khalidi's intended meaning. For now, al-Khalidi's source for the term remains something of a mystery.

What we have found here, I suggest, is that even in al-Khalidi's internal and sensitive reading of Jewish history, he read this history from the perspective of one whose understanding of religious systems is grounded in Islam. The Islamic shade of al-Khalidi's theory of Jewish history is perfectly natural, not only because of the multitude of similarities and parallels between the religious-legal structures of Judaism and Islam,[109] but also because one inevitably perceives others through the paradigms of reality with which one has been endowed by one's culture.

The latter is an insight that has been compellingly explored in the field of translation studies. Lawrence Venuti argues:

> Translation never communicates in an untroubled fashion because the translator negotiates the linguistic and cultural differences of the foreign text by reducing them and supplying another set of differences, basically domestic, drawn from the receiving language and culture to enable the foreign to be received there. The foreign text, then, is not so much communicated as inscribed with domestic intelligibilities and interests.[110]

In the course of translating a text from one language into another, according to Venuti, the translator cannot simply or seamlessly "communicate" the text or its content into a new language. The imagined, "literal translation" ideal-type is necessarily an impossibility because of the inevitable differences between the languages and their corresponding cultures. The translator must negotiate these differences in order to render the text into the new language. Venuti labels this not "communication" but "inscription," where the foreign is "inscribed with domestic intelligibilities and interests." Al-Khalidi's overall project in this

[108] Eliezer Ben-Yehuda, "Haskamah," in *MBY*, 2:1136–37. One of these definitions is "agreement between two things, such as ideas and the like—accord, Einverständnis." Carmilly-Weinberger seems to be referring to this same usage of *haskamah* when he notes that "in the philosophical literature of the Middle Ages," the word can mean " 'consensus,' 'harmony between entities,' 'pre-established harmony.' "

[109] See Ackerman-Lieberman, "Comparison between the Halakha and Shariʿa"; Neusner and Sonn, *Comparing Religions through Law*; Neusner, Sonn, and Brockopp, *Judaism and Islam in Practice.*

[110] Venuti, "Translation, Community, Utopia," 482.

manuscript may indeed be understood as one of translation: to translate Jewish history and Zionism into Arabic, making use of non-Arabic sources. In so doing, al-Khalidi "inscribes" Judaism "with domestic intelligibilities and interests," and this example of asqāmah–ijmāʿ is an acute case of this process. As al-Khalidi works to understand the course of Jewish history, he inscribes onto Judaism his (and his audience's) preconceptions and assumptions, from a knowledge of Islam, about how religions function. Asqāmah may thus be seen as al-Khalidi's domestication of the Islamic ijmāʿ.

Complicating the standard notion of translation, this case problematizes the presumed direction of translation, showing the ability (or even inevitability) of the receiving language and culture to impose its assumptions on that which is ostensibly translated. This case suggests that a translator might not only inscribe domestic meaning onto the foreign text but actually inscribe the domestic concept into the foreign text. This discussion further highlights the issue of inter*religious* translation: that is, the translation not simply between *languages* but between *religions* as well. In translating Jewish history into Arabic in Late Ottoman Palestine, al-Khalidi translates Islam into Judaism, interpreting the Jews' internal history from the perspective of one whose understanding of religious systems is grounded in Islam.

What is critical to stress, though, and what is too often overlooked in the scholarship on this period, is that in the encounter between Zionists and Arabs (be they Muslim or Christian) in Palestine, there was an encounter between individuals of different religions who, to some extent at least, understood each other in religious terms (and on their *own* religious terms); these religious terms were critical to al-Khalidi's "intelligibilities and interests." Ignoring religion, then, prohibits the scholar from recognizing and analyzing some of the most fundamental tools of understanding, or misunderstanding, with which these individuals and communities operated.

Navigating between Sympathy and Fear

Thus far we have seen the extent to which al-Khalidi turns to Jewish history in his effort to understand the modern phenomenon of Zionism. Al-Khalidi accepts the biblical and ancient Jewish narratives of two independent Israelite commonwealths in Palestine, and he acknowledges the subsequent, persistent hope of a return to the Holy Land. Of Jewish messianic expectation in the Talmud, he writes that

> the rabbis of the Jews repeatedly predicted this time, and the Jews repeated in their prayers and at the end of every one of their Zionist congresses the holy Hebrew phrase the Arabic translation of which is:
>
> "Next year in Jerusalem [al-Quds]."
>
> This indicates their affection for[111] Palestine and the extent of their desire to possess it.[112]

For al-Khalidi—relying as he does on Jewish sources as he traces the Jews' historic link to Palestine—the contemporary Zionist congresses are just the latest manifestations of the ancient aspiration articulated in the "holy Hebrew" prayer for "Next year in Jerusalem." This aspiration extends back to Sabbateanism, the medieval Jewish poets, the Talmud, Bar Kokhba, and, originally, the prophets of the Hebrew Bible themselves. For the son and nephew of Jerusalem mayors, and for one of Jerusalem's representatives in the Ottoman Parliament, Jews' "affection for Palestine," and especially for Jerusalem, must have been at once eerily familiar and profoundly threatening. Yet al-Khalidi does not withhold this information from his intended readers. Nor does he even question the legitimacy of the Jews' attachment to the land, except in the modern period when, as we have seen, he contends that the Jews themselves declared their former ambition null and void through a religious-legal pronouncement.

However, al-Khalidi does not limit his exposition of Judaism and Jewish history to the Jews' attachment to Palestine. Rather, his manuscript investigates a wide assortment of aspects of Jewish faith and experience. In the pages that follow, I explore the ways in which al-Khalidi's understanding of Judaism is informed by the centuries-old tradition of Islamic-Jewish polemics, on the one hand, and by very contemporary, pressing concerns about Palestine and Zionist ambitions, on the other. Despite its bold attempt to synthesize all Jewish history, al-Khalidi's manuscript is indeed well titled, for "the Zionist question," when not the explicit subject, is generally perceptible just beneath the surface. This is the case, as well, in al-Khalidi's ambivalent attempt to explain European antisemitism. As I will argue, in addressing Russian Christians' hatred of Jews, al-Khalidi undertakes the treacherous task of sensitively accounting for a bigotry that has resulted not only in the victimization of the Jews but also in the Jews' efforts to take control of al-Khalidi's homeland. Al-Khalidi struggles to navigate between his

[111] *Taʿalluqihim bi* can also be translated as "attachment to," "devotion to," or "connection with."

[112] al-Khālidī, "as-Sayūnīzm, ay al-masʾala aṣ-ṣahyūniyya" [copyist version], 24.

sympathy for a mistreated people and his resentment of those very people. Especially when focusing his analysis on the Jews' role in the economy, he at times accepts antisemitic claims as he watches Jews gradually acquiring his homeland by means of their seemingly endless supply of capital. From his vantage point in Jerusalem and Istanbul, al-Khalidi found himself wondering whether some of the blame for antisemitism might belong to the Jews themselves.

Questioning Jewish Faith in an Afterlife

Let us now look more closely at al-Khalidi's treatment of Jewish faith and religion. In the course of his extended account of the books of the Hebrew Bible, which al-Khalidi undertakes so that the reader will have the necessary background to understand the biblical roots of Zionism that Gottheil identifies at the opening of his encyclopedia article, al-Khalidi concludes the following:

> So the Jews do not anticipate reward or punishment after death for their service and their deeds because the prophets of the Children of Israel did not promise them compensation for their deeds other than worldly, earthly, physical happiness.[113] In some phrases of the Torah, there is allusion to the future life, but this allusion is not as clear as it was to the ancient Egyptians who professed an accounting and punishment after death.

Acknowledging a verse from the book of Daniel (12:2) that declares that "Many of those who sleep in the dust of the earth shall awake," al-Khalidi insists that "in this expression, there is a hint of the resurrection[114] but there is no elucidation of it nor is there insistence upon it as there is in the Holy Gospels [*al-injīl ash-sharīf*] and the Holy Qur'an, in terms of verses and proofs that are mentioned repeatedly," several of which al-Khalidi proceeds to quote.[115]

Though al-Khalidi does not typically cite his sources in this work,[116] he does do so in this case. For the general notion that the Jews do not have a firm belief in reward and punishment or in an afterlife, al-Khalidi points to a thirteenth- to fourteenth-century Muslim historical

[113] Al-Khalidi's footnote here references Abu al-Fida', the thirteenth- to fourteenth-century compiler of history, who quotes ash-Shahrastani.

[114] Here al-Khalidi uses two of the classical Qur'anic terms for this concept: *al-ba'ath* and *an-nushur*.

[115] Ibid.

[116] In the 124 pages of the copyist's text, there are only thirteen source footnotes, at least two of which are the sources cited in Gottheil's *Jewish Encyclopedia* entry.

compiler, Abu al-Fida᾽, who in turn quotes Abu al-Fath Muhammad ibn ᶜAbd al-Karim ash-Shahrastani (d. 1153–1154). A Persian-born Sunni Muslim, ash-Shahrastani wrote *Kitāb al-milal wa-n-niḥal* (The Book of Religions and Systems of Thought, c. 1127–1128), comparing the other religions of his day to Islam. For al-Khalidi's comparison of the Torah's relative silence on the afterlife as compared to the ancient Egyptian faith, he cites a contemporary 1878 French work on the ancient history of the peoples of the Orient by Emmanuel van den Berg.[117] These two sources—ash-Shahrastani and van den Berg—are illustrative of al-Khalidi's dual education: in the Arab-Islamic tradition, on the one hand, and the nineteenth-century European Orientalist tradition, on the other.

Beyond showing the sources for al-Khalidi's understanding of Judaism, however, this passage also reveals a telling choice of focus and terms of comparison. Al-Khalidi's decision to highlight the absence of the concept of the afterlife and resurrection in the Hebrew Bible, and the lack of the doctrine of reward-and-punishment, was not accidental, I would suggest, nor without particular resonance. Rather, this was a conventional trope of Muslim-Jewish polemics from the medieval period, and it has clear roots in the Qur᾽an.[118] Indeed, the second sura of the Qur᾽an emphasizes the centrality of the principle of the afterlife; it actually identifies the Qur᾽an as a guide for the righteous who "have firm faith in the Hereafter" (Q. 2:4).[119] In the Qur᾽an, belief in divine judgment on the Last Day is critical for the self-definition of the believer, and in defining the nonbelieving Other:

> As for those who disbelieve . . . God has sealed their hearts and their ears, and their eyes are covered. They will have great torment. Some people say, "We believe in God and the Last Day," when really they do not believe. They seek to deceive God and the believers but they only deceive themselves. (Q. 2:6–9)

In the ninth sura of the Qur᾽an, we read of the call to "fight those of the People of the Book who do not [truly] believe in God and the Last Day" (Q. 9:29). Jews, of course, are among Islam's People of the Book, *ahl al-kitāb*, and yet, al-Khalidi insists, in the tradition of the Qur᾽an and subsequent polemics in the Muslim-Jewish ideological encounter, Jews do not believe in the Last Day on which divine judgment will be

[117] Van den Berg, *Petite histoire ancienne des peuples de l'Orient*. This small volume can still be found in the Khalidi Library.

[118] See Perlmann, "The Medieval Polemics between Islam and Judaism," 123–24.

[119] Unless otherwise noted, the translations of the Qur᾽an provided here generally follow Abdel Haleem, *The Qur᾽an*.

meted out to all.[120] This assessment of Judaism would certainly have resonated with Muslim readers of al-Khalidi's text.

The presence within al-Khalidi's manuscript of conventional Islamic anti-Jewish tropes, though, does not necessarily imply that his "as-Sayūnīzm" should itself be viewed as a religious polemic. Identifying the genre of al-Khalidi's text is a difficult task, both because of its composite nature (at times, as noted, it is a synthesis of unattributed sources) and because it generally presents itself in what seems like an objective, textbook style. The question here is, in part, one of intentionality: when al-Khalidi employed anti-Jewish themes and tropes, did he do so consciously in order to engage in an act of polemics, or was he simply utilizing and imparting his own conception of Judaism that was unselfconsciously informed by such polemics? Given the methodological challenges of determining authorial intent, this question cannot be answered with certainty, but we might safely conclude that the text is operating within a rich tradition and language of discourse concerning Judaism that do have religious polemical qualities, regardless of whether al-Khalidi intended them as such.

Realigning Interreligious Polemics in Palestine

In al-Khalidi's passage on the absence of discussion of the afterlife, resurrection, and ultimate reward-and-punishment in the Jewish scriptures, Judaism is not contrasted with Islam exclusively. Rather, the points of comparison are Islam *and* Christianity. While al-Khalidi only makes passing reference to the "Holy Gospels," it is clear that in this "us-and-them" statement, Christians are part of his "us." Al-Khalidi's linking of Christianity to Islam is not to be taken lightly. After all, the tradition of Muslim-Christian polemics is at least as extensive and severe as that of Muslim-Jewish polemics.[121] It begins, as does its Muslim-Jewish counterpart, in the Qurʾan itself. "Those who say, 'God is the Messiah, the son of Mary,' are defying the truth" (Q. 5:17). And later, within the same sura, "unbelievers" are identified as "those who say that God is the third of three." The Qurʾan contends, rather, that "there is only One

[120] While the Qurʾan here suggests that only a subgroup of People of the Book fails to believe, al-Khalidi implies that this quality applies to the Jews broadly. On the possible inclusion of Jews among Muhammad's category of believers, see Donner, *Muhammad and the Believers*, especially 68–74. On the apocalyptic orientation of the Qurʾan, see 59, 78–82.

[121] As polemics scholar Moshe Perlmann explains, "the polemic literature of Islam is directed, for the most part, against the far more numerous and powerful Christians; the Jews are considered only in passing." Perlmann, ed., "Samauʾal al-Maghribī," 18.

God," and if these unbelievers "persist in what they are saying, a painful punishment will afflict those of them who persist." Once more emphasizing this point, the sura continues that "the Messiah, son of Mary, was only a messenger; other messengers had come and gone before him; his mother was a virtuous woman; both ate food [like other mortals]. See how clear We make these signs for them; see how deluded they are" (Q. 5:73–75). Scholars have enumerated five aspects of Christianity rejected by the Qurʾan: Jesus and Mary as gods, man as a "son" of God, tritheism, complete identity between Jesus and God, and *al-masīḥ* (the messiah, i.e., Christ) being independent of God.[122] While the Qurʾan does offer a certain degree of praise of Jesus and Christianity in its imagined precorrupted form, later medieval Muslim perceptions of Christianity were more uniformly unsympathetic. Medieval Muslims, according to Jacques Waardenburg, "identified Christianity as a religion opposed to Islam as a religion; the truths of these two religions were thought to be mutually exclusive."[123] Muslim polemicists attacked Christianity for the latter's forgery of scripture, its errors of thought and doctrine (including the notions of incarnation, the trinity, and original sin), and its faults in religious practice (especially for its alleged idol worship and its laxity in circumcision and other aspects of ritual purity).[124]

Muslim anti-Christian writings, moreover, did not cease in the medieval period. They continued into al-Khalidi's own day, and not exclusively among the religiously conservative. Such prominent late nineteenth- and early twentieth-century Muslim thinkers as the reformer Muhammad ʿAbduh (whose notion of evolving ijmāʿ was discussed above) and his younger, more politically oriented collaborator Muhammad Rashid Rida—both contemporaries and acquaintances of al-Khalidi—wrote extensively on and against Christianity. ʿAbduh's *al-Islām wa-n-naṣrāniyya maʿ al-ʿilm wa-l-madaniyya* (Islam and Christianity with [reference to] Science and Civilization) challenged the purported rationality of Christianity (in contrast to Islam's alleged irrationality), and Rida's *Shubuhāt an-naṣārā wa-ḥujaj al-islām* (The Specious Arguments of the Christians [against Islam] and the Proofs of Islam) set out to highlight the polytheistic contaminations of Christianity.[125] Al-Khalidi's apparent desire to see the unity of Islam and Christianity is thus most remarkable as it is at odds with a long history of opposition. On the fundamental religious issues, al-Khalidi's comment suggests, Christians and Muslims are in accord, in contrast to Jews.

[122] See Waardenburg, *Muslim Perceptions of Other Religions*, 9.
[123] Ibid., 40.
[124] Ibid., 49–51.
[125] See ibid., 77–79.

This grouping of Christianity and Islam is suggestive of a move in Late Ottoman Palestine toward conceiving of the Arab population as a coherent body—even in religious terms—despite the apparent religious diversity among its constituent Muslims and Christians. Thus this passage on the Jews' lack of faith in divine retribution and the afterlife is an illuminating piece of contemporary evidence that can inform the historiographical debates concerning the consolidation of Arab identity and Palestinian nationalism—and, in particular, the place of Zionism within this process.[126]

This distinction between Judaism, on the one hand, and Islam and Christianity, on the other, in their theological or eschatological beliefs is of utmost importance as it has real consequences related to the ultimate subject of al-Khalidi's manuscript. In reading the Jews' Bible, writes al-Khalidi,

> one does not find any bit of the reports of the pleasantness of paradise nor of the torment of hell [*jahannam*] that appear in the Holy Qurʾan and no reports of the eternal life and the kingdom of heaven that appear in the Holy Gospels,[127] but rather all of the excitement, intimidation, fascination, warning, promise, and threats that appeared in the Old Testament are limited to *Zion*. Religious happiness [in the Old Testament] is in possessing and ruling it [i.e., Zion], and using foreigners to cultivate its land and herd its livestock, and eat its general riches, and lord over their magnificence, and multiply in it through procreation and so on. Suffering is in its [Zion's] destruction, the departure from it, and the rule of others in it.[128]

It is not merely that Jews differ from Christians and Muslims—whose Scriptures, once again, are linked and, for these purposes, equated—in their theoretical beliefs about the afterlife and divine retribution. The Hebrew Bible and, it is implied, the People of *that* Book focus instead on Zion as the fundamental source of happiness and see punishment not in "the torment of hell" but in expulsion from Zion while others rule it. Al-Khalidi contends that the Jews, at least in the premodern period, were obsessed with the earthly possession of Palestine, while denying all otherworldly concerns. Thus he raises the lack of Jewish doctrine in the afterlife not necessarily to defame Jews in the eyes of

[126] On the formation of Palestinian identity and nationalism, see Khalidi, *Palestinian Identity*. See also Muslih, *The Origins of Palestinian Nationalism*.

[127] Al-Khalidi uses the term *al-injīl ash-sharīf* here, while in other instances he refers to *kutub al-ʿahd al-jadīd* (the books of the New Testament).

[128] al-Khālidī, "as-Sayūnīzm, ay al-masʾala aṣ-ṣahyūniyya" [copyist version], 11. Emphasis added.

those for whom belief in the afterlife, resurrection, and retribution is central to their self-identity but as part of the project of explaining to the reader the biblical basis of Zionism, and, consequently, the gravity of the dangers it portends.

Indeed, as noted, al-Khalidi quotes the Hebrew Bible, in Arabic translation, frequently and extensively in his manuscript.[129] The remarkable line above about Jews' religious joy in "using foreigners to cultivate" the land of Zion, for example, is duly supported by al-Khalidi's subsequent excerpt from the sixty-first chapter of the book of Isaiah (verses not cited in Gottheil's encyclopedia article). Comforting the mourners of Zion, Isaiah predicts that they "shall build up the ancient ruins, they shall raise up the former devastations." Isaiah offers a promise to Zion's mourners (which al-Khalidi underlines) that "strangers shall stand and feed your flocks, foreigners shall till your land and dress your vines; but you shall be called priests of the Lord, you shall be named ministers of our God; you shall enjoy the wealth of the nations, and in their riches you shall glory" (Isaiah 61:4–6).[130] While this Israelite prophecy may have been received in its biblical day as a fantasy of righting injustice and exacting revenge, to an Arab of Palestine in the early twentieth century it was understood as a threat of the gravest proportions. Zionist Jews have come not only to *settle* Palestine, al-Khalidi apparently concluded, but to *exploit* its population and use the Jews' great wealth to do so. Isaiah's prophecy was coming to pass before al-Khalidi's own eyes: al-Khalidi had systematically surveyed the Jewish colonies and was intimately familiar with the Zionist *moshavot* (especially those that are known, in retrospect, as First Aliyah colonies) that depended on inexpensive Arab labor.[131] The fact that, in his reading, the Hebrew Bible and the Jewish religion conceived of divine justice and religious satisfaction as enacted solely in the theater of Palestine had consequences too real and immediate to ignore.

[129] The Khalidi Library holds more than ten copies of various Arabic translations of the Hebrew Bible. By comparing al-Khalidi's quotations from the Hebrew Bible to the various available Arabic versions, I have found that al-Khalidi used an Arabic Bible published in Beirut. The title of this pocket-sized volume reads: *al-Kitāb al-muqqadas ay kutub al-ʿahd al-qadīm wa-l-ʿahd al-jadīd* (The Holy Bible, i.e., The Books of the Old Testament and the New Testament). Beneath the title, a note indicates that this Bible was "translated from the original languages, namely, Hebrew, Chaldean, and Greek." On the history of Arabic translations of the Bible, see Griffith, *The Bible in Arabic*. Though Griffith focuses on premodern translations, see 204–7 on the nineteenth-century versions.

[130] These lines are underlined in both al-Khalidi's original draft and the copyist's version. al-Khālidī, "as-Sayūnīzm, ay al-masʾala aṣ-ṣahyūniyya" [author's version], 4; al-Khālidī, "as-Sayūnīzm, ay al-masʾala aṣ-ṣahyūniyya" [copyist version], 12.

[131] See Shafir, *Land, Labor, and the Origins of the Israeli-Palestinian Conflict, 1882–1914*; Morris, *Righteous Victims*, 39.

CHALLENGING THE INTEGRITY OF BIBLICAL PROPHECY

Al-Khalidi's concern with the Bible is not limited, however, to issues that explicitly pertain to Palestine and the problem of Zionism. Throughout his manuscript, for instance, al-Khalidi casts doubt on the divinity and antiquity of the Jews' Torah. He begins a section of his text called "The Torah and Those Zionist Promises That Appear within It" with the following description of biblical prophecy:

> The People of the Book believe that the ideas of heavenly books were received by prophets in a state of revelation and that they [the prophets] gave expression to them [the ideas] in their usual speech after their return to the human state, in contrast to the Qurʾan, which was revealed in its words and its composition.[132]

The implication that the words of the Jewish (and, indeed, Christian) prophets[133] are not directly divine, as opposed to the unfiltered language—*ipsissima verba*—of God found in the Qurʾan, betrays something of al-Khalidi's religious chauvinism.[134]

Al-Khalidi was well aware that at least some Jews understood Jewish prophecy rather differently. In addition to Gottheil's article from the *Jewish Encyclopedia*, one of al-Khalidi's main sources for information about the Jews, and apparently his primary source for details of their religious beliefs, was a 148-page Arabic work called *at-Talmūd: Aṣluhu wa-tasalsuluhu wa-ādābuhu* (The Talmud: Its Origin, Its Transmission, and Its Morals). *At-Talmūd*, published in 1909 in Cairo, was the work of the Jewish intellectual Shimon Moyal, a member of a distinguished Sephardic family based in Jaffa. Moyal's book, which will be dealt with in detail in chapter 5, sets out to introduce Arabic readers to the Jewish concepts of the written and oral Torahs before offering an Arabic translation of and commentary on the entire Talmud. In his section on prophecy, Moyal elaborates on the characteristics of prophecy as understood, in his mind, by Jews:

> The sign of prophecy was the loss, during the descent of revelation [*nuzūl al-waḥy*], of all senses except that of speech. The prophet would present his sayings and would recite his prophecy while he was absent from existence, like a dead person. But aside from the times of the descent of revelation upon him, he was

132 al-Khālidī, "as-Sayūnīzm, ay al-masʾala aṣ-ṣahyūniyya" [copyist version], 6.

133 Al-Khalidi appears to be referring not merely to the biblical books known as "the Prophets" but to the Pentateuch as well.

134 See William A. Graham, "Scripture and Qurʾan," in *EQ*, 4:558–69. On the common Jewish and Muslim views of *ipsissima verba*, see Peters, *The Children of Abraham*, 5.

> rational, fully aware, and fulfilled all the religious and civil duties required by the Torah.[135]

For Moyal, the Jewish prophets would receive revelation from God in an ecstatic, otherworldly state, but they would not wait until the cessation of the revelation before expressing their prophecy in language; this was done during the very moment of ecstatic revelation. Though he read Moyal's account of biblical prophecy, al-Khalidi apparently rejected it, preferring a view that imagines a delay between the prophetic experience and the presentation of the prophecy in human terms. Moyal's description of biblical prophecy[136] closely accords with al-Khalidi's account of Muhammad's revelation—in both, the words of the prophet are the revealed words, unfiltered and with no delay. To insist on the superiority of Muhammad's prophecy requires al-Khalidi to offer a different view of pre-Islamic prophecy. Whether it was to please his intended audience or to express his own beliefs and faith, al-Khalidi wrote his work with clear Islamic sensibilities.

Al-Khalidi's skepticism about the divinity of the words of the Torah extends beyond the imagined experiences of the scriptural prophets. In fact, following a long tradition of Islamic biblical criticism, al-Khalidi suggests that the true author of the Torah in its present form was not Moses, but rather Ezra the Scribe.[137] Al-Khalidi inserts this view into sections of his manuscript that are adapted from Moyal's book. Consider, for instance, the way in which Moyal describes Ezra: "Ezra the Priest and the Scribe, to whom is ascribed the script method known as the square or Assyrian method, and he is called the elder of that national renaissance [*an-nahḍa al-qawmiyya*]."[138] A corresponding passage in al-Khalidi's manuscript depicts Ezra and his biblical counterpart Nehemiah as follows:

> They were the ones who undertook that Israelite national renaissance [*an-nahḍa al-qawmiyya al-isrāʾīlīyya*] and rebuilt Jerusalem and the Temple. They were the first to gather the books of the Torah and the Prophets, and they recorded them for the first time. The collection of the books of the Old Testament occurred in the fifth century BC, that is, after the return of the Children of

[135] Mūyāl, *at-Talmūd*, 14.

[136] This view, it should be noted, might itself have been informed by Islamic perspectives on prophecy, given Moyal's upbringing in Muslim-dominated society and culture.

[137] Jewish rabbinic literature sees Ezra as having played the central role in restoring the Bible after the Babylonian exile. Certain early modern and modern European biblical critics, most famously Benedict Spinoza, supported this view. See, e.g., Spinoza, *Theological-Political Treatise*, 127–28.

[138] Mūyāl, *at-Talmūd*, 26.

> Israel from the Babylonian exile. Ezra the Scribe, possessor of the book, had the greatest hand in the composition [*tadwīn*] of the Torah; to him is attributed the Hebrew script method, known as the square or Assyrian method.[139]

Though al-Khalidi's manuscript does not cite Moyal's work here (it does do so, however, elsewhere in the text), this passage from "as-Sayūnīzm" seems to offer al-Khalidi's elaboration and emendation of Moyal's account in *at-Talmūd*. Several basic elements are present in both passages: Ezra the Scribe, the national renaissance, and the alternative names for the Hebrew script attributed to Ezra. What al-Khalidi has added to Moyal's original, however, is of critical importance. Following an Islamic understanding of Ezra popularized by the great medieval Muslim polemicists ibn Hazm (994–1064) and as-Samawʾal (c. 1130–1180),[140] al-Khalidi sees Ezra as the true author of the Jews' Torah, which was thus written long after Moses's death and far from Mount Sinai.[141] As as-Samawʾal put it in his *Silencing the Jews*, "now this Torah that they have is in truth a book by Ezra, and not a book of God."[142] Given this long-standing polemical tradition, one cannot draw any definitive conclusions from al-Khalidi's inclusion of this charge in his narrative. Nonetheless, one wonders to what extent al-Khalidi's

139 al-Khālidī, "as-Sayūnīzm, ay al-masʾala aṣ-ṣahyūniyya" [copyist version], 7.

140 On as-Samawʾal al-Maghribi, see Perlmann, ed., "Samauʾal al-Maghribī," 5–136.

141 Moyal, in his exposition on *Pirkei avot*, emphasizes the centrality, for the talmudic rabbis, of the belief in Moses's reception of the Torah from the heavens. It is for this reason, Moyal explains, that the first line of *Pirkei avot* is "Moses received the Torah from Sinai." Moyal writes that "the basis of saving faith is the faith in the truth of the descent of the Torah to Moses from the heavens, because the religious leaders decreed salvation for the Israelite who does not believe in the descent of the Torah from the heavens." Moyal, to be sure, ascribes an important role to Ezra in "preserving" the Torah. In discussing the figure of Rabbi Akiba, Moyal writes: "After the destruction of Beitar, only he [Rabbi Akiba] remained among all of the scholars of the Children of Israel. And the Roman government forbade the Israelites from studying Torah [*an-namus* is the term Moyal typically uses for Torah study]. He [Rabbi Akiba] risked his life and taught five exceptional young men. . . . Thus Akiba's relationship to the Talmud is like the Ezra's relationship to the Torah." In other words, in Moyal's view, Ezra perpetuated knowledge of the Torah, though he certainly did not write it ex nihilo, just as Rabbi Akiba perpetuated the study of the Talmud, though he was not its author nor even its compiler. Another line concerning Ezra that al-Khalidi takes from Moyal nearly verbatim is "And it is said that there are three fathers to the Torah—the first is the prophet Moses, the second is Ezra the Scribe, and the third is Judah the Nasi." Mūyāl, *at-Talmūd*, 60, 136, 49, respectively. The corresponding line in al-Khalidi's manuscript reads: "it is said that there are three fathers to Torah—the first is Moses peace be upon him, the second is Ezra the Priest, and the third is Rabbi Judah the Nasi, the compiler of the Mishna." al-Khālidī, "as-Sayūnīzm, ay al-masʾala aṣ-ṣahyūniyya" [copyist version], 29.

142 Perlmann, "Samauʾal al-Maghribī," 55 (English), 51 (Arabic).

aversion to the latter-day "Israelite national renaissance" informed the way in which he perceived and portrayed Ezra the "nationalist" and Torah-forger.

JEWS AND MONEY IN "AS-SAYŪNĪZM"

Al-Khalidi asserted publicly that his antagonism was not against Jews but against Zionism.[143] Nonetheless, elements of his manuscript betray a sentiment that is difficult to characterize as mere anti-Zionism.[144] Such is particularly the case when it comes to his presentation of the relationship among Jews, money, and commerce. After quoting a number of Qur'anic passages concerning the afterlife, al-Khalidi contrasts these with the beliefs of the Jews, for whom "religious happiness, rather, is worldly happiness, which, in their opinion, is abundant money and children. The holiest duties, for them, are two: the first is increasing descendants and children, and the other is the acquisition, accumulation, and increase of money."[145] This is not the first instance in which al-Khalidi describes what brings Jews "religious happiness." As we found earlier, he contends that Jews find "religious happiness" in the possession of Zion. Now he adds two additional sources of Jewish religious happiness: the accumulation of wealth and the proliferation of offspring. Importantly, in accounting for the values of Jews, al-Khalidi appeals to their *religion*.

The theme of the Jews' obsession with money reappears throughout al-Khalidi's manuscript. Writing of the Jews living under the rule of Alexander the Great, al-Khalidi contends that they "were infatuated with profit and money-changing and the rest of the commercial activities, as was their habit from antiquity in Egypt and Babylonia."[146] He perceives Jewish financial greed throughout Jewish history, and he seeks to highlight this phenomenon even when it does not appear in his literary source. Once more, a comparison of al-Khalidi's manuscript to Moyal's *at-Talmūd* is instructive. In a passage concerning Antiochus's reign over Judea, Moyal writes:

> When the force of Antiochus's oppression increased upon the Israelites in Judea, large groups [*jamm ghafīr*] of them emigrated to

[143] This was the case, for instance, in his speech before the Ottoman Parliament. See Khalidi, *Palestinian Identity*, 80–81, 238n.88.

[144] On the complicated question of the origins of antisemitism among twentieth- and twenty-first-century Muslims, see Cohen, "Muslim Anti-Semitism."

[145] al-Khālidī, "as-Sayūnīzm, ay al-mas'ala aṣ-ṣahyūniyya" [copyist version], 14.

[146] Ibid.

> Egypt, where they found the freedom and safety that they lacked in their land, and where they enjoyed civil rights nearly equivalent to the rights of the Greeks themselves. So their numbers increased to the point that Alexandria itself came to have more than one million of them, i.e., approximately one-third of the population, if the Jewish scholar Philo's estimate is correct.[147]

Clearly utilizing Moyal's work as his source, al-Khalidi offers a version of this account that is, for the most part, a verbatim reproduction of his source. The changes he makes, therefore, are of great interest:

> When the oppression of Antiochus, King of Syria, increased upon the Israelites, large groups [*jamm ghafīr*] of them emigrated to Egypt as there was safety and freedom there and they enjoyed civil rights nearly equivalent to the rights of the Greeks themselves. They worked in [the fields] that they loved—money-changing, resale for profit, monopoly, and all types of commerce and jewel trading—and they amassed much money. Their numbers increased to the point that Alexandria itself came to have more than a million of them, i.e., approximately a third of the population, if the Jewish scholar Philo's estimate is correct.[148]

As can readily be seen, al-Khalidi's version takes Moyal's text about the retreat of masses of Jews to Egypt, and especially Alexandria, and inserts within it a claim not only about the ways in which they earned their livelihood—namely, in commercial and financial fields—but also a statement that these were the economic spheres they "loved."

Moyal himself offers a different theory about the concentration of Jews in commerce. "The Jewish nation," writes Moyal, "at the origin of its creation, worked in raising cattle and farming the land. It did not concern itself with commerce, which, in the period of this nation's independence, was in the hands of the Canaanites." The extent of Israelite aversion to commerce, he contends, is recognizable in the Hebrew prophets' rebuke—"more than once"—of those who engage in trading. Acknowledging that the contemporary Jewish professional profile does not correspond with this supposed hostility toward commerce, Moyal concludes:

> And if we see that the members of the Israelite nation are now strongly inclined toward commerce and working with money, this is because of the bigotry of the nations in the Middle Ages. This is what forced them to abandon making a livelihood through

[147] Mūyāl, *at-Talmūd*, 52.
[148] al-Khālidī, "as-Sayūnīzm, ay al-masʾala aṣ-ṣahyūniyya" [copyist version], 30.

> crafts. Their fathers only found before them commerce and occupations in finance and commerce. They thus excelled in them [these fields] to the point that these became a talent passed from one generation to the next within the nation.[149]

Moyal's apologetic defense of Jews' disproportionate involvement in finance and commerce points to the history of restrictions on Jewish professions, beginning in the medieval period.

Al-Khalidi, in contrast, contends that the Jewish inclination toward commerce began long before the Middle Ages; indeed, this phenomenon already existed "in antiquity in Egypt and Babylonia" and resulted, it would seem, from Jews' own preferences and interests. In Babylonia, the Jews "worked in usury and money changing and monopoly"; under the Islamic kingdoms, the Jews "amassed great wealth and they ascended to the highest salaries in the country"; in early modern Italy, "they worked in large trade and the sea trade and they amassed great wealth, which they hoarded. They were skilled in the works of the bank, and the production of loans and money-changing." Al-Khalidi's emphasis on Jews' disproportionate presence in finance extends into his own period. "It is rare for Jews in Russia to work in agriculture and farming," he explains, "because of their disinclination and unwillingness to do it and because of the prejudice of the laws that deal with their rights. Rather, they live mainly from commerce, then from manufacture. They are superior to the Christian in commerce because of their small expenses and [the fact that they are] content with [having] very little."[150] Like Moyal, al-Khalidi acknowledges, at least in the case of nineteenth-century Russia, the impact of laws that limit the areas in which Jews can seek their livelihoods. However, the first of the two explanations al-Khalidi offers for the Jews' engagement in commerce is their own "disinclination and unwillingness" to participate in other fields. While he notes the legal restrictions on Jews' economic activity, they are secondary.

An Ambivalent Assessment of (Russian) Antisemitism

A close reading of this manuscript suggests that al-Khalidi was struggling with himself, or with his sources, in trying to account for the condition of the Jews. On the one hand, he is acutely aware of and

[149] Mūyāl, *at-Talmūd*, 77–78.
[150] al-Khālidī, "as-Sayūnīzm, ay al-masʾala aṣ-ṣahyūniyya" [copyist version], 28.

sensitive to the effects of antisemitic prejudice and legislation in Europe. On the other hand, he seems unable or unwilling fully to absolve Jews of responsibility for their situation.

In a long passage on the position of Jews in nineteenth-century Russia, al-Khalidi details the various discriminatory laws imposed against the Jewish population[151]—additional taxes exclusively for Jews, fees for the right to wear certain types of clothing,[152] duties on Sabbath candles and kosher slaughtering,[153] prohibitions against Jews' working on Sundays and Christian holidays,[154] and regulations permitting a Jewish convert to Christianity to divorce his or her Jewish spouse. Al-Khalidi offers three explanations for Russia's harsh treatment of Jews. The first is Russians' "religious animosity and their Christian fanaticism [*taʿaṣṣubuhum*[155]] as they believe that the Jews killed Christ, peace be upon him." Because the Jews murdered Christ, Christians

[151] Ibid.

[152] In al-Khalidi's description of this particular tax, one finds a fascinating insight into the way he perceived the Jewish population in his native Jerusalem: "And if a Jew wishes to wear a fur hat and a jubbah [a long outer garment, open in front, with wide sleeves], that is, the dress of the Polish nobles and their neighbors in the country, he must pay another tax of five rubles a year. Therefore, you see the Ashkenazim [*saknāj*] in Jerusalem and the rest of the cities of Palestine dressing up in this clothing on the Sabbath and holidays and they do not pay the tax." It is not clear to which Russian law al-Khalidi refers here. The *Jewish Encyclopedia*'s article on "Costume" notes that, in nineteenth-century Russia, one of the taxes specifically targeting Jews "was that collected for wearing jarmulkas, which seems to have been collected in various places in an irregular manner, but was finally compounded, by a special decree of Feb. 11, 1848, for a tax of five rubles annually, the proceeds to go to the fund of the 'korobka' (basket tax)." Perhaps this is the law al-Khalidi has in mind.

[153] Al-Khalidi explains for his reader the concept of kosher slaughtering: "A tax was also imposed on slaughtering performed according to the Mosaic law of separating between 'the kosher and the tref' [transliterated into Arabic] as the Jews do not eat any [meat] other than their own slaughtering commissioned [supervised?] on the part of the rabbi, who permits them to eat it. That which he does not permit them to eat, they sell for a fifth of the price to non-Jews."

[154] "In 1882," al-Khalidi recounts, "a law was issued that forbade Jews from engaging in commerce on Sundays and Christian holidays. Through this [law] they forced the Jews to be idle for two days each week and during Christian and Mosaic holidays."

[155] *Taʿaṣṣub* can also have a more benign sense, of solidarity. It is the term Jamal ad-Din al-Afghani uses for the force that binds a society together. Expounding on the tenuousness associated with this term in al-Afghani and Muhammad Abduh's *al-ʿUrwa al-wuthqā*, Albert Hourani writes: "Like all human attributes, it [*taʿaṣṣub*] could be perverted; it was not a law unto itself, it was subject to the principle of moderation or justice, the organizing principle of human societies. Solidarity which did not recognize this principle and was not willing to do justice turned into fanaticism." Hourani, *Arabic Thought in the Liberal Age, 1798–1939*, 117. It would seem that in al-Khalidi's mind, Christian Russian solidarity, lacking the "principle of moderation or justice," had become plain fanaticism.

eternally despise them, al-Khalidi explains. In this passage, al-Khalidi does not clearly denounce this religious hatred, but his use of the term *taʿaṣṣub*—fanaticism, bigotry, or chauvinism—in this context suggests his negative judgment of Christian religious antisemitism.

The second cause al-Khalidi cites for these discriminatory laws is Russians' "animosity based in economics," their hatred of "people who are satisfied with small profit and insignificant prices compared to the Christian Russians." When a Jew opens a store next to that of a Christian, al-Khalidi explains,

> it does not take long before the Christian has no market for his merchandise and declares bankruptcy due to his inability to keep up with the Jews in the field of commerce. This is especially so because the Jew does not work in hard labor, agriculture, farming, or mining, which are the basis of the acquisition of wealth. Rather, the Jews acquire preexisting wealth and the children of the foreigner are his plowmen and his vine-trimmers as was mentioned earlier in the Book of Isaiah: and they shall enjoy the wealth of the nations and glory in their riches.[156]

Jews are described as aggressive businesspeople willing to accept low standards of living as they force their gentile competitors out of the market.[157] In this second, economic explanation for Russian antisemitism, al-Khalidi does not quite blame Russian Jewry for the bigotry they face, but his analysis of their economic situation, and particularly his assessment of their resistance to those "productive" fields that are the actual "basis of the acquisition of wealth," suggest that al-Khalidi perceived their plight to be at least partially self-inflicted. Importantly, even in his discussion of the economic motivation for anti-Jewish bigotry, al-Khalidi again cites Isaiah's prophecy of Jewish exploitation of gentiles; the Bible remains central for al-Khalidi's understanding of the Jews, even in his explanation of their economic activities and inclinations.

[156] al-Khālidī, "as-Sayūnīzm, ay al-masʾala aṣ-ṣahyūniyya" [copyist version], 68. This is another reference to the previously cited passage from Isaiah 61.

[157] This accusation has a lengthy history in Christian Europe. Writing of a particular form of European Christian economic antisemitism, Derek Penslar explains that "Jewish competition was particularly distressing because of the alleged Jewish practices of cutting margins to the bone, selling a wide variety of wares and engaging in many different enterprises simultaneously, and aggressively seeking customers." Penslar, *Shylock's Children*, 16. Cf. Theodor Herzl's explanation of the causes of antisemitism: "For we had, curiously enough, developed while in the Ghetto into a bourgeois people, and we stepped out of it only to enter into fierce competition with the middle classes." Herzl, *The Jewish State*, 22.

The third explanation for antisemitism that al-Khalidi proposes is Russians' alleged "racial hatred" (*ʿadāwatuhum fī al-ʿunṣur wa-l-ʿirq*) of Jews. "The Jewish race (*al-ʿunṣur*)," writes al-Khalidi, "is very populous, with many children. Where they settle, their numbers increase and they multiply in a short period. In the cities of Poland, for example, they are more numerous than the Christians."[158] The ever-increasing Jews differ from the gentiles not only in religion, al-Khalidi explains, but also "in their language, nationality (*qawmiyyatihim*), customs, and particular interests," and thus Jews "consider the people among whom they live to be strangers." "Therefore"—note the direction of the causality that al-Khalidi perceives to be driving this phenomenon—"the Russians look at them [the Jews] as foreigners and they do not bestow upon them all of the rights that are bestowed upon the Christian Russian people."[159] In pointing to Russian Christians' "racial hatred," al-Khalidi appears to evince a certain sympathy for Jews, yet that appearance is tempered by his suggestion that this racial hatred stems from the fact that the populous Jews perceive their gentile neighbors as "strangers." The Russian government's discrimination against its Jewish population is understandable, perhaps even justifiable, given Jews' own chauvinistic attitudes. Moreover, the reader notices that these two supposed characteristics of Jews—their insatiable appetite for wealth and unceasing biological reproduction—are at once the cause of antisemitism and, as al-Khalidi explains earlier, that which provide Jews with true "religious happiness." Even in al-Khalidi's analysis of the economic and racial motivations of contemporary antisemitism, religion remains at its core.

Jews from East and West

Al-Khalidi recognized, however, that the condition of Jews was not uniform across all countries, even in Europe. When his presentation of Jewish history reaches its ultimate focus, "the Zionist Question," al-Khalidi discusses the means taken by the Ottoman government to halt Jewish immigration through the so-called Red Slip policy. This policy allowed foreigners to enter Palestine with the equivalent of a three-month visitor's visa. The foreigner would yield his or her passport to the Ottoman authorities upon entry and would receive, in its place, a red-hued permit that provided entry for up to three months. Some time before the end of the term, the visitor was expected to leave

[158] al-Khālidī, "as-Sayūnīzm, ay al-masʾala aṣ-ṣahyūniyya" [copyist version], 69.
[159] Ibid.

Palestine and retrieve his or her passport from the Ottoman authorities. Explaining that the Ottoman policy targeted Jews from Eastern Europe, al-Khalidi writes:

> The Ottoman government took this measure against the Jewish immigrants from Russia and Romania because the immigration of the Jews to Palestine came, for the most part, from Eastern Europe because of the humiliation and poverty in which they live. Those [Jews] who reside in western European countries, however, live comfortably with freedom and equality, and they are in control of finance and commerce.[160] It therefore does not cross their minds to leave their profits and to settle in the arid lands of Palestine, deprived of most of the conditions of civilization.[161]

Al-Khalidi stresses the distinction between the Jews of Eastern Europe and those of western Europe. The former, he argues, live in squalid conditions under antagonistic regimes, isolated and alienated from their non-Jewish neighbors. These are the Jews against whom the Ottoman Red Slip policy is aimed, as these are the ones who are trying to immigrate to Palestine. The latter, the Jews of western Europe, al-Khalidi contends, are quite satisfied with their situation, enjoying full civic equality while they dominate the financial world and assimilate among gentiles. So content with their status, they have no interest in "backward," "unfertile" Palestine. "Nevertheless," al-Khalidi acknowledges, "the Zionists aroused the Jews of Italy, who have influence on the government because of their intermingling and assimilation among the people." As a result of the pressure from powerful, assimilated Italian Jews, explains al-Khalidi, the Italian government "protested against the prevention of Jews from settling in Palestine and said that it does not distinguish between its Christian and Jewish subjects."[162]

In these words about the Red Slip policy, the disparate elements of al-Khalidi's perception of contemporary Jewry are united, however uneasily, and linked to the problem of Palestine and Zionism. First, al-Khalidi recognizes a distinction between the Jews of Eastern Europe and those of the West. Whether because of distinct external conditions—a more liberal and tolerant gentile host society—or because, in internal mindset, the Jews of western Europe were more prepared and eager to be accepted within their host society, western Jews have fully

[160] Literally: "they hold the monetary and commercial reins."

[161] Ibid. Cf. Gottheil, "Zionism," 676, and Naṣṣār, *aṣ-Ṣahyūniyya*, 29.

[162] Al-Khalidi took this final quotation from Gottheil's "Zionism" entry. Gottheil, however, did not discuss the assimilation or financial power of Italian Jewry; this was al-Khalidi's explanation.

embraced "Mendelssohn's theory." They have shed their particularities in all but religion, "intermingling and assimilating" with their gentile neighbors. The fact that these western Jews continued and have succeeded in their efforts to dominate finance and commerce is only evidence that they have maintained their religion in which, as al-Khalidi sees it, amassing wealth is among the greatest religious joys. Though western European Jews have abandoned the age-old desire of a return to Palestine, the impoverished and persecuted Jews of Eastern Europe have not, and because of the wealth (and consequent influence) of the former, the Ottoman government faces pressure, such as that from the Italian government, to admit the latter.

In al-Khalidi's appraisal, money is central to the Zionist effort. "With their money," he explains, "they supported newspapers that defend Zionism and that broadcast the benefits of the colonization" of Palestine. He names a Turkish newspaper, for example, which, he alleges, takes from the Zionists' Anglo-Levantine Bank "whatever it needs in terms of expenditures," as much as "one hundred and fifty thousand francs per year." It is thus no surprise that this newspaper's office, its management, and its printing house are found in "one of the most famous and expensive streets of Istanbul." This particular newspaper, moreover, is not the only one bankrolled by Zionists, al-Khalidi asserts; they support many others, "they compensated those authors and writers who served them," and they bribed those governors and rulers who did their bidding.[163]

The immense wealth of the Jews, as al-Khalidi saw it, had an impact on Palestine in even more tangible ways than the Zionists' suspected bribes of newspapers and government officials. Al-Khalidi had personally surveyed the Zionist colonies in Palestine; these "twenty-eight colonies covering 279,491 dunams" were founded "with the money of Rothschild and other rich men like him."[164] From al-Khalidi's perspective, the Jews' money was a direct threat to Palestine, as it was the means Jews employed to appropriate increasingly large tracts of Palestine. With this wealth, Jews

[163] al-Khālidī, "as-Sayūnīzm, ay al-masʾala aṣ-ṣahyūniyya" [copyist version], 4–5. The reference to the specific Ottoman paper, *Jeunes Turcs*, does not appear to be in al-Khalidi's original draft; it seems to be present only in the copyist's version. See chapter 5 below on Zionist "subventions" for sympathetic Arabic newspapers.

[164] The copyist's version adds bitterly that these lands were purchased "at a very low price with the assistance of the governors and the wealthy of the region." The Arabic press from Cairo and Beirut is peppered with articles about the Rothschilds; this fascination with this wealthy Jewish family is explored in chapter 4. On the place of the Rothschilds in the European gentile imagination, see Penslar, *Shylock's Children*, 47–48.

> are still wandering in this gradually-expanding colony [*istiʿmār tadrījī*] on the lookout for opportunities to achieve a large colony, such as the purchase of the Beisan Valley or taking a concession in the colonization of the Jordan Valley and the nearby vast, fertile lands and plains that resemble the land of Egypt and the Nile Valley, or the colonization of the district of Beer Sheba to the Egyptian borders and the Sinai Peninsula. They have already purchased substantial land in Beer Sheba and they are trying to purchase the Wadi Hawarith . . . and Kfar Saba in order to link these two colonies and take possession of all of the coasts from Haifa to Jaffa and the border of Egypt.[165]

In this passage, one observes al-Khalidi's sense of gloom as he considered the predicament of Palestine. The Jews are engaged in a process of "gradual colonization," and with boundless financial resources at their disposal, they will continue to acquire the most fertile and strategically valuable areas of the country, first in isolated locations, but eventually with expansive territorial contiguity. If Zionism's efforts are not checked, so al-Khalidi implies, there will be no room for Palestine's Arabs.[166]

Just as al-Khalidi raises the traditional Islamic polemical attack on Judaism concerning Jews' lack of faith in the afterlife to account for their obsession with Palestine, so too does he employ the common European-Christian charge of Jewish money-hunger[167] to explain to his reader how Jews have succeeded in advancing Zionism despite the

165 al-Khālidī, "as-Sayūnīzm, ay al-masʾala aṣ-ṣahyūniyya" [copyist version], 5.

166 In Europe, especially in the late eighteenth and nineteenth centuries, there developed the "myth of the powerful Jewish *Landfresser* (landgrabber)" as fear spread that Jews were "descending on indebted peasant holdings and wresting them from their rightful owners." Penslar, *Shylock's Children*, 46. While the *Landfresser* myth is similar to al-Khalidi's claims about Jews in Palestine, Zionists were indeed engaged in a systematic effort to purchase land in Palestine.

167 In labeling this charge Christian (and not merely European), I follow Derek Penslar's understanding of the Christian element of European economic antisemitism. Penslar argues that "in Europe, where culture was profoundly influenced by Christianity, economic antisemitism was in part the product of the representation of Jews in Christian texts as the embodiment of avarice. This representation began with the Gospels, in which the critique of the Pharisees as legalistic and hypocritical is undergirded by accusations of greed and materialism. Through certain stories, such as that of Jesus driving the moneychangers out of the Temple compound, or of Judas's betrayal of Jesus for thirty pieces of silver, not only the Pharisees but the Jews as a whole were associated with a stifling and pernicious materialism." Ibid., 13. Of course, Christianity was not the only factor involved in the common economic antisemitism, and it may be argued that the Christian religion and its sacred texts were manipulated, misconstrued, and misused for antisemitic ends. Nonetheless, whether or not Christianity served any sort of causal role in creating European economic antisemitism, it was certainly important in this discourse.

apparent opposition of the Ottoman government and the local Arab population. In both cases, conventional prejudices from disparate sources are utilized not for the sake of defamation—or at least not *only* for this purpose—but as explanatory tools in al-Khalidi's effort to understand Zionism.

Najib Nassar, Jewish Territorialism, and "Mendelssohn's Theory"

Al-Khalidi recognized that Zionism was not the only Jewish movement seeking a new home for the Jews. Other movements—territorialism or non-Palestinocentric Jewish nationalism—sought refuge for Jews in regions outside of Palestine.[168] Interestingly, al-Khalidi's uncle Yusuf Diyaʾ, in the same 1899 letter to Theodor Herzl mentioned above, appeared to endorse the idea, at least in theory. "That one searches for a place somewhere for the unfortunate Jewish people—nothing would be more just and fair," wrote Yusuf Diyaʾ. He continued: "My God, the earth is big enough. There are still uninhabited lands where one could place the millions of poor Jews who maybe would be happy there and would constitute a nation one day. This would perhaps be the best and most rational solution of the Jewish question. But, by God, leave Palestine alone."[169] Yusuf Diyaʾ was not opposed to the idea of an ingathering of impoverished and persecuted Jews from across their Diaspora to a single location. Moreover, he imagined the future possibility of these Jews' becoming a "nation," by which he appears to mean the creation of their own political state. Ruhi al-Khalidi's uncle and intellectual mentor, in other words, did not insist on the inviolability of "Mendelssohn's theory" eliminating the Jews' sense of constituting a distinct nation;[170] in fact, he believed that the migration of Jewish masses to an "uninhabited land" might well be "the best and most rational solution" to the problem of the Jews. Zionism's flaw is that it has chosen a land that is decidedly *not* uninhabited. Jews, following Yusuf Diyaʾ's reasoning, need not abandon their ambitions for an independent territory; they must simply shift their collective gaze elsewhere.

[168] For a collection of primary sources on the subject, see Rabinovitch, ed., *Jews and Diaspora Nationalism.*

[169] CZA H197.

[170] Following Ruhi al-Khalidi, I use this phrase here as a shorthand for the claim that Jews in the modern period constitute only a religious group, not a national one. There is no reason to assume that Yusuf Diyaʾ al-Khalidi would have recognized this view as "Mendelssohn's theory."

Before turning to the younger al-Khalidi's position on this issue, we must recall that he was not the only Arab in Palestine to undertake a translation of Gottheil's extensive "Zionism" article. In 1911 Najib Nassar, editor of *al-Karmil* newspaper in Haifa and an outspoken opponent of Zionism, published a sixty-four-page pamphlet called *aṣ-Ṣahyūniyya: Tārīkhuhu, gharaduhu, ahamiyyatuhu (mulakhasan ʿan al-ensyklūbīdiyya al-yahūdiyya)* (Zionism: Its History, Purpose, and Importance [excerpted from the *Jewish Encyclopedia*]). In publishing this translation, Nassar made his own purpose explicit: he sought to show that, contrary to the view recently expressed by the Ottoman grand vizier, Zionism was not merely a dream[171] of fanatics, but a very real threat that required decisive and sustained opposition from the highest levels of the Ottoman administration. There could be no better source to demonstrate the serious nature of Zionist intentions and activities, Nassar reasoned, than the Jews' own encyclopedia.

In his analysis of Nassar's *aṣ-Ṣahyūniyya*, Neville Mandel contends that Nassar engaged in a systematic manipulation of Gottheil's article. According to Mandel, Nassar slashed from his translation most of Gottheil's references to internal discord within the Jewish and Zionist ranks and to Jewish territorial projects outside of Palestine.[172] It strikes me that Mandel overstates his case. After all, Nassar acknowledges that Herzl's *Judenstaat* proposed either Palestine or Argentina for the site of the Jewish state; he mentions the al-Arish suggestion as well as the East Africa considerations; and twice he even adds mention of a supposed English rabbinic decree against Zionism.[173] Nonetheless, it is true that Gottheil's article emphasizes these events and movements more than Nassar does. Nassar's thesis—asserting that Zionism must be deemed a grave menace to the Ottoman Empire in general and to Palestine in particular—guided the way in which he selected the passages from Gottheil's encyclopedia entry and led him to excise those parts that undermined his perception of the serious threat of Zionism.

Al-Khalidi's aim in writing his manuscript was different from that of Nassar, as we have discovered, even though al-Khalidi certainly agreed that Zionism was a genuine danger for Palestine. One way to discern the difference between the two works is to compare them on the very issues that Mandel has highlighted concerning Nassar's pamphlet. We have already seen that al-Khalidi writes unreservedly about Jewish opponents of Zionism. In contrast to Nassar, who leaves out from his translation Gottheil's discussion of the Jewish Reform movement's opposition to

171 *Riwāya.* Literally: "a play, story, or drama."
172 Mandel, *The Arabs and Zionism before World War I*, 108–9.
173 Mandel acknowledges these two references in a footnote. See ibid., n.68.

Zionism,[174] "Mendelssohn's theory" and the so-called asqāmah against Jewish nationalism are central to al-Khalidi's narrative.

The comparison between Nassar's pamphlet and al-Khalidi's manuscript is somewhat more complicated when it comes to Jewish territorialist ventures beyond Palestine. While Nassar consistently minimizes these ventures, al-Khalidi discusses some extensively and downplays others. Just like Nassar, al-Khalidi does not give much attention to the explosive East Africa controversy, for instance, even though Gottheil's entry deals with it at great length. Unlike Nassar, though, al-Khalidi presents a protracted discussion of Baron Maurice de Hirsch's project of moving masses of Jews to Argentina, a scheme mentioned only in passing in Gottheil's article. After laying out the details of the scheme and the 1892 negotiations with Russian officials, al-Khalidi takes pains to emphasize that de Hirsch's Argentina plan was quite different from Herzl's Zionism. "There was not the slightest Zionist attachment, neither morally nor politically," in de Hirsch's plan, writes al-Khalidi, "nor was there a thought in his mind of establishing a Jewish state, neither then nor in the future. Rather, his project was the incorporation of the Jewish immigrants into Argentinean citizenship quickly and easily."[175] De Hirsch, in other words, was a philanthropist who fully abided by "Mendelssohn's theory" in all respects: he did not attempt to reconnect the severed link between the Jews and Palestine and he did not treat the Jews as a nation.[176] He simply wished to transfer suffering Jews to a new country, the nationality of which they would immediately adopt.

Perhaps al-Khalidi passed over the East Africa plan because it complicated his theory of Jewish history. Al-Khalidi, like his uncle Yusuf Diyaʾ, recognized the suffering of the masses of Jews in Eastern Europe; as we have seen, he records their oppression under the czar in minute detail. He therefore understood the impulse to find a refuge for Jews wherever it might be. Yet, as one who acknowledged and comprehended the historical Jewish link to Palestine, the notion of the Jews' seeking *nationally* to settle a territory other than Palestine (as was the case with the East Africa plan) must have been somewhat mystifying. The *nationalist* "territorialist" position undercut the premodern bond between the Jews and Zion, while simultaneously violating the modern "theory of Mendelssohn" by still maintaining Jewish peoplehood and the will for Jewish self-rule.

[174] See ibid., 108n.64.

[175] al-Khalidi, "as-Sayūnīzm, ay al-masʾala aṣ-ṣahyūniyya" [copyist version], 75.

[176] This was perhaps merely accidental, though, since Ruhi al-Khalidi emphasizes that de Hirsch rejected the settlement of Palestine for economic and political (i.e., not necessarily ideological) reasons.

Al-Khalidi treats de Hirsch's Argentina plan sympathetically, yet he underscores its ultimate failure. In the end, it helped to sustain "1,200 families, or twenty thousand people," writes al-Khalidi, "which is hardly worth mentioning relative to the Jews who remained in Russia, whose numbers exceeded four million." Al-Khalidi concludes, "If we add this example to the earlier examples of colonies in Palestine, we are able to foresee the destiny of the Jewish kingdom of which the Zionists dream."[177]

Conclusion

In his manuscript, al-Khalidi was struggling with a number of competing, sometimes contradictory impulses, informed by the various components of his complex identity. He was a serious scholar; he had studied Jewish history from sources written by Jews in multiple languages, and he did not question the Jewish historical claim to Palestine. He was also a Muslim, highly educated in his own religious tradition. This religious heritage brought with it particular perspectives on how religious systems function as well as ideas (including rather unflattering ones) concerning Jews. At the same time, al-Khalidi had spent much time—both during his later education as well as during his professional life—in fin de siècle Europe, where he found yet another prevalent image of Jews. Indeed, al-Khalidi was in France during the Dreyfus Affair. Though he might well have sided with the Dreyfusards, the antisemitic stereotypes he encountered in Europe, willy-nilly, appear to have found their way into his thinking about Jews. Nonetheless, al-Khalidi was a liberal democrat, and he sympathized deeply with the suffering of Jews in Eastern Europe. Finally, he was a patriot of the Ottoman Empire, and he felt enduring loyalty to Palestine and its Arab population. He desperately sought to protect his homeland and its people from foreign domination. All these competing impulses find expression in al-Khalidi's manuscript. Though the particular combination or configuration of these impulses cannot be generalized to the entirety of the Arab or Muslim population of Late Ottoman Palestine, many of al-Khalidi's fellow Arabs and coreligionists would have experienced at least some of them. In al-Khalidi's manuscript, then, we are able to witness how one individual negotiated these competing impulses as he tried to make sense of his new neighbors in Palestine and of Zionism, the political movement that brought them there.

[177] Ibid.

CHAPTER 3

"Concerning Our *Arab* Question"? Competing Zionist Conceptions of Palestine's Natives

In a 1913 internal Zionist memorandum, "Concerning Our Arab Question," the Galician-born Hebrew writer and educator Yehoshua Radler-Feldmann, who had immigrated to Palestine in 1907, explained that "in Palestine we can hear two contradictory opinions: the one underrating the Arab question, the other perhaps exaggerating it."[1] Indeed, in the final years of Ottoman rule in Palestine, there was regular discussion in Zionist circles about what it meant for Zionist ambitions that there were hundreds of thousands of non-Jewish natives in the Land of Israel.[2] Radler-Feldmann's simple assertion, however, was not merely a description of reality; it was an *interpretation* of that reality. For Radler-Feldmann, the "question" was an *Arab* question. The problem the Jews faced in Palestine, his choice of words presumed, was their confrontation with "Arabs," a group that constituted the majority of Palestine's population. Radler-Feldmann was certainly not alone in interpreting the question as he did, and subsequent history and historiography have generally reified his view regarding the fin de siècle as the first years of the Zionist-*Arab* conflict.[3] But in the Late Ottoman period, there were other, competing interpretations as well.

[1] Cited in Roʾi, "The Zionist Attitude to the Arabs 1908–1914," 235. Yehoshua Radler-Feldmann (1880–1957), known by the pen name Rabbi Benjamin, was born in eastern Galicia. After living briefly in London, where he worked with Yosef Hayim Brenner, he settled in Palestine in 1907. David Tidhar, EḤY, 4:1711.

[2] On the various positions articulated in the pre–World War I era, see Gorni, *Zionism and the Arabs 1882–1948*, 40–77.

[3] See, for instance, Cohen, ed., *Ẓiyonut ve-ha-sheʾelah ha-ʿarvit*; Beʾeri, *Reshit ha-sikhsukh yisraʾel-ʿarav, 1882–1911*; Rodinson, *Israel and the Arabs*; Roʾi, "The Zionist Attitude to the Arabs 1908–1914," 198–242.

In this chapter I explore the various ways in which Zionists of Late Ottoman Palestine conceived of their non-Jewish neighbors,[4] primarily through a study of three Zionist newspapers in the five years preceding the Great War. I read these newspapers with an eye to the ways in which their respective editors and authors identified and classified the Zionists' non-Jewish neighbors. My analysis reveals that, in these years, there was no clear consensus among Zionist writers about whom Zionists had found in Palestine; there was no agreement, that is, about the natives' defining characteristics and how they might best be classified and conceptualized, and, in turn, how Zionists ought to relate to them. While for some the category of "Arab" was meaningful, even central, for others religious divisions (between Muslims and Christians) were more consequential and thus the primary way in which to perceive their neighbors. Many of Radler-Feldmann's Zionist contemporaries perceived his "Arab Question" as actually a "Christian and Muslim Question" or even two separate Christian and Muslim questions. Zionist authors, in other words, often deemed religion to be the relevant social category to describe the non-Jewish natives of Late Ottoman Palestine. In other cases, the non-Jews of Palestine were characterized in "racial" terms—terms that linked some of those non-Jews to the Jews while further distancing others. Toward the end of the chapter, I will discuss a racial theory concerning the natives of Palestine that first emerged during the prewar years but began to be articulated most clearly in the period immediately following the war by none other than the leaders of Palestine's Zionist community. This theory, we shall see, questioned both the Arab *and* the Muslim nature of those who were generally viewed as Muslim Arabs and asserted that the majority of these were, in fact, Jews.

We will discover in this chapter that the boundaries between the various categories—indeed, the ways in which the categories themselves were to be defined—were contested and in flux. Zionists were struggling, sometimes explicitly and at other times implicitly, with the questions of what it meant for one to be an Arab or a Muslim or a Christian—even with what it meant to be a Jew or a Hebrew. Where did these categories overlap and when did one exclude another? I contend that Zionists' varying conceptions of themselves—as Jews, Zionists, Hebrews, Ottomans, Sephardim, Ashkenazim, and so on—were often

[4] I ask the reader's forbearance with the awkward locutions I have employed in this discussion (e.g., "non-Jewish neighbor," "non-Jewish natives of Palestine," "whom the Zionists found in Palestine"). I use these phrases so as not to prejudice my analysis of how Zionists conceptualized these communities, even as I recognize that the phrases are themselves problematic and would certainly not have been the way the communities described themselves.

linked to the ways in which they imagined and defined their neighbors (hence the double meaning of this book's title, *Defining Neighbors*, as groups both define and are defined by their neighbors). Through my analysis of the three newspapers, I will suggest that while Ottoman Sephardic Zionists and First Aliyah Ashkenazim often conceived of their neighbors in religious terms, the socialist nationalist ideologues of the Second Aliyah were apparently less comfortable doing so. In the minds of those Second Aliyah Zionist ideologues, they were engaged in a national-class encounter; as in their own self-conception, religion for these materialist-secularists could not be a "real," defining feature.

These terminological variations have important implications for our understanding of the early years of the Zionists' encounter with the natives of Palestine. Knowing whom the Zionists believed they had met in Palestine—rather than taking one particular categorization of this population for granted—is critical for comprehending how Zionists related to Palestine's natives, then and later. To begin to understand the ways in which the editors, authors, and, ultimately, readers of these three newspapers conceived of Palestine's native non-Jews, it is valuable to look carefully at the specific terminology the newspapers use in referring to them. As George Lakoff and Mark Johnson have argued, "a categorization is a natural way of identifying a *kind* of object or experience by highlighting certain properties, downplaying others, and hiding still others." This means that "when we give everyday descriptions, for example, we are using categories to focus on certain properties that fit our purposes."[5] If asked whether an individual was "an Arab," a Zionist may have answered affirmatively, but we learn something about how the Zionist views his or her world if, unprompted, he or she identifies that individual as "a Muslim," for instance, or as "a Christian."[6] Indeed, though I make use here of a wide variety of types of articles—including explicitly politically oriented pieces—I draw extensively from daily reportage and other nonprogrammatic accounts. I take these relatively unguarded descriptions of quotidian events as key windows into how their authors viewed their world (rather than how they may have wanted others, for more self-consciously political reasons, to view this world). While I would caution against presuming a precise equivalence

[5] Lakoff and Johnson, *Metaphors We Live By*, 163.

[6] Lakoff and Johnson demonstrate how descriptions "highlight, downplay, and hide" with this list of statements: "I've invited a sexy blonde to our dinner party"; "I've invited a renowned cellist to our dinner party"; "I've invited a Marxist to our dinner party"; "I've invited a lesbian to our dinner party." They write: "Though the same person may fit all of these descriptions, each description highlights different aspects of the person. . . . In making a statement, we make a choice of categories because we have some reason for focusing on certain properties and downplaying others." Ibid., 163.

between the terminology Zionists used to describe their non-Jewish neighbors and the ways in which they perceived these neighbors, studying the terminology is critical in discerning those perceptions.

Newspapers and Their Neighbors

Zionist newspapers represent an exceptionally useful source for this discussion. Though each was edited by a different small group of intellectuals, many people from across Palestine's Jewish society and beyond participated in them—as correspondents, advertisers, letter-writers, and, of course, readers (as the Jewish population enjoyed a high literacy rate). From the earliest period of Jewish nationalist settlement in the Holy Land in the 1880s (the First Aliyah), Zionists established newspapers that combined news reports from Palestine, Diaspora Jewish communities, the Ottoman Empire, Europe, and elsewhere, along with opinion pieces that argued for a variety of political, religious, ideological, or cultural positions. The Zionist press in Palestine was especially vibrant and expansive in the years following the Young Turk Revolution of 1908, the bloodless political uprising in Istanbul that restored the Ottoman Constitution and Parliament and promised increased freedoms, including freedom of the press. Given the loosened restrictions on the press and the new wave of Zionist immigration that had begun in 1904 (the Second Aliyah), the final years of Ottoman rule in Palestine witnessed a marked expansion of Zionist papers: new newspapers were founded, and veteran weeklies became semiweeklies and even dailies.

The three papers I have chosen to analyze here offer certain insights into the worlds and worldviews of the three main Zionist communities in Late Ottoman Palestine: Sephardim, Ashkenazic immigrants of the First Aliyah, and the more recent Ashkenazic arrivals of the Second Aliyah. *Ha-Ḥerut* was founded and edited by Sephardic Zionists in Jerusalem, beginning in 1909; *ha-Ẓevi* (which at various times also went under the title *ha-Or* or *Hashkafah*) was founded by the Ashkenazic First Aliyah immigrant Eliezer Ben-Yehuda and edited by members of his family beginning in 1884;[7] and *ha-Aḥdut* was founded in 1906 and edited by leading members of the socialist Poʿalei Ẓiyon (Workers of Zion) Party, including individuals who came to play central roles in the history of the Yishuv and the State of Israel such as David Ben-Gurion, Yitzhak Ben-Zvi, and Rachel Yanaʾit Ben-Zvi.

[7] See Kressel, *Toldot ha-ʿitonut ha-ʿivrit be-ereẓ yisraʾel*, 71ff.

Though I have chosen these particular papers as a cross-section of the prewar Zionist community, we should not assume that the Zionist subgroup that led the editorial board was representative of the elements of the Zionist community that participated in writing the paper or, all the more so, of the population that read the paper. Consider, for example, *ha-Ḥerut*, which scholars often regard as a "Sephardic newspaper."[8] Though *ha-Ḥerut* was run by Sephardic Zionists and on occasion the Sephardic identity of the newspaper's leadership was proudly displayed,[9] as scholar Yitzhak Bezalel has noted, labeling *ha-Ḥerut* a "Sephardic newspaper" is a complicated matter and cannot be done without qualification. First of all, in its self-definition the paper was not explicitly Sephardic. In the paper's mission statement, published in its first issue in May 1909, the editor, Avraham Elmaleh, declared that the paper would be a "Hebrew and general paper." As a Hebrew paper, he explained, *ha-Ḥerut* would try to "give voice to the feelings and hopes of our people and, with a powerful hand, to raise the Zionist flag." Moreover, *ha-Ḥerut* would "devote large space to matters concerning Jerusalem, the four holy cities [i.e., Jerusalem, Hebron, Tiberias, and Safed] and the colonies, the development of trade, industry, and agriculture in the Land of Israel, the cradle of our ancestors." As a "general paper," *ha-Ḥerut* would strive to provide news from around the world with a particular focus on issues concerning "Turkey" (i.e., the Ottoman Empire) at "the historic moment in which we live."[10] The paper would be "free," that is, independent, and would be bound to "no person or party," only to "the truth." Of course, part of this "truth," for the editors of *ha-Ḥerut*, was the righteousness of the Zionist movement (or their particular interpretation thereof), but it is worth noting here that the words "Sephardic" and "Ashkenazic"[11]

[8] See, e.g., "*Ha-Herut* as a Sephardi National Newspaper" in Jacobson, *From Empire to Empire*, 87–89. Jacobson acknowledges that "*ha-Ḥerut* did not view itself as targeting exclusively the Sephardic community," but she argues that "from its content it was clear that the Sephardi community was its main target population, and that it served as an opposition to the traditional Sephardi leadership."

[9] Consider, for instance, the notice issued in *ha-Ḥerut* on March 1, 1912, upon the paper's conversion to a daily, that referred to the paper as "the Hebrew national newspaper" but also declared that, "as is well-known, it is the first Hebrew paper to be published by Sephardim." That notice further highlighted the fact that "its editor is Sephardic and the majority of its authors are Sephardim. And this is the glory of the community of the Sephardic Jews." See Beẓalʾel, "ʿAl yiḥudo shel '*ha-Ḥerut*' (1909–1917) ve-ʿal Ḥayim Ben-ʿAtar ke-ʿorkho," 127.

[10] Literally: "At this hour of the birth of the world in which we live."

[11] The one possible reference to these internal Jewish divisions is the claim that "our entire purpose, we repeat, is only to benefit our readers, our communities [*ʿedoteinu*], our land, and our language."

are absent from *ha-Ḥerut*'s stated mission. The paper was meant to be "an important Land of Israel newspaper [*ʿiton ereẓ yisraʾeli*]," not a "parochial" Sephardic organ. Furthermore, as we shall see, though the editors remained Sephardim throughout the run of the newspaper, several of *ha-Ḥerut*'s regular contributors were actually Ashkenazim.[12] Bezalel, in his monograph on Sephardic Zionists in Ottoman Palestine, aptly describes *ha-Ḥerut* not as a Sephardic newspaper but rather as "a national newspaper with Sephardic ownership."[13] While one must not disregard the Sephardic identity of the owners, editors, and many of the writers of *ha-Ḥerut* in analyzing this newspaper, one would be mistaken to link the views presented in the paper exclusively with Palestine's Sephardic community. For this reason, I endeavor to highlight the identities of the authors of particular articles when they are noted; at the same time, it is important to read these articles in the contexts of the papers in which they appeared and the cultural worlds of the leaders of those papers.

In the pages of *ha-Ḥerut*, the Christians of Palestine are often denoted simply as "Christians," even when religion—as we might understand it[14]—does not appear to have any connection to the story. For instance, in August 1909, *ha-Ḥerut* reported that "many families of Jerusalem's youth from among our nation [i.e., Jews] left our city this week. Many Christian youths from Bethlehem also left our land and traveled to America [or] to Argentina to seek work."[15] Indeed, Palestine's Christians were a disproportionately urban community and shared a number of socioeconomic characteristics with their Jewish counterparts. While these similarities bred competition and, at times, strife, they also led, or at least permitted, Jews and Christians to act in similar ways—such as emigrating in response to economic hardships. Jews and Christians were also similarly affected by the Young Turk Revolution, after which both communities were legally subject to Ottoman military conscription. In this context, *ha-Ḥerut* reported on the drafting of many Bethlehem Christians: "The number of Greek, Latin, and Protestant Christian residents of Bethlehem whose time has arrived to serve in the army has reached four hundred."[16] In another 1909 article, *ha-Ḥerut*

[12] Bezalel lists Yehoshua Radler-Feldmann (Rabbi Benjamin), A. M. Heimann, Mordecai Ben Hillel ha-Cohen, Y. M. Tukachinsky, Samuel Tiktin, Y. H. Teller, Menashe Meirovitz, M. M. Bronstein, Nahum Maltzen, Mikhael Nekhes, Moshe Smilansky, Mendel Kraemer, A. Z. Rabinovitz, Aryeh Roznik, and Samuel Rafaelovitz. See Beẓalʾel, "ʿAl yiḥudo shel '*ha-Ḥerut*' (1909–1917) ve-ʿal Ḥayim Ben-ʿAtar ke-ʿorkho," 129.

[13] Beẓalʾel, *Noladetem ẓiyonim*, 305ff.

[14] See my discussion of these categories in the introduction.

[15] *ha-Ḥerut* 1:33. The author is Mendel Kremer.

[16] *ha-Ḥerut* 2:6 (October 12, 1909), 3. The author is Mendel Kremer.

reported on a young man who drowned off the coast of Jaffa. The Jaffa correspondent refers to the victim not as an Arab but as "a Christian lad."[17] In these examples, the matters discussed are not in any apparent way related to religion (whether theology or practice). Rather, they would seem to be "secular," worldly matters: levels of emigration to the Americas, conscription rates, and an accidental death. That the individuals discussed were Christian, that they prayed in churches rather than mosques, might seem inconsequential. But in the minds of the authors, being Christian was relevant far beyond the narrow domain twenty-first-century Westerners might impute to religion. For these authors, that is, Christianity was a primary mark of distinction, not a modifier of some other, supposedly more fundamental characteristic.

The same is often the case in Ben-Yehuda's papers from this period. For instance, in a report in a November 1910 issue of *ha-Or*, we read of the beating of an elderly Jew by "a rash gentile" in Jerusalem in broad daylight. Hearing the screams of the victim, many came to the aid of the old man, "but the Christians who were there stood from afar and watched how the seventy-year-old man was beaten by the wild youth." (The author does not limit the accusations to the Christian bystanders; the article immediately notes that "to our shame, there were also two Jews who, out of fear, did not dare to protect their brother."[18]) Similarly, a letter to the editor in an earlier issue (when the newspaper was called *ha-Ẓevi*) reports on "Hebrew among the Christians." The writer requests that Ben-Yehuda, who was already renowned for devising neologisms in his attempt to modernize the Hebrew language, "create a fitting Hebrew word for the French word *Papeterie*,[19] as we have been asked here by misters *Sayegh et Selim*,[20] who would like to use it for the 'stamp of their business' and are not satisfied with only the French and Arabic. The Jews should know that the Christians consider Hebrew a living language more so than do the Hebrews themselves."[21]

This example is particularly informative as it reveals that, in this newspaper, "Christian" is not a code word for European. When individuals are described simply as Christians, after all, there is at least the possibility that European Christian residents of Palestine are the referents; as discussed in chapter 1, in the Late Ottoman period there were small populations of European Christian missionaries and other

[17] *ha-Ḥerut* 1:44 (September 8, 1909), 3. The author is listed as Ben-Avraham.

[18] *ha-Or* 2:14:189 (November 4, 1910), 3.

[19] French for "stationery," the word is recorded in Latin script.

[20] The names are written first in Hebrew script (including *et* for "and") and then in Latin.

[21] *ha-Ẓevi* 25:103 (February 12, 1909), 3.

settlers in Palestine.[22] The fact that the "Christians" who were seeking the Hebrew word for "stationery" are named Sayegh and Selim suggests that they were not Europeans.[23] In these cases, and numerous others, residents of Palestine are classified as "the Christians" when religion or religious identity would appear to be irrelevant to the incidents described.

It is worthwhile noting here that the letter to Ben-Yehuda was signed by David de Boton, a member of an illustrious Sephardic family. There was not, as is sometimes imagined, a rigid separation between the social, intellectual, and cultural worlds of Sephardim, on the one hand, and Ashkenazim, on the other; the Sephardic de Boton knew of and respected the Ashkenazic Ben-Yehuda's Hebrew language project, and he clearly read Ben-Yehuda's newspaper. Because of the Sephardic identity of its author, this letter can obviously not be taken as a direct indication of the perceptions of First Aliyah Ashkenazim. However, the title provided for it by the First Aliyah Ashkenazic editors—"Hebrew among the Christians"—uses the same terminology.

Just as *ha-Ḥerut* and *ha-Or / ha-Ẓevi* frequently identify the Christians of Palestine solely by their religious affiliation, the same is often true of their discussion of Palestine's Muslims. In midsummer 1910 there was a stabbing in Jerusalem. *Ha-Ḥerut* reported that "the Jew Shlomo Babel stabbed a young man who was from among the Muslim notables in our city."[24] In December of that year *ha-Ḥerut* reported on the elections for an administrative council (the *majlis ʿumumī*) in the mutasarriflik of Jerusalem. Here, too, the categories the article cites are Muslim (or, more precisely, "Ishmaelite"), Christian, and Jewish: "from Jerusalem, two Ishmaelites, one Christian, and one Jew were elected"; "from Hebron, three Ishmaelites and one Jew"; "from Jaffa two Ishmaelites and two Christians"; and "from Beersheba four Ishmaelites."[25]

Ben-Yehuda's newspapers use this religious mode of classification of Palestine's Muslims as well. In a November 1908 article titled "Killed," we read of the spread of rumors about a man who had been murdered. At first, the author explains, the man was believed to have been a

[22] For a brief overview of the activities of British, German, French, and Russian settlers and missionaries in Jerusalem, including those of the German Templers, see Ben-Arieh, *Jerusalem in the Nineteenth Century*, 58–71.

[23] Given their knowledge of the French word, though, it is possible that they were natives of Lebanon (where the French presence was more expansive) and not of Palestine. However, this is certainly not necessarily so; after all, well-educated Arabs in Palestine (especially those who attended missionary schools) were taught French.

[24] *ha-Ḥerut* 2:122 (July 20, 1910), 3. The author is Mendel Kremer.

[25] *ha-Ḥerut* 3:18 (December 2, 1910), 3. The author is, again, Mendel Kremer. See further in this chapter for a discussion of this contributor.

Jew. "One hour later," however, "the rumors had changed." In fact, the victim was not a Jew. "Then who was he?" asks the author rhetorically. He was actually "a Muslim!"[26] A report from Hebron in December 1908 proudly tells of the happiness shared "by all" in the celebration of "the holiday of freedom" (*ḥag ha-ḥerut*) that followed the Young Turk Revolution. In Hebron, the correspondent relates, "Jews and Muslims walked together arm-in-arm, in brotherhood." The correspondent, listed simply as "R," notes that this scene was all the more exceptional given the fact that an anti-Jewish boycott was ongoing in Hebron. "We hope," he concludes, that "beginning today, after the celebration, they will cancel it. This boycott has deprived several of our brothers of a livelihood."[27]

The term Ishmaelite also appeared in Ben-Yehuda's papers. For instance, in the "Jerusalem Daily" section of a late 1910 issue of *ha-Or*, the author describes a piece of prime Jerusalem real estate (including the Carmel Hotel) that was owned by "more than thirty Ishmaelite families."[28] Later that same month, also in the "Jerusalem Daily" feature, an article reported on "The Sale of a House from a Jew to Ishmael [*sic*]."[29] This article also comments on the unfairness of the land-purchasing system, pointing to "the speed and swiftness" with which the transaction was completed in the court ("in three hours"), while "in cases of transactions between Jews, and all the more so from an Ishmaelite to a Jew . . . many days are wasted running back and forth to court and much money spent unnecessarily." Interestingly, the author does not object, on principle, to the sale of land by a Jew to a non-Jew; the article does not mention this issue.[30]

Intriguingly, in the Second Aliyah paper *ha-Aḥdut*, such singularly religious categorizations—neither qualifying nor qualified by any other terms—are much less prominent in the paper's descriptions of the non-Jewish natives of Palestine. The relative absence of such categorization is particularly remarkable when seen in the context of their regularity in *ha-Ḥerut* and *ha-Ẓevi / ha-Or*. I shall return to *ha-Aḥdut* below. For now, let us simply note that to the extent that we can gauge perceptions by terminological usage, at least at times, this is how the authors of *ha-Ḥerut* and *ha-Ẓevi / ha-Or* authors perceived their world: the Jews of Palestine were living among Christians and

[26] *ha-Ẓevi* 25:40 (November 25, 1908), 2.

[27] *ha-Ẓevi* 25:57 (December 20, 1908), 2.

[28] *ha-Or* 2:27:202 (November 20, 1910), 2.

[29] The article title indeed reads *yishma'el* (Ishmael) not *yishma'eli* (an Ishmaelite), though in the article itself the author uses the term Ishmaelite. I presume that the missing *yud* was the result of a typographical error.

[30] *ha-Or* 2:27:209 (November 29, 1910), 3.

Muslims; that they were also Arabs often seems irrelevant or unworthy of mention.

But not always, to be sure. At other times, even in *ha-Ḥerut* and *ha-Ẓevi / ha-Or*, the non-Jewish natives of Palestine are referred to simply as Arabs. In Hebron in June 1909, for example, there was a public celebration on the visit of a high-level official from the Russian Orthodox Church. According to *ha-Ḥerut*'s correspondent, Arabs and Jews joined in the celebration (a fascinating scene of Palestinian social history in its own right), and all was proceeding delightfully. The festivities were interrupted, however, when an intoxicated "Arab" with "a good heart" shot his pistol and accidentally killed a young Jewish woman. The details of this incident are intriguing—vigilante pursuit of the killer, threats of revenge and counterrevenge, and so on—but the important point for the present discussion is that the killer is identified merely as "one of the Arabs."[31] The fact that he was intoxicated perhaps suggests that he was not a Muslim—or not a strictly observant one[32]—but, regardless, for this *ha-Ḥerut* author's purposes, he was simply an Arab. The same is true in multiple other *ha-Ḥerut* reports, including, for instance, a brief account from the Galilee of "the Arabs of the region" who allegedly planted the "body of a murdered Arab" in the Jewish Kinerret colony near Tiberias in order to accuse the Jews of being "the Arab's murderers."[33] In these cases, *ha-Ḥerut*'s authors use the term Arab without reference to the subjects' religious identity.

As with *ha-Ḥerut*, Ben-Yehuda's papers also often refer to non-Jewish residents of Palestine simply as "Arabs." In a report entitled "The Arabs in Jaffa," published in January 1909, *ha-Ẓevi* explains that, in the wake of the newspaper's earlier notice about "an Arab" who allegedly poisoned young Jewish girls, "there erupted among the Arabs great excitement, and on Thursday they burst into the store of a Jewish shopkeeper and beat him murderously, accusing *him*, the Jewish shopkeeper, of poisoning Arab girls."[34] The next month, *ha-Ẓevi* reported on another event in Jaffa, in which "an Arab entered one of the houses in [the neighborhood of] Neve Shalom and kidnapped a young woman." When the "Arab" was finally caught, he brazenly declared, in the language of the Young Turk Revolution, that "there

[31] *ha-Ḥerut* 1:10 (June 11, 1909), 3. The author is listed as M. ʿ. M.

[32] For a report on an 1895 alleged incident in which a Muslim notable visited a Jewish colony and became intoxicated, "something he could not do in an Arab environment," see Asaf, *ha-Yeḥasim beyn ʿarvim vi-hudim be-ereẓ-yisraʾel 1860–1948*, 25. On Islamic attitudes toward intoxication, see Enes Karic, "Intoxication," EQ.

[33] *ha-Ḥerut* 1:25 (July 26, 1909), 2. The author is listed as Y. B. Sh.

[34] *ha-Ẓevi* 25:92 (January 31, 1909), 2. Emphasis corresponds to a repeated pronoun.

is freedom [*ḥuriyya*] today!” The author of this report asks rhetorically: “Where are the Jaffa police? And if they are not to be found, where are the enlightened of the Arabs? Why are they not teaching the masses knowledge and ethics [*deʿah u-musar*]?”[35] The problem is identified here as the absence of enlightened and ethical *Arabs*. The journalists who wrote for Ben-Yehuda’s newspapers, like those in *ha-Ḥerut*, sometimes defined their neighbors as “Arabs,” displaying no interest in distinguishing between Arabs of different religions, even concerning matters of ethics, when one might have expected religion to enter into the discussion.

How might we account for this alternation between nonreligious categorizations of Palestine’s natives (as Arabs), on the one hand, and religious classification (as Christians or Muslims), on the other? A regional explanation does not fit; there does not appear to be a geographical pattern of terminology choice, correlated, for instance, to whether the location described included both Muslim and Christian populations. Moreover, because articles from these newspapers are frequently written anonymously or signed merely with initials, it is difficult to determine any pattern related to characteristics of the authors: Ashkenazim versus Sephardim, religious versus more secular Jews, Arabic-speaking versus non-Arabic-speaking Jews, or Jews more familiar with native life in Palestine versus those less versed in such affairs.

Simpler explanations might apply. Perhaps, if authors knew the religions of the individuals involved, they would note them; otherwise, “Arab” would have to do. But even this explanation is unsatisfactory, as illustrated in a *ha-Ḥerut* article entitled “A Christian Stabs a Hebrew” from 1910.[36] The article describes an incident in Jerusalem in which Jewish schoolchildren were allegedly surrounded by “Arab youths,” one of whom stabbed a Jewish boy in his side, inflicting a deep wound. The article never mentions the religion of the assailant; the two times he and his friends are identified, they are denoted as “Arab youths” or simply “Arabs.” That the perpetrator was Christian appears only in the article’s title, suggesting yet another possible explanation for variations: the newspaper’s editors, who presumably titled the article, may have been more likely than other writers to view their neighbors in religious terms. Regardless of the explanation, for some of Palestine’s Zionists, at least at times, their encounter with Palestine’s natives was an encounter with members of two religions.

[35] *ha-Ẓevi* 25:98 (February 7, 1909), 2.

[36] *ha-Ḥerut* 3:23 (December 14, 1910), 2–3. There is no named author.

Mendel Kremer and the "Ishmaelites"

A curious fact in this regard is that the author of many of the reports concerning Palestine's natives in *ha-Ḥerut* (the newspaper often characterized simply as "Sephardic") was a journalist named Mendel Kremer, an unambiguously Ashkenazic name. Though he wrote frequently for *ha-Ḥerut* and occasionally for other Zionist papers in Palestine, little is known about Kremer.[37] One source we do have about Kremer is Theodor Herzl's diary entries from his visit to Palestine in 1898. During the trip Herzl met Kremer. Just after Herzl's much-anticipated audience with the German kaiser, who was also visiting Jerusalem, Herzl records that "outside stood the secret-service agent and supposed Zionist Mendel Kremer, who has been accompanying us since Jaffa—by order of the Turkish government, it seems to me."[38] Later, in Jaffa, Herzl explained his preference to remain on a ship so as to stay "out of reach of the Mendel Kremers, Mazies,[39] and all those people who, with good intentions or bad, might have got me into trouble with the Turkish misgovernment—whether in order to save imperiled Jewry, earn their thirty pieces of silver, or get into the good graces of Rothschild or some pasha."[40] Herzl perceived Kremer as an Ottoman spy in Zionist guise, a claim that may reveal more about Herzl's paranoia or ignorance of the realities of Ottoman Palestine than it does about Mendel Kremer himself.[41] Herzl's suspicions about Kremer do, however, suggest that Kremer was highly familiar with Ottoman culture and presumably spoke Ottoman Turkish, if not Arabic

[37] He sent a letter to Ben-Yehuda's *ha-Ẓevi* concerning the decree that Muslim women boycott Jewish-owned stores in Hebron (*ha-Ẓevi*, November 23, 1908) and another concerning the devastating December 28, 1908, earthquake in Italy and Italy's benevolent treatment of its Jewish population (*ha-Ẓevi*, January 19, 1909). At the close of the latter letter, Kremer's name is signed in Latin script, so I have chosen here to spell his name accordingly. Yoseph Lang writes that Kremer was *ha-Ẓevi*'s Jerusalem correspondent and became an editor of *Hashkafah*. Lang, *Daber ʿivrit!*, 405, 513. At various points, Campos identifies Kremer as "the Jaffa-based correspondent for the Hebrew paper *ha-Hashkafa*," "an Ottomanized Jew," and "a *mukhtar* of Ashkenazi Jews in Jerusalem." Campos, *Ottoman Brothers*, 77, 155.

[38] Herzl, *Complete Diaries*, 757. Herzl spells the name Krämer.

[39] The reference here is to the physician Aaron Meir Masie (1858–1930). Born in Eastern Europe, he studied in Mir, Zurich, and Paris before immigrating to Palestine in 1888. He was appointed chief medical officer for the Rothschild settlements. See Joseph Gedaliah Klausner, "Masie, Aaron Meir," EJ[2].

[40] Ibid., 762.

[41] Herzl's accusation is, as far as I have been able to tell, nowhere corroborated nor repeated.

as well.[42] This impression is confirmed, it would seem, by the fact that one decade later, Kremer was one of *ha-Ḥerut*'s main correspondents on issues concerning Palestine's native non-Jewish population, further indicating that there were Ashkenazim who were viewed by the Sephardic editors of *ha-Ḥerut* as experts on the affairs of Palestine's natives. For the present discussion, it is relevant to note that Kremer typically used religious categorizations of Palestine's Arabs in his articles.

Kremer was in fact the author of the *ha-Ḥerut* article, noted above, that listed the representatives elected to the Ottoman Parliament as Jews, Christians, and Ishmaelites. Though the term Ishmaelite does not necessarily have religious connotations, in these newspapers it is used interchangeably with Muslim.[43] In an issue of Ben-Yehuda's *ha-Or* printed just ten days after *ha-Ḥerut*'s report on the elections, there is a small notice on "the Holiday of the Sacrifice" (the Hebrew translation of the Islamic holiday *ʿīd al-qurbān*, i.e., *ʿīd al-aḍḥā*): "Monday will be the first day of the holiday of 'the Sacrifice' for the community of the Ishmaelites. The holiday will last four days."[44] This notice may also have been written by Kremer, as it is signed with his initials M.K.[45] In 1909, also in *ha-Ẓevi*, Kremer published a letter with his full name that insisted that under the new Ottoman regime, the Jews had the same right to serve in the highest levels of government "just as all [other] Ottomans." In this letter, Kremer was particularly concerned that in Jerusalem's administrative council—in which "all important matters" of government would be addressed, including "many issues that affect the Jewish community [*ʿedat ha-yehudim*] of Jerusalem"—"there is not a single Jew, but there are seven from the community of Ishmaelites and five from the community of Christians."[46] Kremer, an influential journalist in both the Sephardic-edited and Ashkenazic-edited Zionist newspapers, was interested in religious distinctions and brought these

[42] The fact that Kremer was in Palestine in 1898, of course, also indicates that he was either a member of the pre-Zionist Jewish community of Palestine or that he had come to Palestine in the first wave of Zionist immigration.

[43] On the generally ethnic usage of the term Ishmaelites, see Israel Ephʿal, "Ishmaelites," EJ[2]; "Ishmael," EQ; and "Races," EQ. On Ishmael in rabbinic sources, see Bakhos, *Ishmael on the Border*.

[44] *ha-Or*, December 12, 1910.

[45] Kremer, in *ha-Ẓevi* 25:56 (December 18, 1908), 3, acknowledged that he sometimes published with these initials, though he claims that someone else had done so as well, and that, as a result, to avoid confusion and so as not to be associated with another's views, he would cease to do so. However, given that this 1910 article is on the same subject as Kremer's typical articles, it would seem that, sometime between 1908 and 1910, Kremer had reclaimed his initials for the purposes of articles in Ben-Yehuda's papers.

[46] *ha-Ẓevi* 25:75 (January 10, 1909), 2.

matters to the attention of the readers across Palestine's diverse Zionist community.

DUAL LABELS: MUSLIM ARABS AND (NOT QUITE) ARAB CHRISTIANS

In addition to characterizing native non-Jews either by their religion or simply as Arabs, certain Zionist journalists elected at times to use both, with the phrases "Christian Arabs" or "Muslim Arabs." Such terms are also found in *ha-Ḥerut* articles from the period, usually in the context of comparing the communities' attitudes toward Jews and Zionism. Relative to other Hebrew newspapers in Late Ottoman Palestine, *ha-Ḥerut* was exceptionally concerned with the anti-Zionist Arabic press. While the paper had already published many notices and warnings about the Arabic press in Palestine—especially concerning the newspaper *al-Karmil*, edited by Najib Nassar, a Greek Orthodox Arab in Haifa—*ha-Ḥerut*'s full-scale, front-page literary war against this phenomenon began in earnest in November 1910 with a two-page article titled "The Great Danger."[47] *Ha-Sakanah ha-gedolah*, "the Great Danger," subsequently became *ha-Ḥerut*'s watchword for the problem of the anti-Zionist Arabic press. Nassar, as discussed in chapter 2, was the journalist-activist who, like Ruhi al-Khalidi, translated Gottheil's "Zionism" encyclopedia entry. In describing Nassar, *ha-Ḥerut*'s editorial claims that his paper was the work of "the Christian Arab enemies, who hate us religiously and racially." The true problem, asserts *ha-Ḥerut*, is that the effects of anti-Zionist agitation among the Christian Arab papers extend to "our good Muslim Arab neighbors." *Ha-Ḥerut* accuses these Christian Arab enemies of using all sorts of tactics to cause "our Muslim neighbors to come in conflict with us, to awaken among them a hatred against the Jew who had always been considered like a brother to the Arabs and a member of the same race [*neḥshav le-aḥ u-le-ven geza*ᶜ *le-ha-*ᶜ*arviyim*]." *Ha-Ḥerut*'s editors saw a marked distinction between the natural attitude toward Jews and Zionism of Christian Arabs, on the one hand, and of Muslim Arabs, on the other. The former, owing to their "religious and racial hatred" of Jews, were deemed instinctively antagonistic; the latter, because of their feelings of common race with Jews, were regarded as welcoming and supportive. Only on the instigation of the "Christian Arab enemies" and the deception they perpetrate might otherwise naturally sympathetic Muslim Arabs turn against Zionism.

[47] *ha-Ḥerut* 3:6 (November 4, 1910), 1–2.

There is something peculiar, and noteworthy, in this editorial's racial reasoning. Christian Arabs hate Jews religiously and racially, *ha-Ḥerut* explains, whereas Muslims view Jews amiably because Jews and Arabs are thought to be racially linked.[48] There is no systematic racial theory articulated in this article (though, as we shall see, such theories were being developed by certain Zionist ideologues at the time), but one wonders whether *ha-Ḥerut* considered the Christian Arabs to be not "fully Arab" in racial terms. It is not clear what sort of definition *ha-Ḥerut*'s editors had in mind when they used the term "Arab" for Christian Arabs. Is it, in the Christian case, merely a linguistic quality as opposed to Muslim Arabs, who are "racially" Arab? There is in fact some evidence suggesting that, at least in the minds of some of *ha-Ḥerut*'s contributors, Christian Arabs were not seen as being "authentically" Arab. In one article, for instance, a new orphanage in Egypt is described as being designed as a shelter for "abandoned Arab, Jewish, and Christian children."[49]

This occasional distinction between Arabs and Christians was not unique to *ha-Ḥerut*. In a front-page essay in his *ha-Ẓevi* newspaper in November 1908, Eliezer Ben-Yehuda discusses the new policy of military conscription for non-Muslims. As "heavy and difficult" a burden conscription is for Muslims and Christians, Ben-Yehuda writes, it is all the more so for Jews. After all, "nearly all the Christian natives of the land here," he explains,

> are similar in their way of life to the Arabs. Nearly all speak Arabic, and they are all accustomed to the Arabs. And there is no doubt that every Christian among the people of the army feels himself almost as though among people of his own age and his own nation (*benei ʿamo*). As for the Jews, they are so distant, at least for now, from the life of the natives of the land. They do not even know the Arabic language nor the Turkish [language]. Certainly, a Jewish man would feel himself to be totally strange among his fellow Christian and Muslim members of the army.[50]

Ben-Yehuda's essay presumes that Palestine's Christians are not quite Arabs. Though he is not perfectly explicit, Ben-Yehuda seems to take

[48] Cf. Gad Frumkin, who retrospectively wrote that in this period "the Muslims among the Arabs saw themselves as close to the religion and race [la-dat ve-la-geza'] of the Jews." Frumkin, *Derekh shofet bi-rushalayim*, 218. Cited in Bartal, "Du-kiyum nikhsaf," 10.

[49] *ha-Ḥerut* 3:13 (November 21, 1910), 3. It is also possible, of course, that the term Christians here refers to *non-Arab* Christians, such as British Christians who were then in control of the region, but this is left ambiguous.

[50] *ha-Ẓevi* 25:30 (November 13, 1908), 1–2.

Arabs to be, by definition, Muslims.[51] We infer this assumed definition not only by process of elimination—if "true" Arabs are neither Christians nor Jews, they must, in the context of Late Ottoman Palestine, be Muslims—but also because the essay is about military service, which had previously been the exclusive domain of Muslims. Palestine's Christians, Ben-Yehuda contends, share many cultural traits with "real" Arabs, not least their common Arabic language, a commonality that Ben-Yehuda (who perceived the Hebrew language as a sine qua non of Jewish nationality) did not underestimate. But ultimately, as much as Palestine's Christians shared with Arabs, as similar as their way of life and customs might be, they were nonetheless something other than proper Arabs.

The distinction between Arabs, on the one hand, and Christians, on the other, was not employed consistently. As we have already seen, *ha-Ḥerut* reports not infrequently on a group deemed to be "Christian Arabs"; the same is true in Ben-Yehuda's newspapers.[52] For example, in a December 1908 issue of *ha-Ẓevi,* the anonymous editor of the "Special Telegrams" section follows up on an earlier report about the Ottoman interior minister and "the Christian Arabs."[53] The minister had refused to fulfill "even part of the demands" of "the Christian Arabs" concerning " 'the holy grave' " (i.e., the Holy Sepulcher).[54] This refusal, writes *ha-Ẓevi,* "aroused among Jerusalem's Christian Arabs great agitation."[55] In 1909 a *ha-Ẓevi* correspondent with the initials Sh. R. reported on a violent incident in Jaffa: "Old Jews on their way to pray in the synagogue at sunrise were beaten by a group of drunken Christian Arabs who were returning from the bars[56] in which they drank excessively and ran wild." The particular way in which this author conceives of these "Christian Arabs" is highlighted in the article's conclusion, in which he warns that if this phenomenon is left unchecked, it will prove to be "a disgrace to the nation of Arabs [*ʿam ha-ʿarvim*] or to Christianity [*noẓriyut*]." While the author closes optimistically—"We are moving forward, toward the light, toward natural progress, toward a future

[51] The dictionary entry *ʿarvi* in the Ben-Yehuda dictionary was written later by Moshe Zvi Segal. See the editor's note, MBY, vol. 9.

[52] Ben-Yehuda's papers pay particular attention to a specific subset of Christian Arabs, namely, "Orthodox Arabs." See, for instance, *ha-Ẓevi,* November 25, 1908; December 22, 1908; December 24, 1908; January 4, 1909; March 24, 1909.

[53] The editors on the masthead at this point were Eliezer Ben-Yehuda, his wife Hemda, and their son Itamar Ben-Avi. Presumably one of them edited this section.

[54] The phrase used is *ha-kever ha-kadosh,* which the author places in quotation marks. It is not clear whether these marks are meant to be derisive or simply indicate the name of the location.

[55] *ha-Ẓevi* 25:57 (December 20, 1908), 2.

[56] Literally: "houses."

of peace and fraternity"[57]—he is concerned that the "Christian Arab" leadership is not acting appropriately to stem the tide of anti-Jewish attacks in Palestine.[58]

Dividing Neighbors: Muslims versus Christians

Later, in May 1909, one of *ha-Ẓevi*'s Jaffa correspondents reported on the response of the city's residents to violent events two hundred kilometers to Jaffa's north. "On Saturday in Beirut," Ben-Yehuda's paper reports, "they hanged the Muslim army soldier who killed the Beirut delegate, the Christian Arab. The Christian Arabs spread the word in our city [Jaffa], a rousing call to go see the hanging of the enemy."[59] The article explains that they[60] hired sailors to transport people from Jaffa to Beirut and back, "and thus those who went were many."[61] Here we encounter not only *ha-Ẓevi*'s use of the phrase and concept of "Christian Arabs" but also the rather unsubtle implication that Muslims and Christians are enemies. The view that the natural pair of antagonists in Palestine, and beyond, were Muslims and Christians—and not, that is, Jews and Arabs (whether Muslim, Christian, or both)—was at once, it would seem, a description of perceived reality as well as a prescriptive claim, a statement of what *should be*. This descriptive-prescriptive position is a subtext of many Late Ottoman Zionist newspaper reports concerning the non-Jewish natives of Palestine.[62]

[57] *ha-Ẓevi* 25:71 (January 5, 1909), 2.

[58] See also *ha-Ẓevi* 25:155 (April 25, 1909), 2, on the murder of "the Christian Arab representative Arslan Bey." The reference here is to the murder of Muhammad Arslan Bey on April 13, 1909, in Istanbul. For a contemporary observer's account, see McCullagh, *The Fall of Abd-Ul-Hamid*, 316.

[59] *ha-Ẓevi* 25:175 (May 19, 1909), 2.

[60] The article indicates that "the Arabs" made this arrangement. This is presumably a reference to the "Christian Arabs" from the previous sentence, but the fact that they are listed simply as Arabs here is yet another complication in this question of nomenclature.

[61] In telling of the contract they signed with the sailors, the author refers to them here simply as "the Arabs," but the previous paragraph makes it clear that these Arabs are exclusively "Christian Arabs."

[62] The reports of the murder of the "Christian Arab" delegate are all the more curious and revealing because the murdered delegate was not actually Christian. Muhammad Arslan was a Druze emir from Lattakia in the vilayet of Beirut. The presence in Palestine and the broader Levant of a non-Jewish community that was neither Christian nor properly Muslim might have complicated the perspective of some Zionists who viewed their neighbors in dichotomous religious terms. While Zionists (and later Israelis) would come to relate to the Druze very differently from the way they treated Palestine's other non-Jewish residents, at this early stage of encounter some may not have understood the distinctions and presumed that, in the Levant, a non-Muslim non-Jew was a Christian.

The (welcome) antagonism between Christians and Muslims was imagined not merely in the Middle East but far beyond as well. Consider, for instance, *ha-Ẓevi*'s 1908 report on a rumor in Russia that alleged that seventeen Jewish students in Odessa "took upon themselves the Mohammedan religion in order to be accepted to university."[63] *Ha-Ẓevi*'s report relates that three Muslims sent an open letter to a Moscow newspaper, *Moskovskie vedomosti*, expressing their anger against those Jews "who wish to penetrate Islam and destroy it, as they have destroyed Christianity."[64] What is fascinating and telling about the way in which the *ha-Ẓevi* article treats this controversy is that it transforms what is reasonably understood to be a problem between Muslims and Jews into a clash between Muslims and Christians.[65] The article does this by quoting at length the response of *Russkoe znamia*, a conservative Christian Russian newspaper, to the Muslims' letter of protest. "The Mohammedans," the Russian paper insisted, "are not like us, the Christians." Rather, the article declared:

> They are all[66] haters of humanity and haters of all forms of freedom. . . . About humanity[67] they know nothing (about this [inserts the Hebrew author sarcastically] only the *Russkoe znamya* knows!), they respect their faith and demand respect for themselves. And not just "the masses"[68] who have never seen the walls of a school

---

In contrast to their views of Christians and Muslims, Jews generally lacked an inherited discourse or approach to the Druze, members of an esoteric religious sect formed in the eleventh century. On Arslan, see McCullagh, *The Fall of Abd-Ul-Hamid*, 96–97, 148; Akarlı, *The Long Peace*, 153; Prätor, *Der Arabische Faktor in der jungtürkischen Politik*, 60. On the Druze of Palestine, see Falah, "A History of the Druze Settlements in Palestine during the Ottoman Period," 31–48. On the relationship between the State of Israel and the Druze, see, for instance, Parsons, "The Druze and the Birth of Israel"; Frisch, "The Druze Minority in the Israeli Military"; Gelber, "Antecedents of the Jewish-Druze Alliance in Palestine." I am grateful to Jens Hanssen for pointing out the Zionist newspapers' mislabeling of Arslan as a Christian.

[63] Some version of this report was apparently first published in *Hod ha-zman*, a periodical published first in St. Petersburg, then in Vilnius.

[64] The terms used here are *muslimiyut*, literally "Muslimness," and *noẓriyut*, which might be translated as either "Christianity" or "Christianness."

[65] Even if this article was simply copied verbatim from *Hod ha-zeman*, the fact that this *particular* article was chosen (from among the countless others in the contemporary press) for inclusion in *ha-Ẓevi* suggests that the editors appreciated its tone and implication.

[66] The text reads: "All of them—*milvad be-rosham*—all of them are haters of humanity." The phrase *milvad be-rosham* is ambiguous but may mean "aside from their leader." I am uncertain whom the author has in mind here.

[67] The term used is *humaniyut*, which might also be rendered "humanism."

[68] *ha-ʿam*: literally, "the people" or "the nation."

> but also the intellectuals who have received higher education. Now that they hear sounds of happiness from the Jews upon the acceptance of Jewish-Muslims to the university, three Muslim intellectuals publish this letter to the editor of *Moskovskie vedomosti*.[69]

By including this extensive quotation, the author suggests that the real adversaries of Muslims in Russia in this matter were not Jews but Christians[70] (and, read in *ha-Ẓevi*, the implication would seem to be that the same was true in Palestine as well).

Identity at the Borders

Regardless of the political implications involved in emphasizing distinctions between groups, found in the pages of Ben-Yehuda's newspapers in the postrevolutionary years is a strain of interest in and anxiety concerning the borders of identity in Late Ottoman Palestine. Consider, for instance, the small, rather cryptic paid notice[71] in *ha-Ẓevi* in an issue from November 1908 (mentioned in chapter 1) that reads: "To the Arab Hebrew woman [*la-ʿivriyah ha-ʿarviyah*]! If you are a Hebrew, you are not an Arab. If an Arab, not a Hebrew. So, you are neither a Hebrew nor an Arab. C.Q.F.D."[72] The author who submitted this note appears to be writing to question, on logical grounds, an earlier note that was signed by "an Arab Hebrew woman." Just six notices below this dismissal, there is yet another enigmatic notice that reads: "To M.M.: I saw you, I knew you, I respected you. I will leave you, I will remember you, and I will not forget you," signed "Arab Hebrew" (*ʿivri ʿarvi*).[73] These brief, mysterious notices suggest that, at this point in Palestine's history, the borders between "Hebrew" and "Arab" were still being delineated.[74] Though there were surely those who forcefully disagreed,

69 *ha-Ẓevi* 25:47 (December 8, 1908), 3.

70 Indeed, *Russian* Christians, a population particularly despised in the Ottoman context.

71 The section titled *Doʾar ha-Ẓevi* was a sort of classifieds section of *ha-Ẓevi*, for which advertisers and other correspondents paid a small fee (a tenth-piece) per line. See, e.g., *ha-Ẓevi* 25:39 (November 24, 1908), 3, for an explanation of the system.

72 *ha-Ẓevi* 25:42 (November 27, 1908), Supplement, 2. C.Q.F.D. is the French equivalent of the Latin term of logic Q.E.D. The continuation of this notice becomes even more inscrutable.

73 Ibid.

74 The related idea of the Jewish Arab or the Arab Jew has been the subject of much discussion in recent years. See, e.g., Shenhav, *The Arab Jews*; Somekh, *Baghdad, Yesterday*; Gottreich, "Historicizing the Concept of Arab Jews in the Maghrib," 433–51; Levy, "Historicizing the Concept of Arab Jews in the Mashriq," 452–69; Jacobson, *From Empire to Empire*, 111–16.

whether on logical, political, cultural, or other grounds, some clearly did not consider Hebrew and Arab to be mutually exclusive.

Hebrew and Arab were not the only categories to be questioned in Ben-Yehuda's papers. In one issue of *ha-Or* from 1910, a report is found with the title "A Christian Muslim Woman." *Ha-Or*'s correspondent explains that there was great commotion in the market after a peasant woman, "a Christian from Ramallah, who had been persecuted relentlessly by the residents of the village, decided to leave her faith and enter under the wings of Islam." This only aroused further fury among her former coreligionists, who wished to execute her for her betrayal. Brought before the court, she repeated her desire to enter, as the author puts it, "the religion of Ishmael" and beseeched the judges to protect her from the wrath of "her nation" (*benei ʿamah*).[75] The author and the editor who titled the article were clearly intrigued by the possibility of a Christian Muslim, a concept, like the Arab Hebrew, that angered many by challenging the exclusiveness of supposedly contradictory categories.

Yet another such liminal figure in Late Ottoman Palestine was the Karaite. Karaites were members of a Jewish sect that had separated from the dominant Jewish community beginning around the ninth century. In the early twentieth century, the largest single population of Karaites was found in the Russian Empire, but communities existed in a number of Middle Eastern cities, including Istanbul, Jerusalem, and Cairo. Those Karaites who spoke Arabic and had been living for generations in Arabic-speaking lands generated some identity confusion, as is evidenced on the pages of *ha-Or* in 1910. In an article titled "The Arabic[76] Theater," *ha-Or* informs its readers that

> the troupe of the famous Arab[77] actor, Rahamim Bibas—a Karaite Jew—performed several shows in Jerusalem with great success. Among the actors, there are also many women, and this is undoubtedly the first time in Jerusalem that an Arab audience hears such beautiful words from both men and women together. Anyone interested in the Arabic language, in its advancement and development, is well served to head to the theater across from Jaffa

[75] *ʿAm* here could also be taken as "people."

[76] The phrase is *ha-ḥezyon ha-ʿarvi*. Because the term *ʿarvi* can mean both Arab and Arabic, that is, both an ethnic group and a language, there is always a degree of interpretation in which one engages in translating the word. This is especially treacherous in a project such as that of this chapter, which aims to be sensitive to the choice of terminology in these newspapers. I therefore render the present phrase as "Arabic Theater" and not "Arab Theater" with an awareness that the intended meaning may have been the latter, even though, in my view, this would seem unlikely.

[77] See previous note.

> Gate. . . . It is fitting for the members of our nation (*benei ʿameinu*) to give Rahamim Bibas a round of applause.[78]

Here *ha-Or* describes the actor, Rahamim Bibas, as both an Arab and a Karaite Jew.[79] Several days later, *ha-Or* felt compelled to issue a correction. In fact, "the Arab actor" is not a Karaite but "a Jew like all others, who takes pride in his Jewishness and follows his religion." By referring to "the excellent actor" as a Karaite, *ha-Or* emphasizes, it meant no offense. "For us," the author explains, "the Karaites are also an important part of the greater Jewish race [*ha-gezaʿ ha-yehudi ha-gadol*], and we hope that the day will yet come . . . when the Karaites will join us in all of our hopes and deeds." After all, the article concludes rhetorically, "Are we not one nation?"[80] In these early years of Zionist national formation and consolidation in Palestine, Middle Eastern native-Arabic-speaking Karaites presented Zionists with the quandary of whether they belonged to the Jewish nation. While Jewishness defined by a shared religion—or the perception of such—might exclude the Karaites from the Jewish nation, the Karaites, despite any religious deviance, nonetheless retained their place within the "greater Jewish race," at least for this author. Especially for those Zionists who, perhaps like the *ha-Or* author, viewed their own Jewishness in nonreligious terms, expanding the bounds of Jewishness to groups whose religious practice diverged from what was understood to be "normative" Judaism was not an insuperable challenge. In fact, as we shall discover below, some prominent Zionists claimed for their "greater Jewish race" far more unlikely groups than the Karaites.[81]

But even certain Rabbinate (i.e., non-Karaite) Jews had the potential to test the boundaries of Jewishness, at least in the minds of European Zionists in Palestine. Karaites were not the only ones who had lived for generations in the Middle East, shared customs associated with Arabs,

[78] *ha-Or* 2:55:230 (December 22, 1910), 3.

[79] On the Bibas visit, see Snir, "Arabness, Egyptianness, Zionism, and Cosmopolitanism," 139; Yehoshua and Yehoshua, *Yerushalayim ha-yeshanah ba-ʿayin u-va-lev*, 220–21.

[80] *ha-Or* 2:58:233 (December 26, 1910), 3. Interestingly, the advertisement that this acting troupe subsequently placed in *ha-Or* does not mention Bibas's ethnic or religious identity, nor, for that matter, the language of the play. The title of the play is listed as *The Vision of Joseph the Righteous*, and the ad offers only these details: "In the light of day on Thursday, the 28th of Kislev, the Egyptian organization headed by the famous actor Rahamim Bibas will perform the interesting story of Joseph the Righteous in five acts." The ad further indicates that the proceeds will benefit the Society of Love and Brotherhood, a Hebrew nationalist organization primarily of Jerusalemite Sephardim (though there were some Ashkenazim as well) that, at its peak, counted about two hundred members. The organization existed from 1910 to 1913. See Bezalel, *Noladetem ẓiyonim*, 217–18.

[81] See below on Yitzhak Ben-Zvi and David Ben-Gurion's World War I–era writings on Palestine.

and, not least, spoke Arabic. Consider, for instance, the report in *ha-Ẓevi* about an encounter with a Jew from Gaza. "By chance," writes the correspondent, "we met this week one of those Jews about whom we were unsure whether they are members of our nation [*mi-vnei ʿameinu*] or children of the land [*mi-vnei ha-areẓ*], Arabs descended from Arabs." Such ambiguous figures are, just like Arabs, "tall-statured, sun-tanned, slightly thin but nevertheless healthy, and quite proud." The author explains that this was a Jew from Gaza, a city that seemed to most Jews in Palestine more distant than America and less familiar than Australia. The article reports that this Arab-like Jew noted that, in Gaza, "the Arabs and Jews live in brotherhood" and complained only that the Jews there lack a synagogue and a cemetery.[82] Likewise, after the immigration of about 150 Yemenite Jews to Palestine, *ha-Ẓevi* explained that "in their customs and their ways, they are similar to the Bedouin Arabs, and some also have four wives."[83] The writers in this newspaper were struck by the similarities between Arabs and certain Middle Eastern–born Jews. These liminal types challenged Zionists' preconceptions of what constituted a Jew, on the one hand, and an Arab, on the other. In Late Ottoman Palestine, ethnic, racial, national, and religious categories were all in some degree of flux.

Christians and Muslims, Christianity and Islam

Earlier we found that one of *ha-Ḥerut*'s explanations for what it perceived to be more intense animosity toward Zionism among Palestine's Christians than among its Muslims was that Muslims and Jews were linked by race, while Christians, of another race, "hated the Jews racially." More common than racial arguments, though, are discussions of *religious* differences in *ha-Ḥerut*'s attempts to account for the perceived divergent approaches of Christian and Muslim Arabs toward Jews and Zionism. In an article called "The Enemies of Judah," published in early 1911, Mendel Kremer argues for the founding of a Jewish newspaper in Arabic and Turkish that would set out to prove that the Christian opponents of Zionism were motivated not by concern for the Ottoman government and the integrity of the Empire, as the Christians claimed,

[82] *ha-Ẓevi* 25:64 (December 28, 1908), 2. The author ends with what seems to be a critique of Jewish values: "How strange is the nation of Israel, satisfied with so little indeed: prayer and death, death and prayer. For what does it need to live?"

[83] *ha-Ẓevi* 25:75 (January 10, 1909), 1. On the waves of Yemenite Jewish immigration to Palestine in this period, see Druyan, *Be-ein "marvad-kesamim"*; Druyan, "ʿAliyatam vehitʿarutam shel yehudei teiman ba-ʿaliyah ha-rishonah."

but rather by "the religious hatred that they have for the Jews."[84] In another issue of *ha-Ḥerut*, a reader sent a letter to the editor concerning the oft-repeated proposal for a Jewish-edited Arabic-language newspaper. "It will be the responsibility of the newspaper," writes this reader, "to show the source of the hatred" against the Jews of Palestine. The paper would have "to explain that it is not the benefit of the nation and the land"[85] that motivates the new enemy press, but rather "Christianity's hatred of Judaism." "It will be possible to prove this," the reader concludes, "from the fact that the Muslim Arabs, who are far from religious hatred, understand the benefit that the Hebrew settlement has brought."[86] In other words, Christian Arabs oppose Zionism because of their religion's hatred of Jews' religion. Muslim Arabs, members of a faith that, according to this author and others in *ha-Ḥerut*, is by nature tolerant of other religions, acknowledge the supposed material benefit that Zionism bestowed on Palestine.

Recent scholars have questioned the claim commonly expressed by Zionists during the Ottoman period (and later) that Palestine's Christians were more resistant to Zionism than were their Muslim counterparts.[87] We might further wonder whether any differences that did exist stemmed from religion or, alternatively, from Christians' socioeconomic status as competitors with Palestine's Jews or from a more developed nationalist consciousness engendered by European-style education. Nonetheless, in the minds of many Zionists, the Christians' motivation for opposing Zionism was religious.

One wonders to what degree Zionists may here have been projecting their own religious hostility onto others, as evidence in the Hebrew press suggests that among some of Palestine's Zionists, there was indeed religious antipathy against Christianity. Take, for example, an article provocatively titled (in large, bold letters) "Jesus of Nazareth Never Existed" in a March 1910 edition of *ha-Ḥerut*.[88] "Neither a fire nor an earthquake nor even a plague could inflict such terror and fear upon the Christians of Germany as did the actions of Professor Arthur Drew[s]," a German intellectual who enraged and scandalized many within Germany and the broader Christian world with his claims that Jesus had actually never lived, that is, that there was no historical

[84] *ha-Ḥerut* 3:43 (January 30, 1911), 3–4.

[85] Here, as throughout the literature of this period, the definition and thus referent of the terms "nation" and "land" are ambiguous. The context of the letter suggests broad definitions of both, namely, the Ottoman "nation" and the Ottoman Empire, respectively, but other interpretations might be reasonable as well.

[86] *ha-Ḥerut* 2:100 (May 30, 1910), 2–3.

[87] See Khalidi, *Palestinian Identity*.

[88] *ha-Ḥerut* 2:67 (March 2, 1910), 2.

Jesus. The article reports on a public lecture Drews delivered in Berlin the previous month to an audience of "tens of thousands," in which he contended that the Christian idea of a "half man, half God" was simply "impossible."[89] Great scholars in the audience, writes *ha-Ḥerut*'s correspondent, A.B.G. Triwaks, attempted to counter Drews's argument, but he "stood and showed, with historical evidence, that 'Jesus never existed' and that all faith in him was as meaningless as the dust of the earth." The author explains Drews's position in terms with which *ha-Ḥerut*'s readers would comfortably relate: "Professor Drew[s] is one of those Christians in Germany who believes only in the verse: 'Hear O Israel, the Lord is our God, the Lord is one' " (Deuteronomy 6:4).[90] One readily detects the glee in *ha-Ḥerut*'s account of the women who fainted "upon hearing Professor Drews's heresy." Even after one woman reached toward the heavens and called on her Lord to send a plague upon Drews's head, "a plague," the author notes wryly, "did not fall on his head and so he continued on with wisdom." The article's author felt heartened by this "excellent lecture," seeing how "great, learned men are finding within themselves sufficient strength to come out against Christianity and the so-called 'Son of God' based on historical research." The news was not unambiguously rosy, however; it was not clear, the author acknowledged, whether Drews was motivated by opposition to Christian orthodoxy—an apparently praiseworthy impulse—or by an antisemitism that could not stomach the notion of a Jew at Christianity's core.[91]

This article, ostensibly concerning events nearly three thousand kilometers from Palestine, must be understood within the context in which it was meant to be read: Palestine, 1910. It is one small piece of evidence of Jewish hostility toward Christianity in Late Ottoman Palestine. Just a few months after the Drews article appeared, *ha-Ḥerut* opened with an editorial titled "Heresy or Incitement?"[92] The editorial describes "a new danger." Whereas previously Christian missionaries had preached to Jews by pointing to concepts within the Hebrew Bible—such as the lamb, Adam's sin, or an atoning sacrifice—as proof of Christianity, they have, *ha-Ḥerut* asserts, recognized that such methods have failed. Now the missionaries are engaging in a new tactic: using Jews, former yeshiva students, to perform their mission. As proof, *ha-Ḥerut*'s editorial cites an article published in the newspaper

[89] These lectures were published in Drews and Loofs, *Hat Jesus gelebt?* See also Drews, *Die Christusmythe*; Drews and Burns, *The Christ Myth*.

[90] The suggestion here would seem to be that the notion of the trinity violates true monotheism.

[91] In other words, it would be better to have no Jesus than a Jewish Jesus.

[92] *ha-Ḥerut* 3:18 (December 2, 1910), 1.

ha-Poʿel ha-ẓaʿir in which a Jew declared that "the New Testament is our book, bone of our bone, flesh of our flesh," contending that "the ascetic worldview and the submission to the God of the prophet from Anathoth [i.e., Jeremiah] and [the God] of the prophet from Nazareth [i.e., Jesus]—they are from the selfsame source."[93] The goal of this article, asserts *ha-Ḥerut*, is not simply heresy but the conversion of Jews to Christianity. How, *ha-Ḥerut*'s editor wonders, can a Jew accept "the fabricated stories, the nonsensical myth of 'the son of God'?" After all, in the Jews' historic determination "not to believe such nonsense, we have been slaughtered, killed every day until now."

On the one hand, there is nothing surprising about a Jewish writer opposed to the threat of Christians proselytizing to Jews. The threat was real. After all, the Jews of Palestine were a primary target of the Society for the Promotion of Christianity among the Jews (SPCJ), along with other less descriptively named missionizing organizations. In 1908, assessing the accomplishments of his organization in its first hundred years, SPCJ president John Kennaway wrote proudly: "More remarkable perhaps than everything else is the evidence of the changed attitude of the Jews toward Our Lord. No longer is He denounced and cursed as an impostor, but He is held up by the thoughtful among them as one of the highest types of humanity, an inspiring ideal of matchless beauty."[94] Clearly, early twentieth-century Christian missionizers were eager for Jews to think positively of Jesus. That there were Jews who were expressing such views—and in the Hebrew Zionist press in Palestine, no less—was thus a source of anxiety for those Jews who considered it critical to keep Jews entirely alienated from Christianity. Recognizing the contemporary Jewish fear of Christian proselytizing, then, is necessary for understanding the strong response to the appearance of sympathetic words about Jesus in a Zionist newspaper. On the other hand, the language *ha-Ḥerut*'s editor uses in describing Christianity—fabricated stories, nonsense, myth, the derisive quotation marks surrounding "the son of God"—is indeed the language of anti-Christian polemics and appears to reflect a severe, visceral aversion to Christianity.[95]

[93] The reference here is likely to Yosef Hayim Brenner. On the Brenner Affair, see Govrin, *"Meʾoraʿ Brener"*; Knaʿani, *ha-ʿAliyah ha-sheniyah ha-ʿovedet ve-yaḥasah la-dat ve-la-masoret*, 71–81. See also Almog, "The Role of Religious Values in the Second Aliyah," 240–41.

[94] Gidney, *The History of the London Society for Promoting Christianity amongst the Jews*, viii.

[95] On the medieval antecedents of anti-Christian polemics in Islamic lands, see Lasker, "The Jewish Critique of Christianity under Islam in the Middle Ages."

Reports of this kind are not the exclusive domain of *ha-Ḥerut*. In February 1909 Ben-Yehuda's *ha-Ẓevi* published a brief report on a "Rabbi for the Jews and Christian Devotee" (*rav la-yehudim ve-ḥasid noẓri*).[96] The article describes a certain Rabbi Fleisher in New York who is alleged to have sermonized in support of Christianity and even claimed that "Jesus was the greatest of Israel's prophets." The article notes that the American Jewish newspapers criticized this rabbi and all those "liberal rabbis who have recently begun to praise Christianity in their synagogue sermons." That the author shares the sentiment of the American Jewish press is demonstrated in the article's description of the offender: "Fleisher, rabbi, so to speak, of a community of liberal Jews." The contempt here is not quite as vivid as in *ha-Ḥerut*, but "so to speak" (*kivyakhol*) leaves little room for doubt that, in this author's view, a rabbi worthy of the title would never praise Jesus or Christianity.

That one finds no parallel anti-Islamic polemic in these newspapers can be ascribed, at least in part, to the context of the Ottoman Empire: the editors and contributors might well have self-censored criticism of Islam, fearing the newspaper's closure and the editors' imprisonment should an article deemed offensive to Islam have been published. Such fears would not have been baseless paranoia. In August 1909, for instance, after *ha-Ẓevi*'s editors were taken to court for criticizing the Ottoman government's alleged neglect of the welfare of Palestine's Jews, Mendel Kremer reminded the readers of *ha-Ḥerut* that articles in the Hebrew press were translated into Arabic and Hebrew by government officials. It is thus the responsibility of newspaper editors, warns Kremer, to know the proverb "Wise people, be careful with your words, and especially in your newspapers!"[97]

At the same time, it is unlikely that the distinction drawn repeatedly between the natural propensity of Muslims toward religious tolerance and that of Christians toward religious bigotry was simply lip-service paid to the paper's Ottoman censor. After all, there was no need to raise the issue of religious differences between these communities in the first place. Rather, for Sephardim in the Ottoman Empire in particular, this distinction was central to their collective memory and identity. In expressing his loyalty to Hebrew as the national Jewish language, for instance, *ha-Ḥerut*'s editor smeared Ladino, the Judeo-Spanish that was presumably among his native tongues, as "the language of the Inquisition and Torquemada."[98] For this community, a reference to the Inquisition was guaranteed a strong negative reaction.

[96] Literally: "a rabbi for Jews and a Christian Hasid."

[97] *ha-Ḥerut* 1:29 (August 4, 1909), 3.

[98] *ha-Ḥerut* 1:3 (May 18, 1909), 1.

And as descendants of refugees from Christian religious intolerance who found safety in an Islamic empire,[99] the Sephardim associated not just the Ottoman regime nor even Muslims but Islam itself with tolerance and respect. Consider these words, quoted approvingly by *ha-Ḥerut*:

> It is known that in all Christian countries, they hate the Jews with the deepest religious hatred. . . . But the Muslim world has not known such feelings and never will. Islam was born on the knees of Judaism. These two nations [Jews and Muslims] are close to one another in blood and language, and the religion of Islam is filled with Jewish traditions. Because Islam recognizes all monotheistic religions, it is not possible to enroot in the heart of its believers hatred and animosity toward the very nation that first taught monotheism. This is the reason that the Jews living among Muslims did not suffer religious persecution by Muslims such as the oppression they experience in the Christian countries. The Inquisition, the *auto-de-fé* and other horrors are entirely unknown in the Muslim context.[100]

Note the stark contrast between this laudatory language about Islam and the derogatory words and tone the newspaper used regarding Christianity. Whereas Christianity is an essentially bigoted religion, it implies, Islam is fundamentally tolerant (this, in addition to racial proximity, the shared "blood," of Jews and Muslims). Christians and Muslims have treated Jews differently because Christianity and Islam are fundamentally different, explains the author, and *ha-Ḥerut*'s editor agrees. Because of this *religious* difference, anti-Zionism—or, as

[99] See Cohen, "Fashioning Imperial Citizens," 3. Cohen identifies a number of myths developed by Ottoman Jewish elites to claim a special relationship between the Ottoman state and the Jews. One of these myths is that "*the Jews* of Ottoman realms had been mercifully received by the empire in 1492, when they had nowhere else to go." Cohen astutely draws our attention to the fact that this "picture necessarily excluded Jewish communities who had lived in the area before the Ottoman conquest—such as Greek-speaking *Romaniot* Jews of the eastern Mediterranean basin or the Arabic-speaking communities spread across the empire—as well as those who had found their way to the empire for reasons unrelated to the Spanish expulsion. In other words, this approach allowed the Judeo-Spanish communities of the empire's European and Anatolian provinces to stand in as a synecdoche for 'Ottoman Jewry' as a whole." *Ha-Ḥerut*'s articles might be understood as both participating in this ideological project and working within the discourse already created by the success of the project.

[100] *ha-Ḥerut* 3:45 (February 3, 1911), 2–3.

ha-Ḥerut often dubs it, antisemitism—has taken root specifically within the *Christian* Arabic press.[101]

Though the claim that essential religious differences between Islam and Christianity largely accounted for the respective communities' attitudes toward Zionism is found most prominently in *ha-Ḥerut*, Jerusalem's Sephardic-edited newspaper, it was not only Sephardim who held this view. In fact, as we have seen, Ashkenazim—such as Mendel Kremer—perceived the same distinction between Palestine's Muslims and Christians and also attributed this disparity to their respective religions.[102] And this, too, is understandable, for, perhaps no less than Sephardic natives of the Ottoman lands, Ashkenazic Zionists from Europe who had recently arrived in Palestine were well aware that they themselves had sought refuge from persecution in countries ruled by Christians in a land governed by Muslims. For those Zionists who imagined that their non-Jewish counterparts in Palestine acted in accordance with their respective religions, it was only reasonable to link Christian opposition to Zionism to the Christian faith and Muslim goodwill to Islam.

Socialist Zionists and Arab Differences

Not all Zionists in Palestine attributed the divergent treatment of Jews under Christendom and Islam to the greater tolerance supposedly inherent in the Islamic faith. In the newly founded *ha-Aḥdut* (Unity) workers' newspaper, David Ben-Gurion, a recent immigrant to Palestine and a leader of the Second Aliyah socialist Zionist group Poʿalei Ẓiyon (Workers of Zion), wrote:

> Among all of the lands of the Diaspora to which members of our nation were dispersed, Turkey was the only one in which a "Jewish Question" did not arise. In all of the lands of Europe, the Jews were imprisoned in the narrow and suffocating ghetto, lacking

[101] In her discussion of the distinction these papers drew between Christians and Muslims, Abigail Jacobson highlights another important context: the Balkan wars (1912–1913). In the course of these wars, Muslims suffered greatly, and, Jacobson argues, Ottoman Sephardim "may have been influenced by the anti-Christian feelings throughout the empire and developed hostile feelings toward the Christians as well." Jacobson, *From Empire to Empire*, 110. While this perceived distinction between Christians and Muslims preceded the Balkan wars, the earlier tensions between Christians and Muslims in the Ottoman Empire's European territories surely informed Ottoman subjects' views of religious differences, and the Balkan wars certainly exacerbated these tensions across the empire.

[102] *ha-Ḥerut* 3:43 (January 30, 1911), 3–4.

> rights, ceaselessly pressed and persecuted[103] by the governments and nations among which they lived. At the same time, the Jews in Turkey enjoyed complete freedom and knew nothing of special limitations and oppression. The entire land, in all directions, was open to them, and they were permitted to settle and work as they chose. And when the Jews of Spain were expelled from their land, they found in the Ottoman kingdom a place of refuge and personal treatment that they did not find anywhere else. The Turkish nation did not only open the gates of its land to the Hebrew exiles; it also offered them all civil rights. Aside from military service, which was reserved [*mukdash*] for the "believers," the Jews were able to attain all of the government and public positions, from the lowest level to the very highest.[104]

In this opening paragraph to his article "Clarifying Our Political Situation," Ben-Gurion points to the same discrepancy *ha-Ḥerut* noted between the treatment of Jews in Europe, on the one hand, and in the Ottoman Empire, on the other. But there are key differences between the ways in which these two articles identify and account for this divergence. In *ha-Ḥerut*, "Christian countries" are juxtaposed with "the Muslim world." In other words, the societies were labeled by their dominant religious affiliations. The explanation for the difference between the Jewish condition across the two societies is, correspondingly, tied to religion: Jews were respected in the "Muslim world" "because Islam recognizes all monotheistic religions," whereas in "Christian countries" they were hated "with the deepest religious hatred." In contrast, Ben-Gurion presents the distinction as one between "the lands of Europe" and "Turkey" or "the Ottoman kingdom," geographic and political designations. That Europe was a predominantly Christian society and Turkey and the Ottoman Empire were ruled by Muslims was not relevant to Ben-Gurion in his assessment of the political situation. Indeed, religion is almost completely absent from his discussion, except in one instance. In the (prereform) Ottoman Empire, Ben-Gurion explains, the Jews were not deemed proper "believers" (*ma'aminim*, a term he places

[103] The phrase Ben-Gurion uses here, *nirdafim bli ḥasakh* ("ceaselessly persecuted"), is likely borrowed from Isaiah 14:6. The prophet writes of the punishment that is suffered by the "wicked" and "tyrants" "that belabored nations in fury, in relentless pursuit (*murdaf bli ḥasakh*)." Though I am arguing here that Ben-Gurion, like his fellow Second Aliyah socialist Zionists, did not tend to use religion as an interpretative tool for understanding his non-Jewish neighbors in Palestine, he was nonetheless famously interested in the Bible. For some of his addresses to his Bible study group, see Ben-Gurion, *Ben-Gurion Looks at the Bible.*

[104] *ha-Aḥdut* 1:3, 87.

in apparently derisive quotation marks[105]) and thus were prohibited from joining the military. Ben-Gurion's single allusion to religion, that is, points to an *intolerant* aspect of the Ottoman Empire's Islamic identity, which he does not appear to take particularly seriously. Overall, however, he does not conceive of the two "civilizations" in religious terms. The contrast between the article in *ha-Ḥerut* and Ben-Gurion's piece in *ha-Aḥdut* thus could hardly be more pronounced.

To be clear, Ben-Gurion, like the authors in *ha-Ḥerut*, also considered the Christian-edited Arabic press to be exceptionally anti-Zionist. "Just as freedom had been declared and newspapers were able to write about whatever they pleased" as a result of the Young Turk Revolution, he writes, "immediately, the Christian press began strong propaganda against the Jews." While this hostility was evident elsewhere in the Ottoman Empire, he contends, it was especially so "in the newspapers of the Christian Arabs," opposing "the Jewish settlement in the Land of Israel."[106] However, when he tries to explain what he perceives to be anti-Jewish hatred in Palestine, Ben-Gurion has difficulty accounting for why it has taken root in one religious community more so than in another. "The source of this hatred," he insists, is

> the Arabs who work in the [Jewish] colonies. Like every worker, the Arab worker also hates his taskmaster and exploiter. But because there is not only a class opposition here but also a national difference between the workers and the farmers—this hatred takes the shape of a national hatred. In fact, the national element dominates the class element and so in the hearts of the Arab working masses, a fierce hatred flares against the Jews.[107]

There is an obvious disconnect between Ben-Gurion's class and national theory of Arab opposition to Zionist settlement in Palestine, as he articulates it above, and his perception that *Christian* Arab journalists and intellectuals (not undifferentiated Arab laborers) were the ones who most forcefully opposed Zionism. The "Arab workers" about whom Ben-Gurion writes were, after all, mostly Muslim, not Christian.

[105] While these quotation marks may merely indicate a borrowing of terminology (from the Arabic *muʾminīn*), later in the same article Ben-Gurion uses quotation marks in a way that obviously connotes derision. He refers to "the 'Zionists' abroad" (outside of the Land) for whom "the yishuv is nothing more than a propaganda tool for 'their Zionist work.' " It would seem that the same sense applies to these quotation marks as well.

[106] In this sense, I disagree with the assertion that *ha-Ḥerut*'s insistence on distinguishing between Muslim and Christian Arabs was "unique and uncommon." Jacobson, "The Sephardi Community in Pre–World War I Palestine," 24. See, for example, Ben-Gurion, "Clarifying Our Political Situation," *ha-Aḥdut* 1:3, 89–90.

[107] Ben-Gurion, "Clarifying Our Political Situation," *ha-Aḥdut* 1:3, 90.

As ideological secularists and materialists,[108] the socialist ideologues of the Second Aliyah tended to perceive themselves and others in a way that minimized categories and phenomena, such as religion, that they regarded as nonbasic cultural superstructures. A most extreme example of this approach, to which I briefly alluded above, is a theory held by Ben-Gurion but articulated most clearly by his senior partner in the leadership of Poʿalei Ẓiyon, Yitzhak Ben-Zvi. Ben-Zvi (originally Shimshelevich) was born in 1884 in Poltava in the Ukrainian region of the Russian Empire. A socialist Zionist from an early age, he immigrated to Palestine in 1907, during the Second Aliyah. In his first years there, Ben-Zvi founded the Bar Giora (1907) and ha-Shomer (1909) defense organizations as well as the socialist Zionist newspaper *ha-Aḥdut*, which he coedited with his wife Rachel Yanaʾit and Ben-Gurion.[109] In 1913 Ben-Zvi and Ben-Gurion relocated to Istanbul to study law in the university, though they were soon to return to Palestine upon the outbreak of the Great War. Suspicious of all nationalist movements in their midst, the Ottomans imprisoned and then deported the two, and by 1915 they were in New York. There they cowrote a Yiddish book, *Erets yisroel in fargangenheit un gegenvart* (The Land of Israel in the Past and the Present), to which we shall return shortly.[110] Toward the end of the Great War, the pair joined the Jewish Legion and returned once more to Palestine, where they soon resumed leadership of the Zionist community.

Shortly after the war, Ben-Zvi published a small booklet of his own about the Arabs of Palestine, *ha-Tenuʿah ha-ʿarvit* (The Arab Movement). Like Ruhi al-Khalidi in his conception of his Jewish contemporaries, Ben-Zvi turned to distant history in seeking to understand his Arab neighbors. While he devotes much of his analysis to the various nationalist movements among Arabs in the Middle East, it is his ethnographic survey of Palestine's Arabs that is most relevant here. He divides the Palestinian Arabs into several different categories. The Bedouin, in Ben-Zvi's view, are the only element in Palestine that is of "pure Arab racial origin" (*she-moẓʾo mi-gezaʿ ʿarvi naki*).[111] "The same," he asserts, "cannot be said of the rest of the elements—the fellahin and the urbanites—who are, of course, Arabs in terms of language and culture, but by origin and race (*moẓʾam ve-gizʿam*) are mixed and

[108] For an influential revisionist reading of the place of socialism in socialist Zionism, see Sternhell, *The Founding Myths of Israel*.

[109] For an English translation of the founding statement of ha-Shomer, see Kaplan and Penslar, eds., *The Origins of Israel, 1882–1948*, 54–56.

[110] On the joint composition of this text, and for related correspondence, see Mintz, "Beyn David Ben-Gurion le-Yiẓḥak Ben-Ẓevi."

[111] Ben-Ẓevi, *ha-Tenuʿah ha-ʿarvit*, 1:19.

composed from different elements." "The Arabs who conquered the Land of Israel," Ben-Zvi explains, "did not destroy the earlier settlement, nor did they themselves engage in colonization. They simply seized lands and levied taxes upon the residents." Along with the Bedouin, some of these "racial" Arabs, he suggests, did remain in Palestine, settling primarily in the larger cities and mixing with the natives.

But who are the fellahin, the masses that account for the vast majority of the residents of Palestine? "The fellahin," Ben-Zvi writes, "are the descendents of the laborers of the land who remained in Palestine from before the Islamic conquest."[112] And who were those pre-Islamic fellahin of Palestine? Here Ben-Zvi draws on the argument he had made in his Yiddish collaboration with Ben-Gurion.[113] "The primary source of this agricultural settlement was the ancient *Jewish* agricultural settlement." This settlement "certainly absorbed a mix of blood from all of the conquerors of Palestine who left their traces within it: among them the Byzantines, the Mongols, the Syrians, the Bedouin, and the Crusaders. However, the core of the present agricultural settlement has its source in the fellahin, Jews and Samaritans, the 'people of the land' (*ʿam ha-areẓ*) then and always, who remained connected to the land and did not go into exile."[114] Ben-Zvi explains that these Jews "were torn from the Jewish nation through wars and revolts—lasting six hundred years, always ending in slaughter and plunder—and finally submitted to their conquerors and became servants to tribute."[115] Under Christian rule, "they ultimately accepted, if only in appearance, the Greek religion that was . . . the majority religion of the Palestinian community in the generation before the conquest of ʿUmar. After this conquest, they accepted Islam." However, Islam "has not penetrated into them even until the present day. [Rather] they have a mix of customs: Muslim, Christian, Jewish, and Canaanite all together."[116] Those seemingly Muslim Arab peasants, Ben-Zvi argues, are hardly Muslim or even Arab beneath the surface, neither in faith nor in racial origin. "The fellahin were material that was dragged toward the conquering religion," he explains, and this means that their identity remains malleable at present as well. "They might become a distinct nation (*ʿam meyuḥad*), or they might be dragged toward one of the nations (*eḥat*

112 Ibid.

113 For Ben-Zvi's earlier writing on the matter, see Ben-Gurion and Ben-Ẓevi, *Erets Yisroel in Fergangenhayt un Gegenvart*, 37–38. For Ben-Gurion's discourse on this same issue, see ibid., 319, 326ff. See also Belkind and Ben-Gurion, *ha-ʿArvim asher be-ereẓ-yisraʾel*, 43ff.

114 On Jewish-Samaritan relations, see Knoppers, *Jews and Samaritans*.

115 The term here is taken from Genesis 49:15.

116 Ben-Ẓevi, *ha-Tenuʿah ha-ʿarvit*, 20.

ha-umot) that are established in the Land of Israel in the process of national differentiation (*ha-proẓes shel ha-diferenẓiya ha-le'umit*) that has begun in our time."[117] The fellahin, understood here as a mass of people still lacking national affiliation, might just as easily—and all the more naturally—join the Jewish nation as they might any Arab or Muslim nation, if only the right efforts were made.

The political interests that inform and motivate this eccentric—though not unprecedented nor uncommon[118]—theory are sufficiently clear: if the majority of the *seemingly* Muslim Arab population of Palestine was in fact *Jewish* in "racial" origin and could consciously become Jewish by nationality once again, then the Zionist project instantaneously attained greater demographic feasibility. But what is most intriguing about Ben-Zvi's theory in this context is not the politics that may have driven it but what it suggests about this Zionist's encounter with the Arabs of Palestine. Ben-Zvi glanced at his Arab neighbors—not the more politically conscious Christians and Muslims in the cities but the peasants working the land—and found hidden Jews. Indeed, he did not merely find hidden Jews; these were the *ideal* Jews, the prototypes of the treasured New Hebrew, Jews who had never abandoned the Land of Israel and never stopped tilling its soil. Ben-Zvi identified only the land-working Palestinian *peasants* as Jews, explicitly denying the city-dwelling elites any substantial Jewish heritage. If European Jewry was overly bourgeoisie for this socialist, the Zionist project would not only restore Europe's Jews to their homeland but would also reintegrate the truly Jewish fellahin of Palestine into their natural nation—the Jewish nation—thereby making this nation natural, that is, endowing it with the demographic building blocks for its missing worker class.

Moreover, the fellahin were descendants of the sort of Jews, like Ben-Zvi and many of his fellow Second Aliyah Zionists, who were not overly concerned with religion. They could nominally adopt or shed

---

[117] Ibid., 20–21. In this sentence, one sees how early twentieth-century Hebrew writers used the terms '*am*, *umma*, and *le'um* fairly interchangeably, all with the sense of nation and nationalism.

[118] Tracing the history of this theory and its alternative political uses might yield intriguing results. Two of its early exponents were Yisrael Belkind and Ber Borochov. On the earlier versions, see Gorni, *Zionism and the Arabs 1882–1948*, 103; Zerubavel, "Memory, the Rebirth of the Native, and the 'Hebrew Bedouin' Identity"; Shavit, *The New Hebrew Nation*, 123–24. See also Barnai, *Historiyografiyah u-le'umiyut*, 31–32. Israel Bartal suggested that "the modern political conflict between the Jews and Arabs put an end to the possibility of searching for Jewish roots within the local population" in Palestine. Bartal, " '*Am*' ve-'*Areẓ*' ba-historiyografiyah ha-ẓiyonit," 132. The search continues, but now with different political ends. See, e.g., Sand, *The Invention of the Jewish People*, 182–89.

one religion or another if necessary, so long as they were able to remain on their land.[119] In his Yiddish collaboration with Ben-Gurion, Ben-Zvi was responsible for the chapter called "History," in which he explained that the Jewish masses who remained in Palestine after the Roman destruction of the Jewish commonwealth—the "Jewish fellahin," as he calls them—"paid little interest to the refined, artful hairsplitting argumentation [*pilpulim*] of the learned [class]. These people of the land[120] used to neglect even the most basic commandments, such as laying phylacteries and praying." One can only assume that Ben-Zvi shared these imagined Jewish fellahin's antipathy toward such religious *pilpulim*. In seeking to understand the Arabs of Palestine—to study their history and their society—Ben-Zvi came to the radical conclusion, employing theories of race and genealogical origin, that these were the real Jews.

The Arabic Press, the "Great Danger," and the Claim of a Sephardic-Ashkenazic Divide

One question that has interested recent scholars of this period in Palestine is whether Sephardic Zionists had a discernibly different attitude toward the Arabs of Palestine from that of their Ashkenazic counterparts. An increasingly common view is that the Middle Eastern Sephardim—given their knowledge of Arabic, their typically longer heritage living among Muslims, and their deep-rootedness in the Ottoman Empire—related to their non-Jewish neighbors differently from, and more positively than, the way in which the Ashkenazic newcomers to Palestine did. In making the case for this distinction between Sephardim and Ashkenazim, Abigail Jacobson has pointed to the various newspapers that each of these communities produced to argue that the differences between the papers reflect "essential differences between the Sephardi and Ashkenazi Jews in Palestine," and that, in contrast to the Ashkenazim, "the Sephardim seem to have realized the importance and necessity of coexisting and co-operating with the Arab inhabitants of Palestine."[121] In making her argument, Jacobson studied three newspapers: *ha-Ḥerut*, *ha-Aḥdut*, and another Second Aliyah Zionist paper,

[119] On the "secularity" of this theory, see also Bartal, " 'ʿAm' ve-'Areẓ' ba-historiyografiyah ha-ẓiyonit," 128–29. Bartal highlights Ben-Zvi's tenacious commitment to this theory over the course of decades.

[120] The phrase *amei horetz*, which generally carries a negative connotation of ignoramus, here is subverted and regarded positively as those who remained on the land.

[121] Jacobson, "Sephardim, Ashkenazim and the 'Arab Question' in Pre–First World War Palestine," 126–27.

ha-Poʿel ha-ẓaʿir, founded and staffed by members of the eponymous workers' party, Histadrut ha-poʿalim ha-ẓeʿirim be-ereẓ yisraʾel (Organization of Young Workers in the Land of Israel).[122] Given these sources, Jacobson notes that the differences she observed between *ha-Ḥerut*, on the one hand, and *ha-Aḥdut* and *ha-Poʿel ha-ẓaʿir*, on the other, should be regarded as differences between Sephardic Zionists and Second Aliyah Ashkenazic Zionists (rather than Ashkenazic Zionists broadly).[123]

By adding the Ben-Yehuda family's newspapers into the analytical frame, my study both builds on and complicates Jacobson's provocative analysis and conclusions. To be sure, I mined the newspapers for different sorts of material (especially the terminology and categories employed in referring to the non-Jews of Palestine) rather than focusing on more programmatic statements. I would suggest, however, that the commonalities we noted between the Sephardic-edited *ha-Ḥerut* and the newspapers of Eliezer Ben-Yehuda, a First Aliyah Ashkenazic Zionist, support Jacobson's intuition that the differences she identified between *ha-Ḥerut*, on the one hand, and the socialist Second Aliyah papers, on the other, caution against imagining a clear divide between Ashkenazim and Sephardim.

While some Sephardim during the Late Ottoman period, and still more thereafter, charged the Ashkenazim with callousness toward Palestine's Arabs and an unwillingness to learn Arabic or understand local culture,[124] it must be noted that for the editors of *ha-Ḥerut*, the differences were not black and white. The primary concern that the editors voiced regarding their non-Jewish neighbors was, as noted above, that the Arabic press was vociferously anti-Zionist. As *ha-Ḥerut*'s editors made their case about the degree to which the Arabic press posed formidable challenges to the future of the Jewish settlement in Palestine and the consequent need to create a Zionist-edited Arabic newspaper to respond to the alleged slander, they declared: "of the newspapers of our city, we can say that the truth is that *ha-Aḥdut* is the only one

[122] Ha-histadrut ha-poʿalim ha-ẓeʿirim be-ereẓ yisraʾel (known by the shortened name ha-poʿel ha-ẓaʿir) was founded in Petah Tikvah in 1905. For an English translation of the organization's founding document, see Kaplan and Penslar, *The Origins of Israel, 1882–1948*, 39–41.

[123] In her recent monograph, Jacobson argues that "Zionism indeed played out differently among the Sephardi elite and the European Jewish immigrants to Palestine, especially those of the second *ʿaliya*." Jacobson contends that the Sephardic Zionists advocated an "inclusive Zionism" (viewing the Arabs as "possible partners for a future life in the country") in contrast to the Second Aliyah Ashkenazic Zionists, who advocated an "exclusive Zionism" (one that "excluded the Arabs from the discussion about future life in Palestine"). Jacobson, *From Empire to Empire*, 97–98.

[124] Ibid., 105, 111.

that has awoken to our words."[125] In other words, the only local Zionist paper that listened to *ha-Ḥerut* and thus also understood the problems associated with the Arabic press was none other than *ha-Aḥdut*, one of the very papers that has at times been portrayed as the antithesis of the Sephardic approach. Whether or not we accept *ha-Ḥerut*'s claim of credit for "awakening" *ha-Aḥdut* to this problem, the fact that, according to *ha-Ḥerut*'s editors, one of these Second Aliyah Ashkenazic papers joined *ha-Ḥerut*'s campaign suggests the need for qualifying the fundamental distinction that has been posited between Ashkenazim (even Second Aliyah Ashkenazim) and Sephardim in Late Ottoman Palestine.

The claim that the Sephardic Zionists were particularly or uniquely sympathetic to Palestine's Arabs is still more complicated. Jacobson argues that "throughout its discussion of the ways to influence Arab public opinion," *ha-Ḥerut* "reflected hopes for coexistence and co-operation between the Jewish and Arab community in Palestine." While I generally agree with Jacobson, it is important to recognize the terms on which this coexistence and cooperation were meant to be based. Recall that *ha-Ḥerut*'s worries about the impact of the anti-Zionist Arabic press led the newspaper to call for a large-scale apologetic propaganda campaign. The newspaper issued this plan: "We will show to the Arab masses what the Jews have done for the land [Palestine] and the homeland [Ottoman Empire].[126] We will prove to them . . . that we have enriched the production and labor and [we will show] the great advances that we have brought in commerce and in everything, and the great benefit that we have brought through this for the good of the Ottoman homeland."[127] *Ha-Ḥerut*'s answer, in other words, was to convince "the Arab masses" that they have only benefited—and would only continue to benefit—from the Jewish immigration to Palestine. While to a certain degree this response reflects a desire for peaceful coexistence, I would suggest that it was not merely "paternalistic," as Jacobson acknowledges,[128] but essentially delegitimized any criticism of the Zionist endeavor.

In their articles, *ha-Ḥerut*'s editors expressed no interest in a mutual exchange of ideas concerning Zionist settlement or the future of Palestine. Rather, all who sought to question the ideological or political compatibility of Zionism and Ottomanism, who perceived within Zionism a separatist movement seeking Jewish sovereignty in Palestine, who highlighted the trappings of statehood that the Zionist movement

[125] *ha-Ḥerut* 3:16 (November 28, 1910), 2. Cf. Ben-Ẓevi, "On the Question of Founding a Newspaper in Arabic," *ha-Aḥdut* 3:4–5 (November 10–17, 1911).

[126] *Ha-Ḥerut* frequently uses the term *moledet* ("homeland") to refer to the Ottoman Empire, as can be seen explicitly in the concluding words of this passage.

[127] *ha-Ḥerut* 3:7 (November 7, 1910), 1.

[128] See Jacobson, "The Sephardi Community in Pre–World War I Palestine," 32.

created for itself (including a flag, an anthem, and postage-like stamps) were dismissively and derisively labeled "the enemies" (*ha-ẓorerim*) and "the informants" or "the libelers" (*ha-malshinim*). Consider, for instance, a November 1910 *ha-Ḥerut* report entitled "The Libel of our Enemies." The author explains:

> It has come to our attention from a trusted source that, following the celebration of the anniversary [of the arrival in Palestine] of Mr. [Eliezer] Ben-Yehuda, a telegram was sent from here [Jerusalem] to Haifa, to the newspaper *al-Karmil*, saying: "In the *beit ha-ʿam* [House of the Nation] of the Jews an anniversary party was organized in honor of Ben-Yehuda, one of the scholars of the Jews. There, they raised the flags of the Zionists, sold Zionist stamps, and sang the Zionist national anthem. As the Zionists are arousing this movement (?), the residents of the Land of Israel are slumbering in a deep sleep."[129]

Here *ha-Ḥerut* cites an Arabic newspaper from Haifa that fairly accurately described the celebration of the anniversary of this most prominent Zionist's immigration to Palestine. Some of the details are corroborated just one page earlier in the same issue of *ha-Ḥerut*; the rest, in Ben-Yehuda's own paper, *ha-Or*.[130] The description recorded in the telegram to *al-Karmil* was, if anything, understated in its portrayal of the nationalistic nature of the party for Ben-Yehuda; *ha-Or* described the festivities as "the first national, living celebration after two thousand years of exile and destruction" at which, inter alia, Ben-Yehuda "cried tears of joy" on hearing the singing of the Zionist national anthem *ha-Tikvah*. What is clear, then, is that it was not any inaccuracy in the description of the event that disturbed *ha-Ḥerut*'s writer; it was rather the Arabic newspaper's cautionary rhetorical conclusion, that while the Zionists were pursuing their national plans, Palestine's (non-Jewish) residents were "in a deep sleep." *Ha-Ḥerut* thus challenges the reader: "Now . . . do you still doubt our words? Do you still not wish to understand the deep disaster [*ha-shoʾah*] that can come upon us if we do not act preemptively? Will we be deaf and pass silently over these vulgar lies that have the potential to destroy our standing here in the land?"[131] *Ha-Ḥerut*'s editors were offended by any criticism of Zionism; it was the

[129] *ha-Ḥerut* 3:7 (November 7, 1910), 3. This anonymous article was probably written by the then-editor, Hayyim Ben-Attar. The parenthetical question mark is found in the *ha-Ḥerut* article, indicating the author's or editors' apparent (if perhaps feigned) bewilderment as to what is meant by "this movement."

[130] See *ha-Or* (November 7, 1910).

[131] For an analysis of the Ben-Yehuda anniversary celebration, see Saposnik, *Becoming Hebrew*, 202ff.

critical tone, it would seem, not the alleged facts (which, the author presumably recognized, were true), that constituted the "vulgar lie." *Ha-Ḥerut* viewed any sign of opposition to Zionism as a "Great Danger" (the catch-phrase consistently attached to its reports on the anti-Zionist Arabic press) that demanded a strong, countervailing response.

While *ha-Ḥerut*'s editors may have desired peaceful relations with their non-Jewish neighbors in Palestine, they appear to have desired such relations only on their own terms, leaving no room for critical attitudes toward Zionism, its methods, or its goals. In this sense I differ from Jacobson, who contends that this position represents "an interesting alternative to the more dominant approach of the European Zionist leadership" and "an alternative way of living with the Arabs."[132] If the non-Jewish residents of Palestine were willing uncritically to accept Zionist immigration to the country and the prevalence of Jewish national symbols in their developing culture and institutions, only then, it would seem, would *ha-Ḥerut* advocate cooperation. The supposed Sephardic-Ashkenazic divide vis-à-vis Palestine's native non-Jews seems to be far less pronounced on closer inspection.

Conclusion

Palestine's Hebrew newspapers offer critical insight into Zionist perceptions of the Zionists' neighbors in Palestine. Whether in the simple terminology the authors and editors employed in describing Palestine's natives as they narrated events or in more explicit discussions of the nature of and distinctions between these communities, these journalistic texts reveal that Zionists in Late Ottoman Palestine perceived their neighbors through a variety of lenses. For these Zionists, Palestine's non-Jews were not merely some generic, nondescript indigenous population wrongfully living in the Jews' rightful homeland. Rather, these populations were communities with which Jews had long and complex histories, as members of interconnected religious civilizations or as members of the same race. There is also a sense of uncertainty that emerges from some of these newspaper pages—an uncertainty about (if not a conscious desire to challenge) the boundaries of identity that were forming during this period. There is no doubt that there was already a clear sense of political danger in the Zionists' encounter with Palestine's non-Jews. However, if we retrospectively identify in this period a simple Jewish/Zionist-Arab/Palestinian encounter, or nothing more than seeds of "Arab-Israeli conflict," we miss the intriguing complexity and fluidity of this moment.

[132] Jacobson, "The Sephardi Community in Pre–World War I Palestine," 31.

CHAPTER 4

Imagining the "Israelites": Fin de Siècle Arab Intellectuals and the Jews

"Among the peculiarities of history is that Egypt has today become a place of refuge for the Jews coming from Palestine," notes the author of "The Jews and the War," an article published during the First World War in the Egypt-based Arabic journal *al-Hilāl*. After all, "in antiquity," the author elaborates, "Palestine was the place of refuge for those who escaped after their exodus from Egypt."[1] During the Great War, many Jews fled Palestine while others were expelled by the Ottoman authorities who were suspicious of all nationalist activity within their realm.[2] Between 1914 and 1915, in the months before the *al-Hilāl* article was published, more than eleven thousand Jews who had been expelled from the district of Jaffa by the local Ottoman commander sought refuge, if only temporarily, in Alexandria, Cairo, and Suez.[3] The irony of Jews' escaping Palestine and fleeing to Egypt—an Exodus-in-reverse—was not lost on the author of this wartime Arabic journal article.

The unsigned article was likely written by *al-Hilāl*'s new editor, Emile Zaydan, the son of the journal's founder, Jurji (George) Zaydan

[1] *al-Hilāl* 24 (1915–1916), 404.

[2] As Justin McCarthy explains, "some 600 [Jews] had been deported from Jaffa to Egypt by the end of 1914, later to be joined by their families, who were transported on the American warship *Tennessee*. The deported Jews were considered political threats by the Ottoman government because they were subjects of Russia (at war with the Ottomans) or because they were Zionists who, it was believed, advocated the separation of Palestine from the Ottoman Empire. For a time, it appeared as if all Jews who had retained their Russian nationality would be deported. However, the German and American governments prevailed upon the Ottomans to allow the Russian Jews to become Ottoman subjects." McCarthy, *The Population of Palestine*, 20.

[3] See Krämer, *The Jews in Modern Egypt, 1914–1952*, 10–11. See also Krämer, *A History of Palestine*, 151–52; Rachel Simon, "Zionism," in *The Jews of the Middle East and North Africa in Modern Times*, ed. Simon, Laskier, and Reguer, 169.

(1861–1914).[4] Writing during the tumultuous early years of the First World War, Emile Zaydan observed the mass emigration of Jews from Palestine to Egypt and wondered what would become of the Zionist colonies that had been established there over the previous three decades. Though he expected his readers already to know about Zionism,[5] Zaydan reminds them that it is the movement through which "a group of Jewish leaders set out to assemble their scattered [brethren]." The Zionists have created "colonies [*mustaʿmarāt*] in Palestine to realize their hopes." So successful were the Zionists in their propagandistic efforts, Zaydan asserts, that by one estimate they raised "at least one hundred million guineas [pounds]."[6] The current war, however, had radically altered the situation, such that "no one knows the fate of the approximately forty colonies that were founded in Palestine." Zaydan contends that according to "the Jewish intellectuals," "the war has crushed their hopes, especially after the oppression by the rulers in Turkey [i.e., the Ottoman Empire] that led to the mass migration [of Jews] to Egypt." Despite Zionism's early accomplishments—whether in fundraising or in the colonization of Palestine—the movement, in Zaydan's view, now had a most uncertain and tenuous future.

What is most important about these comments for our purposes is what they reveal about how Zaydan perceived and interpreted contemporary Jewish history. The Zionists were, for Zaydan (consistent with the claim of the Zionists themselves), the descendants of the biblical Israelites; indeed, "Israelites" (rather than *yahūd*, i.e., Jews) is the term he prefers in this article.[7] The current fortunes, or misfortunes, of the Jews and especially of Zionism are thus read through the prism of the Bible.

Not unlike Muhammad Ruhi al-Khalidi, who, as we discovered in chapter 2, attempted to explain—and counter—Zionism through an understanding of Judaism and Jewish history, Zaydan also interprets Zionism, and notes the irony of its condition, through the lens of Jewish scripture. While important and influential, al-Khalidi was only one man, and his "as-Sayūnīzm" never reached the wide audience for which it was intended. This chapter analyzes many of the themes and arguments concerning Jews and Zionism that did reach Late Ottoman Palestine's literate, intellectual Arabic-reading public through regional

[4] See Philipp and Zaydān, *Ǧurǧī Zaidān, His Life and Thought.*

[5] "The readers know about the Zionist movement," writes Zaydan. See below for an analysis of the ways in which Zionism was addressed in *al-Hilāl* over the preceding decades.

[6] On the guinea and the history of Egyptian currency, see Goldschmidt and Johnston, *Historical Dictionary of Egypt*, 119–20.

[7] See below for a discussion of those who insisted on the distinction between the terms.

Arabic journals. In so doing, the chapter widens the scope of this study and shows that al-Khalidi's contemporaries were reading and writing about many aspects of the Jews' religion and history, proposing theories and perspectives no less fascinating than those we discovered in "as-Sayūnīzm."

In an effort to understand what Arab intellectuals in Palestine and beyond knew and thought about Jews, Judaism, and Zionism, I examine three of the most widely read and influential Arabic journals of the late nineteenth and early twentieth centuries—*al-Hilāl* (The Crescent), *al-Muqtaṭaf* (The Digest), and *al-Manār* (The Beacon)—as well as a monograph on Jewish history written by one of these journals' editors. Jews, we will find, were a frequent topic of interest for the journals' editors and readers.[8] No single, consistent image of Jews emerges from the varied pages of these journals; they were presented sympathetically by some and more hostilely by others. Nonetheless, certain problems and themes recurred frequently; these, I suggest, both reflected and informed the ways in which the journals' readers, including those in Palestine, perceived Jews and understood the Zionist project in Palestine. The themes were as varied as the racial relationship between Jews and Arabs; the origins of the Hebrew Bible and the historicity of its stories; the morality of the Jewish religion; the causes of antisemitism; the conditions of Jews in Christendom vis-à-vis those in the Islamic domain; the link between Jews and finance; and, increasingly as time progressed, the Zionist settlement of Palestine.

Ultimately, in presenting this analytical snapshot of the variety of Arab intellectual conceptions of Jews during the Late Ottoman period, this chapter aims to unearth and explore the complexities of the intellectual encounter between Arabs and Zionists in Palestine. For the editors, contributors, and readers of these Arabic journals, Zionists were not a foreign, unfamiliar group of European colonists; in fact, as we shall see, even those from Europe were generally not considered "European" at all. Rather, as Jews, the Zionists were known from the Bible and the Qurʾan, and they were often viewed as relatives—racial or otherwise—of the Arabs. Traditional religious polemical tropes were certainly incorporated into the way Jews and Zionists were perceived, but so too were the arguments of modern biblical criticism. In this analysis, we again discover the fluidity between self-perception and the perception of the other; that is, we find that the way in which an

[8] The interests of readers, while obviously difficult to determine with any certainty, might be gauged not only by what the editors published (based on their assessment of their readers' interests) but also by letters to the editor, which will be discussed in some detail below.

author defined himself was often intimately connected to the way in which he defined the Jew. To the extent that we may distill a general sense of the Jews from the wide variety of texts studied below, we might conclude that Jews and, not least, Zionists were viewed with a striking combination of respect and fear, sympathy and resentment.[9]

Regional Journals and Their Reach in Palestine

First, a word about the journals and editors I have chosen to analyze. *Al-Muqtaṭaf* was founded in 1876 in Beirut but was restarted in Cairo in 1884; *al-Hilāl*, which began in 1892, and *al-Manār*, the first issue of which appeared in 1898, were also based in Cairo. At first glance these three journals may seem a peculiar source for a book primarily concerned with the mutual perceptions and intellectual encounters among Zionists and Arabs. Not only were they all published outside of Palestine, the presumed center of the Zionist-Arab encounter, but their founders and editors were themselves not from Palestine. Rather, they were all Syrian-born (originating from areas in current-day Lebanon); *al-Hilāl*'s Jurji Zaydan and *al-Muqtaṭaf*'s founders Yaʿqub Sarruf, Faris Nimr, and Shahin Makaryus were Christians from around Beirut, while *al-Manār*'s editor Rashid Rida was a Muslim from a village near

[9] The pioneering study of the image of the Jew in the Arabic press is Sehayik, "Demut ha-yehudi bi-reʾi ʿitonut ʿarvit beyn ha-shanim 1858–1908," which reviews tens of Arabic journals from the half-century preceding the Young Turk Revolution. Sehayik seeks to portray this period as " 'a golden age' in relations between Jews and Arabs in the Middle East." In so doing, he overlooks or minimizes evidence to the contrary. Moreover, to explain what he perceives to be a marked and abrupt deterioration in attitude toward the Jews after 1908, he points to the rise of Zionism. However, 1908 was a transformational year not for Zionism but rather for the Ottoman Empire, as it was the year of the Young Turk Revolution. In other words, any dramatic change in attitude, if there had been one, would more reasonably be attributed to changes that came with the revolution, including (and most important in this context) the liberalization of the Ottoman censorship regime. Even the opposition to Zionism that was expressed in the Arabic press, Sehayik contends, was limited exclusively to the political realm. He asserts that "even this opposition did not, at that time, stem from a religious or racist background, but rather from a fear of creating a political problem in a period of the weakening of the Ottoman Empire, which symbolized Arab-Islamic pride. In addition, the local Christian zealots feared that the Zionist movement would harm them and their economic and political position in the region." Sehayik is unwilling to see in early Arab opposition to Zionism anything other than the expression of political or economic interests, notwithstanding his characterization of the post-1948 Arab-Israeli conflict as "the war of annihilation that the Arabs declared against the state of Israel that is accompanied by an extreme, uncompromising Islamic-religious, anti-Jewish flavor" (221).

Tripoli.[10] In other words, these journals were not intended to represent nor to address *Palestine's* Arabic-readers in particular.

As I argued in chapter 1, however, attempting strictly to isolate Late Ottoman Palestine's Arab intellectual life from that of the broader Middle East, especially Egypt and the Levant, is a problematic, even futile, endeavor. The biographies of many of Palestine's intellectuals in this period include close connections with figures and movements beyond Palestine, and it was common for these individuals to spend significant periods of their lives studying or working in surrounding lands. Late Ottoman Palestine's Arab intellectuals were part of a wider intellectual community and culture; understanding what members of this same community—even those without origins in Palestine—thought about the Jews is therefore helpful in gaining a more complete picture of the general discourse in which Palestinian Arab intellectuals participated. It is for this reason that I have also included in this study a monograph on Jewish history written by Shahin Makaryus, one of *al-Muqtaṭaf*'s editors. This recognition of a broader fin de siècle Arab Nahḍa culture, of course, does not discount and must not obscure the fact that Palestine's Arabs necessarily had particular concerns about the Jews, most notably the question of Zionism, even if, as we shall see, those based outside of Palestine were becoming increasingly interested in the Jews and their nationalist movement as well.

Beyond revealing the broader, regional Nahḍa discourse on the Jews, these journals also represent a rich source for an understanding of the knowledge and beliefs of the Arabic-speaking and Arabic-reading society in Palestine. First, as Ami Ayalon has noted in his work on literacy in Palestine, one finds evidence of Palestinian readership of *al-Muqtaṭaf* and *al-Hilāl* in the noticeable number of letters to the editor of the respective journals that were signed by readers who lived in Palestine.[11] Other evidence confirms that these three journals were certainly present in Palestine during the Late Ottoman period. All likely had agents in Jerusalem. We know of *al-Hilāl*'s agent by name:

[10] See Ayalon, *The Press in the Arab Middle East*, 52–55.

[11] Ayalon writes that "during the 24 years of its publication until 1900, *al-Muqtaṭaf* handled 81 queries from Palestine, while *al-Hilāl*, launched only in 1892, responded to queries of 20 different Palestinian readers." Ayalon acknowledges, though, that "the extent of Palestinian presence in the questions-and-answers sections was, unsurprisingly, markedly smaller than that of Lebanese and Egyptian readers" and, in fact, "also smaller than the presence of queries sent from Damascus, Aleppo, or even Baghdad." Nonetheless, "though limited in scope, such involvement did reflect active Palestinian interest in the fruits of the *nahdah*." Ayalon, *Reading Palestine*, 52–55. Suggestive of the wide reach of these journals, letters arrived from as far off as Natchez, Mississippi. See *al-Hilāl* (October 1910–July 1911), 53–54.

Eftim Effendi Mashbek is mentioned in one of the journal's 1910 volumes.[12] Near-complete sets of the journals are extant in the Khalidi Library and the al-Aqsa Library, the two Jerusalem libraries where I read them while researching this book.[13] Palestine's intellectuals, such as Muhammad Ruhi al-Khalidi, surely followed these journals, and the journals, in turn, followed al-Khalidi and his counterparts in articles on Palestinian society and politics.[14] Al-Khalidi wrote articles for these journals, typically under the pseudonym "al-Maqdisī," "the Jerusalemite."[15] The journals, then, are a critical source for an analysis of not only the broader Middle Eastern intellectual environment during the Late Ottoman period but also that of Palestine in particular.

Before proceeding to the analysis of the journals, we might highlight one important implication that emerges from this study. It is commonly claimed, as discussed in chapter 3, that Muslims were more sympathetic to Jews (and perhaps even to Zionism[16]) than were Christians. A close reading of these journals suggests that greater nuance must be acknowledged in the sharp distinction that is often drawn between Muslim and Christian intellectuals in this period vis-à-vis Jews.[17] *Al-Manār*, which was edited by a devout, if reform-minded,[18] Muslim, regularly expressed deeply anti-Jewish views, while the Christian editors of *al-Hilāl* and *al-Muqtaṭaf* repeatedly came to the Jews' defense when readers questioned Judaism's decency.[19] To be clear, this study

[12] *al-Hilāl* (October 1910–July 1911), 21.

[13] On the presence of these journals in these libraries, see also Khalidi, *Palestinian Identity*, 54–55. According to Rashid Khalidi, the copies in the Khalidi Library likely belonged to Muhammad Ruhi al-Khalidi.

[14] See, for example, *al-Hilāl* (October 1908–July 1909), 177.

[15] The revelation of al-Maqdisī's identity as al-Khalidi occurs in *al-Hilāl* (October 1908–July 1909), 181–82.

[16] Rashid Khalidi has convincingly challenged this dichotomy vis-à-vis Zionism in *Palestinian Identity*, 134ff. Cf. Mandel, *The Arabs and Zionism before World War I.*

[17] Noting the role of Christians in discussions found in the Islamic journal *al-Manār*, Daniel Stolz has commented on "the confessionally porous boundaries of Islamic discourse" in this period. Stolz, " 'By Virtue of Your Knowledge,' " 224.

[18] On Rashid Rida and the Salafiyya movement, see Hourani, *Arabic Thought in the Liberal Age, 1798–1939*, 222ff. See also Adams, *Islam and Modernism*; Commins, *Islamic Reform.*

[19] While the editors of *al-Hilāl* and *al-Muqtaṭaf* were Christians, these journals were not "Christian journals" in an exclusive sense, even as matters related to the Hebrew Bible and the New Testament occupied significant space in them. Internal evidence within the journals confirms that their contributors and readers included many Muslims. *Al-Manār*, in contrast, may more reasonably be regarded as an "Islamic journal" insofar as it devoted much space to Qurʾanic commentary that would be more likely to alienate non-Muslim readers (leaving aside the potentially disturbing substance of that commentary relating to non-Muslims). On the relationship between Rida and the editors of *al-Hilāl* and *al-Muqtaṭaf*, see Ryad, *Islamic Reformism and Christianity*, 76–86.

does not argue for the opposite claim—that this period's Muslims were *less* sympathetic to Jews than were Christians. First of all, these journals cannot be taken as representative of the religious communities of their editors (*al-Muqtaṭaf* and *al-Hilāl*, for example, fashioned themselves as modern, scientific journals and included non-Christian contributors). Second, one sometimes finds anti-Jewish views expressed in the Christian-edited journals and tolerant perspectives articulated in the Muslim-edited journal. A more nuanced view—one sensitive to the complexities and contradictions associated with these communities—is clearly necessary.

Who Is a Yahūdī? Who Is an Isrā'īlī?

To understand the various perceptions of Jews exhibited in these journals, we must begin by investigating what precisely was meant by the term "Jew" (or its frequent alternative, if not equivalent, "Israelite") in this journalistic discourse. At least for some writers, there was a meaningful distinction between the terms Jew and Israelite. In an *al-Muqtaṭaf* article on "The Jews of France," the author explains that

> some members of the Israelite nation [*al-umma al-isrāʾīliyya*] consider labeling them "Jews" to be an insult to them. They prefer to be called "Israelites" following the example of the Jews of France.[20] But their scholars and writers disagree with this view and, from antiquity until the present, always called themselves "Jews" in all their books and letters. Despite this, we will use the label "Israelites" in this article because most of them who reside here in Egypt prefer this name.

The author later explains that technically, "Israelite" refers specifically to "the ten tribes that were exiled during the first exile [by the Assyrians in the eighth century BCE] and whose location is now unknown," and that "it is likely that contemporary Jews are not [descended] from them but rather from the tribes of Judah and Benjamin."[21] Even *al-Muqtaṭaf*, however, did not uphold this terminological distinction with

[20] Phyllis Cohen Albert has investigated the history of the uses of these terms in the French context. Cohen Albert rejects the conventional wisdom that "in the wake of the Revolution emancipated French Jews began calling themselves *Israélites*, in preference to *Juifs*, thus indicating that they had denationalized their Jewish identity, and limited it to a newly narrowed definition in the religious sphere." Instead, she contends that this distinction was first articulated in 1890 in an article entitled "Juifs et Israélites." See Cohen Albert, "Israelite and Jew," 91–96.

[21] *al-Muqtaṭaf* 43:6 (December 1913), 561.

any consistency. In a brief entry in August 1916 entitled "New York: Capital of the Nations," *al-Muqtaṭaf* opens by identifying New York as "the largest Jewish city [*madīna yahūdiyya*] because it has a million Jews." Just two months later, though, *al-Muqtaṭaf* published another short article on New York. This time it opened by stating that "New York is the largest Israelite city."[22]

The question that had by that point been discussed in Europe for over a century—are the Jews a religion, a nation, a race, or something else?[23]—concerned the authors of these fin de siècle Arabic journals, whether they referred to their subjects as Jews or Israelites. Consider, for instance, the view proposed in *al-Hilāl*'s five-page piece on "The Jews and the War: Their Influence on It and Its Influence on Them," the same article that noted the irony of Jewish migration from Palestine to Egypt. The essay opens by identifying the Israelites:

> The Israelites are distinguished from among the rest of the peoples [*ash-shuʿūb*] by their preservation of their nationality [*jinsiyyatihim*] and their customs and practices, despite the passage of time and their subordination to different states. Israelitism [al-isrāʾīliyya[24]] is simultaneously a religion [*dīn*] and a nationality [*jinsiyya*], unlike Christianity and Islam.

The author perceives a distinction between the categories of religion and nationality. A Christian Frenchman would thus be Christian by religion and French by nationality, and a Muslim Egyptian would, likewise, be Muslim by religion and Egyptian (or, depending on the ideology of the classifier, Arab) by nationality. But for Jews, this author contends, there is no such dichotomy; "Israelitism" is both religion *and* nationality. This unique nature of Israelitism is relevant for an article on "The Jews and the War" because, the author explains, "if we are surprised by fighting between Christian and Christian in this war, we are all the more shocked by fighting between Jew and Jew." The implication here is that the solidarity among Jews, who share both religion and nationality, is, or would be expected to be, stronger than that among Christians (or among Muslims), who are united solely by

[22] See *al-Muqtaṭaf* 49:2 (August 1916), 205, and 49:4 (October 1916), 409.

[23] A brief but useful survey of this discussion can be found in Silberstein, "Religion, Ethnicity, and Jewish History."

[24] In more familiar parlance, we might render this term as "Judaism" or, perhaps more precisely, "Jewishness." Given the ambiguity, however, and the fact that each of these terms has different nuances, I have chosen to use the more literal though obviously more cumbersome "Israelitism."

religion. How strange, then, Zaydan suggests, to find Jews on opposing sides of the battlefields of this war.[25]

For Emile Zaydan and, as we saw earlier, Ruhi al-Khalidi, the question was whether Jews were a nationality or a religion. According to Zaydan, Jews constitute both a religion (*dīn*) and a nationality (*jinsiyya*), while al-Khalidi contended that in the past Jews had possessed both national and religious qualities, but they had permanently abandoned their national qualities in accepting "Mendelssohn's theory." For still other Arab intellectuals, however, there was yet another category—namely, race—that was even more decisive in defining Jews. As addressed in chapter 1, race entered the discourse of the late nineteenth- and early twentieth-century Middle East through multiple sources: (1) European—the centrality of race-thinking in fin de siècle European intellectual and nationalist thought (including varieties of Zionism);[26] (2) Ottoman—the question of the dominance of Turks, defined racially, in the Late Ottoman Empire; (3) Egyptian—the place of race in contemporary debates about Egypt's relationship to the Sudan; and (4) Syrian—the role of Darwinian and Social Darwinist theories in the formative experiences of the Syrian-born editors of the major Arabic intellectual journals of the period.

One of those Syrian-born intellectuals who moved to Egypt in the wake of the controversy over Darwinism was Shahin Makaryus, a founding editor of *al-Muqtaṭaf*.[27] In 1904 Makaryus published a monograph called *Tārīkh al-isrāʾīliyyīn* (History of the Israelites). The introductory chapter of this 270-page book, published by *al-Muqtaṭaf*'s press, is called "The Origin and Lineage of the Jews" (*aṣl al-yahūd*

[25] Cf. *al-Muqtaṭaf* 46:3 (May 1915), 504, for the editor's response to a question about what happens when Freemasons find themselves on opposite sides of a battlefield.

[26] Certain Zionists employed race-thinking in making the argument for a Jewish race (and, by extension, nation). Zionist race-thinkers were compelled, though, to consider the implications of the Jews' race for their relations with Palestine's Arabs, ostensible racial relatives. One of Efron's subjects, Jewish race scientist Elias Auerbach (b. Posen 1882; moved to Palestine 1905), employed the Jews' Semitic race as an argument for the "appropriateness of a mass return to the Middle East," to be in their natural racial environment. "Buoyed by ample anthropological evidence and by theories of Semitic unity, Auerbach's Zionist vision," Efron explains, "projected a peaceful and harmonious future for Jews and Arabs in the Land of Israel." In other words, the Jews' race was, in Auerbach's case, an argument for Zionism, but for a Zionism that stressed peaceful coexistence with Palestine's Arab natives. Efron, *Defenders of the Race*, 139–40. On race-thinking among Jews and Zionists, see also Hart, *Jews and Race*; Falk, "Zionism and the Biology of the Jews," 587–607.

[27] See discussion of the Lewis Affair in chapter 1. On Makaryus's racial thought, see also Gribetz, " 'Their Blood Is Eastern,' " 143–61.

wa-nasabuhum). The chapter opens with this statement describing what Makaryus considered to be the current state of race-thinking:

> Most scholars say that mankind is divided into four branches [*furūʿ*] to which all sects [*ṭawāʾif*] and generations may trace their origins. Their evidence of this division is the differences that exist in moral, intellectual, and physical qualities. These four branches are the Caucasian [*qawqāsī*], Mongolian [*manghūlī*], Negroid [*zanjī*], and Malay [*malqī*].[28]

Though he employs certain medieval Arabic terminology,[29] Makaryus follows a conventional European breakdown of the races of humanity that began to be developed in the eighteenth century.[30]

As is generally the case with race-thinking, Makaryus's brand was not simply a mode of classification; he asserted a hierarchy.[31] "Clearly," Makaryus insists, "what is meant by the history of humanity is actually the history of the Caucasian branch. This is because the rest of the branches did not influence civilization [*al-ʿumrān*] as did [the Caucasians]. Civilization [*al-madaniyya*] is indebted to it [the Caucasian 'branch'] as to no other branch for the way in which it has developed."[32] Of the four races, the most influential in the rise and development of human civilization, Makaryus claims, is the Caucasian race.

Given his acceptance of the claim that the Caucasians are the most advanced of the races, it is hardly a surprise that Makaryus, a Christian Arab from Syria, regards "Semites" as one of the three large constituent groups of Caucasians, along with "Arians or Indo-Europeans" and "Hamites."[33] According to Makaryus, Semites include "the Hebrews or Jews, the Phoenicians, the Assyrians, the Arabs, the Babylonians, and the Chaldeans."[34] Indeed, Makaryus not only classifies Semites among humanity's superior race, Caucasians, but he also locates Semites at the creative, spiritual helm of their many fellow Caucasians. "It is clear,"

[28] Makaryus, *Tārīkh al-Isrāʾiliyyīn*, 1.

[29] On the negative image of the so-called zanjī in medieval Arabic writing, see Lewis, *Race and Slavery in the Middle East*, 31–34, 50–53, 92–95. On the zanjī in medieval Jewish imagination, see also Goldenberg, " 'It Is Permitted to Marry a Kushite.' "

[30] Cf. Johann Friedrich Blumenbach (1752–1840), a professor of anatomy at Gottingen University, who classified humanity into five groups: Caucasian, Mongol, Ethiopian, American, and Malay. For key passages of Blumenbach's 1775 dissertation *On the Natural Variety of Mankind*, see Bernasconi and Lott, *The Idea of Race*, 27–37. For a contemporary review of the work, see Augstein, *Race*, 58–67.

[31] As Eric Weitz notes, "unlike ethnicity, race always entails a hierarchical construction of difference." Weitz, *A Century of Genocide*, 21.

[32] Makaryus, *Tārīkh al-isrāʾīliyyīn*, 2.

[33] Ibid.

[34] Ibid.

he asserts, that "the Semites have an important place in the history of civilization and the state of contemporary human society. From them, the three great religions emerged among the civilized: Judaism, Christianity, and Islam. . . . The Aryans and similar groups borrowed these religions from them."[35] The Semites, with whom Makaryus would certainly have identified not only the Jews (the subject of his book) but also himself, as an Arab, are the source of the world's most important "civilized" religions. Even the "Aryans"—who, in the minds of many nineteenth-century European race-writers, were the most superior of all races—borrowed their religions from their Semitic originators.[36]

Concluding his discussion of the place of Jews among the races, Makaryus explains that "the Jews, then, are Caucasian Semites." He traces the Jews' lineage "back to Shem the son of Noah." Makaryus, notably, does not question contemporary Jews' direct descent from the ancient Semites. "During the days of the expansion of their sovereignty in Palestine," he writes, the Jews "preserved their lineages and recorded them in books that were kept for this purpose." When Israel was exiled and scattered, these lineage records were lost, according to Makaryus. "Despite this," he contends, "they preserved their existence. Wherever they went, they did not assimilate much [*wa-lam yukthirū min al-ikhtilāṭ*] among the foreign peoples who surrounded them." The Jews avoided assimilation to such an extent that "it is said that those of them who settled in Europe many centuries ago still have a distinct pronunciation of European languages from that of Europeans, even to the present day."[37] In other words, for Makaryus, the Jews of his day—whether his Jewish neighbors in the Middle East or those farther off in Europe—were authentic, racial Semites, the progeny of the biblical Israelites, and were best understood in this racial context.

Like Makaryus, Jurji Zaydan, founder of *al-Hilāl* and father of Emile Zaydan, also came to embrace race-thinking. Indeed, as mentioned briefly in chapter 1, the elder Zaydan published a full book on the subject of human races in 1912. In this book, *Ṭabaqāt al-umam aw as-salāʾil al-bashariyya* (Classes of the Nations, or Races of Man), Zaydan explained that, while throughout history people have been interested in understanding the different nature and morals of man in different

[35] Ibid., 3.

[36] Cf. Ernest Renan, who credits the Semites "with bringing about the discovery, 'without reflection nor reasoning,' of the purest religious form humanity had ever known. This discovery," explains Gil Anidjar, "was, to be sure, anything but an invention. . . . Rather, a kind of 'primitive intuition' enabled the Semites to part from the world in a unique way and arrive, 'without any effort' or meditation, at the notion of the Supreme God.' " Anidjar, *Semites*, 31.

[37] Makaryus, *Tārīkh al-isrāʾīliyyīn*, 3.

places, it is only in recent decades that these can be studied not through "fables and exaggeration," but rather as "a true science (*ʿilman haqīqiyyan*) based on observation and research."[38] Zaydan relies on a number of English-language scholars in crafting his book; indeed, much of the book is a translation of A. H. Keane's *The World's Peoples*, published just four years earlier in New York in 1908.[39] Zaydan explains that, of the five books he reviewed in order to write his book, he preferred Keane's because "it organized the peoples [*al-umam*] by classes, meaning that it graded them on the ladder of humanity as per the laws of evolution [*nāmūs an-nushūʾ wa-l-irtiqāʾ*]."[40] In his work, Zaydan translates faithfully most of Keane's section on the Jews, including the Irish scholar's argument against those who claim that, given the variety in color and height among contemporary Jews, "the Israelite race [*al-ʿunṣur al-isrāʾīlī*] has been lost," leaving only "the Jewish sect [*aṭ-ṭāʾifa al-yahūdiyya*]." Though some believe that Jews no longer constitute a race but rather a religious community of mixed racial characteristics, Zaydan follows Keane in insisting that they remain racially distinct. He highlights their shared features, "the most important of which are the large, hooked nose and the prominent, watery eyes," along with "a protrusion under the chin and coarse, curly hair."[41] Jews are not all the same, to be sure, as "among them there is a sect[42] in the lands of the Maghreb and Palestine that is distinguished for its beauty and these [general] features have already left them."

Keane was particularly interested in what he considered to be the Jews' remarkable adaptability; he referred to them as the "most versatile perhaps of all peoples."

> Originally pure nomads, the Israelites became excellent husbandsmen after the settlement in Canaan, and then they have given proof of the highest capacity for poetry, letters, erudition

[38] Zaydān, *Ṭabaqāt al-umam aw as-salāʾil al-bashariyya*, 5.

[39] On Zaydan's work on race and his use of Keane, see El Shakry, *The Great Social Laboratory*, 58–60.

[40] Zaydān, *Ṭabaqāt al-umam aw as-salāʾil al-bashariyya*, 6. See Keane, *The World's Peoples*. On Keane, see "Dr. A. H. Keane," *Nature* 88 (February 8, 1912), 488. The other works Zaydan cites are Bettany, *The World's Inhabitants, or Mankind, Animals, and Plants*; Bettany, *The World's Religions*; Moncrieff, *The World of to-Day*; Tylor, *Anthropology*.

[41] Zaydān, *Ṭabaqāt al-umam aw as-salāʾil al-bashariyya*, 235. Keane's original reads: "One observer even asserts that there are all kinds of Jews—brown, white, dark, tall, short—so that there is no longer any question of a Jewish race, but only a Jewish sect. Nevertheless certain marked features—large hooked nose, prominent watery eyes, thick pendulous under lip, rough frizzly lusterless hair—are sufficiently general to be regarded as racial traits." Keane, *The World's Peoples*, 331.

[42] For consistency, I translate *ṭāʾifa* again here as "sect" as I do earlier in this passage, but in this case "group" or "part" might be more precise.

> of all kinds, philosophy, finance, music, and diplomacy. The reputation of the medieval Arabs as restorers of learning is largely due to their wise tolerance of the enlightened Jewish communities in their midst. In recent years the persecutions, especially in Russia and Rumania, have caused a fresh exodus, and flourishing agricultural settlements have been founded in Argentina and Palestine. Efforts have also been made to direct the current of migration to the British possessions in East Central Africa.[43]

Zaydan reproduces nearly all these lines in close Arabic translation, openly praising the Jews for their intelligence and resourcefulness. There are two noteworthy changes Zaydan makes in his rendition of this narrative. First, while he notes the British efforts to "transplant" Jews to their East Africa protectorate, he omits mention of the "flourishing settlements" in Argentina and Palestine. Later in this chapter we will return to the issue of the presentation of Zionism by these journalists; for now, we might simply note that Zaydan apparently preferred not to broach the topic here. Second, while Keane presents Jews as the ultimate source of the revival of scholarship and culture in medieval Arab society—crediting Arabs with nothing more than not interfering with the Jews' intellectual creativity—Zaydan offers a different perspective. For him, Jews merely "had a hand in the renaissance [*nahḍa*] of the Arabic language during the Islamic civilization."[44] Zaydan acknowledges the role played by Jews in medieval Arabic culture, but he is loathe to attribute all of this culture's accomplishments exclusively to Jews.

Jewish and Arab Race against European Prejudice

Implicit in these journalists' conception of the Jews in racial terms is the link between Jews and Arabs. Five years before publishing his monograph on human races, Jurji Zaydan was already considering the relationship between Jews and Arabs and the phenomenon of Jewish Arabs. In a 1903 volume of his *al-Hilāl*, Zaydan published an article entitled "The Jews in the Lands of the Arabs" (*al-yahūd fī bilād al-ʿarab*) in response to a reader's inquiry about "the Arab tribes who converted to Judaism before Islam." Under the rubric of "Jews in the Lands of the Arabs," Zaydan includes both people of biblical Israelite origin who immigrated to the Arabian Peninsula as well as natives of these *bilād*

[43] Keane, *The World's Peoples*, 332.

[44] Zaydān, *Ṭabaqāt al-umam aw as-salāʾil al-bashariyya*, 235.

al-ʿarab, the "lands of the Arabs," who converted to the Jewish religion. He explains that "Judaism is ancient in the Arabian Peninsula, for Jews continued to immigrate to Arab lands from their earliest period, whether fleeing violence or searching for livelihood." This "earliest period" of Jewish history in Arabia may well have begun as early as the Pentateuchal period. "It is not unlikely," he claims, "that a group of them immigrated there during their wanderings in the wilderness at the time of Moses." A Jewish presence in the "lands of the Arabs," in other words, could be as ancient as the Jewish presence in the Holy Land.[45]

Relying on traditional sources composed between the ninth and the fifteenth centuries, Zaydan presents his readers with three possible origins of the Jews in Arab lands. The first source he cites is Abu al-Faraj al-Iṣfahānī (ninth–tenth centuries). In *Kitāb al-aghānī*, Zaydan explains, al-Iṣfahānī notes that the first Jews in Arab lands were those who fought the biblical Amalekites. In sparing the Amalekite prince, these Jews failed to annihilate the people completely as had been commanded and thus were refused entry to "ash-Shām," i.e., Greater Syria (including the Land of Israel). They decided to settle the land of those they had decimated, and this included the city of Yathrib (i.e., Madina). Next, Zaydan discusses the theory of al-Maqrizi (fourteenth–fifteenth centuries) that Jews arrived in Yathrib during the time of Samuel the Prophet, and again after the Roman conquest. At the latter time, al-Maqrizi suggests, Jews undertook to spread their religion among the native peoples. "By the eighth century CE," he writes, "the Jewish religion was widespread in many Arab lands." Finally, Zaydan mentions the position of Ibn Khaldun (fourteenth–fifteenth centuries), who argued that the first to bring the Jewish religion to the Arabs was Dhu Nuwas, a king of Yemen who, along with his people, converted to Judaism at the end of the fifth century, "though in a different version, the people of Yemen converted to Judaism at the beginning of the fourth century."[46] Whether through immigration or by native conversion, there had been Jews living among Arabs, and even Arabs living as Jews, Zaydan argues, beginning no less than a millennium and a half earlier.

The same year in which Zaydan published his article, Makaryus addressed the question of the relationship between Jews and Arabs in a fascinating footnote in *Tārīkh al-isrāʾīliyyīn*. Identifying the biblical figure Abraham as the paterfamilias of the Jews, Makaryus writes that

[45] For a modern scholarly account of the Jews in pre-Islamic Arabia, see Newby, *A History of the Jews of Arabia*.

[46] *al-Hilāl* (October 1903–July 1904), 85–86.

"some European writers think that the Jews [come] from the Arabs."[47] Makaryus highlights the merits of this position, explaining:

> The ancestor of the Jews after Abraham was Isaac his son, and the ancestor of the Arabs was Ishmael, the son of Abraham and the half-brother of Isaac. The kinship [between the Jews and the Arabs] is thus clear. Some of the Arab tribes were Jewish, both before and after [the advent of] Islam. . . . Abraham somewhat resembles a leader [*shaykh*] of an Arab tribe as is made clear from his biography in the Torah. . . . His morals and customs that are recorded are similar to the customs and morals of the Arabs, such as hospitality, pride, courage, bravery, generosity, protecting neighbors, and other such customs and ways of life.[48]

The biblical patriarch Abraham, in other words, might well have been an Arab himself; his son Ishmael, after all, is "the ancestor of the Arabs." The Jews, according to this theory, are simply an Arab tribe that broke off from the rest of the Arabs in the biblical era, at the time of Abraham's two sons, though even then not fully so; there remained Arab tribes that professed the Jewish religion in the periods both before and after the rise of Islam. Ultimately, however, the biblical narrative is just one piece of evidence of the familial kinship between the Jews and Arabs, and perhaps not the most compelling one at that. Makaryus insists that his discussion of Abraham and his two sons "is besides the fact that the Jews and Arabs are of one species and one race [*jins wāḥid wa-farᶜ wāḥid*]. The relationship between the two [i.e., Jews and Arabs], according to science, then, is apparent and clear, and it is confirmed by the religious histories and the traditional stories."[49] It is the "science" of race that, for Makaryus, proves the link between Jews and Arabs; "religious histories and traditional stories" merely corroborate this connection.

Investigating and highlighting the relationship between Jews and Arabs was not merely a matter of intellectual curiosity for these journal editors. There were certain practical or ideological concerns that made Arabs' association with Jews especially important and useful at this particular moment. The fin de siècle was the age of the Nahḍa, the Arab renaissance in which various influential Arab thinkers, exposed to European culture, were eager at once to embrace elements of that

[47] The Arabic reads *min al-ᶜarab*, which might be rendered as "are among the Arabs" or "are of the Arabs." The example Makaryus offers of this perspective is Benjamin Disraeli's 1847 political novel *Tancred*, which had been translated into Arabic by Makaryus's own journal *al-Muqtaṭaf*.

[48] Makaryus, *Tārīkh al-isrāʾīliyyīn*, 4.

[49] Ibid.

culture and to show that Arabs were just as *capable* of societal progress as their European counterparts, if not more so, even if Arabs at present were not as advanced.[50] The problem was that race-thinking, which was then so deeply embedded in European thought, and which these intellectuals duly accepted, suggested that, as members of a non-European race, Arabs might inherently lack the capacity for the intellectual, social, and cultural progress that Europeans had experienced.

To solve this conundrum, the Jews became a critical link.[51] Claiming a close association with Jews offered Arabs proof that members of their own race, as they conceived it, could be as successful and "advanced" as Europeans. This logic is evident in an extended *al-Muqtaṭaf* article about the Egyptian Jewish businessman Felix Suares that was written just after his death in 1906.[52] (Though unsigned, the article was probably written by Makaryus, who dedicated his monograph on Jewish history to his friend Suares in a preface that is markedly similar to this article.) The introduction to the article, part of a series on the world's leading businesspeople, offers us some insight into the way in which the author—and *al-Muqtaṭaf* more broadly—viewed Jews in relation to Easterners, or, in the language of the day, "Orientals." At times, the author writes, circumstances demand that one "silence the arguments of some Europeans who claim that the nations of the East [*umam al-mashriq*] are inferior to them, or that they [these nations] have aged, that their demise is nearing, and that they will not endure." For this author, the most compelling refutation of such a claim is found in the example of "the Israelites," that is, the Jews. After all, the Jews who settled in Europe and were granted full civil rights "nearly equaled or even excelled beyond" their non-Jewish neighbors in the areas of science, philosophy, manufacturing, and commerce. Especially in the fields of philosophical sciences and financial activities, "every European bows" to the Jews because "the balance of money is in their hands, despite their small numbers." This is the case not merely in one country but "in every country in which they are given equal civil

[50] On the Nahḍa, see the classic work on the subject, Hourani, *Arabic Thought in the Liberal Age, 1798–1939*. In 1899, the editors of *al-Muqtaṭaf* wrote that "the West borrowed from us when we were once great and now it is our turn to take from the West." "The Egyptian Princess," *al-Muqtaṭaf* 23 (1899), 66. Cited in Elshakry, "Darwin's Legacy in the Arab East," 111.

[51] On other Arabic journal responses to European condescension toward the Arab/Islamic world—including highlighting the glorious past of the Arab world, the intolerance and violence of medieval European/Christian society, as well as self-critique—see Sehayik, "Demut ha-yehudi bi-reʾi ʿitonut ʿarvit beyn ha-shanim 1858–1908," especially 43–52.

[52] Suares died in April 1906, and the article about him appeared at the opening of the May edition of *al-Muqtaṭaf*.

rights to others, as is clear in France, Austria, and America, and as is obvious as well in Egypt,[53] since security has been strengthened and the rights of foreigners preserved."[54] To use European Jewry as proof of the potential for Easterners to excel even beyond Europeans—so as to encourage his fellow Easterners and to rebuff the condescension of Europeans—the author must assert the fundamental "Eastern-ness" of Jews, including and especially the Jews of Europe.

This was a theme to which *al-Muqtaṭaf* returned in greater detail in 1913, in an article on "The Jews of France":

> Our purpose in publishing these lines is for Easterners to see that a group of them, i.e., the Israelites who immigrated to Europe and settled France—the mother of the sciences and arts and civilization—matched or even surpassed the French in every pursuit. Given this, we do not know how the Europeans can claim that the Eastern mind is inferior to the Western mind and that if an Easterner were to compete with a Westerner with equal means, the Westerner would prevail.[55]

For evidence of Jewish success in France, *al-Muqtaṭaf* relies on an article by the French author Eugene Tavernier.[56] The article describes the spread of Jews throughout the various parts of French public life, from the military to the government to the police to the press. Tavernier's article, it seems, caught the eye of *al-Muqtaṭaf*'s editors because it showed that "the Israelites, who are a pure Eastern nation," are able to excel in France to a degree far disproportionate to their small numbers, with Jews holding positions of prominence in "the sciences, literature, politics, and finance." And this success came "despite the fact that their history in France is one of continuing oppression," from medieval slaughters to ritual murder accusations to economic discrimination to, most recently, the Dreyfus Affair.[57] If the Jews, "a pure Eastern nation," could achieve such feats of success even while suffering persecution and deprivation, other Easterners (especially, for *al-Muqtaṭaf*'s purposes, Arabs) could have confidence that they too have the ability to excel in the modern world.

[53] Literally: "in this region." *Al-quṭr*, in the Egyptian context, though, generally refers exclusively to Egypt.

[54] *al-Muqtaṭaf* 31:5 (May 1906), 361.

[55] *al-Muqtaṭaf* 43:6 (December 1913), 561.

[56] Tavernier's 1913 article "The Jews of France in the XIXth Century," 393–407, is mentioned in Philipp, *Die Juden und das Wirtschaftsleben*, 120. On Tavernier's view of France as "the daughter of the Grand Orient," see Kedourie, "Young Turks, Freemasons and Jews," 98.

[57] *al-Muqtaṭaf* 43:6 (December 1913), 563.

What was implicit in the 1906 article on Suares is explicit in this 1913 article on the Jews of France: the Jews can be viewed as role models for the Arabs especially (if not only) when Jews are defined in *racial* terms. Here, explains the author, "we consider the Israelites as an Eastern people [*shaʿb sharqī*] in the sense that they are a race of humanity [*jins min ajnās al-bashar*] and not as a people with a particular religion [*ahl dīn khāṣṣ bi-him*]." As a result, there is, for these purposes, no distinction between Jews who practice Judaism and "those who have converted to Christianity or Islam."[58] For example, "the rise of [Benjamin] Disraeli to prime minister of England is the rise of a member of the Jewish nation [*al-umma al-yahūdiyya*] or of an Eastern nation, even though he was born a Christian."[59] The same is true for all Christian "scholars and ministers in European countries whose origins are Jewish [*aṣluhum yahūdī*] and for those with Jewish origins who converted to Islam in Muslim countries. All of these people have Eastern blood [*damuhum sharqī*] and are of the Semitic race like Arabs, Assyrians, Syrians and others of the Semitic nations."[60] Viewing the Jews in racial terms, even deeming their religious affiliation irrelevant to their fundamental identity, the author asserts an Arab-Jewish connection that is intrinsic and irrevocable. "If researching this topic does nothing more than convince the readers of their natural ability as an Eastern people who are not prevented from reaching the highest ranks of the advanced nations," such a result would be "more than enough." For *al-Muqtaṭaf*, the Jews were a model of a successful "Eastern nation" and "Semitic race"[61]—at once inspiration and proof that success was within reach.

This perspective on the close familial kinship between Jews and Arabs was not the interest exclusively of *al-Muqtaṭaf* or its Christian coeditor, Shahin Makaryus. In 1910 Rashid Rida, editor of the Islamic journal *al-Manār*, noted in passing the relationship between Jews and Arabs in his discussion of the Jewish role in finance. Rida remarked that it is well-known that finance is concentrated "in the hands of the Jews and [that] they are [part] of us (i.e., the Easterners) in kinship [*nasab*] and homeland [*mawṭin*]." Moreover, in Europe, the Jews' "skill in establishing justice and freedom has become clear." In fact, Rida concludes, Jews "are superior to the rest of their Syrian and Palestinian

[58] Ibid., 564.

[59] The author's choice to highlight Disraeli in particular from among all of history's converts from Judaism was not accidental, for Disraeli himself, "a Romantic Orientalist" in the words of scholar Ivan Kalmar, held this racialist view. Kalmar, "Benjamin Disraeli, Romantic Orientalist."

[60] *al-Muqtaṭaf* 43:6 (December 1913), 564.

[61] Ibid.

brethren in their abilities."[62] For Rida and *al-Manār*, as for other contributors to these journals, Jews were a model of modern success to be respected and emulated by other "Easterners" and fellow members of the "Semitic race."

Race and the History of Jewish-Arab Coexistence

Though the *contemporary* implications of Jewish-Arab racial kinship (i.e., providing evidence for hope in Arabs' own potential for "progress") were clearly important for these editors, the journals employed this theory to explain earlier historical moments as well. For some, the racial link between Jews and Arabs helped to account for the relatively good relations between Jews and Arabs in previous periods. (These supposed good relations were themselves a common theme in these journals). For example, in February 1908 *al-Muqtaṭaf* published a six-page article on "Philosophy among the Jews." In the middle of the article, after discussing various ancient Jewish "philosophical movements" such as the Pharisees, Sadducees, Essenes, and rabbinic Judaism, the author reaches the subject of Jews' first interactions with Arabs, and then, with Islam. Some Jews, the author explains, "refused to remain under the Roman yoke, suffering from chauvinistic oppression." These Jews "came to the land of the Arabs, before Islam, and settled there." In contrast to the Roman-controlled lands from which they fled, in "the land of the Arabs" there was "harmony between them [the Jews] and the natives because they were similar in language and close in race [*al-jins*], and because of the absence of a state that distinguished between native and foreigner."[63] With the advent of Islam, "its oppression of the Jews was not severe." In fact, Jews "welcomed the conquerors," and their spirit—which had been distressed by "the tyranny of the Romans and Persians"—"was revived." This article on Jewish philosophy highlights that under Arab-Islamic rule a group of Jews "devoted themselves to knowledge and literature." Such Jewish scholars included the famed thinkers Saadiah bin Yusuf (Saadiah Gaon) and Samuel bin Hofni.[64] In other words, one of the reasons for the "harmony" between Jews and Arabs (and thus Muslims) was the fact that they were "close in race," that their *racial* connections facilitated a natural coexistence and permitted Jews to reach great philosophical heights.

[62] *al-Manār* 13:5 (1910), 355.

[63] *al-Muqtaṭaf* 33:2 (February 1908), 125.

[64] Samuel bin Hofni (d. circa 1034) is regarded as the last Gaon of Sura. On the Geonic period, see Brody, *The Geonim of Babylonia and the Shaping of Medieval Jewish Culture.*

As it was expounded in *al-Muqtaṭaf*, this theory was meant to offer further proof that Jewish philosophy is best developed within Arab-Islamic culture and civilization. Not only were the Jews who first fled to Arab lands from the "chauvinistic oppression" of Roman rule the ones who attained the pinnacles of Jewish philosophic inquiry, but the demise of Jewish philosophy can be traced to the moment at which European Christendom destroyed the great Jewish community that had flourished under Islam. "At the end of the fifteenth century,"[65] the author explains, "the Jews were expelled from Spain and, in their expulsion, Jewish philosophy disappeared." For this author, Jews have a special bond with Arab and Islamic civilization, tied, at least in part, to their shared racial origins. Moreover, the two societies are conceived in opposition to the imagined Other of Europe. Jews are second only to Arabs in "the history of philosophy" and share the glory with Arabs for together having "preserved science and philosophy during a period in which Europe was lost in the darkness of ignorance." Explicitly linking Jewish philosophy (and, more generally, the achievements of Jewish culture) to Arab or Islamic rule, the article expresses pride in the shared Arab-Jewish philosophical past in contrast to the ignorant past of Europe.[66]

Crescent, Cross, and the Causes of Antisemitism

The notion that historically Jews thrived and prospered under Arab and Islamic rule—especially as compared to the oppression and persecution they suffered in Christian Europe—was a leitmotif of nearly all comments on the course of Jewish history articulated in these journals.[67]

[65] The author writes that the expulsion took place in 1494. It is not clear why the author identifies this date, rather than 1492, as the date of expulsion.

[66] *al-Muqtaṭaf* 33:2 (February 1908), 127.

[67] Mark R. Cohen dubs this "the 'myth of an interfaith utopia' in Islam," which was propagated by both Jews and Arabs (especially, though not exclusively, Muslims) for various purposes at different times. "Frustrated by the tortuous progress of their own integration into gentile society in what was supposed to be a 'liberal' age of emancipation," writes Cohen of nineteenth-century European Jews, "Jewish intellectuals seeking a historical precedent for a more tolerant attitude toward Jews hit upon a time and place that met this criterion—medieval Muslim Spain," and, more broadly, the Jewish experience under Islam. Cohen contends that this myth has been employed more recently "by Arabs as a weapon in their propaganda war against Zionism." He explains that "according to this view, for centuries, Jews and Arabs lived together in peace and harmony under Islamic rule" and thus "modern antipathy toward Israel began only when the Jews destroyed the old harmony by pressing the Zionist claim against Muslim-Arab rights to Palestine." He claims that Christian Arabs "have felt a need to affirm historical Islamic

In a 1908 volume of *al-Manār*, the condition of the Jews is discussed in the course of Rida's Qurʾanic commentary on a verse (Q. 3:112) that describes the "shame" (*adh-dhilla*) and "destitution" (*al-maskana*)[68] with which the Jews have been punished for having "persistently disbelieved in God's revelation and killed prophets without any right." The first condition, "shame," writes Rida, "has been removed from them [the Jews] in the Muslim countries and, more recently, in European countries as well (except, that is, for Russia), with laws that granted equality to all residents." To be sure, "they have enemies in Europe." Among these enemies, there are those in Germany who "might withhold the title 'German' from them [the Jews] and designate them [simply] as 'Jew.' "[69] In Rida's view, the Jews in Islamic lands have lived without the veil of "shame" under which they were forced to endure in Europe. The recent improvements in the condition of European Jewry do not constitute a model for the way in which Jews ought to be treated under Islamic rule, but comprise merely a long-delayed "catching up" on the part of Europe to the more decent, tolerant policies and attitudes under Islam.

The questions of religious tolerance and the place of Jews (as well as Christians) in the Islamic ordering of the modern world came to the fore in the early twentieth century. This was due in large measure to the increased interaction between Muslims and non-Muslims, especially Europeans, whom many Muslims viewed as possessing certain knowledge and skills that could not, or should not, be denigrated and dismissed.[70] In 1910 a Tunisian scholar wrote to *al-Manār* to inquire about Rida's views on the status of Jews and Christians after the advent of Islam. The questioner expresses surprise at Rida's earlier suggestion that in order for a person to be redeemed, Islam demands "faith in God and in the Last Day, and good deeds," regardless of the practitioner's nation, historical era, or geographical location. This Tunisian respondent

---

tolerance of the non-Muslim for their own sake" and points to Emile Zaydan's *al-Yahūd fī at-tārīkh* (*al-Hilāl* 22:4 [January 1914], 243–56) as evidence. Cohen concludes with his own "suspicion" that "the author wished to praise Islam for providing a more comfortable home for the Jews than did Christendom, with a hoped-for continued Muslim tolerance of Arab Christians in mind." While this suspicion may be correct, I have found no evidence in Zaydan's writings to substantiate it. Rather, I would suggest that Zaydan was simply rehearsing here the commonly accepted narrative of the alternative experiences of the Jews under Islam versus those in Christendom. Cohen, *Under Crescent and Cross*, 3–8, 205n.15.

[68] For these two terms, I follow the translation of Yūsuf ʿAlī, *The Meaning of the Holy Qurʾan.*

[69] *al-Manār* 10:11 (January 1908), 814.

[70] See Hourani, *Arabic Thought in the Liberal Age, 1798–1939*. See also Commins, *Islamic Reform.*

contends that, from his perspective, Islam requires "belief in God and in the Last Day, *as well as faith in [His] messengers* [*ar-rusul*]." As such, one who believed in Moses and Jesus before the advent of "our prophet" Muhammad was, "beyond a doubt," a Muslim. But does Rida truly think, asks this reader, that a contemporary twentieth-century Jew or Christian will be redeemed if he "believes in God and in the Last Day, and performs good deeds" but "rejects that which was revealed to Muhammad"?[71] The reader wishes to understand how Rida could consider a Jew or a Christian to be deserving of redemption in the afterlife when he denies the legitimacy of "the seal of the prophets," Islam's Muhammad.

In his reply, Rida appeals to the writings of an early Islamic exegete, Muhammad ibn Jarir at-Tabari (838–923). Rida cites the story of a meeting among Jews, Christians, and Muslims, each professing the superiority of their own religion. The Jews say that "our religion is better than yours, for our religion preceded yours, and our scripture preceded yours, and our prophet preceded yours. Ours is the religion of Abraham." They conclude from this that "only those who are Jewish will enter paradise." The Christians, the tale follows, say the same thing concerning their own religion. Finally, the Muslims assert that "our book came after yours and our prophet followed yours. You were instructed to follow us and leave your religion." Therefore, reckon the Muslims, "only those who follow our religion will enter paradise." At the climax of the story, God joins the conversation and reveals the Qur'anic passage (Q. 4:123–25):

> It will not be according to your hopes or those of the People of the Book: anyone who does wrong will be requited for it and will find no one to protect or help him against God; anyone, male or female, who does good deeds and is a believer, will enter Paradise and will not be wronged by as much as the dip in a date stone. Who could be better in religion than those who direct themselves wholly to God, do good, and follow the religion of Abraham, who was true in faith? God took Abraham as a friend.[72]

Rida takes this story as evidence that the Qur'an "has conditioned entry into paradise and happiness in the afterlife upon faith and good deeds while denying boasting between the People of the Book and the Muslims."[73] Rida articulates an Islamic argument for religious toleration

[71] *al-Manār* 13:8 (1910), 572.

[72] Rida does not provide the full Qur'anic passage here but cites the beginning and end with the equivalent of an ellipsis ("—until his words—") in the middle.

[73] *al-Manār* 13:8 (1910), 573.

that mirrors certain eighteenth- and nineteenth-century European Enlightenment writings.[74] Late Ottoman Palestine's intellectuals, especially those Muslim elites such as Ruhi al-Khalidi, must be understood in the context of an Islamic world in which one of the most renowned and respected Islamic scholars of his day would not only argue for religious toleration but also insist that there is room for Jews and Christians in heaven.

Rida at once disparages European anti-Jewish persecution—viewing it as decidedly un-Islamic—and yet, similar to al-Khalidi, explains it in such a way that suggests it is understandable and perhaps even the fault of the Jews themselves. In 1903 Rida wrote at length about the Jews in a passage that links a number of themes already discussed in this chapter:

> The people of Israel are unique among the peoples of the world in the tenacity of their religious bond and their racial solidarity [*tamassukihi bi-r-rābaṭa al-milliyya wa-l-ʿaṣabiyya al-jinsiyya*]. They like to and try to divert toward themselves all of the advantages of the peoples among whom they live. Were it not for the fact that they believe that their religion is exclusively for them and thus they do not have to proselytize, they would try to turn all of the religions back to it [Judaism] with the [same] determination with which they try to transform the strengths of all of the people to the benefit of the Children of Israel. All of this—were it not for its excessiveness—are excellent qualities. However, excessive self-love, just like insufficient self-love, is

[74] Cf. Gotthold Ephraim Lessing's play *Nathan the Wise* (1779). On Rida's place within the Nahḍa, the Arab Enlightenment, see Hourani, *Arabic Thought in the Liberal Age, 1798–1939*, 222–43. Hourani points to Rida's attempts to revise and moderate certain conventional rulings in Islam. Related to the issue of religious freedom, Hourani writes of Rida's position on Muslim religious apostasy. Rida, Hourani explains, "gave up the traditional view that the Muslim who abandoned Islam should necessarily be put to death. Instead, he made a distinction between the apostate who revolts against Islam and is therefore a threat to the *umma*, and him who abandons it quietly as an individual: the first should be put to death if captured, the second not. His reasoning in favor of this conclusion shows the principles of his thought. The condemnation of the apostate to death is supported, it is true, by the unanimous *ijmaʿ* of the jurists; but one must go beyond this, and ask if the *ijmaʿ* is based on a clear text of the Qurʾan or not. In this case, there is no text of the Qurʾan stating that all apostates should be killed; on the contrary, there is a text [Qurʾan 2:256] condemning all compulsion in religion (*lā ikrāh fī ad-dīn*). The *ijmaʿ* is therefore in contradiction with the principles of Islam, and must be rejected." Ibid., 237. Hourani shows the way in which Rida similarly limited other Islamic concepts and practices, such as that of jihād. For more recent studies of Rida's perspective on other religions, see Ryad, *Islamic Reformism and Christianity*; Wood, *Christian Criticisms, Islamic Proofs*. On the relationship between Jews and the Nahḍa, see Levy, "Jewish Writers in the Arab East."

> harmful. For this reason, we find that this people is oppressed by all peoples and nations that do not extend to it the tolerance of the Muslims. Have you not seen that those who have been expelled by countries and evicted from their lands overwhelmingly have found refuge only in the countries of the Ottoman Empire, even in Palestine, where they seek to become independent and establish a new state?[75]

Here, Rida first alludes to the dual definition of the Jews, considering them to be linked by both a "religious bond" and "racial solidarity." This twofold tie that binds the Jews together, Rida claims, is exceptionally strong, and he appears to admire this. However, his is far from a philosemitic proclamation. After all, the Jews are characterized not only by a deep sense of unity but also by greed, an "excessive self-love" that leads them to try to channel everything of value they find among other peoples toward themselves. Writing in strikingly psychological terms, Rida asserts that "just like insufficient self-love," an overabundance of self-love is also harmful. And it is this excessive, harmful self-love among Jews that, in Rida's rendering, accounts for the way Jews are treated by non-Muslims rather than any condemnable Christian inclination toward intolerance. Though Rida is not advocating anti-Jewish persecution, this explanation of the phenomenon treads closely to a justification. Muslims, by contrast, owing to their deep-seated quality of "tolerance," have dealt more favorably with the Jews, despite the latter's loathsome behavior. It is for this reason, concludes Rida, that Jews have so frequently fled from non-Muslim countries and sought refuge in the lands of Islam. For the moment, let us leave aside Rida's passing reference to Palestine and the Zionist movement; we might simply note that, in these revealing lines, he portrays Zionism as fitting into a broader pattern within Jewish history, a movement of overly self-interested Jews from non-Muslim countries migrating toward the lands of Islam because of the relative tolerance found there.

Rida's premise of Jewish self-interest as the cause of antisemitism was followed by a more developed theory of the Jewish psyche by a different author in *al-Hilāl* in 1906. The context this time was not a Qur'anic commentary, as was typically the case in Rida's *al-Manār*, but a lead story on what these journals found to be the ever-intriguing

[75] *al-Manār* 6:5 (May 1903), 196. In this discursive context, the term *jinsī* seems most appropriately translated as racial. Sylvia Haim has read this passage as evidence that Rida "sometimes imputed to the Jews the faults with thich they are usually taxed." Haim, "Arabic Antisemitic Literature," 309.

Rothschild banking family.[76] This article, "The House of Rothschild: The Most Renowned Financial House in Europe," was part of a series on "The Most Famous Events and Most Important People." After a general introduction on the subject of wealth, the author turns to the topic of "The Jews and Wealth," implying from the start not only that the Rothschilds were a Jewish family, but that their Jewishness was relevant to their financial position. At the opening of this section, the author identifies Jews in positive terms: "The Jews are among the oldest and most intelligent peoples [*shuʿūb*]." The author next offers a barebones narrative of Jewish history, revealing those aspects he deems to be most important. The Jews, he explains, "had a state in antiquity, and some of them were distinguished as judges, kings, and prophets." Eventually the Jews' "sovereignty was wrested from them" and "their city (Jerusalem) was destroyed." The result was that "they were exiled throughout God's lands, leaving them without a country or a government." Until this point, the narrative reads very much like a Jewish nationalist appraisal of Jewish history: a glorious period of Jewish sovereignty that came to a cataclysmic end and was followed by a period defined by the absence of a country and of sovereignty.

For this *al-Hilāl* author, though, Jewish history in the Diaspora was principally characterized by the pursuit of wealth. In his assessment of the Jewish people's perseverance to cohere even in exile, the author considers the Jews' "intelligence, ambition, and courage" to be traits that kept them from reaching the same fate as "many ancient nations that grew old and then assimilated among living, youthful nations and thereby perished and disappeared." To survive as a people in exile, the Jews transformed themselves into "a religious community [*jamāʿat ad-dīn*]," the unity of which was only enhanced by "oppression [at the hands] of other nations." Having "despaired of achieving sovereignty," Jews in the Diaspora "directed their intelligence and interests toward the accumulation of wealth." The Jews' single-minded focus on money is thus linked directly to their loss of sovereignty. Deeming unrealistic any hope of the restoration of Jewish sovereignty, Jews sought power through a means that did not require a state. Over many generations, they developed the "skills" of wealth acquisition that ultimately made them, in this author's estimation, "the nation most capable of gaining wealth."[77] This phenomenon was discernible, the author contends,

[76] This was not the first time *al-Hilāl* published an article on "the House of Rothschild." See, e.g., the brief report on "the origin of the House of Rothschild," focusing on the six purported elements of Amschel Rothschild's will to his children, *al-Hilāl* (1904–1905), 492.

[77] *al-Hilāl* (October 1906), 5–6.

"even during the pre-Islamic era."[78] Indeed, soon after the Jews' arrival in the Arabian Peninsula, to which they fled from "Roman oppression," "commerce and money-changing were virtually their monopolies." And the situation was much the same, the author explains, in Iraq, Syria (ash-Shām), and Egypt.

While for Rida, as we saw above, a primary cause of antisemitism was the Jews' excessive self-interest, this *al-Hilāl* author explains the widespread hatred of Jews in a related but somewhat more sympathetic way. "It is possible," the article suggests, that the Jews' "wealth was one of the most significant reasons for their persecution, due to envy and jealousy." As opposed to attributing anti-Jewish sentiment to a negative quality of Jews, the author instead blames non-Jews' "envy and jealousy." The Jews' "enemies poured wrath upon their [the Jews'] religion and seized, expelled, and killed them." Though the Jews' wealth was a target of gentile jealousy, those responsible for the hatred and violence were the coveters, not the coveted.

Though the *al-Hilāl* author and Rida differed in their apparent degree of sympathy toward the Jews and in their explanations of the Jews' persecution, they agreed in one important regard. In the minds of both the Muslim Rida and the writer for the Christian-edited *al-Hilāl*,[79] the Jewish experience under Islamic rule was fundamentally distinct from (and superior to) that under non-Muslim domination. The Jewish condition was so grave in the pre-Islamic Middle East, writes *al-Hilāl*'s author, "that when Islam arrived, they [the Jews] saw in it relief for themselves, and they assisted the Muslims in their goals and helped them with the means of conquest." In turn, the Muslims "were kind" to the Jews; "they became close with them and many [Jews under Islamic rule] were distinguished in science and politics even though their endeavors were mostly devoted to trade, money-changing, and usury." Indeed, the author explains, they constituted a number of the famous financial houses in the Abbasid state in Iraq, the Fatimid state in Egypt, and the Umayyad state in Andalusia. In contrast to this remarkably comfortable coexistence within the Islamic realm, the Jews of Europe

> continued to suffer persecution under the rule of Christian kings to the point that oftentimes official orders were issued to take their money, burn their books, and expel them, based on charges that were mostly fabrications. Some of these accusations are still leveled [against them] until the present day, such as the charge of kidnapping Christian children, poisoning drinking wells and the

[78] Literally: the period of Arab "ignorance."

[79] As this article was anonymous, the religious affiliation of its author is unknown.

> like. The Jews did not bear this disgrace patiently but rather conspired against their enemies with various tricks for which there is no space here.[80]

According to the *al-Hilāl* author, anti-Jewish persecution was (and remained) a distinctly Christian and European phenomenon, one wholly foreign to Islam. Overall the author is highly critical of Christian Europe's persecution of Jews, though his claim that it was "based on charges that were *mostly* fabrications" suggests that, in his mind, perhaps not *all* the accusations were unwarranted. While the author contends that Jews were not altogether faultless in their relations with European Christians, he interprets Jews' "tricks" as a *reaction* to antisemitism, not its cause—a stark contrast to Rida's perspective. For this *al-Hilāl* author, the cure for antisemitism is not Islam—the journal was, after all, edited by a Christian[81]—but "modern civilization" and the "spirit of individual freedom." Once these ideals reached parts of Europe in the modern period and Jews "were granted their civil and personal rights and freedom of occupation," they were able to achieve success in many areas of public life, most prominently in finance. (With this the author returns to the subject of his article, the Rothschilds.[82])

These two articles—the first in Rida's *al-Manār* and the second in Zaydan's *al-Hilāl*—are suggestive of a consensus spanning the spectrum of Muslim and Christian fin de siècle Arabic writers on the fundamentally superior treatment of Jews by Muslims than by Christians. (To be sure, many Jewish writers of the period shared this view.[83]) For an article published in a journal edited by a Muslim, it is perhaps unsurprising that this view is expressed unabashedly. However, in a journal edited by a Christian, this forthright statement of Islam as inherently more tolerant than Christianity is remarkable.

Tolerance as a Quality of Islam or of Arabs?

Not every Christian-edited journal, however, was apparently satisfied with the wholesale criticism of Christendom that was implied by this comparison between the treatment of the Jews under Islam and those under Christendom. *Al-Muqtaṭaf* proposed a more nuanced stance on the question. In "The Jews of France," its 1913 article cited above, the

80 *al-Hilāl* (October 1906), 6.

81 Though not only Christians wrote for or read *al-Hilāl*, this is not the forum in which one would find explicitly proselytizing arguments on behalf of Islam.

82 *al-Hilāl* (October 1906), 6.

83 See chapter 3 and Cohen, *Under Crescent and Cross.*

discussion extends beyond France and into Europe more broadly. The history of Europe's Jews, the author explains, was comparable to, or even worse than, that of French Jewry. The only exception, notably, is the history of the Jews "in Spain during the period of Arab rule," where Jews were treated "like all other residents, and famous scholars and doctors arose from among them." At first glance, this highlighting of Spain in the medieval period, i.e., when Muslims ruled, appears entirely consistent with the distinctions drawn in *al-Manār* and *al-Hilāl*. However, it is critical to note the terminology the author uses here. The benevolent treatment that Jews received in medieval Spain occurred "during the period of *Arab* rule," not *Muslim* rule. In other words, tolerance, for this author, was an Arab quality rather than a Muslim one (that is, a quality belonging to Christian Arabs no less than to Muslim Arabs).

The author then compares the status of Jews in different Christian countries. Lest readers associate anti-Jewish persecution exclusively with Catholics (such as those of France), he insists that "the Protestants were no more tolerant than were the Catholics." In fact, "the opposite was the case." For instance, "the situation [of the Jews] in Italy was always superior to their situation in the Protestant countries." Supporting this contention, the author notes: "In 1588, Pope Sixtus V abrogated all the orders of his predecessors to oppress them [the Jews]. He permitted them to live and trade in all the lands that submit to his rule and to observe their religious rituals without harassment. He made them equal to the rest of his subjects in their rights and obligations."[84] The author presents a fascinating and revealing interpretation of Jews' distinct experiences in the various regions of their Diaspora.

[84] *al-Muqtaṭaf* 43:6 (December 1913), 564. Cf. Heinrich Graetz, *History of the Jews*, Vol. 4 (Philadelphia: Jewish Publication Society of America, 1897), 655–656. Graetz writes that "the condition of the Jews in Rome was apparently altered" under Pope Sixtus V (1585–1590). Sixtus V "allowed Jews to be around him, and harbored Lopez, a Jewish refugee from Portugal, who made various suggestions as to the improvement of the finances. He went still further; he issued a bull (October 22, 1586), which did away with almost all the restrictions made by his predecessors. Sixtus not merely granted Jews permission to dwell in all the cities of the Papal States, but also to have intercourse with Christians and employ them as assistants in business. He protected their religious freedom by special provisions." It is certainly possible that this author or others relied on Graetz for their knowledge and interpretation of Jewish history. Graetz's work was introduced into the curriculum of Alliance Israélite Universelle schools in the Middle East as early as 1892–1893. See Rodrigue, *French Jews, Turkish Jews*, 83; Rodrigue, *Jews and Muslims*, 110. Especially given Graetz's espousal of the "myth of the interfaith utopia" in Islam, his writings might well have served as a critical source for some of the authors of these Arabic journal articles. On Graetz and the "myth of the interfaith utopia," see Cohen, *Under Crescent and Cross*, 3–4, 203n.3–4.

On the one hand, he acknowledges that they fared better in the Muslim world (most notably Spain) than in Christendom, but when making this comparison, he does not employ religious categories (i.e., Muslims vs. Christians); it was *Arabs* who were more tolerant than *Europeans*. On the other hand, the author obviously recognizes that these ethnic (or perhaps, in the language of the day, "racial") groups have various religious affiliations, and he is keen to dissociate Catholicism (as in France) from anti-Jewish persecution. In this sense, he appears eager to portray Catholicism more sympathetically than Protestantism. While one may suspect that this inclination is tied more to the author's own religious affiliations (perhaps he was a Catholic) than to his understanding of the historical record, it is necessary to recall that at least the editors of *al-Muqtaṭaf* were converts to Protestantism.[85] In any case, what we have found in this article is, specifically, a *Christian* Arab (and perhaps more precisely a *non-Protestant* Christian Arab) version of the theory accounting for the distinctions in how Jews have been treated in their Diasporas. The author maneuvers through his knowledge of Jewish history to portray Jews as better off under both Arab and Catholic rule, while subtly leaving Islam out of the equation altogether.[86]

Defending Judaism against Libel

Though the consensus among these Arabic journals held that Jews were treated more favorably under Islam (or under Arab rule) than in Christian Europe, Judaism was generally treated more respectfully by the two Christian-edited journals analyzed here than by Rida's *al-Manār*. Indeed, the editors of *al-Muqtaṭaf* and *al-Hilāl* frequently went out of their way to defend the Jewish religion against defamation. Such defenses often came in response to ritual murder accusations that arose periodically in Europe and the Middle East. In 1903, for instance, a reader from the American city of Worcester[87] wrote to the editors of *al-Muqtaṭaf*, noting that "newspapers write constantly of Jews murdering children and draining their blood to fulfill certain religious duties." The reader inquires, "Is this true?" The editors' answer is brief (only seven short lines) but forceful. "The Jewish religion," they assert, "is

[85] Asher Kaufman claims that they had converted from Maronism. See Kaufman, *Reviving Phoenicia*, 41. However, Rashid Khalidi noted, in private correspondence, that they came from the Marjeyoun region where there was no Maronite community. Khalidi contends that they were originally Greek Orthodox or Catholic.

[86] *al-Muqtaṭaf* 43:6 (December 1913), 564.

[87] Presumably, this refers to the city in Massachusetts, though there are places by the same name in New York, Vermont, Wisconsin, Maryland, and Pennsylvania as well.

built upon the Torah and there is nothing in the Torah that requires or permits the murder of children for a religious purpose." The editors then address the root of such allegations. "For those who envy and despise the Jews," they write, "these accusations are easily leveled and are, with little difficulty, believed." However, "the evidence that is mustered to prove" these allegations, insists *al-Muqtaṭaf*, "will not convince the fair-minded." Rather, the charges are "baseless" and those who make them should be punished.[88]

Similarly, in 1910–1911, *al-Hilāl* was asked a question about the Jews by a reader in Natchez, Mississippi.[89] This reader had heard that Jews took "the blood of a Christian to add it to their matzah" for Passover,[90] and that "this is one of the laws of their religion." The reader considered these claims unlikely and wished to consult with *al-Hilāl*. The editor begins his answer by noting that he had been asked a similar question fifteen years earlier and published a discussion on the topic then. The journal concluded then that the "alleged horrors to which you alluded" are simply

> the remnants of superstitions of the Dark Ages, when mutual hatred spread between Christians and Jews and each sect ascribed aspects of indignity upon the other. We do not believe that an entire people [*umma*] would be able to agree to commit such horrors, and especially not the Jewish people [*al-umma al-yahūdiyya*] that was coeval with both ancient and modern civilization, and was the source of law and the foundation of the true religions, particularly after the light of civilization dawned and the rays of freedom and knowledge rose. Incidents such as these are not impossible among some individual Jews just as they are not impossible among non-Jews. However, on the question of whether these horrors are required or permitted by the official religious law, the answer is "no."[91]

Al-Hilāl permits the theoretical possibility that there may be some Jews who engage in horrifying acts such as ritual murder but insists that Jews were no more likely than non-Jews to commit such misdeeds. Importantly, the editors of both *al-Muqtaṭaf* and *al-Hilāl* agree, and state as much with forceful conviction, that the Jewish religion is unequivocally innocent in this regard. But the defense of Judaism, at least as articulated by *al-Hilāl*'s editor, is actually much more significant. Not

[88] *al-Muqtaṭaf* 28:9 (July 1903), 616.

[89] A potentially fruitful area for future research would be an investigation of the participation of American (or Arab American) readers in these Arabic intellectual journals.

[90] Identified here not as Passover but as "the great holiday."

[91] *al-Hilāl* (October 1910–July 1911), 53–54.

only is Judaism not a murderous religion; it is, in fact, "the source of law and the foundation of the true religions." This, to be sure, is a sweeping statement of approval for Judaism, extending far beyond the narrow scope of denying ritual murder charges.

CHALLENGING JUDAISM IN *AL-MANĀR*

Wholesale favorable evaluations of the Jewish religion of the sort found in *al-Hilāl* are generally absent from *al-Manār*, a periodical that was an amalgamation of a religious Qurʾanic commentary and an intellectual journal.[92] The first pages of each edition of *al-Manār* were always composed of a Qurʾanic exegesis, which Rida attributed to *al-ustādh al-imām*, Rida's teacher and mentor Muhammad ʿAbduh. In one such commentary, published in April 1907, Rida accuses the Jews of having "preserved only part of the book that God revealed to them." The rest of the original Torah was lost. Worse yet, Rida asserts, the Jews do not properly fulfill even the portion of the Torah they *have* preserved. Deepening his critique of the Jews and their Torah, Rida adds that "there is no evidence that the five books attributed to Moses, peace be upon him, which they call the Torah, were actually written by Moses or memorized by him." Explicitly invoking the research of European biblical scholars, Rida contends rather that the evidence suggests that these books "were written hundreds of years after him [Moses]." In fact, "there is no evidence that Moses, peace be upon him, knew the Hebrew language; his language, rather, was Egyptian." Where, Rida asks rhetorically, "is the Torah Moses wrote in *that* language and who translated it?"[93]

This insistence that Moses was not the author of the Torah, or, more precisely, that he was not the author of the book the Jews now refer to as the Torah, is familiar to us from al-Khalidi's manuscript.[94] Moreover,

[92] In this regard I differ with Sylvia Haim, who discounts the anti-Jewish references in *al-Manār*. Though Rida "writes of the wealth of the Jews, their meanness, their treacherous relations with the prophet, their danger to the Ottoman Empire, etc.," Haim contends that "this usually occurs in his commentary on the Koran when he is trying to expound some *sura* or *hadith* which refers to the Jews and to illustrate the superiority of Islam over Judaism." Haim, "Arabic Antisemitic Literature," 309. In my view, there is no reason to discount Rida's comments about Jews, whether ancient or contemporary, regardless of the genre of texts in which these comments appear. In a later essay, Haim acknowledges Rida's "ambivalent attitude towards the Jews." Haim, "Islamic Anti-Zionism," 49.

[93] *al-Manār* 10:2 (April 1907), 83.

[94] This, of course, was not an original theory of either Rida or al-Khalidi; the notion that the Torah was not written by Moses has ancient precedents. My point here is simply to highlight that both Rida and al-Khalidi chose this same theme in their early twentieth-century writings about the Jews and Judaism.

the integration of contemporary European biblical scholarship's claims into traditional Islamic anti-Jewish polemics is a phenomenon we also encountered in al-Khalidi's "as-Sayūnīzm." Like al-Khalidi's (generally more subtle) critique of Judaism and the Torah, Rida's assault progresses from what he considers to be the dubious provenance of the Torah to the book's contents and lacunae. "In the books that the Jews possess," alleges Rida, "there is neither promise nor threat of the afterlife [*al-ākhira*]." Rather, the implications of actions in the Jews' scripture are confined to "wealth, fertility, and rule over the land"; punishment, in turn, is limited to the loss of these blessings and "the rule of the nations over them." Al-Khalidi, we recall, notes precisely this same alleged absence in the Torah of a discussion of the afterlife. For al-Khalidi, in his work on Zionism, the implication of this absence was clear: the Zionist movement was all the more to be feared, and actively opposed, given the fact that the *this-worldly* possession of Palestine was the ultimate religious aim of Jews. Rida, who was engaged in a different sort of project in his Qurʾanic commentary, does not immediately link this claim with Zionism (though, as we shall see, Zionism was indeed on his mind). At this point, however, Rida's interest is in a more basic Jewish-Islamic polemic. Islam, he explains, teaches that "every prophet commanded belief in the Last Day."[95] Given this Islamic maxim, Rida supposes that the original Torah also actually included such a belief, but that it was "neglected and forgotten" and thus did not find its way into the contemporary, flawed Torah of the Jews.

Pondering the Prospects of Zionism

Though Rida generally focuses his exegesis on elucidating Qurʾanic passages, contemporary events and problems of his day are often perceptible just beneath the surface. Zionism was one such phenomenon that caught Rida's attention and occupied his interest even as he commented on the Qurʾan. In January 1908, after claiming that Jews no longer experience shame (*adh-dhilla*) in the lands of Islam, Rida asks about the other term of castigation that the Qurʾan (Q. 3:112) attaches to the Jews: *al-maskana*, "destitution." "Might the *maskana* ever disappear from them [the Jews]?" he asks. "Might they, one day, have power and sovereignty?" Rida contends that this question of the potential for Jews to return to power is a complex one.

In setting out to answer the question, Rida begins "from a religious perspective" and explains how Jews, Christians, and Muslims think

[95] *al-Manār* 10:2 (April 1907), 84.

"religiously" about the matter. The Jews, according to Rida, say that the restoration of their glory "has been foretold with the appearance of their 'messiah,' "[96] a term Rida defines as "the one [who brings] dominion and law." For Christians, this messiah is "Jesus Christ the son of Mary, peace be upon him, and the 'dominion' that he brings is 'spiritual dominion' "; that is, the Jews' expectation that a messiah will restore them to *political* sovereignty is misguided. Finally, citing the Gospel of Barnabas,[97] Rida explains that the Muslim position is that "the promised one is Muhammad . . . the one who came with the prophecy that resulted in dominion." The problem with the Jews' interpretation, then, is not its assumption of the *political* nature of the dominion but rather the presumption that it will be *Jewish* political dominion.

Setting aside the "religious perspective," Rida then addresses the issue from a "social point of view." Here he suggests that one must consider the Jews' "dispersion throughout the world as a minority" and the challenges this dispersion would necessarily pose to their prospects of renewed sovereignty in any one place. Moreover, given Jews' "abandonment of the arts and practice of war, and their weakness in agricultural work due to their interest in amassing money from the nearest, most profitable, least difficult source, such as usury," Rida wonders how they might succeed in regaining political power.[98] How might a people that has devoted itself to "usury" suddenly begin a life of agriculture, as would necessarily be demanded, were it to gain a country of its own? Though Zionism is not mentioned here by name, it is clear that Rida's concern about the movement motivated his exploration of the subject in this exegesis.

Two years later, in 1910, Rida developed these views more extensively, still within the framework of his Qurʾanic commentary. He begins again with the contention that the Torah, in the form in which it now exists, is not the true word of God. This time, he offers further details about the process by which the Torah was transformed from the version that God revealed, and he explicitly contrasts Jewish infidelity to their scripture with Muslim faithfulness to theirs. The Jews, he explains, "did not memorize it by heart at the time of its revelation, as we [i.e., Muslims] memorized the Qurʾan, and they did not write many copies of it at first, as we did so that if some copies were lost others would remain." Rather, "the Jews had only one copy of the Torah—the one that Moses . . . wrote—and it was lost." Then, citing his teacher

[96] Rida offers both the Arabic *masīḥ* and the transliteration of the English "messiah."

[97] On this apparently early modern pseudepigraphic text and Rida's Arabic edition of it, see Ryad, *Islamic Reformism and Christianity*, 213–42; and Sidney H. Griffith, "Gospel," EQ.

[98] *al-Manār* 10:11 (January 1908), 814–15.

Muhammad ʿAbduh, Rida explains that Jews abandoned many of the original Torah's laws while adding others that were never commanded. For instance, the Torah "prohibited them from lying, harming people, and taking usury," but, insists Rida (citing ʿAbduh), Jews commit all these offenses. Similarly, "their scholars and leaders added many religious laws, ceremonies, and customs, to which they [Jews] adhere, even though they are not in the Torah nor are they known from Moses, peace be upon him."[99] The Jews' Torah is a corrupted text, argues Rida, and the religious practice that developed among Jews in the subsequent generations veered significantly from that which was originally mandated by God.

As before, but now in a more systematic way, Rida's assault on the authenticity and divinity of the Torah blends traditional Islamic polemics with contemporary European biblical criticism. He refers, for example, to the relationship between the Bible and Hammurabi's Code (which European Egyptologists had unearthed less than a decade earlier in Persia). In the very same paragraph, Rida rehearses the accusation that the Jews removed references to Muhammad that had been found in the original Torah.[100] Later in the article, Rida cites the writings of Rahmat Allah al-Hindi (1818–1891), an Indian Muslim biblical critic[101] who in turn relied on the work of, among others, the British Methodist biblical scholar Adam Clarke (1762–1832). Rida explains Clarke's theory that marginal notes written by subsequent readers of the Torah came to be incorporated into the text itself by even later readers who were unaware of the marginalia's original purpose; these additions came to be regarded as original elements of the Torah.[102] Rida further highlights the theories that attribute to Ezra the Scribe many explanatory phrases found in the Torah and insists that the *taḥrīf* (corruption) of the biblical text is abundantly clear from the many cases of Babylonian terms found in the text. The presence of these terms is taken as evidence that the biblical text could not have been completed before the Babylonian exile.[103] Rida's critique of Judaism and the Jews' Torah is an eclectic assortment of conventional polemical tropes known from the earliest Jewish-Islamic religious encounter along with modern European academic perspectives that together, in Rida's mind, undermined contemporary Jews' claim to an authentic book of God.

[99] *al-Manār* 13:10 (November 1910), 723.

[100] Ibid., 724.

[101] The work cited here is Rahmat Allah ibn Khalil ar-Rahman [al-Hindi], *Iẓhār al-ḥaqq* (Cairo, 1877).

[102] *al-Manār* 13:10 (November 1910), 727. See Clarke, *The Holy Bible, Containing the Old and New Testaments.*

[103] *al-Manār* 13:10 (November 1910), 727.

Even in the course of his own polemic against Judaism, Rida holds fast to the contention that Jews were treated more favorably under Islam than in Christendom. He notes that the Islamic conquest of "Syria, Palestine, and then Andalusia" benefited the Jews, freeing them from "Christian oppression." They continued to be oppressed in Russia and Spain "because the governments there were religious." The Jews thus "conspired, and still conspire, in the name of freedom and civilization, to remove the influence of the Christian religion from these two states."[104] As evidence, Rida cites Jewish involvement in the recent revolutions in Russia and Spain.[105] As we shall see, when Rida writes that Jews "conspire" to bring down various Western governments, ostensibly "in the name of freedom and civilization," his real concern is a parallel "conspiracy" in which he believes Jews have been engaged, a conspiracy much closer to home and of much greater consequence to his readers: the 1908 Young Turk Revolution against the Ottoman sultan.

Rida does not argue that the Jews are opposed, in principle, to *religious* rule. They are opposed, rather, to *non-Jewish* religious rule. Indeed, their aim is to establish Jewish religious domination. Jews "revolt against anyone who resists [their efforts] to establish a religious government [*sulṭa dīniyya*] of their own," asserts Rida. It is for *this* reason that they "had a hand in the Ottoman [Young Turk] Revolution, not because they were oppressed or persecuted in the Ottoman Empire." After all, they were so secure in the Ottoman Empire that "they fled to it from persecution in Russia and elsewhere."[106] Thus, Rida reasons, their opposition to the Ottoman sultan's government was due to its opposition to the Jews' efforts to create their own religious state.

It is at this point that Rida openly directs his comments to the subject of Zionism. Jews participated in the Young Turk Revolution, he insists, "because they want[ed] to rule Jerusalem [*bayt al-muqaddas*] and its environs, and to establish Israelite sovereignty there." The Ottoman sultan's government had sought to prohibit Jews from acquiring land in Palestine, and, Rida hastens to add, any land purchases that Jews did manage to carry out were accomplished "through subterfuge, bribery, and other monetary schemes." As a result, Rida charges, Jews helped carry out the Young Turk Revolution that overthrew the sultan, and they are assisting the new government in an effort to realize their own aims. Rida then implores "the Ottoman nation [*al-umma al-ʿuthmāniyya*]" to recognize that "the danger of their influence is great

[104] Ibid., 725.

[105] Rida presumably refers here to the Russian Revolution of 1905 and Spain's so-called Glorious Revolution of 1868.

[106] *al-Manār* 13:10 (November 1910), 725.

and immediate." The Jews are, after all, "a nation [*qawm*] that engages in excessive usury." Through their deception and money, the Jews have been able to control France "like a ball in their hands and end the rule of the Church"—despite the fact that France stands at "the pinnacle of science, civilization, politics, wealth, and power." How much more facilely, Rida warns, will Jews be able to dominate the Ottoman government, given its state of "ignorance and weakness and its need for money."

Before returning to his discussion of the corruption of the Torah, Rida allows himself one further remark on contemporary events: a warning, or threat, concerning the consequences of Zionism's success. The Jews' desire to rule Palestine is so intense, and the danger so alarming, because "Jerusalem [bayt al-muqaddas] holds great importance for both Muslims and Christians." If Jews succeed in gaining control there, Rida contends, "they will establish Israelite sovereignty and transform the al-Aqsa Mosque (the Temple of Solomon)—which is the direction they face when praying[107]—into a temple exclusively for them." And this, Rida suspects, will "ignite the fires of riots, prophesied clearly in the traditions regarding the End of Days." Rida insists that "the Ottoman nation [*al-umma al-ʿuthmāniyya*] must strive to prevent" this Jewish attempt to gain control over Palestine. If not, "this will prove lethal to Ottoman power, may God protect us."[108] And with this, Rida resumes his exegetical discourse on a Qurʾanic sura that deals with the Jews' corruption of their scripture.

For Rida, Zionism represents the Jewish effort to replace the al-Aqsa Mosque with a new Jewish temple. Jews are willing to use any means at their disposal, and in particular illicit, sinister financial means, to gain control of Palestine. Rida portrays the potential consequences of Zionist success in terrifying, explicitly eschatological terms. Critical to note here is that for Rida, as for al-Khalidi, the Zionist movement was a religious phenomenon—i.e., Zionists were acting out of religious motivations[109]—and, especially for an Islamic scholar such as Rida, the movement was most appropriately understood and assessed through a Qurʾanic exegetical lens.

One month later, in *al-Manār*'s final issue of 1910, Rida once more turned to the subject of Zionism in his opening Qurʾanic commentary. He writes not only of the Jews' desire "to restore their dominion

[107] *al-masjid al-aqṣā (haykal Sulaymān) wa-huwa qiblatuhum.* Clearly, al-Khalidi's equation of the al-Aqsa Mosque and the Temple of Solomon, discussed in chapter 2, was not entirely idiosyncratic in this historical and cultural context.

[108] *al-Manār* 13:10 (November 1910), 726.

[109] Al-Khalidi, however, viewed the movement as a violation of the *proper* understanding of modern Judaism, as we saw in chapter 2.

to Jerusalem and its surroundings" but also of their intentions to "evict the Muslims and Christians from that holy land and to leave them with nothing." The Jews have sought to accomplish this mass eviction of Palestine's natives—identified, significantly, in religious categories—by "cutting off the means of livelihood" from non-Jews. Because of the financial assistance of the Jews' political and philanthropic organizations, Jews are able to work, Rida claims, at lower prices than non-Jews, and thus exclude Christians and Muslims from the workforce.[110]

Rida again addresses the question he expected to be on readers' minds: will the Jews succeed in their ambition of "restoring their dominion" in Palestine? To the disappointment, no doubt, of his readers in Palestine, the Qur'anic verse under analysis in this issue of *al-Manār* leaves such an eventuality as an open question. "The verse neither confirms nor denies it," Rida explains, though there are numerous factors militating against the realization of the Jews' goals, especially those he had already mentioned in his earlier commentaries: "they are scattered and consumed with their money in all countries," and they lack "abilities in war and agriculture." Nonetheless, insists Rida, Jews "believe with religious faith that they will eventually establish sovereignty in the Holy Land."[111] In other words, while this Qur'anic verse lacks assurances of the ultimate success or failure of Zionism, Jews themselves are certain, with *religious* faith, that they will eventually achieve their aims. Because of this religious certainty, and the Jews' consequent decisive moves toward achieving their Zionist ambitions, Ottoman citizens must take the threat seriously. The Jews "have already amassed a great deal of money" for these purposes, writes Rida, who concludes his commentary on the Qur'anic phrase with this exhortation: "the Ottomans must not give them [the Jews] power over Palestine, nor should they facilitate their purchase of its land and their mass immigration to it." This movement represents "a great danger,"[112] insists Rida, "as we have recently warned in the exegesis of the previous verses."[113]

110 *al-Manār* 13:11 (December 1910), 806. It is typically assumed that Jewish immigrant laborers demanded higher wages than Palestine's non-Jewish population. If this particular aspect of Rida's accusation is correct, i.e., if Jews were indeed working for lower pay than their non-Jewish neighbors in Palestine, this would require a significant revision of the commonly held views of the economic relations between Zionists and Arabs in the Late Ottoman period. On labor issues during this period, see Shafir, *Land, Labor, and the Origins of the Israeli-Palestinian Conflict, 1882–1914*.

111 *al-Manār*, 13:11 (December 1910), 806.

112 *khaṭaran kabīran*. Cf. the term used by *ha-Ḥerut* to describe the anti-Zionist press in Palestine and beyond (*ha-sakanah ha-gedolah*).

113 *al-Manār* 13:11 (December 1910), 806.

While Rida argues forcefully against Zionism, he, like al-Khalidi, does not cast doubt on the fundamental Jewish historical claim that, in antiquity, a Jewish state existed in Palestine. Even in the course of polemicizing against the Jews, Rida consistently accepts this historical assertion. For instance, in September 1907 Rida's Qurʾanic commentary confronted "the two great specious arguments that the Jews used against Islam." The first concerns the Jews' alleged accusation that Muhammad could not possibly be part of the prophetic tradition of Abraham, given that Muhammad sanctioned the consumption of foods—such as camel meat—prohibited in this tradition. The second "specious argument" relates to Muhammad's privileging of Mecca over Jerusalem. "God promised Abraham that his blessing would come in the progeny of his son Isaac," claimed the Jews, "and all of the prophets from Isaac's seed privileged Jerusalem and prayed toward it." Jews are thus alleged to have reasoned that if Muhammad were truly part of this tradition, he too would have favored Jerusalem; by selecting Mecca as his *qibla* (direction of prayer), "he contradicted all of them."[114] The answer Rida cites to the latter accusation is that

> the Sacred House,[115] to which we direct our prayers, was the first building that was made a temple for man. It was built by Abraham and his son Ishmael, peace be upon them, exclusively for worship. Then, the al-Aqsa Mosque [al-masjid al-aqṣā[116]] was built in Jerusalem [bayt al-muqaddas[117]] centuries later by Solomon the son of David. . . . It is thus correct that Muhammad was [part] of the religious community [*al-milla*] of Abraham and in his worship he faced [the same place] where Abraham and his son Ishmael had faced.[118]

In this passage, Rida exhibits no interest in denying the Israelite link to Jerusalem. Like al-Khalidi and other Muslim intellectuals of his day, Rida freely acknowledges that the Temple was built by the Israelite king Solomon, as recounted in the Bible and in Islamic tradition, even if Rida chooses to refer to the Temple as al-masjid al-aqṣā, the distinctively Qurʾanic name for Jerusalem's central sanctuary.[119] Rida opposed

[114] *al-Manār* 10:7 (September 1907), 482.

[115] This title is used to refer to the Kaʿba in Mecca.

[116] Literally: "the furthest place of worship."

[117] Literally: "the Holy Temple."

[118] *al-Manār* 10:8 (September 1907), 485.

[119] Rida often identified the Temple of Solomon with the al-Aqsa Mosque. In 1903, in his discussion of the secret Masonic associations, Rida explained that the founders included Jews and Christians, and, as a result, its symbols are taken from their "shared book called the Holy Bible" and the founders "traced these [symbols] back to the

Zionism because it threatened to dislodge Muslims and Christians from Palestine and to replace the al-Aqsa Mosque with a new Jewish temple. He questioned aspects of the Jews' religion, to be sure—even aspects as fundamental as the provenance of their Torah—but he took for granted that Jews once had a sovereign state in Palestine.

The Bible in *al-Hilāl* and *al-Muqtaṭaf*

Like Rida in *al-Manār*, the editors of *al-Hilāl* and *al-Muqtaṭaf* were keenly interested in the Bible. As Christians in less overtly sectarian journals, however, they approached the text in a way that was rather different from Rida's approach. They frequently reported on contemporary scholarship and discoveries that either confirmed or cast doubt on biblical claims. In July 1906, for instance, *al-Muqtaṭaf* presented a six-page article called "The Exodus and Number of the Children of Israel." The article is a selective summary of a chapter by Egyptologist and archaeologist W. M. Flinders Petrie in the newly published *Researches in Sinai.*[120] The chapter, "The Conditions of the Exodus," argues that the number of Israelites generally believed to have departed Egypt in the biblical Exodus is grossly exaggerated. Among the different proofs cited, *al-Muqtaṭaf* mentions the claims that there is no archaeological evidence for the Exodus, that sources suggest that the Israelites were in Palestine (not Egypt) at the time of the Exodus, and that the Sinai Peninsula does not contain enough water to sustain the millions of people and their animals that, according to the traditional view, fled Egypt with Moses.

If one initially suspects that this article aims to argue that the entire Exodus story was a nonhistorical fabrication, and thus to undermine an important element of the Jews' historical claim to Palestine, one soon realizes that this is not the intention of Petrie or *al-Muqtaṭaf*'s editors. Instead, Petrie proposes a theory that interprets the census numbers offered in the Bible in a radically different way, reading the Hebrew word typically rendered "thousands" instead as "tents," that is, families, thus yielding only a small fraction of the number of Israelites traditionally believed to have participated in the Exodus. Petrie's opinion in this "most difficult question," *al-Muqtaṭaf* predicts, is likely to be "rejected and discredited" by "most religious biblical scholars." Such scholars, *al-Muqtaṭaf* writes derisively, routinely "reject any new idea,"

---

construction of the Holy Temple, the Temple of Solomon, peace be upon him. This is the al-Aqsa Mosque." *al-Manār* 6:5 (May 1903), 197.

[120] Petrie and Currelly, *Researches in Sinai.*

but "it is not long before they return to it and accept it."[121] The author finds Petrie's theory—that many fewer Israelites actually entered Palestine in the biblically recounted Exodus than is generally believed—to be compelling and anticipates that it will eventually gain wide acceptance. This particular view, to which the journal offers such extensive space and attention, is interesting in that it at once challenges traditional beliefs about the Bible while still accepting (through reinterpretation) the Bible's literal claims.

To be sure, these journals also often highlighted what contributors believed to be confirmatory evidence of traditional biblical claims. Several examples might suffice. In 1895 *al-Muqtaṭaf* offered a brief note on "The History of the Torah." The author cited an article from the English *Fortnightly Review*, which contended that archeological discoveries in Egypt, Assyria, and Canaan had proved that, "in contrast to what biblical critics say," the Children of Israel were literate before they settled the Land of Canaan. Apparently responding to assertions that Moses could not have written the Bible owing to his and his people's illiteracy, the *al-Muqtaṭaf* article declares that "the attribution of the Five Books to Moses is no more unreasonable than its attribution to anyone else."[122] A decade later, in 1906, *al-Muqtaṭaf* published an article on "The Excavation of the Antiquities of Palestine." Here the author reports on the recently convened annual meeting of the Palestine Exploration Fund in London and recounts the speech of its director, R. A. Stewart Macalister, on the discoveries in the ancient city of Gezer. The article emphasizes the implications of these excavations for an understanding of the death of the biblical figure of Samson and mentions, inter alia, the unearthing of the fortress of Simon the Maccabee.[123] In 1912–1913, *al-Hilāl* published a brief article on the origins of the Philistines, the people mentioned in the Bible who "resided in Palestine and against whom the Israelites fought." Recent research "conducted by the English scientific expedition," *al-Hilāl* reports, "has shown that their origins are in the island of Crete."[124] A 1913 piece in *al-Muqtaṭaf*, also translated from an English-language journal, discusses archaeological discoveries in Jericho, Samaria, Jerusalem, and the Mount of Olives. The author relates the Jericho findings to the story of Rahab

[121] *al-Muqtaṭaf* 31:7 (July 1906), 541.

[122] *al-Mutaṭaf* 19:21 (November 1895), 876.

[123] *al-Muqtaṭaf* 31:7 (July 1906), 614.

[124] *al-Hilāl* (October 1912–July 1913), 444. There appears to be a typographical error here, as the article actually indicates that the Philistines came from the "newspaper" (*jarīda*) of Crete rather than the "island" (*jazīra*).

in the biblical book of Joshua.[125] At least some *al-Muqtaṭaf* writers not only accepted the historicity of biblical narratives but were eager to show that there was compelling, "scientific" reason to do so.[126]

On the other hand, the journals' editors and writers did not uniformly accept the historicity of biblical accounts. One *al-Hilāl* reader in 1907 inquired of the journal's editors as to whether they had found "in the history of ancient Egypt anything that corroborates the Torah's writings about the stories of Joseph and Moses." This prompted an extended discussion in which the editors cite, among others, the ancient Christian and Jewish authors Eusebius and Josephus from Palestine and concede that the archaeological evidence is wanting.[127] Similarly, in a review of a 1907 book by the British orientalist scholar David Samuel Margoliouth, *Cairo, Jerusalem, and Damascus*, *al-Muqtaṭaf* notes that "though the Torah records the history of the Jews and their ancestors in detail, from Creation until around the time of Christ [*al-masīḥ*]," nonsectarian historians ("neither Jewish nor Christian nor adherents of any other religious community") "treat the Torah's historical accounts as they do the historiographical writing of Herodotus." That is to say, such historians "only accept from either [the Bible and Herodotus] that which is corroborated by [archaeological] remains, conforms to reason, and does not contradict science." In their work, explains *al-Muqtaṭaf*, these historians are comparable to "doctors, astronomers, chemists, and physicists."[128] For this reviewer, Margoliouth, described as "our dear friend, professor of Arabic at Oxford University," represented a biblical scholarly approach that (quite rightly, in this reviewer's opinion) refused to presuppose the accuracy or historicity of the biblical text.

Al-Muqtaṭaf's discussion of this work by Margoliouth, the son of an English Jewish convert and missionary to Anglicanism, may indicate an interest on the part of the reviewer in portraying the Jews' connection to Jerusalem as more limited than Margoliouth claimed. Jerusalem, which the reviewer describes as "the capital of the Jews and the *qibla*

[125] The article was by Harold Shepstone in *The World's Work*. *al-Muqtaṭaf* 42:3 (March 1913), 272.

[126] On the role of Protestant missionaries—such as those who taught *al-Muqtaṭaf*'s editors at the Syrian Protestant College—in promoting the idea of science as a buttress for faith, see Elshakry, "The Gospel of Science and American Evangelism in Late Ottoman Beirut," 173. "Education in the natural sciences was promoted as one way to aid pupils on the path to God," Elshakry explains (183).

[127] *al-Hilāl* (October 1907–July 1908), 172–74.

[128] *al-Muqtaṭaf* 33:1 (January 1908), 81.

[the direction of prayer] of the Christians,"[129] is the subject of the only paragraph of Margoliouth's book that *al-Muqtaṭaf*'s article translates in its entirety. Though the translation is placed in quotation marks, there is a significant difference between the original English and the Arabic translation. Margoliouth writes that "the period during which the city could claim the title imperial was very short, extending no longer than the reigns of David and Solomon, the former of whom appears to have brought several of the surrounding peoples into subjection."[130] In this sentence, he is commenting on the *imperial* position of Jerusalem, a status defined by the subjugation of non-Israelite peoples under the power of the Israelite sovereign. In *al-Muqtaṭaf*'s rendering, the sentence reads: "The period in which this city was the capital [*'āṣima*] of the country of the Jews was extremely brief, limited to the reigns of David and Solomon."[131] *Al-Muqtaṭaf*'s reviewer, in other words, translates Margoliouth's line as a statement of the limited nature of the historical claim on Jerusalem as the Israelite capital. One wonders whether this mistranslation may have resulted from a deliberate misconstrual of Margoliouth's statement to serve a particular political (perhaps anti-Zionist) interest.

These journals thus exhibited a strong interest in the Bible, biblical archaeology, and the question of the historicity of biblical narratives. Like the (usually European) researchers on whose work they reported, some of the articles aimed to prove the reliability of biblical accounts, while others were more skeptical. For most, the fact of an Israelite past in Palestine was accepted without question, though, as we find in the mistranslation of Margoliouth's text, opposition to Zionism at times may have colored the way in which the Bible and related research were presented to readers.

Makaryus and the Statelessness of the Jews

The journals and their editors, as we have already seen in *al-Manār*, also addressed Jewish ambitions in Palestine more explicitly and directly. Even before Herzl founded the World Zionist Organization in

[129] Though referring to Jerusalem as the Christian *qibla* is unusual, the idea is grounded in a long-standing tradition and connected, one presumes, to the eastward orientation of many churches. As Reuven Firestone noted in private correspondence, the ninth- to tenth-century scholar Muhammad ibn Jarir at-Tabari mentions in his commentary on Q. 2:145 that both Jews and Christians prayed facing Jerusalem. See also Firestone, "Rituals: Similarities, Influences, and Processes of Differentiation," 703.

[130] Margoliouth and Tyrwhitt, *Cairo, Jerusalem, and Damascus, Three Chief Cities of the Egyptian Sultans*, 295.

[131] *al-Muqtaṭaf* 33:1 (January 1908), 81.

1897, *al-Muqtaṭaf* considered the prospect of a Jewish return to Palestine. In 1895, in its "Opinions of Scholars" section, *al-Muqtaṭaf* included an extended discussion on a proposal by a certain "Dr. Mendes in a North American newspaper."[132] Mendes, the journal reports, argued that "the only way to bring about the end of wars and disputes between the world's countries and to link the nations with bonds of love and brotherhood is to return Palestine to the Jews." According to *al-Muqtaṭaf*, Mendes offered a number of different arguments in defense of this proposal. Among other benefits, granting Palestine to the Jews would solve the "Eastern Question," he claimed, by removing Palestine—"the primary ambition of European countries"—from the claws of the European powers. It would also end the quarrel between the various Christian sects in Jerusalem, as the goal of dominance for any one of them would be rendered unrealizable. Finally, it would solve the "Israelite Problem," that is, the problem of antisemitism in Russia, Germany, and France. Mendes's arguments are presented without comment or criticism until the last revealing line: "Perhaps, were he [Dr. Mendes] to consult with the Jews about their return to Jerusalem, he would find that many of them do not want this."[133] For this *al-Muqtaṭaf* author, the utopian idea of a Jewish return to Palestine was unrealistic because Jews themselves were uninterested in pursuing it (a fair assessment, no doubt, in 1895).

At least one of *al-Muqtaṭaf*'s editors—Shahin Makaryus—looked more favorably on the Jewish nationalist movement to return to Palestine. Let us return to Makaryus's *History of the Israelites*, the text in which Makaryus described Jews in explicitly racial terms. Perhaps related to his racial perspective on Jews, Makaryus evinces a discernible sympathy for their desire to restore their sovereignty in Palestine. To write the history of the ancient Israelites, Makaryus employs "the Torah," a term that by Arabic convention includes the entire Hebrew Bible, as his primary source. The Torah, he explains, narrates the Jews' "slavery and oppression as well as the power, success, and sovereignty that they achieved." In this sense, the Torah is the book of the Jews' "consciousness, their beliefs, and religious and civil laws." For the post-biblical period, or, as he names it, the period "after the destruction of Jerusalem," Makaryus contends that the history of the Jews is not found in any one book; rather it is "dispersed among the histories of

[132] Neville Mandel suggests two possibilities as to the identity of this "Dr. Mendes": either Henry Pereira Mendes or Frederick de Sola Mendes, brothers and Sephardic rabbis in New York. Mandel, *The Arabs and Zionism before World War I*, 40n.35. Henry Pereira Mendes was one of the founders of the Federation of American Zionists. See Sefton D. Temkin and Eugene Markovitz, "Mendes," in EJ[2].

[133] *al-Muqtaṭaf* (October 1895), 795.

the nations [*al-umam*] among which they resided as a people without a homeland or country [*shaʿban lā waṭan lahu wa-lā bilād*]," a people with nothing but "the memory of the past and their beliefs."[134] Makaryus presents this statement about Jewish history, one surmises, to explain to readers the challenges he faced in writing the Jews' history. But the way in which he describes postbiblical Jewish history is significant for our understanding of his perception of the Jews and, in particular, their relationship to Palestine. The lack of "a homeland or country" is, in Makaryus's view, a—perhaps *the*—defining feature of the history of the Jews after the Bible. Moreover, this lack not only defined but necessarily limited their history. All that Jews had left during their many centuries of exile was the "memory" of their former political achievements and their beliefs. Makaryus appears to assume that the history of the Jewish Diaspora was not a genuine history because it lacked national, political sovereignty (an assumption Makaryus shared, it should be noted, with many Jewish nationalist historians of the fin de siècle period and beyond).[135] The Jews' history, he suggests, must be culled, in a most undignified way, from the "proper" histories of other nations that had their own states.

In the passage cited above, Makaryus apparently distinguishes between *shaʿb* and *umma*, terms that are often used interchangeably and ambiguously. If we may infer definitions from this passage, a *shaʿb*, for Makaryus, is a people that lacks a sovereign state, whereas an *umma* (pl. *umam*) is a people that has achieved sovereignty. This particular distinction between these terms is peculiar and reflective of the fin de siècle emphasis on the relationship between nations and sovereignty.[136] One notices this restrictive definition of *umma* again in Makaryus's chapter on "The Dispersion of the Jews after the Destruction of Jerusalem." The chapter opens with the explanation that "the history of the Israelites as an *umma* ends here. After the destruction of Jerusalem, as was noted earlier, they were dispersed throughout all of God's lands."[137]

Before continuing with this discussion of Makaryus's perspective on the Jews' homelessness, it is worth briefly noting that an alternative (if not contradictory) view of Jews' stateless condition was expressed in Zaydan's *al-Hilāl*. In one of this journal's numerous articles on the Rothschilds, the author addresses the Jewishness of the famed banking family. He explains:

[134] Makaryus, *Tārīkh al-isrāʾīliyyīn*, 77.

[135] On this subject, see the work of David N. Myers, including *Re-Inventing the Jewish Past* and *Resisting History*.

[136] See Ami Ayalon's discussion of these two terms and the relationship between them. Ayalon, *Language and Change in the Arab Middle East*, 48–52.

[137] Makaryus, *Tārīkh al-isrāʾīliyyīn*, 77.

> Among the things that assisted the success of this house was the fact that its members were Jewish, because Jews were known for their remoteness from political parties that were common in those days. Because they were neutral, people did not fear that they would engage in conspiracies or betrayal. They were concerned, rather, with acquiring money for themselves and the rulers would compete to obtain their assistance and to earn their confidence in order to benefit from their service. [The Jews'] neutrality and wisdom helped them and they benefited from both.[138]

For this *al-Hilāl* author, the Jews' lack of political connection to any state, their fundamental political neutrality, was a boon for them in the Diaspora, permitting them to profit simultaneously from warring states with no suspicions as to their political allegiances. The indignity that Makaryus associates with this condition of "homelessness" is entirely absent in this rendering.

"From Barrenness to Fertility": Makaryus and Zionism

Returning once more to Makaryus's monograph, let us consider the way in which he directly addresses the phenomenon of Zionism. In his chapter on Jewish organizations, he devotes less than two pages to the Zionist Organization, but in his concise description he seems to exhibit respect, and even sympathy, for the movement. "Among the large organizations of the Israelites these days," writes Makaryus, "is the Zionist Organization, the goal of which is to colonize the land of Palestine and to rule it." Makaryus writes that Theodor Herzl, the organization's founder, sought to convince the Jews to "transport their brethren from Russia, Romania, and the places in which they are oppressed to the land of their fathers and grandfathers in Palestine." Makaryus continues with details about Herzl and other Zionist leaders, followed by descriptions of various branches and institutions within the Zionist movement. At the conclusion of the section, Makaryus indicates that he chose "not to go on at length about the history of this significant organization [*al-jamʿiyya al-ʿaẓīma*]."[139] Instead, he hopes that in a second edition of the book he will "expand the explanation

[138] *al-Hilāl* (October 1906), 9.

[139] Though the adjective *ʿaẓīm* typically has positive connotations, I render it here as "significant," that is, fairly neutrally, so as not to prejudice the analysis and because the term occasionally is used in a negative sense.

of this [matter], God willing."[140] But before ending the passage on the Zionist Organization, Makaryus adds:

> It behooves us not to disregard the fact that among the effects of these organizations and their charities is the purchase of the village of al-Mutallah[141] in the district of Marjayoun in the vilayet of Beirut and the Israelites' settlement there; and the purchase of lands in the areas of Hula, Tiberias, Jaffa, Haifa and so on, which the Jews settled. They transformed their conditions from poverty to prosperity [*min ʿusr ilā yusr*] and from barrenness to fertility [*min jadb ilā khiṣb*].[142]

Remarkably, Makaryus, cofounder and coeditor of one of the most important Arabic journals of the time, expresses a strikingly positive attitude toward the Jewish colonization of Palestine. Indeed, the description of the Zionists' success in making the desert bloom,[143] as it were, could easily have been written by a Zionist.

Why would Makaryus write so admiringly of the Zionist movement? His expectations about the book's readership may have played a role. One indication of the identity of this readership comes from the book's dedication to Felix Suares (1844–1906),[144] scion of one of the most affluent Jewish families in Egypt. In his dedication,[145] Makaryus writes that Suares is among the greatest of a people that includes "distinguished men of religion, science, and politics." Of this people,[146] Makaryus writes:

[140] One wonders whether Makaryus intentionally avoided the subject so as not to upset readers of one political perspective or another; the anticipated second edition never appeared.

[141] The Jewish Colonization Association's purchase of al-Mutallah (Hebrew: Metullah) and the removal of its primarily Druze residents from the land sparked a significant controversy among Zionists concerning the impact of Zionist colonization on Palestine's natives and the ways in which the negative effects might be mitigated. The conflict with the Druze fellahin of al-Mutallah after the purchase of the land was a primary subject of Yitzhak Epstein's 1905 speech, published two years later as "A Hidden Question." See Dowty, " 'A Question That Outweighs All Others.' "

[142] Makaryus, *Tārīkh al-isrāʾīliyyīn*, 202–3.

[143] For a critical examination of this trope, see George, " 'Making the Desert Bloom.' "

[144] On Felix Suares and his family, see Krämer, *The Jews in Modern Egypt, 1914–1952*, 39ff.; Beinin, *The Dispersion of Egyptian Jewry*, 256.

[145] Strangely, the dedication page is missing in one of the two copies of Makaryus's book that I was able to locate (though the dedication is listed in the table of contents). The tattered copy found in Columbia University's Butler Library includes the dedication page.

[146] Makaryus uses the term *umma* here in reference to the Jews, suggesting that he was not quite consistent in his distinction between *umma* and *shaʿb* and in his insistence that the Jews no longer constitute an *umma*.

> They have sat on the thrones of kings, and ruled their subjects justly for long periods of time. God blessed their wisdom and increased their people in their days. They have achieved wide fame and reached the pinnacle of glory and honor in their virtuous work. There is no need to mention those great philosophers, celebrated poets, exacting historians, authors and philanthropists.

From this dedication—before the body of the text even begins—we find that Makaryus intends this book to be a glorification of the Jews, in honor of his friend Suares. "The reader of this book," Makaryus declares, addressing Suares, "will see the badge of truth, faithfulness and diligence represented in the nation of which you are a part." He chose to dedicate the book to Suares in recognition of "our years of friendship, and because I observed your glorious work that benefited all the residents of this happy region [i.e., Egypt]. You should accept it as a reminder of kindness and as an acknowledgment of your favor. May God grant you a long life." The final 50 pages of the 260-page book focus on the contemporary Jewish community of Egypt and offer biographical sketches of prominent individuals and families (6 pages on religious leaders, the rest on the financial elites).[147] The book was unmistakably designed to interest (and delight) the Jewish community of Egypt. It is certainly possible that Makaryus thought this audience would appreciate kind words about Zionism.[148]

The positive, noncritical nature of this work was noticed, and highlighted, by one prominent early reviewer, Rashid Rida. In *al-Manār*, Rida describes Makaryus as "widely knowledgeable in history." He outlines Makaryus's book[149] as a work on "the lineage and origin of the Jews; their spread and history before and after the exodus from Egypt; their scattering throughout the world, east and west; their religion, law, sects, and holidays; their famous members from the distant and recent past; their associations; and their distinguished and notable men at present." While Rida's summary accurately represents the book's contents, the brief review is not without its critique. "In his writing about the sects and religious communities [*aṭ-ṭawāʾif wa-l-milal*]," Makaryus's style, contends Rida, is "to focus on that which is good and

[147] The religious leaders described are Rūfāʾīl Hārūn bin Shimʿūn (the hahambaşi of Egypt), Iliya Ḥazān (the hahambaşi of Alexandria), and Masʿūd Ḥāy bin Shimʿūn. Makaryus also provides biographical sketches of members of the following families: Menashe, Qatawi, Rolo, Moseiri, and de Lathermeres.

[148] On "Early Zionism in Egypt," see Landau, *Jews in Nineteenth-Century Egypt*, 115–24.

[149] Without any remark, Rida renders the title *Tārīkh al-yahūd* (History of the Jews) instead of the actual title *Tārīkh al-isrāʾīliyyīn* (History of the Israelites). This substitution points to the synonymous nature of "Israelite" and "Jew" in the Arabic lexicon of this period, even though some did highlight the distinction between the two terms.

praiseworthy" in the respective religion, "and to pay no attention to the negative." As a result, Makaryus "never mentions anything blameworthy" about the Jews. Rida concludes by noting that "some Jewish leaders have praised the book and approved its use for teaching in their elementary schools due to its brevity and its simplicity."[150] One wonders—as it seems Rida did—to what extent Makaryus offered a sympathetic reading of Zionism simply to appeal to his intended audience, regardless of any negative attitude he may have held toward the movement. At the same time, it is overly simplistic and anachronistic to attribute any positive words about Zionism by a non-Jew in the Arab world to the author's financial interests. After all, Makaryus knew that the book would also be read by non-Jews (and could have expected it to be reviewed by none other than Rashid Rida), and other interests could have dictated a different approach. Makaryus's perspective on Jews and Jewish history, as articulated in his writings in *al-Muqtaṭaf* and his *Tārīkh al-isrāʾīliyyīn*, along with his relations with Jewish contemporaries, might well have given him a more sympathetic estimation of the Jewish national movement. His admiring language about Zionism may have been at least partly related to his perception of the Jews as the Arabs' *racial* relatives, as Semitic, Eastern cousins returning home.

The subject of Palestine and Zionism continued to interest these journals. At the start of 1914, before the Great War began, *al-Muqtaṭaf* published a three-page article called "The Colonization of Palestine." The article, though not written in support of the Jewish settlement enterprise, is not particularly critical of it either. The article focuses on the agricultural advances made by the Jewish colonies in Palestine. The penultimate paragraph makes clear that the primary grievance the author has is not against the Jews but rather against the local Ottoman regime: "What we demand of the Israelites in this regard is much less than what we demand of the local government." The writer calls on the Ottomans to "strengthen security, protect rights, ease traffic routes, found agriculture schools throughout the country on its [the Ottoman government's] vast lands so that the fellahin will actually learn the principles of agriculture." In this way, it would seem, the Arabs of Palestine might *also* be able to flourish along with the Jews. The author acknowledges, however, that merely establishing security and preserving rights are not simple tasks for a government that has so many other states covetous of its possessions.[151]

[150] *Al-Manār* 7:12 (August 1904), 472–73.
[151] *al-Muqtaṭaf* 44:1 (January 1914), 51.

Certainly by 1917, well into the Great War and on the eve of the Balfour Declaration and Britain's conquest of Palestine, *al-Muqtaṭaf* presented a firmer, though still hardly vehement, stance against Jewish colonization of the Holy Land. An article entitled "The Country of Palestine" relayed the conclusion of the secretary of the British Palestine Society, E.W.G. Masterman, that Palestine in its current condition "is not suitable for European colonization." The article ends with a quotation attributed to Masterman: "the country, in its current condition, cannot sustain an increase in its population and therefore I consider the gate of colonization there to be [closed] tight after the war if there is a desire for extensive colonization."[152] One cannot be certain whether this was a view shared by all *al-Muqtaṭaf*'s editors or just certain contributors; regardless, it was an assertion printed in *al-Muqtaṭaf* without criticism and suggests that the writers and readers were concerned about the prospect of mass Jewish immigration to Palestine at the close of the war. Makaryus's praise of the fruits of Zionist colonization was not a unanimously held attitude on the pages of his journal.

"Brothers Fighting Brothers": *Al-Hilāl* and the Jews in the Great War

I conclude this chapter by looking, once more, at the same article in *al-Hilāl* with which we began: Emile Zaydan's "The Jews and the War." This intriguing piece ties together many of the disparate themes discussed throughout the chapter, including the presumed link between ancient Jewish history and the contemporary Jewish experience, sympathy for the plight of the Jews of Europe, and, at the same time, intense anxieties about Jews' seemingly boundless power.

Zaydan points to a number of ways in which Jews are connected to the Great War, but the first he notes is (like the ironic fact that Palestine's Jews have fled to Egypt during the war) also a historical curiosity:

> Among the strangest of coincidences is that the fourth of August, namely, the day of the outbreak of the war, corresponds to the memorial day of the destruction of the Jews' Great Temple

[152] *al-Muqtaṭaf* 51:3 (September 1917). Masterman's article includes the line: "It is useless for any to settle in Palestine who are not prepared to be themselves practical agriculturalists and also to face, especially in the immediate future, very many difficulties. There will not be immediate openings on an extended scale after the war." Masterman, "Palestine," 26. On the concept of "absorptive capacity" in Palestine, see also Reichman, Katz, and Paz, "The Absorptive Capacity of Palestine, 1882–1948."

> and their captivity—both the first time, by Nebuchadnezzar the Babylonian, and the second time, by Titus the Roman. Some of them [the Jews] call this war [i.e., World War I] the third Jewish captivity because it has increased their poverty and their dispersion and was even more woeful upon them and more thorough in thwarting their dreams and hopes.

According to Zaydan, August 4, 1914, marked both the start of the Great War and the Jewish day of mourning for the destruction of the ancient Jerusalem Temples (Tishʿah be-Av, i.e., the ninth day of the lunar month of Av).[153] By linking the consequences of the Great War for contemporary Jews to the Jews' ancient past and their religious calendar, Zaydan displays a conception of his Jewish contemporaries that, as we have found in this chapter, was common among Arab intellectuals of the time. Contemporary Jews were understood by these intellectuals in light of their own perceptions of Judaism and Jewish history. Jews were imagined to be living within a historic Jewish drama that began, in many Arab authors' minds, with the Bible. Moreover, this passage from Zaydan reflects the widespread acceptance on the part of these Arab intellectuals of the basic Jewish claim to a historic link to Palestine.

Highly sympathetic to the Jews' historic plight, Zaydan's article employs one particularly interesting, uncommon medium to highlight the challenges facing the Jews. In the middle of the first page, there is a drawing of a Jew with a globe in his hands (see figures 3 and 4). The image was a common motif of late nineteenth- and early twentieth-century European antisemitic art and caricature that alluded to the theory that Jews controlled, or at least sought to control, the entire world. The cover of the French journal *Le Rire* in 1898, for instance, famously portrayed Alphonse de Rothschild, crowned with a golden calf, grasping the globe in his taloned hands.[154] (Above we encountered

[153] In 1914 Tishʿah be-Av was observed on August 2, the tenth day of Av (the ninth day of Av fell on August 1, but this was a Sabbath). Zaydan's confusion can likely be explained by the fact that he had presumably encountered a Jewish source that noted that the war began on this Jewish day of mourning (a claim that has indeed become part of modern Jewish lore). For Russian Jews (among whom, one assumes, this calendrical coincidence was first observed), the war did effectively begin on the ninth of Av, as Germany declared war on Russia on August 1. For Zaydan, however, living in British-occupied Egypt, August 4 was understood to be the beginning of the war, namely, the day Britain declared war on Germany. Thus Zaydan, having heard the Jewish claim that the war began on Tishʿah be-Av, appears to have mistakenly assumed that this referred to August 4.

[154] See, e.g., the caricature of de Rothschild on the cover of *Le Rire: Journal Humoristique Paraissant le Samedi*, copied in Albert Lindeman's entry on "Rothschilds" in Levy, *Antisemitism*, 625; of a Jewish monster holding a globe, from the 1901 Vienna newspaper *Kikeriki* (1901), copied in Arie Stav, *Peace*, 41.

Figure 3. Cartoon from *al-Hilāl* 24 (October 1915–July 1916), 401.

Figure 4. Cartoon from cover of *Der Groyser Kundes* (January 20, 1911). Courtesy of YIVO.

this sort of image expressed verbally in Rida's remark that Jews controlled France "like a ball in their hands.") Zaydan, however, chose this image to express a rather different message. Beneath the picture there is a caption in Arabic that reads: "An old Israelite [*shaykh isrāʾīlī*] asks himself: Where is the promised land?" Zaydan interprets the drawing as follows:

> We have copied here a cartoon [*ṣūra ramziyya*][155] that portrays an old Jewish man [*aḥad mashāyikh al-yahūd*] holding the globe in his hand, searching for a stable place where his people will be safe. He says to himself: "In Russia, they do not want me. Likewise in France, England, America, and Palestine! The world is vast and beautiful, but it seems as though there is no place for me."[156]

Underlying Zaydan's interpretation of the image are two elements. First is his sympathy for the predicament of the Jews, unwelcome throughout the otherwise "vast and beautiful" world. This sympathy, to be sure, is not to be taken lightly in an era in which racial antisemitism was spreading in many regions of Europe and, indeed, in the Middle East as well. Zaydan, like his father (who, as we have seen, defended the Talmud against antisemitic libel), could hardly be accused of antisemitism. However, the second important element of Zaydan's interpretation of the cartoon is its highlighting of the Jews' willingness to consider places other than Palestine as their "Promised Land." In asking "where is the Promised Land," the Jew might be understood to be conceding either that he does not know where Palestine is, that he is so far removed from the land that he has to scour a globe to locate it, or that the Jewish national movement is not truly concerned with "returning" to the ancient homeland but merely with finding "a stable place where his people will be safe." For Arabs unsympathetic to the Zionist movement's attempts to settle and control Palestine, the Jews' openness to other places could surely have raised suspicions as to the sincerity of the Jewish claim of a "return" to their Promised Land.

Zaydan's selection and interpretation of this cartoon are especially interesting when one considers the cartoon's origins: the cover of a January 1911 New York-based Yiddish-language satirical journal, *Der Groyser Kundes* (The Big Stick).[157] The artist's name, Lola, the pseudonym of Leon Israel (1887–1955), is visible in English in the corner of

[155] Literally: "a symbolic picture or image."

[156] *al-Hilāl* 24 (October 1915–July 1916), 401.

[157] *Der Groyser Kundes* (January 20, 1911). I thank my colleague Eddy Portnoy for his help in finding the source of this cartoon. On Lola, see Portnoy, "The Creation of a Jewish Cartoon Space in the New York and Warsaw Yiddish Press, 1884–1939," chap. 3.

al-Hilāl's version. Obscured, though, in *al-Hilāl* are the Yiddish words that appear on the (cartographically imprecise) globe in the *Der Groyser Kundes* version. In the original, Amerika (America), Frankraykh (France), Rusland (Russia), Daytshland (Germany), and Holand (Holland) are identified as the journal exclaims: "A big world and nowhere to go!" Lola's cartoon was not concerned with the Promised Land but with any land, and Palestine is noticeably absent from the potential places of refuge. Zaydan, in other words, through the caption he created and the interpretation he offered, transformed this American Yiddish cartoon from one about the inability of Jews to find a haven in Europe to one about the Jews' search for the Promised Land.

Zaydan's compassion for Jewish suffering during the war is notable. He emphasizes that more than 550,000 Jews are on the battlefields, with "brothers fighting brothers." At least four million Jews, moreover, have been "forced to emigrate from their countries and to endure the hardships of long-distance travel to flee approaching armies." These refugees include "old men, women, and children who have left their homes, their land, and their possessions in order to save their lives."[158] It is evident that Zaydan pities Europe's Jews for their unfortunate situation in the war.

But immediately after Zaydan expresses this concern, he proceeds to quote, with no apparent disapproval, an article from an unidentified journal that takes a decidedly anti-Jewish stance. After citing statistics indicating the disproportionate involvement of Jews as soldiers in the various warring armies, the quoted article adds: "If we consider the influence of the Jews in this war and the important positions that they hold, we are shocked at the obedience of the nations to their [the Jews'] power and their confidence in their abilities." The article then discusses the prominence of Jews in Britain (e.g., the Rothschilds), Belgium (e.g., the first Belgian taken prisoner during the war was a Rothschild), Italy (e.g., Prime Minister Luigi Luzzatti), Germany (e.g., Karl Marx, Ferdinand Lassalle), Austria (e.g., high-ranking Jewish military officers), and Russia (e.g., the dense population of Jews).[159] All this is to highlight the extent to which Western countries are dominated by Jews.

How can we make sense of Zaydan's lengthy quotation of a most unsympathetic article about Jews' domination over and exploitation of Europe when we know that Zaydan generally viewed Jews favorably and repeatedly expressed pity for their misfortunes? Given the many texts we have reviewed in this chapter, one may conclude that this seeming contradiction was very much the norm among these Arab

[158] *al-Hilāl* 24 (October 1915–July 1916), 401–2.
[159] Ibid., 402–4.

intellectuals of the period. They recognized and acknowledged the adversity that the Jews faced, both historically and at present, especially in Europe, and respected them for persevering and maintaining their distinct identity (whether they viewed it as racial, religious, or both). Indeed, they saw the Jews as a model to be emulated. At the same time, in their respect for the Jews' success in the face of adversity, these Arab intellectuals also discerned reason to fear the Jews, not least because of the Jews' renewed interest in achieving sovereignty in Palestine. For many of Palestine's *al-Muqtaṭaf*, *al-Hilāl*, and *al-Manār* readers, the latter factor—the fear of Jews and their power and ambitions—came, as time progressed, to outweigh the former—the sense of kinship, sympathy, and respect. Yet the prominence of the perception of commonality at this early stage of encounter necessarily cautions us against projecting far back into this period the deep, seemingly impermeable divisions that developed later.

CHAPTER 5

Translation and Conquest: Transforming Perceptions through the Press and Apologetics

And now, the known Christian enemy, owner of al-Karmil, published a pamphlet that he claims is drawn from the English Jewish Encyclopedia. He is spreading it among the masses and sending it to the officers of the government and the representatives so that they deal with it in the upcoming meeting of parliament!

I would like to translate this book into Hebrew and print it in Hebrew periodicals so that our brethren will see the extent of our Arab enemies' hatred. I am also ready to accept responses from anyone who wishes to answer it and to assemble all of the ideas along with my own and to make from the material one forceful answer.[1]

One could hardly fathom a more evocative example of the complex role of language and translation in the encounter between Zionists and Arabs in Late Ottoman Palestine: an urgent call in Hebrew by a Palestine-born, Arabic-speaking Sephardic Zionist for a Hebrew translation of an Arabic translation prepared by a Palestine-born Christian Arab of an English text by a British-born Ashkenazic American Zionist. The three individuals involved in this 1911 affair are already familiar to us from previous chapters. The original, English text in question was Richard Gottheil's 1906 entry on "Zionism" in the *Jewish Encyclopedia*, one of the main sources for Ruhi al-Khalidi's manuscript analyzed in chapter 2. "The known Christian enemy" referred to here was Najib Nassar, whose 1911 Arabic pamphlet entitled *Zionism: Its History, Purpose, and Importance (Excerpted from the Jewish Encyclopedia)* served as a point of comparison in our analysis of al-Khalidi's text and whose *al-Karmil* newspaper sparked *ha-Ḥerut*'s "Great Danger" campaign, studied in chapter 3.[2]

[1] *ha-Ḥerut* 3:157 (September 22, 1911), 2.

[2] Naṣṣār, *aṣ-Ṣahyūniyya*.

Finally, the author of the exhortation cited above was Shimon Moyal, whose *at-Talmūd* of 1909 was, as we have seen, another of al-Khalidi's sources for information on Jewish history and beliefs. Although it is unclear whether he had already read Nassar's *Zionism* or had simply heard about it, Moyal was in any case certain that it was no mere literal Arabic rendering of Gottheil's article but rather a willful distortion designed to misrepresent and vilify Zionism. Moyal, a native of Jaffa, believed it to be of critical importance that his fellow Zionists—most of whom could not read Arabic—were made aware of this slander disguised as translation because of its potential to influence how its readers perceived Zionism.[3] So Moyal decided to translate it—again.[4] Translation was thus a tool used to expose Arabs to the dangers of Zionism, on the one hand, and to expose Zionists to the dangers of Arab perceptions of Zionism, on the other—*both* ostensibly based on the same text.

The translation and retranslation of the *Jewish Encyclopedia*'s "Zionism" entry is an acute case of the central and problematic place of language and translation in Late Ottoman Palestine and in the Arab-Zionist encounter more broadly. While the contested nature of language in internal Zionist debates is well-known and well studied,[5] the position of language and translation in the encounter between the Zionists and Arabs of Palestine has received relatively little scholarly attention.[6] Through a study of two very different but related projects—the varied attempts to make the Arabic press more sympathetic toward Zionism and the publication of two Arabic books about the Jews and Judaism—this chapter argues that translation served not only as a means of relating information in a different language but also as a tool of influence, defense, persuasion, apologetics, and polemics.

A Third Conquest: The Arabic Press

The years of the Second Aliyah (1904–1914) are associated with two Zionist projects of "conquest," namely, "conquest of labor" and

[3] Although it contained anti-Zionist commentary and was selective in the passages it chose to translate, the pamphlet was a reasonably faithful rendering of Gottheil's original. In this regard I disagree with Neville Mandel, who reads the pamphlet as a more extreme polemical distortion. See Mandel, *The Arabs and Zionism before World War I*, 108–9. See my critique in chapter 2.

[4] On the politics of translation, see Seidman, *Faithful Renderings*.

[5] The so-called Language War of 1913 surrounding the language of instruction at Haifa's Technion is the most obvious example. See, e.g., the chapter "Language Wars and Other Wars" in Saposnik, *Becoming Hebrew*, 213–37.

[6] One notable exception is Halperin, "Orienting Language."

"conquest of land."[7] The former denotes the effort to have Jewish-owned farms and places of employment exclusively employ "Hebrew" (that is, Jewish, as opposed to Arab) laborers; the latter refers to the attempt by Jews and Zionist organizations to purchase as much of Palestine's territory as possible. There was, however, another project of Zionist "conquest" during this period, one that aimed to "conquer the Arabic press."[8] This third conquest had a number of different versions and permutations and generated passionate discussion and debate among Palestine's Zionists. Translation, as we shall see, was at the center of this discourse.

After the 1908 Young Turk Revolution, Arabic-reading Zionists in Palestine began to notice a disturbing trend. With the liberalization (though not cessation) of the Ottoman press censorship regime, there was an explosion of new Arabic newspapers throughout the empire. Some of these new papers openly challenged Ottoman government policies and criticized other populations within the empire, acts that were generally proscribed before the revolution.[9] The newly voiced criticism included among its targets the mass Jewish immigration to and settlement of Palestine and the imperial government's inability or unwillingness effectively to oppose Zionism.[10]

An articulate Arab opposition to Zionism evoked significant anxiety among many of Palestine's Zionists. First among those to express alarm about this phenomenon were those Zionists, like Shimon Moyal, who actually read the Arabic press articles about Zionism. To identify who these first readers were, we must consider the state of Arabic literacy among Late Ottoman Zionists. As late as January 1914, Moshe Smilansky wrote of his fellow Zionists in Palestine:

> In the course of thirty years [since the first wave of Jewish nationalist immigration to Palestine], we have not learned the language of the land. In the entire new Hebrew yishuv, there are not even ten people [a *minyan*] who know how to read and write Arabic. This may seem absurd to the reader, but it is a fact, to our shame. Many of us know how to speak Arabic. But even

[7] See, e.g., "From 'Conquest of Labor' to 'Conquest of Land': The Identity of Soldier and Settler, 1907–1914," in Shafir, *Land, Labor, and the Origins of the Israeli-Palestinian Conflict, 1882–1914*, 135–45; Gelvin, *The Israel-Palestine Conflict*, 65–66.

[8] Shimon Moyal uses the phrase "conquest of the Arabic press" in his argument against Abraham Ludvipol, *ha-Ḥerut* (October 25, 1911). See below.

[9] On the flourishing of the Arabic press in this period, see Ayalon, *The Press in the Arab Middle East.*

[10] For a detailed analysis of the various positions on Zionism articulated in the Arabic press, see the chapter "Elements of Identity II: The Debate on Zionism in the Arabic Press," in Khalidi, *Palestinian Identity*, 119–44.

> this knowledge is extremely limited. Most of the [Jewish] Arabic speakers are from the masses of the nation; our intelligentsia in the land is entirely alien to it [Arabic]. Therefore, even the knowledge of "those who know" Arabic is extremely limited. Two years ago, there was an incident in which a high official, an Arab patriot, wished to speak with the Hebrew leaders and asked to speak Arabic. There was not a single person in Jaffa or its surroundings who was able to take up this task and so the residents of Jaffa needed to bring a "speaker" from Jerusalem. And even in Jerusalem, the number [of new Hebrew yishuv members] who know Arabic is two or three.[11]

Even if Smilansky overstated his claim for rhetorical effect, the basic point—that few Ashkenazic Zionist immigrants in the Late Ottoman period mastered Arabic—is not disputed. As Smilansky suggests, many members of the "new Hebrew yishuv" had learned some Arabic after their arrival in Palestine, but most acquired only the essentials necessary to carry on life in an Arabic-speaking environment (giving them the ability, for example, to engage in simple commerce or to instruct laborers). There were certain notable exceptions, of course, such as the journalist-linguist Eliezer Ben-Yehuda, who not only learned Arabic but used it as one of his sources for expanding the modern Hebrew vocabulary.[12] However, the vast majority of Ashkenazic Zionists in Palestine never became literate in Arabic; learning to speak one new language, namely, Hebrew, was a sufficient challenge for most of the immigrants who were at the same time struggling to make a living in a new and foreign environment.[13]

There were, of course, some Zionists who did not need to learn Arabic as they already knew the language. As discussed in chapter 1, these were the mostly Sephardic Jewish natives of Palestine, as well as Jewish immigrants from Arabic-speaking lands, many of whom affiliated with the Zionist enterprise.[14] To be clear, though, not all Jews born in the Middle East were *literate* in Arabic.[15] Arabic literacy, after all, was limited among the population of the Middle East as a whole, and in any

[11] Moshe Smilansky, "Maʿaseinu yekarvunu, maʿaseinu yeraḥakunu," *ha-ʿOlam* (January 1914).

[12] See Eliezer Ben-Yehuda, *ha-Mavo ha-gadol*, MBY. See also Avishur, "ha-Markiv ha-ʿarvi ba-lashon ha-ʿivrit bat zemanenu u-vi-sifrutah me-Eliʿezer Ben-Yehuda ʿad Netivah Ben-Yehuda (ve-Dan Ben-Amoẓ)," 9.

[13] There were certainly efforts to introduce Arabic instruction in Jewish schools in Palestine. See Lang, *Daber ʿivrit!*, 626.

[14] On the Yemenite immigration to Palestine, for instance, see Druyan, *Be-ein "marvad-kesamim."*

[15] On Arabic literacy in Palestine, see Ayalon, *Reading Palestine*.

case, for many Sephardic Jews, Ladino (not Arabic) was the language spoken at home while Hebrew was the language of prayer and most writing.[16] Nonetheless, Sephardic Jews who were born in the Middle East, including of course the Zionists among them, were generally able comfortably to communicate at least orally in Arabic.

Some of these native Middle Eastern Jews, though, were in fact literate in Arabic.[17] Two such Arabic-reading and Arabic-writing Jews were Shimon Moyal and Nissim Malul, both central figures in Zionist efforts related to the Arabic press and also the authors of the two Arabic works on Judaism that will be studied in this chapter. Moyal and Malul were colleagues with similar life trajectories.[18] Both were Sephardic Jews born in Palestine who spent years in Egypt before returning as passionate Zionists to the Holy Land toward the end of the Ottoman period.[19] Moyal was born in 1866[20] to a wealthy Moroccan Jewish family that had recently arrived in Jaffa. Malul, twenty-six years younger, was born in 1892 to a Tunisian Jewish family in Safed. Moyal was educated in Jewish religious schools in Palestine until the age of sixteen, after which he traveled to Beirut to study Arabic and French and later to Cairo for medical school. During his years in Egypt, he wrote for a number of Arabic newspapers and journals, as did his wife Esther al-Azhari Moyal, herself an influential author and editor of an Arabic women's journal. The Moyals returned to Palestine in 1908, and Shimon died there less than a decade later, in 1915, at the age of forty-nine.[21] Malul and Moyal probably first met in Cairo, where their lives overlapped for several years. During his youth, Malul's family moved from Jaffa to Tanta (in Lower Egypt) so that his father, Moshe (Musa) Hayyim Malul, could take up the post of rabbi of the community. They then moved to Cairo, where Musa was appointed judge (*dayan*) on the

[16] See Beʾeri, *Reshit ha-sikhsukh yisraʾel-ʿarav, 1882–1911*, 53. Louis Fishman challenges the presumption that most of Palestine's Sephardic Jews spoke Arabic. See Fishman, "Palestine Revisited," 140–44.

[17] These included Ashkenazim (members of the so-called old yishuv) as well.

[18] On Moyal and Malul, see also Jacobson, "Jews Writing in Arabic."

[19] As discussed in chapter 3, recent scholarship has focused great attention on an alternative (less exclusivist) version of Zionism espoused by certain Sephardic Zionists. See especially Campos, *Ottoman Brothers*; Jacobson, *From Empire to Empire*. The particular views of Moyal and Malul are analyzed below.

[20] According to Beʾeri, *Reshit ha-sikhsukh yisraʾel-ʿarav, 1882–1911*, 188; Bezalel, *Noladetem ẓiyonim*, 390; Levy, "Jewish Writers in the Arab East," 197. Yaʿqub Yehoshuaʿ, however, claims that Moyal was born in 1870. See Yehoshuʿa, *Tārīkh aṣ-ṣiḥāfa al-ʿarabiyya fī filasṭīn fī al-ʿahd al-ʿuthmānī, 1908–1918*, 123.

[21] Esther al-Azhari Moyal survived until 1948. She is a primary interest in Levy, "Jewish Writers in the Arab East."

religious court of the local chief rabbi.[22] In Egypt, Nissim Malul continued his education in Jewish religious subjects, but he also formally studied Arabic language and literature. He began publishing frequent articles in the newspaper *al-Muqaṭṭam* before he too returned to Palestine in 1911, where he lived an active intellectual and political life until his death in 1959 at the age of sixty-seven.

We will return to Moyal and Malul in significant detail in the pages that follow; for the moment, though, it is important to note that it was Jews such as these who were the first to express concern about the opposition to Zionism emerging in the newly aggressive and self-confident Arabic press. The Sephardic-edited newspaper *ha-Ḥerut*, analyzed in chapter 3, was preoccupied with the problem of the anti-Zionist Arabic press and was in the forefront of what soon became a Zionist communal and institutional obsession. In its very first month of publication, May 1909, *ha-Ḥerut* printed a supplement on the subject of the Arabic press,[23] and within two months the paper was issuing regular and frequent warnings of the "Danger!" in what it identified as the "anti-Semitic" Arabic press.[24] While several newspapers were discussed, before long the primary target of Zionist concern was the Haifa-based *al-Karmil*, the "known enemy-of-Israel newspaper" edited by Najib Nassar, whose Arabic translation of Richard Gottheil's "Zionism" encyclopedia entry so worried Moyal.[25]

The concern about an assertive Arabic press opposed to Zionism filtered from the alarmist articles on the pages of periodicals such as *ha-Ḥerut* to the Zionist institutional leadership in Palestine, Constantinople, and Berlin. The Zionist Organization's Palestine Office,[26] which had been founded in 1908, took heed of the phenomenon and, in 1911, created its own Press Bureau, charged with, inter alia, preparing regular reports on the Arabic press's articles that related to Jews and Zionism.[27] The Press Bureau paid Nissim Malul a salary to prepare

[22] For some of Malul's biographical details, see the obituary-commentary: Yisraʾel Ben-Zeʾev, "ha-ʿItonaʾi ve-ha-ʿaskan d"r Nissim Malul z"l." See also Jacobson, "From Empire to Empire," 183–184; Naṣṣār, *Mawqif aṣ-ṣiḥāfa al-miṣriyya min aṣ-ṣahyūniyya khilāl al-fatra min 1897–1917*, 110–12.

[23] The supplement featured the editor's interview with Shimon Moyal. *ha-Ḥerut* 1:4 (May 21, 1909), Supplement.

[24] See, for instance, *ha-Ḥerut* 1:24 (July 23, 1909), 1.

[25] *ha-Ḥerut* 2:60 (February 14, 1910), 2.

[26] On the Palestine Office and its head, Arthur Ruppin, see Penslar, *Zionism and Technocracy*, 77, 80–102.

[27] See Ruppin's "Concerning the Establishment of a Press Bureau" letter to the Zionist Central Bureau in Berlin, October 6, 1911, CZA Z3.1447. Though the Press Bureau's primary responsibilities related to the Arabic press, it was also charged with reviewing the Turkish and French press in Constantinople and, "if possible," sending letters to large

translations of relevant Arabic newspaper and journal articles.[28] His extensive expository reports, typically written in Hebrew and translated into French and German (to be sent to the Zionist offices in Constantinople and Berlin), were highly valued by the Zionist leadership.[29] Moyal, whose independent wealth may have permitted him to do the work gratis, was apparently not on the Palestine Office payroll; instead, he generally published his translations of the Arabic press in *ha-Ḥerut*.[30] Through these reports, Zionists in Palestine and their leadership abroad discovered what was being written and published about them by Arab journalists and intellectuals. Translation, that is to say, was the first step in the "conquest" of the press.

Why and How to Influence the Press

The Zionists' focus on the Arabic press merits some reflection. If the underlying concern was not with the press per se but rather more broadly with Arab views about Zionism, were there not other means of gauging Arab sentiments or ideas concerning the Jews and Zionism? Zionists might, for instance, have studied the sermons of religious leaders, surveyed workers in the fields, or interviewed Arab notables to determine the range of beliefs on the subject among Arabs. These or other methods might well have yielded a more representative and accurate picture of what the region's Arabs were thinking about the Zionist movement and its efforts in Palestine.

The preoccupation specifically with the press might be attributed, at least in part, to some of the following factors. First, Zionists and

---

European newspapers as well. See also L2.26.2 for the 1911/1912 Palestine Office budget, including the expenses for the Press Bureau.

[28] Unfamiliar with the Arabic press, the Zionist leadership requested that Malul present a list of the important newspapers and journals to which he wished to subscribe. Such a request was made by Yehoshua Feldman on June 3, 1914. See CZA L2.94.1b. In one budget report from the Press Office, Malul is listed as receiving 1,200 francs for his services. See CZA L2.167. Malul was relieved of his duties in September 1914 because of budget constraints resulting from the war. He appealed the decision directly to Ruppin, pointing to both the achievements of his press work and his poor financial situation. See CZA L2.72.2, September 20, 1914, and September 27, 1914. After the war, Zionist officials once more demanded Malul's Arabic translation services. See CZA L4.999, January 23, 1920.

[29] Hundreds of pages of these reports are extant in the Central Zionist Archives in Jerusalem. See, inter alia, CZA L2.94.1a, L2.94.1b, and L2.94.2. A letter on May 7, 1914, from the Zionist representative Victor Jacobson in Constantinople requested even more detailed and timely reports on the Arabic press. CZA L2.94.1b.

[30] See, for instance, *ha-Ḥerut* (September 22, 1911).

particularly their leadership were an overwhelmingly literate, educated community, and so it was natural for Ruppin's Palestine Office to turn toward a written, textual source such as newspapers as it sought to assess Arab views. Second, the press was easily and inexpensively accessible. The Palestine Office simply needed to pay for subscriptions and hire a translator to evaluate Arab sentiments from throughout the region and across the various demographic sectors. At a time when—notwithstanding al-Khalidi's perception of infinite Zionist capital—funds were limited, this was a more economical option than deploying a team of interviewers and investigators. Third, several of the Arabic-speaking Sephardic intellectuals to whom the Palestine Office appealed, such as Malul, were themselves already active in the general Arabic press in Egypt, Syria, or Palestine; it is thus unsurprising that these Zionist agents believed strongly in the power of the press and argued that the Zionist establishment should take it seriously. Indeed, the writers in *ha-Ḥerut* and the officials in the Press Bureau imagined that the Arabic press did not reflect Arab views so much as the press created (or, at least, strongly influenced) those views.

While there was widespread Zionist agreement that the advent of this anti-Zionist Arabic press constituted a significant threat to the movement, the appropriate reaction to the threat was less clear.[31] Exposing it, by means of translation, was deemed to be a necessary part of the response; for most, however, exposé was not sufficient. One way in which Zionists hoped to improve their portrayal in the Arabic press was financially to assist sympathetic Arabic newspaper editors. The paper that appears to have received the greatest Zionist financial support was *an-Nafīr*, edited by the Christian Arab Iliya Zakka.[32] In 1910 *ha-Ḥerut*'s editor, Avraham Elmaleh, alerted his readers to the fact that "there is in Jerusalem an Israel-loving Arabic newspaper edited by the young, talented writer Iliya Zakka, who disagrees with *al-Karmil* and all of the enemies of Israel." In recognition of Zakka's "beautiful articles in support of Israel" (and by Israel, Elmaleh meant the Jews), *ha-Ḥerut* called on its readers to subscribe en masse to *an-Nafīr*. "Let us create for him just one hundred subscribers, and through him we will be able to respond," Elmalah wrote, to the slander printed about the Jews and Zionism.[33]

[31] For a useful early scholarly article on the subject, see Roʾi, "Nisyonoteihem shel ha-mosadot ha-ẓiyonim lehashpiʿa ʿal ha-ʿitonut ha-ʿarvit be-ereẓ yisraʾel ba-shanim 1908–1914."

[32] On Zakka's *an-Nafīr*, founded in Alexandria and then moved to Jerusalem and then Haifa, see Yehoshuʿa, *Tārīkh aṣ-ṣiḥāfa al-ʿarabiyya fī filasṭīn fī al-ʿahd al-ʿuthmānī, 1908–1918*, 50–53.

[33] *ha-Ḥerut* 2:98 (May 25, 1910), 1–2.

Ha-Ḥerut also supported Zakka's paper more circuitously. The Hebrew paper encouraged members of Jerusalem's Jewish community to study Arabic under Zakka's instruction. "Mr. Iliya Zakka, editor of *an-Nafīr*," *ha-Ḥerut* reported in November 1910, "is thinking about starting evening classes in Arabic language just for Jews, at a low price. Our brothers, and especially the Russian youth, will be able to advance in a short time through this excellent opportunity, as Mr. Zakka knows Russian very well."[34] Having Russian Jewish immigrants study Arabic with Zakka would not only expand the base of Arabic knowledge into the Ashkenazic community (a goal advocated by many of *ha-Ḥerut*'s contributors) but also supplement Zakka's income, permitting him to continue to publish his newspaper and encouraging him to print articles supportive of the Zionists.

It is difficult to determine whether *ha-Ḥerut*'s staff believed that Zakka was actually, as they put it, "one of the righteous gentiles whose great sympathy for the Jews" comes from the fact that he was "a free-thinking and truth-loving man,"[35] or whether they thought they were in reality purchasing support that would otherwise not be forthcoming. If, however, Yaʿqub Yehoshuʿa, historian of Palestine's Arabic press, is correct that Zakka's paper ceased its support and attacked Zionism whenever Zionists' money failed to come Zakka's way, then one assumes that *ha-Ḥerut*'s editors understood the nature of their relationship.[36] In any case, the Zionist institutional leadership apparently did engage in more explicit, direct quid pro quos with certain Arabic newspapers (including, it seems, Zakka's *an-Nafīr*), offering monetary subventions in exchange for their support.[37]

[34] Zakka's knowledge of Russian was likely acquired during his studies in the Russian teachers' institute in Nazareth. See Yehoshuʿa, *Tārīkh aṣ-ṣiḥāfa al-ʿarabiyya fī filasṭīn fī al-ʿahd al-ʿuthmānī, 1908–1918*, 52. *Ha-Ḥerut* noted that the classes will be immersion-style, "Arabic-in-Arabic according to the modern method." *ha-Ḥerut* 3:9 (November 11, 1910), 2.

[35] *ha-Ḥerut* 2:133 (August 16, 1910), 2.

[36] Yehoshuʿa, *Tārīkh aṣ-ṣiḥāfa al-ʿarabiyya fī filasṭīn fī al-ʿahd al-ʿuthmānī, 1908–1918*, 52. See also Khalidi, *Palestinian Identity*, 58.

[37] See, e.g., Jacobson to Frank, October 28, 1913, CZA Z3.1642. For Zionist financial documents naming Zakka, see CZA L2.167. See also CZA J15.6175 for *an-Nafīr* receipts. Given the prevalance of bribery in Late Ottoman Palestine, perhaps these "subventions" should be understood in this context. Before Zionist immigrants even took their first steps in Palestine, while still on their ships, they already found the need for bribery. As Neville Mandel writes, "they simply resorted to the common expedient of bribing the port authorities and anyone else . . . who tried to block their way." "Everything," Mandel asserts, "had its price: entry and release of baggage at the ports, permits to buy land and to build on it could all be bought." Such a culture, he notes, was not unfamiliar to Jewish immigrants from Russia. Mandel, "Ottoman Practice as Regards Jewish Settlement in Palestine," 35.

To have Zionism presented more favorably in the Arabic press, several Arabic-writing Zionists tried another tack as well: they contributed articles to Arabic newspapers and wrote letters to their editors defending the Jews and Zionism against published attacks. The young Nissim Malul was prominent in this effort, writing frequently for *al-Muqaṭṭam* and *al-Ahrām*,[38] and Shimon Moyal participated actively as well.[39] In 1913 a small group of Sephardic intellectuals, including Elmaleh and Malul, met at the Jaffa home of Moyal and formed Agudat ha-Magen (the Shield Society). The goal of this group, as recalled later by one of its members, was to "explain to the Arab world in the Arabic press that the interests of the Jews of Palestine not only do not conflict with Arab interests, but, on the contrary, they bring great economic and cultural benefit to the Arabs."[40]

But the influence Jewish writers could have on an Arabic newspaper in this way was, according to Malul himself, inevitably limited. First of all, from his previous experience in Egypt, where he attempted to use this method to counteract what he deemed to be a growing "antisemitic movement," Malul found that Arab editors ultimately began charging Jewish contributors for printing their articles. "The same thing that happened with the Egyptian press," Malul wrote in October 1911, "has happened to us also with the Syrian and Palestinian press."[41] If Zionists had to pay to have their sympathetic articles published, the distinction between this approach and the "subventions" clearly dissolves. Furthermore, if Arabic newspapers were beginning to refuse even to publish articles written by Zionists, all the more unrealistic—Moyal and Malul argued in adjoining opinion pieces in *ha-Ḥerut*—were calls by Ashkenazic Zionists for Sephardic Zionists to become employed by these newspapers and thus surreptitiously to "infiltrate" their editorial boards and "conquer" them.[42] No less problematic was the fact that, according to Malul, the number of Jews commanding the necessary journalistic and linguistic skills to fill such positions did not exceed ten

[38] See, e.g., the translation of one of Malul's *al-Muqaṭṭam* articles from October 1912 in CZA L2.167. See also Khalidi, *Palestinian Identity*, 249n.35. According to Khalidi, Malul wrote thirteen pro-Zionist articles for *al-Muqaṭṭam* and nine for *al-Ahrām*. On Malul as the Jaffa correspondent for *al-Muqaṭṭam* and his April 1914 interview of the Zionist leader Nahum Sokolow, see Tauber, "Jewish–non-Palestinian-Arab Negotiations," 165.

[39] See Moyal to Ruppin, 5 January 1912, about the meeting Moyal was set to organize concerning his own work in the Arabic press. Moyal requested that Ruppin attend the meeting. CZA L2.167.

[40] On the founding of Agudat ha-Magen, see CZA L2.94.1a. This retrospective quote is from Chelouche, *Parashat ḥayai 1870–1930*, 149–50. On Elmaleh's role in the short-lived organization, see Bartal, Kaniel, and Ẓaḥor, eds., *ha-ʿAliyah ha-sheniyah*, 22.

[41] *ha-Ḥerut* 4:13 (October 25, 1911), 2.

[42] Ibid.

or fifteen, hardly a sufficient number to fill the editorial boards even of just the most important Arabic newspapers.

A Zionist Newspaper in Arabic and the Charge of "Assimilationism"

The answer that Moyal and Malul, along with several other Zionists, proposed instead was the creation of the Zionists' own Arabic newspaper. Such an undertaking would permit Zionists to present their perspective to Arabs on the Zionists' own terms, without subventions or any sort of dependence on otherwise unsympathetic Arabs.[43] This proposal to favorably translate Zionism into Arabic was aired publicly on the pages of *ha-Ḥerut*, and it stirred intense controversy almost immediately among Palestine's Zionist community. One Ashkenazic Zionist—Abraham Ludvipol—accused the scheme's most outspoken early proponent, Shimon Moyal, of being an "assimilationist." By institutionalizing the use of Arabic by Zionists, the Arabic newspaper idea aimed in reality to break down the linguistic and cultural barriers between Jews and their Arab neighbors, Ludvipol contended. The outrage was only intensified when Moyal insisted, in something of a rhetorical flourish, that it would be worthwhile to sell an entire Zionist colony if, through its sale, "we were to found an Arabic newspaper that would fight our war."[44]

The debate between Moyal and Ludvipol exposed tensions within Palestine's Zionist community, between Sephardim and Ashkenazim. Moyal claimed that Ludvipol's attack was based in the latter's irritation that "a Sephardic Easterner dared to prove to him, with evidence, that his European experience and ideas are not always sufficient for him to deal properly with the East." Moyal excoriated Ludvipol for his condescension toward the Sephardim, insisting that he recall that "you are our guest and that the residents of the Land of Israel and their ancestors suffered terribly over many years in order to preserve their nationality among the streams of nations that flowed as they grabbed the reins of the government generation after generation."[45] Having "preserved their nationality" for so long, Moyal implied, the Sephardim could hardly be accused of being "assimilationists." Rather, a Zionist-edited Arabic newspaper would simply be like the Arabic newspapers of the

[43] In addition, as some advocates hastened to highlight, a Zionist newspaper in Arabic would also serve to address Arabic-reading Jews. See Malul, *ha-Ḥerut* (June 18, 1913).

[44] See *ha-Or* 3:2 (October 4, 1911), 1; and *ha-Ḥerut* 4:9 (October 19, 1911), 1–2.

[45] *ha-Ḥerut* 4:9 (October 19, 1911), 1–2.

Ottoman Empire's other ethnic and religious communities: "We find a Sunni Muslim Arabic newspaper, a Shiite Muslim Arabic newspaper, a Coptic Christian Arabic newspaper, a Catholic Christian Arabic newspaper, an Orthodox Christian one and a Maronite Christian one. But we do not have even one Jewish Arabic newspaper!"[46] These other newspapers advanced the interests of their respective communities, Moyal explained, and this was precisely what the Jewish community lacked. Because Jews had thus far failed to establish their own Arabic paper after the extension of press freedoms following the Young Turk Revolution, Muslim Arab public opinion in Palestine was left in the hands of the Christian newspapers. These Christian-edited papers, such as Nassar's *al-Karmil*, introduced "hatred between us and the Muslims," contends Moyal, "through lies, cowardly complaints, and faulty information."[47]

That Moyal's chief antagonist in this debate was Abraham Ludvipol is surprising. A Volhynian-born journalist (who wrote in French and Yiddish as well as Hebrew), Ludvipol had been living in Palestine since 1907.[48] In late 1911, at the very time at which he was engaged in his polemic with Moyal, Ludvipol was hired to direct the Palestine Office's Press Bureau, which, as noted, was charged with, among other duties, monitoring the Arabic press and responding to unsympathetic articles. Ludvipol himself was responsible for following the French press and Malul, Moyal's young protégé, was soon working under him, tracking the Arabic press.[49] Ludvipol presided over a meeting of the "Committee on the Arabic Press" in January 1912 in which he reported on Malul's recent articles in several Arabic newspapers and discussed the topics of the next set of articles the committee wished Malul to submit for publication.[50] Ludvipol apparently believed that the proper way for Zionists to influence Arab public opinion through the press was to write articles for already-existing Arabic newspapers—a project he oversaw—whereas the creation of a new Zionist-edited Arabic newspaper was thoroughly objectionable. In Europe, he explained, Jews cre-

[46] *ha-Ḥerut* 4:13 (October 25, 1911), 2.

[47] *ha-Ḥerut* 4:9 (October 19, 1911), 1–2.

[48] See Getzel Kressel, "Ludvipol, Abraham," EJ[2]. Ludvipol had initially moved to Palestine a decade earlier, in 1897, but he did not remain for long; he returned to Europe for the first Zionist Congress. Tidhar, EḤY, 2:673–74. See also Gorni, *Zionism and the Arabs 1882–1948*, 53n.14.

[49] See Ruppin to Warburg, September 24, 1911, in which Ludvipol is described as "head of the bureau, correspondent for French newspapers"; Ruppin to the Zionist Office in Berlin, October 6, 1911, CZA Z3.1447. See the Palestine Office's accounting book from January 31, 1912, CZA L2.167, in which payments to both Malul and Ludvipol are listed.

[50] "Meeting of the Committee on the Arabic Press, 24 Tevet 5672," January 14, 1912. CZA L2.167.

ated newspapers in non-Jewish languages, but no Gentiles ever read them.[51] Similarly, if a Zionist Arabic newspaper aimed to influence the opinion of non-Jewish Arabic-readers, it would necessarily fail. One wonders whether this was less a debate over principle than a turf battle.[52] After all, were Zionists to establish their own Arabic newspaper, Ludvipol may have feared losing control over his office to the editors of the new paper.

Regardless of the antagonists' motivations, the debate dragged on for a couple of years until finally Moyal and Malul succeeded in founding a short-lived Arabic newspaper. In 1913, under Moyal's leadership, *Ṣawt al-ʿuthmāniyya* (The Voice of Ottomanism) was created. For Moyal, the paper was meant to fulfill the desire he articulated the previous year to

> explain to the Arabs that our ambitions as Hebrew nationalists do not oppose their ambitions, and that we have the necessary qualities to work hard together for the sake of the shared homeland and to enhance the prestige of the Ottoman nation under whose shadow we stand at the same time as we seek to be a distinct Jewish nation concerned for its language, character, past, future, and customs.[53]

Highlighting the consistency between "Hebrew nationalism," defined in distinctly cultural terms—language, character, past, future, customs—and Ottomanism, Moyal hoped, through *Ṣawt al-ʿuthmāniyya*, to allay fears about the Zionists' separatist political ambitions.

Some have seen Moyal and Malul's effort to create an Arabic newspaper as an emblem of a unique Sephardic respect for their Arab neighbors and Arab culture (in contrast to an alleged Ashkenazic disregard, or worse, for Arab culture). It is worth noting, though, that Malul, in a 1913 series of articles defending his Arabic-language activities against charges of assimilationism, including his work for the Zionist Arabic newspaper, explains that the Arabic language could never "penetrate our hearts and destroy the aim of our souls." On the contrary, he insists, "the mind cannot imagine the possibility that this minor culture [*tarbut peʿutah*] will act upon us so much so that it would push us backward."[54]

[51] *ha-Or* 3:2 (October 4, 1911), 1.

[52] In contrast, Yosef Gorni presents this controversy as a case of opposed "ideological outlooks in Palestine." See Gorni, *Zionism and the Arabs 1882–1948*, 53–54. Another factor in this dispute may be connected to the reason Ludvipol came to Palestine in the first place. He had been sent by Hibbat Zion to found a new Hebrew newspaper. Having failed to do so, Ludvipol may not have been eager to see the founding of a newspaper in a different language. On Ludvipol's Hibbat Zion mission, see Tidhar, EḤY, 2: 674.

[53] *ha-Ḥerut* 4:70 (February 2, 1912), 3.

[54] *ha-Ḥerut* 5:221 (June 17, 1913), 2.

It is difficult, surely, to consider Malul's description of Arab culture as "minor" to be an expression of deep respect and admiration for Arabs. While the cultural experiences of Palestine's Sephardic Zionists were obviously different from those of their European counterparts and thus may have helped foster somewhat different Zionist ideologies, the evidence, as we discovered in chapter 3 as well, does not support the thesis that these ideologies were uniformly or unqualifiedly tolerant and respectful of the land's Arabs.

Defending Zionism by Translating Judaism: A Study of Two Apologetics

"Conquering" the Arabic press was not the only way by which Zionists sought to influence Arab views about the Jews and Zionism, though it appears to have been the approach to which the most time and resources were devoted in this period. In the pages that follow, we turn to a different sort of translation project carried out by two of the same individuals involved in the Arabic press efforts: Shimon Moyal and Nissim Malul. In a span of less than three years, each at the moment of his return to Palestine from Egypt in 1909 and 1911, respectively, Moyal and Malul wrote books in Arabic about Judaism and Jewish history. As they translate Judaism and the Jewish experience into Arabic, these texts, I argue, highlight the perception among some Zionists that the Arabs' resistance to Zionism and Jewish settlement in Palestine was aggravated by inherited religious prejudices, and that a proper translation could effectively dispel the misperceptions and alleviate the tensions.

Moyal's *at-Talmūd*

We turn now to the first (and ultimately, the only) volume of what Shimon Moyal intended to be an Arabic translation of the entire Talmud, a 1909 text entitled *at-Talmūd: Aṣluhu wa-tasalsuluhu wa-ādābuhu* (The Talmud: Its Origin, Transmission, and Ethics).[55] In analyzing this text, which as we saw in chapter 2 served as a source for al-Khalidi's understanding of Judaism, I aim to uncover the ways in which Moyal

[55] The cover page of the book offers an English translation of the title as "The Talmud: Its Origine and its Morals." On *at-Talmūd* in its Nahḍa context, see Levy, "Jewish Writers in the Arab East," 199–213. See also Gribetz, "An Arabic-Zionist Talmud."

sought to portray Judaism and Jewish history to non-Jewish readers of Arabic. I argue that Moyal used his exposition in two different, complementary if subtly competing, ways. On the one hand, I contend that Moyal tried to make Judaism appear less foreign and more congenial to Muslim and Christian readers by highlighting, explicitly or implicitly, areas of apparent similarity between the respective faiths and by describing Jewish principles in familiar language and terminology. In this sense, Moyal's work can be understood as part of the broader genre of apologetics—though, on occasion, the text betrays certain indirect polemical aspects as well, especially in relation to Christianity. On the other hand, *at-Talmūd* is not merely a latter-day apology for Judaism (though even if it were, its effort simultaneously to apologize in both Christian *and* Islamic terms in the fin de siècle Middle East context would surely recommend it for sustained examination). Rather, while painting Judaism in the most benign fashion, Moyal continually and consistently recounts Jewish history in distinctly *nationalist* terms; in so doing, he portrays Jewish nationalism as having ancient and, by implication, legitimate roots. This text, in other words, is a work of religious apologetics enmeshed within a nationalist (or Zionist) reading of ancient Jewish history. Moreover, by his choice of terminology as he describes the Jews' antique national past in the contemporary Arabic idiom of nationalism, Moyal may have been suggesting that not only Judaism but Zionism itself (in a particular form) gave Ottoman Arabs little to fear. Analyzing *at-Talmūd*, then, offers a fascinating window into the Arab-Zionist intellectual encounter of the Late Ottoman period.

At first glance, Moyal's *at-Talmūd*, 148 pages long, appears to be a simple and dry introduction to Jewish Oral Law. After his preface, Moyal presents an account of the transmission of the Oral Law from Moses until the compilation of the mishnah. In broad outline, the text proceeds as follows. It begins with a section about the various biblical judges, the prophets, the Great Assembly, and the tannaitic rabbis. It then identifies each tractate of the mishnah. Next, several pages are devoted to a discussion of the ancient Israelite synagogue in Alexandria. Finally, Moyal introduces, translates, and comments on the first three chapters of the book of *Pirkei avot* (known in English as "Ethics of the Fathers"), with a brief interruption before the third chapter for a discussion of the mystical book of the Zohar.

Aside from a number of contemporary Ashkenazic and Sephardic rabbis whose insights Moyal tapped for this work (particularly an Ashkenazic rabbi in Egypt by the name of Mendel Cohen), Moyal acknowledges several literary sources on which he drew. These include

Maimonides's introduction to his mishnah commentary,[56] the Judeo-Arabic commentary on *Pirkei avot* attributed to Maimonides's grandson David ha-Nagid (published for the first time in Alexandria in 1901),[57] and Gedalia ibn Yahya's sixteenth-century *Shalshelet ha-kabbalah*.[58]

In contrast to the works on which Moyal relied, his own text was directed at a *non*-Jewish audience. "This is the fruit of my great labor," writes Moyal in his preface, "which I present to the speakers of Arabic." The "speakers of Arabic" (*an-nāṭiqīn bi-ḍ-ḍād*) whom Moyal had in mind were not other Jews, like himself, who spoke Arabic natively. After all, Moyal explains that the underlying aim of the work is "to remove misunderstanding between them" (that is, Arabic-speakers) and "the most ancient race among them, namely the Israelite race, the source of the prophets."[59] The categories here ("Arabic-speakers" and "the Israelite race") are interestingly ambiguous—mutually exclusive in one phrase, overlapping in the next. The "them" of "misunderstanding between them" appears to refer exclusively to *non-Jewish* Arabic speakers, whereas the "them" of "the most ancient race among them" appears to include Jews (at least Arabic-speaking ones) within the broader category of *an-nāṭiqīn bi-ḍ-ḍād*. Regardless of this ambiguity,[60] it is clear that the readers Moyal wished to reach were non-Jewish Arabic-readers, whom the book was meant to disabuse of

[56] Moyal's version of this text would seem to be a translation back into Arabic from the Hebrew translation of Judah ben Solomon al-Harizi. In any case, it is different from the Arabic version edited by Kafah. Cf., for instance, Mūyāl, *at-Talmūd*, 54–57, to Maimonides, *Zeraʿim*, 29–31.

[57] Maimuni, *Pirkei avot*. Scholars have challenged the attribution of this text to David ha-Nagid on both stylistic and paleographic grounds. See Fenton, "The Literary Legacy of David Ben Joshua, Last of the Maimonidean Negidim," 13–14n.23. I am grateful to Elisha Russ-Fishbane for directing me toward this scholarship.

[58] On the "resurgence of Jewish historical writing in the sixteenth century," including *Shalshelet ha-kabbalah*, see Yerushalmi, 57–75.

[59] Mūyāl, *at-Talmūd: Aṣluhu wa-tasalsuluhu wa-ādābuhu*, 3.

[60] Levy offers a somewhat different reading of Moyal's formulation here, highlighting Moyal's presumption that the relationship between Arabic-speakers and Jews was one "not between two different peoples, but between the whole and one of its parts or elements [*ʿanāṣir*]." Levy concludes that "even as Moyal emphasizes and defends his own Jewishness, he deliberately naturalizes Jewish identity into a history of Arabness, describing Israelites [*al-ʿunṣur al-isrāʾīlī*] as the oldest strain, element or race [*aqdam ʿanāṣirhim ʿahadan*] of Arabic speakers." My reading suggests that, for Moyal, the relationship was more ambiguous. Levy, "Jewish Writers in the Arab East," 207–8, 205n.162, 216n.179. This terminological ambiguity may be considered in the context of recent scholarly discussions of the "Arab Jew." See, e.g., Shenhav, *The Arab Jews*; Gottreich, "Historicizing the Concept of Arab Jews in the Maghrib," 433–51; Levy, "Historicizing the Concept of Arab Jews in the Mashriq," 452–69; Levy, "Mihu yehudi ʿarvi?"

certain "misunderstandings" they had about Jews. The language of Moyal's work is thus not incidental but rather central to its purpose and message.

The Charge of Jewish Ritual Murder

Part of Moyal's agenda in translating the Talmud—which had never been translated in its entirety into Arabic—may be illustrated with a brief line Moyal includes in his review of the ancient Israelite judges. When he reached the figure of Jephtah, who, according to the Bible, slaughtered his own daughter in accordance with his vow to sacrifice the first thing that came to greet him from his home if he was victorious in battle, Moyal writes: "It is said of him in the Torah that he killed his only daughter with his own hands, in fulfillment of his vow.[61] There is a long discussion about him in the Talmud that will be mentioned in the appropriate place. Many have protested against him for having killed his daughter due to the impermissibility of human sacrifices in Jewish law."[62] Moyal was undoubtedly correct in insisting that many biblical interpreters and commentators have criticized Jephtah for fulfilling his vow. Yet, in asserting "the impermissibility of human sacrifices in Jewish law," Moyal was not merely continuing an internal Jewish exegetical debate about this story, nor was it the biblical tale that he likely had foremost in mind. More recent events were paramount.

Accusations of ritual murder perpetrated by Jews, though common in medieval and later Christian Europe, were generally unknown in the Arab Middle East.[63] With the increasing presence and influence of European Christians in the Middle East in the nineteenth century, however, the blood libel began to penetrate into Christian Arab discourse. The most famous of Middle Eastern blood libels was the Damascus Affair of 1840, in which a group of Jews were accused and convicted of having ritually murdered an Italian monk and his Muslim servant who had disappeared together in Damascus.[64] This was not the first such case in the Middle East, though. The accusation had already struck the

[61] The author's footnote refers the reader to Judges 11:34.

[62] Mūyāl, *at-Talmūd: Aṣluhu wa-tasalsuluhu wa-ādābuhu*, 11.

[63] With the Ottoman conquest of Constantinople in 1453 and eastern regions of Europe, the incorporation of these lands' populous Greek Orthodox Christian communities into the Islamic empire introduced the Ottomans to the blood libel. But even then it tended to be used almost exclusively by Christians. See Lewis, *Semites and Anti-Semites*, 132.

[64] On the Damascus Affair and its historical and historiographical implications, especially in Europe, see Frankel, *The Damascus Affair*.

Jewish communities of Aleppo (1810), Beirut (1824), Antioch (1826), Hama (1829), Tripoli (1834), and Jerusalem (1838). Nor was Damascus the last such incident. The blood libel was repeated multiple times throughout the Middle East, extending into the twentieth century.[65] Declaring—in Arabic, and in a work explicitly directed at a non-Jewish audience—that "human sacrifices" were proscribed by Jewish law in the context of a biblical tale, Moyal subtly countered ritual murder accusations against fellow Jews living in Arab lands.

The fact that this implied defense against blood libel accusations appears in a Jewish writer's Arabic commentary on the Talmud alludes to another, related phenomenon in late nineteenth- and early twentieth-century Middle Eastern history. In this period, Arabic polemics against Judaism and the Jews began to conscript the Talmud as weapon, serving as evidence of the Jews' iniquity. This appears to have occurred through the translation of European antitalmudic texts and myths into Arabic, usually by Christian Arabs. Among the earliest was Habib Faris's *Ṣurākh al-barīʾ fī būq al-ḥuriyya* (The Call of the Innocent with the Trumpet of Freedom).[66] Faris's book, published in Cairo in 1890, accuses the Jews of ritual human sacrifice (*adh-dhabāʾiḥ al-bashariyya*) and points to a number of European as well as recent Middle Eastern cases of Jews' alleged horrific acts. Faris, following European sources, ascribes this phenomenon directly to talmudic teaching. Similarly, in 1899 Yusuf Nasrallah published an Arabic translation of a French version of August Rohling's 1871 German work *Der Talmudjude*. In Nasrallah's *al-Kanz al-marṣūd fī qawāʿid at-talmūd* (The Awaited Treasure concerning the Laws of the Talmud),[67] which also includes a translation of Achille Laurent's 1846 anti-Jewish work on the Damascus Affair,[68] the author claims that the Jews engage in ritual murder according to the demands of "the laws of the Talmud." Moyal's attempt to assert that human sacrifices are prohibited by Jewish law in his own Arabic work specifically focused on the Talmud must then be understood in this new polemical context.

In fact, the immediate impetus for Moyal's writing *at-Talmūd* came from a *Christian* Arab intellectual. Curiously, however, and highlighting

[65] See Landau, "ʿAlilot dam u-redifot yehudim be-miẓrayim be-meʾah ha-teshaʿ ʿesreh."

[66] An edited version of this work appeared as Fāris, *adh-Dhabāʾiḥ al-bashariyya at-talmūdiyya*.

[67] Landau appears to misidentify this book as "an apologia on the laws of the Talmud." Landau, *ha-Yehudim be-miẓrayim ba-meʾah ha-teshaʿ-ʿesreh*, 111; Landau, *Jews in Nineteenth-Century Egypt*, 101. It is possible that Landau did not actually see the book but rather relied on a mention of it in *al-Hilāl*.

[68] Laurent, *Relation historique des affaires de Syrie depuis 1840 jusqu'en 1842*. Nasrallah identifies the author as Shārl Lūrān.

the complexities of interreligious relations in the fin de siècle Middle East, the instigator was not Faris nor Nasrallah nor any other Christian anti-Jewish agitator. Rather, it was Jurji Zaydan, the markedly *philosemitic* Christian editor of the Arabic journal *al-Hilāl*, discussed in chapter 4.[69] Zaydan had fielded numerous letters from readers inquiring about the Jews' mysterious Talmud, which Zaydan consistently defended as nothing more than "a large book made up of a number of volumes containing the Jews' laws, rituals, traditions, history, morals, sciences, and personal and civil rulings."[70] Protestations of the Talmud's decency and harmlessness were clearly insufficient, however, as readers' inquiries about the perniciousness of the Talmud continued to arrive at the editor's office. Finally, Zaydan suggested that Moyal, whom he met in Cairo, translate the Talmud into Arabic to dispel the slanderous rumors about the text once and for all.

Who Has "a Share in the World to Come"?

Even as it seeks often rather blandly to review post-Pentateuchal Israelite history so as to explain how the Oral Law received by Moses was transmitted until it was recorded by Rabbi Yehuda ha-Nasi, *at-Talmūd* is, I contend, a deliberately apologetic (and at times subtly polemical) work. Consider Moyal's choice to begin his Talmud translation project not with the first tractate of the mishnah, *Berakhot*, but rather with *Pirkei avot*. This choice highlights Moyal's desire to trace the chain of Oral Law transmission (found at the very beginning of *Pirkei avot*) as well as to show that the Talmud is indeed an *ethical* work (evidenced by the rabbis' ethical exhortations recorded in *Pirkei avot*), not the sort that would guide its adherents to kill innocents. This no doubt accounts for the prominent place of ethics (*al-ādāb*) in the very title of Moyal's work.

Moyal immediately hits a snag, though, because the line traditionally printed and read before the first mishnah of *Pirkei avot*—"All Israel have a share in the World to Come"—does little to refute the

[69] On the Beirut native Zaydan and his *al-Hilāl*, see Ayalon, *The Press in the Arab Middle East*, 53–54. On *al-Hilāl*'s Palestinian readership, see Ayalon, *Reading Palestine*, 50. On Zaydan's central role in the attempt to translate the Talmud, see Sehayik, "Demut ha-yehudi bi-reʾi ʿitonut ʿarvit beyn ha-shanim 1858–1908," 105–7. Levy has also carefully reconstructed the relevant exchanges in *al-Hilāl* and the course of events that led to the Zaydan-Moyal translation project; see Levy, "Jewish Writers in the Arab East," 199–204.

[70] "At-Talmūd wa-tarjamatuhu ilā al-ʿarabiyya," *al-Hilāl* 13, 5 (February 1, 1905), 303–5. I translate *ādābuhum* here as "moral and ethics," though the term could also mean "literature." Cf. Levy, "Jewish Writers in the Arab East," 203.

accusation that the Talmud privileges Jews over non-Jews. Clearly cognizant of this challenge, Moyal historicizes the choice of that line as the *fātiḥa* (opening words) of *Pirkei avot.*[71] He insists that this opening was selected "during a period of successive acts of oppression and persecution against the Israelite nation" because "it promises the grace of another world to this world's most oppressed people, those lacking in all human rights [*al-ḥuqūq al-bashariyya*]." He is not content, however, merely with historicizing the *fātiḥa*; he seeks to disprove the charge that "the Israelite religion" claims "a monopoly on the blessing of the world to come and eternal salvation." On the contrary, Moyal insists, "the Israelites have opened the gates of heaven to all of humanity as long as they follow the ways of moral excellence and kindness." After all, he explains, this one talmudic line does not negate another that says, as Moyal puts it: "Anyone who has merit from among the nations of the world has a share in the world to come."[72] This statement, as Moyal renders it, seems to be based on a line not from the Talmud but from the Tosefta (*Sanhedrin* 13:2), and, more so perhaps, on Maimonides's famous formulation *ḥasidei umot ha-ʿolam yesh lahen ḥelek le-ʿolam ha-ba* (the righteous of the nations of the world have a share in the world to come).[73] Just as Judaism does not discriminate against gentiles in the world to come, Moyal seems to imply, Jews do not discriminate against gentiles in this world.

Moyal emphasizes Jews' obligation to treat all of humanity kindly in his commentary on a line of *Pirkei avot* attributed to the sage Hillel. "Be of the disciples of Aaron," Hillel is reported to have said, enumerating the particular qualities he considered to be associated with the priestly brother of the biblical Moses. One of the traits Hillel ascribes to Aaron is "a lover of creatures."[74] In his phrase-by-phrase discussion of this mishnah, Moyal expounds on this line as follows: " 'A lover of creatures': not excluding foreigners (*al-ajānib*), for if this were not so, then [Hillel] would have said 'a lover of your brethren' or 'a lover of your countrymen [*muwāṭinīka*]' as they say in those instances in which they wish to specify [only] members of the Israelite nation."[75] Moyal presents this egalitarian, nondiscriminatory perspective not as

[71] The term *fātiḥa*, which Moyal uses here, has obvious Qurʾanic resonance as the name used for the first sura.

[72] Mūyāl, *at-Talmūd*, 58–59.

[73] Maimonides uses this phrase several times in his writings; e.g., *Hilkhot Teshuva* 3:5/13, in Maimonides, *Sefer mishneh torah*, vol. 1. On this Maimonidean phrase, see Nehorai, "Ḥasidei umot ha-ʿolam yesh la-hem ḥelek le-ʿolam ha-ba"; Korn, "Gentiles, the World to Come, and Judaism."

[74] Moyal's Arabic translation renders this *muḥibban li-l-khalq*.

[75] Mūyāl, *at-Talmūd*, 80.

his own view but rather as his interpretation of Hillel's aphorism. However, given the variety of ways in which Moyal might have interpreted the words of this mishnah (and all the others as well), we may infer another element of his agenda through these interpretations and comments. Moyal's choice to offer this particular explanation suggests—especially when read in the context of the broader work—that this is indeed the message about Judaism that Moyal was attempting to deliver.

In *at-Talmūd*, Moyal's apologetic agenda extends beyond simply showing that Judaism does not discriminate against gentiles—neither in its understanding of their place in the afterlife nor in the way Jews are instructed to relate to them. In fact, the effort to make Judaism not just palatable but also familiar to Christians and Muslims runs throughout Moyal's text. Whenever he touches on a figure or practice comparable or related to one found in either Christianity or Islam, we will see, he is quick to note the commonality.

Christianity and Moyal's Talmud

Given three factors—the conspicuous role of Christian Arabs in the propagation of antitalmudic allegations, the fact that it was a sympathetic Christian (Zaydan) who initiated this Talmud translation endeavor, and the disproportionate number of Christians in the Arabic-reading public[76]—it is perhaps unsurprising that Moyal frequently focuses on Judaism's similarities (and especially those of the Talmud) with Christianity and the New Testament. About the Jewish custom of reading a section of *Pirkei avot* each Sabbath between the holidays of Passover and Shavuot, for instance, Moyal explains in a footnote that this tradition is comparable to "the custom of spiritual devotions [practiced] by the Christians [*ar-riyāḍāt ar-rūḥiyya ʿind al-masīḥiyyīn*]."[77] More strikingly, consider the way in which Moyal develops his apologetic explanation for the statement, discussed above, that "all Israel have a share in the world to come." "All Israel," he claims, refers exclusively to "those who *deserve* the description 'Israelite,' owing to their good deeds, flawless intentions, and proper morals." In other words, this is not a blanket (chauvinistic) claim that a special place is reserved in the world to come for all Jews. Moyal contends that, on careful

[76] On the difference between Christian and Muslim literacy rates in Palestine, see Ayalon, *Reading Palestine*, 16–17.

[77] Mūyāl, *at-Talmūd*, 59.

examination of the Torah,[78] one finds that the prophets refer to "their nation with the name 'Israel' in matters of encouragement, consolation, and praise," whereas, in instances of "censure and rebuke," the names "House of Jacob," "Children of Jacob," and "Jacob" are used. *Pirkei avot* does not offer a share in the world to come to all of the Children of Jacob (that is, all Jews), but rather only to "all *Israel*" (that is, all who are worthy).

To substantiate his theory that the name Israel is reserved only for the meritorious, Moyal provides a scriptural proof-text, citing the phrase "an Israelite, in whom there is no deceit." This line serves, for Moyal, as further evidence of the use of Israel or Israelite exclusively to denote an ethical individual. The source of this line, intriguingly, is neither a prophet in the Hebrew Bible nor a rabbinic dictum; rather, these are the words of Jesus found in the Gospel of John. "When Jesus saw Nathaniel coming toward him," John 1:47 reports, "he said of him, 'Here is truly an Israelite in whom there is no deceit.' " Moyal makes no effort to disguise the source of this phrase; he openly identifies it as one that appears "more than once in the Gospels [*al-injīl*]."[79] This argument functions on a number of levels. First, of course, is the explicit contention that, when properly understood, the opening line of *Pirkei avot* reveals nothing morally damning about Judaism. Somewhat more subtle is the implication that Judaism and Christianity are so fundamentally linked that the meaning of a phrase in the sacred canon of Judaism can actually be ascertained through a knowledge of Christian scripture. Finally, in responding to Christian attacks on the ethics of the Talmud, Moyal, in a shrewd polemical tactic, attempts to undermine the criticism by using Christian scripture as his definitive proof-text.

In fact, the New Testament appears frequently in Moyal's *at-Talmūd*. In his exegesis of Rabbi Hanina's instruction to "pray for the peace of the government" (*Pirkei avot* 3:2), Moyal notes:

> The speaker did not limit his directive only to the peace of the Israelite government, despite the presence of the Roman occupation at the time and the limitation of legal authority to Roman administrators and, similarly, collecting taxes and tithes. [Rather,] he [Hanina] commanded obedience to the ruler without regard to his religion [*dīnihi*] or nationality [*wa-jinsiyyatihi*]. According to this principle, the author of the Gospel who came after him said

[78] Following common convention in Arabic, Moyal often uses the term Torah to refer to the entirety of the Hebrew Bible, though he is certainly aware of the sense of Torah as the Five Books of Moses. See ibid., 25n.1.

[79] Ibid., 59. Perhaps Moyal has in mind Romans 9:6, in which Paul the Apostle claims that "not all Israelites truly belong to Israel."

> "Render unto Caesar that which is Caesar's and unto God that which is God's."[80]

In his gloss on this phrase, Moyal contends that Jews are instructed to obey the government under which they live, regardless of whether it is their own "Israelite government" or that of another, even a government of "occupation" (*iḥtilāl*). Perhaps with contemporary Christian accusations of Jewish political disloyalty in mind (whether concerning European governments or that of the Ottoman Empire), Moyal is careful to relate this rabbinic dictum to yet another New Testament statement of Jesus, this time a famous line from the synoptic Gospels. Moyal suggests not only that Judaism and Christianity espouse a similar position concerning obedience to governments, but also that Jesus's view corresponded with the view articulated by Rabbi Hanina. From the standpoint of rhetoric, if not logic, a stronger defense against Christian accusations could hardly be imagined.

Although he seeks to link Jesus's New Testament teachings to the Talmud, Moyal is at pains to argue against the contention that Jesus himself is discussed (and, more relevantly, denigrated) in the Talmud.[81] Moyal has occasion to address this matter in his remarks on *Pirkei avot* 1:6. This mishnah records a saying of Joshua ben Perahiah, who is identified by one of Moyal's main sources, David ha-Nagid's Judeo-Arabic commentary, as the teacher of Jesus (*ustedh yeshuaʿ*). Moyal writes:

> Among his students was a man who was called Jesus the Nazarene (*yasūʿ an-nāṣirī*), but he was not Jesus the son of Miriam, the one who proclaimed Christianity. This correspondence of names has caused confusion among some historians who conflated the two. . . . We allude to this error here briefly and perhaps we will return to the details later on, when we discuss the trial of Christ [*maḥkamat al-masīḥ*].[82]

Moyal insists that, in the early rabbinic period, there were two men named Jesus, both from Nazareth. Thus when one encounters a talmudic story concerning a figure named "Jesus the Nazarene," one must not presume that this story concerns "the one who proclaimed Christianity."[83] The alluring possibility of an extended discussion of "the trial

[80] Ibid., 122. See Matthew 22:21, Mark 12:17, Luke 20:25.

[81] For a recent scholarly work on the subject, see Schäfer, *Jesus in the Talmud.*

[82] Mūyāl, *at-Talmūd*, 70–71.

[83] This apologetic strategy of denying the identity of the Talmud's Jesus and Christianity's Jesus is known from—and perhaps informed by—the positions of the Jewish disputant (Yehiel of Paris) in the so-called Paris Disputation of 1240. See Maccoby, ed.,

of Christ" remains unfulfilled; perhaps Moyal intended to return to the matter in a future volume, one of the many he had planned for his grand translation project.

Moyal does not explain why he considers it important to highlight the distinction between the two men named Jesus. The medieval (or pseudo-medieval) source on whom Moyal often relies, David ha-Nagid, was satisfied simply by describing Joshua ben Perahiah as the teacher of Yeshuaʿ. It would seem that Moyal, once again, had antitalmudic polemics in mind and used this textual opportunity to rebut accusations. In particular, both Faris and Nasrallah cited a number of (the same)[84] allegations about the Talmud's approach to Jesus and Christians more generally: that Jesus the Nazarene is "in the abyss of hell between tar[85] and fire"; that he was conceived when his mother Miriam prostituted herself to the soldier Pandera; that Christian churches are places of filth and those who preach within them are like "barking dogs"; that killing a Christian is a commandment; that a contract with a Christian is not binding; and that it is a Jew's duty to curse thrice the leaders of the Christian faith.[86] None of these allegations was novel, to be sure, but, perhaps because of their recent translation into Arabic and diffusion within the Arabic-reading world, Moyal felt a sense of urgency to confront them at the first opportunity afforded him within his commentary.

In his presentation of the history of Hellenized Judaism in ancient Alexandria—a three-page section titled "The Israelite Temple in Alexandria"[87]—Moyal lays out his most developed argument about the historical connection between Judaism and Christianity. After discussing the founding of the city of Alexandria, the creation of the Israelite Temple of Onias,[88] and the mass Israelite emigration from Judea to

---

Judaism on Trial, 153–62. In response to the accusation that "the Talmud contains blasphemies against Jesus," Yehiel is reported to have said: "Wherever Jesus is mentioned in the Talmud, it is the Jesus who was the pupil of Joshua ben Perahiah who is meant. It is quite possible that the Christian deity was also called Jesus, and there were thus two Jesuses, and possibly even two Jesuses from the same town, Nazareth."

[84] A segment of Nasrallah's introduction appears to be lifted from Faris. Cf. Fāris, *adh-Dhabāʾiḥ al-bashariyya at-talmūdiyya*, 45–46; Rohling, *al-Kanz al-marṣūd fī qawāʿid at-talmūd*, 10–11.

[85] This might mean "excrement." See Schäfer, *Jesus in the Talmud*, 13, 85–93.

[86] In both Faris's and Nasrallah's texts, these allegations are explicitly associated with the Paris Disputation of 1240.

[87] The term *kanīsa* might also be translated as "synagogue" and, in Christian contexts, as "church."

[88] The presumed site of the Temple of Onias was first excavated in 1887 and, more extensively, in 1905, just four years before the publication of Moyal's book. Moyal presumably wrote most of *at-Talmūd* while still in Egypt and mentions Alexandrian Jewish

Egypt during the time of Antiochus,[89] Moyal turns to the topic of cultural exchange between the Jews and the Greeks:

> When the assimilation [*ikhtilāṭ*] of the Jews among the Greeks increased, the two groups exchanged their sciences and ideas. Yet the Israelite religious philosophy influenced the Greek philosophy more than the Greek philosophy influenced the Israelite religion. This was because the Alexandrian Israelites accepted, with great pleasure and delight, the philosophy of Plato, which was widespread at the time. They began to reconcile it with the Torah and they worked hard to explain the anthropomorphic expressions as symbols and signs (*allegory*), according to the custom of the Greeks.[90]

There seems to be some confusion in this passage. Moyal insists that "the Israelite religious philosophy" more substantially influenced "Greek philosophy" than vice versa, but the discussion that follows appears to highlight precisely the opposite: the influence of Greek philosophy. Whether this muddle can be ascribed to Moyal's concern about the sensibilities of contemporary Jewish readers,[91] a typographical error, an inconsistency within his sources, or something else entirely, the matter of the direction of net influence between Greek and "Israelite" philosophy does not appear to be at the core of Moyal's interest in this discussion.

Rather, Moyal's concern here seems to be identifying the (Hellenistic) Jewish roots of Christianity, an identification that simultaneously serves apologetic and polemic purposes vis-à-vis Christianity. He explains that Philo of Alexandria was "the one who first created the term *logos*," which Moyal immediately notes is "the term Paul the Apostle used in the New Testament."[92] Similarly, according to Moyal, Philo introduced the term *paraclete*, "which also appears in the Gospels." These terms "indicate the presence of an intermediate power," an idea that "the Christian Church Fathers [*ābāʾ al-kanīsa al-masīḥiyya*] who lived shortly after him [Philo] learned from him." Through his writing

---

communal leaders, so it is likely that he was particularly interested in, and familiar with, the history of ancient Alexandria.

[89] Concerning Moyal's claim that the Israelites in Egypt "enjoyed civil rights similar to the rights of the Greeks themselves," cf. Graetz, *History of the Jews*, 1:503.

[90] Mūyāl, *at-Talmūd*, 52. Moyal transliterates the word "allegory" into Arabic.

[91] This would seem unlikely, however, given Moyal's pride in expressing views not consistent with those of the Jewish religious establishment. See, e.g., Moyal's discussion of the compilation of the Zohar in ibid., 119.

[92] Moyal uses the term *al-injīl* here. Though translated literally as "the gospel," *al-injīl* is used by Moyal (not exceptionally) to refer to the New Testament more broadly.

on the "Israelite temple in Alexandria," Moyal sought to highlight the shared origins of Judaism and Christianity and, in so doing, it would seem, to convince his readers that the two faiths are not so fundamentally opposed as might otherwise be believed.

However, in the same section of the text, Moyal declares that Philo's philosophy, and the "ideas of the Alexandrian Israelite scholars" found in the Septuagint, are "greatly distanced from the true Israelite spirit [*ar-rūḥ al-isrāʾīlī al-ḥaqīqī*]." Moyal goes on to discuss the tensions between the Jewish scholars of Judea and those of Alexandria. His conclusion, indeed the very last remark Moyal offers before beginning his analysis of *Pirkei avot,* once more turns to Christianity. The "Greek Israelite books," he argues, "cleared the way for the spread of the religion that newly came into existence at that time, that is, the Christian religion, which, at first, was nothing more than one of the ways of Israelite theology."[93] Given the contention that these "Greek Israelite books" violated "the true Israelite spirit," Moyal's linking of Christianity to ancient Alexandrian Judaism should not be understood as an attempt to equate true Judaism (as Moyal conceived of it) with Christianity. Moyal's writing on ancient Judaism's relationship with the origins of Christianity thus serves two purposes: on the one hand, to underscore the affinities between Christianity and Jewish concepts (for example, Philo), and, on the other hand, to emphasize that Christianity grew out of a deviant, "inauthentic" form of Judaism, namely, Hellenistic Judaism (of the Diaspora), rather than out of the "true Israelite" religion.

At-Talmūd and Islamic Terminology

Moyal's intended readers, Arabic-speakers, were not, of course, only Christians. Muslims represented the vast majority of the Arab population, and thus, to succeed in his goal of combating "misunderstanding," Moyal would have to address the concerns of Muslim readers as well. In general, Moyal makes fewer direct references to Islam than he does to Christianity. At least three reasons for this disparity might be suggested. First, the translation project, as discussed above, was originally initiated by a Christian, Jurji Zaydan; thus from the start, *Christian*-Jewish matters were paramount. Second, the anti-Jewish sentiment that was percolating through the Middle East was being carried, it was believed, by Christians, whether native Arabs or Europeans. To the extent that Moyal wrote *at-Talmūd* as a response to this phenomenon, he would have reasonably chosen to focus more on Christianity than

[93] Ibid., 53.

on Islam. Finally, we must consider the context in which *at-Talmūd* was written and meant to be read—namely, a predominantly Muslim society (even as the British were in political control of Egypt, where the book was published). Engaging with Islam for a non-Muslim was surely a more perilous enterprise than dealing with Christianity. Given that Christians were in any case viewed as the more critical demographic, Moyal might well have felt it unnecessarily hazardous to discuss Islam in significant detail. Though there are a few explicit references to Islam in the text, there are other more subtle ways in which Moyal addresses a Muslim audience. In particular, he presents Judaism in characteristically Islamic terms[94] and thereby provides the Muslim reader with a sense of comfort and acquaintance with Jewish religion and history.

It is necessary to begin the discussion of the use of Islamic language within Moyal's text with a word of methodological caution. Given the historical relationship between Arabs (and their language) and Islam, religious terminology in Arabic inevitably evokes Islamic connotations and associations. In analyzing Moyal's Arabic presentation of Jewish history and ideas, then, there is a danger of misinterpreting each of his uses of religious (seemingly Islamic) terminology as attempts to make Judaism appear similar to Islam. As vast as the Arabic lexicon is, words with Islamic religious resonance are not always reserved for Islamic contexts; they may also be used to describe aspects of other religions, where appropriate.[95] Thus, we must be careful in this analysis not to overinterpret Islamic-tinted language. However, we must not ignore those instances in which we can decipher uses of classical terms of Islam that appear out of the ordinary and, perhaps, designed to evoke a sense of commonality and shared discourse among a Muslim audience.

One case in which the Islamic sense of a word Moyal uses seems to be relevant, and perhaps intentional, is that of *taḥrīf*. This word, which means "corruption" or "distortion," in Islamic contexts typically refers polemically to the way in which Jews and Christians allegedly distorted their own, originally divine, scriptures. Moyal uses the term in his discussion of the Septuagint. He presents both the traditional myth of the

[94] Levy has correctly noted that Moyal "borrows freely from the Islamic theological lexicon" in his description of the Jews and the Jewish religion. Levy, "Jewish Writers in the Arab East," 209. My aim here is to propose an explanation for this borrowing.

[95] For example, I would argue that Moyal's use of terms related to the word *fatwā* (a formal statement of legal opinon in Islam) falls under this category. Moyal explains that "after the destruction of the Temple and the exile of Israel from its land," Israel "no longer worked in agricultural work and so the study and fatwas (*fatāwā*) on these topics [of agriculture] decreased." Mūyāl, *at-Talmūd*, 40. While a Muslim reader would recognize this word from his or her own tradition, Moyal likely used the term as the most appropriate Arabic word for "religious legal decision."

composition of the Septuagint text (by seventy rabbis for King Ptolemy II Philadelphus) and the skeptical, academic critique (that the Greek translation of the Bible was made for Jews who no longer understood Hebrew). He explains that "the Israelites do not accept the sanctity of the Septuagint." Rather, "they disavow anything within it that contradicts the Torah that is in their hands. They consider anything that is inconsistent to be a corruption [*taḥrīf*] that was introduced later into the Septuagint for religious purposes."[96] In this case, I would argue, Moyal must have had the Islamic polemical concept of taḥrīf in mind as he wrote these words. He appears to be attempting to show that Jews are aware of the problem of taḥrīf and eschew those texts that suffer from it. This may well be a nod to Moyal's Muslim readers, an effort to portray Jews as sensitive to the matters that concern Muslims about Judaism and at the same time to defend Judaism's own scripture.

There is, however, another potential implication of this passage. The Septuagint was, after all, accepted by the Orthodox Church. One standard piece of evidence mustered to support the Islamic accusation of biblical taḥrīf is the fact that there were three different versions of the Bible: the Jews' Hebrew Bible, the Samaritans' Bible, and the Christians' "Greek Bible" (the Septuagint).[97] By associating taḥrīf with the Septuagint, Moyal may be intimating that Muslims were correct in discerning textual "corruption" in the Bible; Muslims were simply mistaken in their assumption that the Jews' Hebrew Bible was not the original. Taḥrīf, in other words, may have occurred, but the results can be found only in the Christians' Bible, the Septuagint, that product of corrupted Hellenistic Judaism. If this reading of Moyal is correct, it would be a case of simultaneous apologetics toward Islam and polemics against Christianity. Perhaps because of Moyal's interest in gaining the sympathy of Christian Arab readers, this point is not made explicit.[98]

Muslim polemicists' charge of Jewish taḥrīf at times extended beyond corruption of the Bible. "Jewish oral tradition, seen as an unauthorized addition to Scripture," explains Hava Lazarus-Yafeh, "is also considered to be part of this falsification."[99] Thus Moyal's decision to begin his *at-Talmūd* not only with *Pirkei avot*, which itself begins with

[96] Ibid., 29.

[97] Ibid. See Hava Lazarus-Yafeh, "*Taḥrīf*," in EI².

[98] The question of the accuracy and authenticity of Bible translations was on the minds of fin de siècle Arab intellectuals. There were two major Arabic Bible translations undertaken in the nineteenth century: the first by Protestants (1856–1865) and the second by Catholics (1876–1880). The respective merits and faults of each were debated widely in Arabic journals through the end of the nineteenth century. See Sehayik, "Demut ha-yehudi bi-reʾi ʿitonut ʿarvit beyn ha-shanim 1858–1908," 98–102.

[99] Lazarus-Yafeh, "*Taḥrīf*."

an account of the transmission of the Oral Law from Moses, but also with his own extensive introduction to the chain of oral tradition in Judaism, might be understood as an attempt at answering Muslims' taḥrīf claim. On a more basic level, the project of tracing the Jewish *shalshelet ha-kabbalah*, the chain of tradition[100] would have particular resonance, and perhaps attraction, to Muslims familiar with their own *isnād* tradition for *ḥadīth* literature.[101] Moyal's choice of the subject for the first volume of his projected translation series may well have been informed, at least in part, by his recognition of this commonality with Islam.

In fact, Moyal's account of the composition of the mishnah employs another term with Islamic associations—a term we considered in detail in chapter 2. To explain how the Oral Torah, which Jews had been forbidden from writing, could suddenly, in the days of Rabbi Judah ha-Nasi, be composed in a book, Moyal appeals to the notion of ijmāʿ, or consensus, found prominently in Sunni Islam.[102] He writes that "the scholars [*al-ʿulamāʾ*] of his [Judah ha-Nasi's] age consented [*ajmaʿ*] upon them [the books of the mishnah] without exception or opposition."[103] Moyal repeats this claim several times in the course of his work. In a subsequent rendition of this account, he explains that, fearing that the Oral Torah be forgotten, "the scholars [*al-ʿulamāʾ*] deliberated on lifting the ban on writing it down and, by a consensus of opinions [*bi-ijmāʿ al-ārāʾ*], allowed the writing of the mishnah."[104] In other words, the prohibition against writing the Oral Torah was overturned by the ijmāʿ of the scholars of Rabbi Judah ha-Nasi's generation. Given

[100] The genre of Jewish succession lists was apparently initially adapted from the Greco-Roman literary genre of scholarly successions. See Amram Tropper, "Avot," EJ².

[101] An *isnād* is the chain of transmission supporting a *ḥadīth*, a traditional report concerning the life and teachings of the prophet Muhammad. As Cyril Glass explains, "the authority, and character, including moral probity, of every member of a chain in the transmission of a given Ḥadīth, and the existence of alternative chains of transmission for a saying, were fundamental criteria for accepting Ḥadīth as authentic." See Cyril Glassé, "Isnād," NEI. See also J. Robson, "Isnād," EI². Moyal uses the term *isnād* in reference to the transmission of a particular mishnah in *at-Talmūd*, 108.

[102] See "idjmāʿ" in EI².

[103] Mūyāl, *at-Talmūd*, 7. Moyal also employs this concept in his exposition on the Sanhedrin: "All these great men in Israel gathered and consented (*ajmaʿū*) to enact the appropriate laws for the life of the nation and they determined the daily prayers." See ibid., 26, 28, 48. Cf. Maimonides's introduction to *Mishneh Torah*. Maimonides does not appear to use the term ijmāʿ here, though he does claim that Rabbi Judah ha-Nasi taught the mishnah "to the scholars in public and it was revealed to all of Israel and they all wrote it down." On the notion of ijmāʿ or parallels to it in Judaism, especially in Middle Eastern Judaism, see chapter 2 above, as well as Goitein, *A Mediterranean Society*, 2:65–66; Levy, *The Sephardim in the Ottoman Empire*, 51; Fishman, "Guarding Oral Transmission."

[104] Mūyāl, *at-Talmūd*, 37.

its use of Islamic legal terminology, this is an account that would—and may well have been intended to—appeal to Muslim readers, a presentation of Judaism not only in their own language, but also in terms that they could be expected to hold in high regard.

Consider two other telling instances in which Moyal uses distinctly Islamic terminology in his writings on Judaism. Well-known are the so-called Pillars of Islam (*arkān ad-dīn*), including profession of faith, pilgrimage, prayer worship, fasting, and alms-giving.[105] In his gloss on Rabbi Shimon's exhortation in *Pirkei avot* to "be careful with the reading of *shemaʿ*," Moyal explains that "*shemaʿ* is the most important pillar [*ahamm arkān*[106]] of the morning and evening prayers [*ṣalātay aṣ-ṣabāḥ wa-l-ghurūb*]."[107] Especially in the context of prayer (*ṣalā*), this use of the term *arkān*, it is fair to presume, was not accidental; it was part of the broader project of the text to emphasize the shared features of Judaism and the other religions of *an-nāṭiqīn bi-ḍ-ḍād* (Arabic-speakers). The same might be said of Moyal's curious use of the term *jihād*. Of Rabbi Ishmael, Moyal writes that he would try to provide sustenance for women whose "fathers and husbands were engaged in holy war [*jihād*]."[108] Jewish legal literature, to be sure, has a developed discourse on the "commanded war," (*milḥemet miẓvah*),[109] but in classical Judeo-Arabic texts, the term jihād is not typically used to refer to these wars.[110] Of course, it is possible that by using jihād, Moyal may have intended nothing more than simply to translate the concept of *milḥemet miẓvah* into Arabic. Regardless of Moyal's intent, however, the impact on the reader would once again likely have been the same, leaving him or her with the impression—a reasonable one, to be sure—that Judaism and Islam are remarkably similar and, by extension, that Judaism need not provoke apprehension or fear.

There are more explicit ways in which Moyal sought to link Judaism with Islam. Consider, for example, his commentary on Hillel's maxim, in the second chapter of *Pirkei avot*, that "one who increases women, increases witchcraft." Moyal explains that "increasing women" refers to polygyny (*taʿaddud az-zawjāt*). Elaborating, he provides the context:

[105] See S. Nomanul Haq, "Rukn," EI².

[106] The term *rukn* (pl. *arkān*) can also be translated as "basic element."

[107] Mūyāl, *at-Talmūd*, 112.

[108] Ibid., 135.

[109] See, e.g., Maimonides's *Hilkhot melakhim* (Laws of Kings) 5:1. On the evolution of the concept of "holy war" in Judaism, see Firestone, *Holy War in Judaism*.

[110] Tellingly, there is no entry for jihād in Joshua Blau, MTAY. I thank Benjamin Hary for confirming, in private correspondence, that he too had not encountered this usage in the Judeo-Arabic literature he has edited.

> It was permitted earlier for each Israelite [man] to take [the number of] wives permitted by the Qurʾan to Muslims, until some leaders [*ayimma*] put an end[111] to this. [But] not all of the nation follows it [the restriction]. There are, even now, a number of places where it is still permitted for any Israelite who wishes to marry two, three, or four women. But what is meant by this maxim [about wives and witchcraft] is clear and does not require elucidation.[112]

Although we might be curious to know what Moyal intends in this final line (is it "clear" to Moyal that polygyny leads to witchcraft or is it simply "clear" that Hillel thought so?), our concern here is rather with the first part of this passage. Moyal plainly identifies and equates the Jewish laws concerning polygyny with those of the Qurʾan's limit of four wives.[113] It must be noted that Moyal somewhat overstates the similarity. The Talmud does record "sound advice" that recommends that men limit the number of their wives to four,[114] but other rabbinic opinions permit as many wives as a man can afford to sustain.[115] Moyal's exaggeration of the correspondence between Islam and Judaism in this regard, I would argue, is another aspect of the apologetic nature of *at-Talmūd*. In his attempt to make Judaism feel more familiar and less threatening to his non-Jewish readers, in this case Muslims, Moyal not only describes Judaism in Islamic terms but even simplifies (or distorts) his presentation to conform to his argument of similarity.

The Challenge of Two Target Audiences

As a work of religious apologetics, Moyal's *at-Talmūd* is particularly intriguing in that, in a single text, it simultaneously addresses both Christians and Muslims. Thus far we have analyzed aspects of the text that appear to be concerned with only one or the other of the religious traditions. In addition, there are instances in which Moyal refers to both religions at once, highlighting the commonalities shared

[111] The word *ḥadd* could also mean "restriction [of number]." Either sense of the word provides the same basic meaning here.

[112] Mūyāl, *at-Talmūd*, 104.

[113] Qurʾan 4:3 reads: "If you fear that you cannot treat orphans with fairness, then you may marry other women who seem good to you: two, three, or four of them." For ʿAbduh's and Rida's approach to polygyny, see Gätje, *The Qurʾān and Its Exegesis*, 248–61.

[114] b. Yevamot 44a records that "sound advice was given: only four [wives] but no more, so that each may receive one marital visit a month."

[115] See b. Yevamot 65a.

by all three faiths. Twice in the course of his introductory review of the transmission of Jewish Oral Law, Moyal stresses that the individuals mentioned are common to all three traditions. Of the biblical prophet Elijah, for instance, he explains that this "famous prophet, who never died but ascended alive to the heavens in a chariot of fire" is the "saint Ilyās of the Christians and a legendary figure for Islam."[116] The insertion of this line serves to provide both Christian and Muslim readers a sense that this story is one that they share. Similarly, Moyal identifies the biblical Jonah as the one "who is mentioned in the Arabic translation of the Bible by the name Yūnān and in the Qurʾan by the name Yūnis."[117] Once more, through these insertions, Moyal attempts to convince his reader, whether Christian or Muslim, that Judaism is not a foreign or shadowy religion. It actually shares some of the same "saints" and "legendary figures" of Christianity and Islam.

The three religions' commonalities are not limited to biblical characters. In his discussion of the book of the Zohar[118] (which Moyal contends, contra one of his rabbinic advisors, is a medieval text, not one written by the tannaitic Rabbi Shimon bar Yoḥai),[119] Moyal defines Kabbalah, somewhat critically, as "inherited customs, that is, a strange mixture of imaginary, hypothetical ideas concerning divinity and the spirit and what lies beyond the grave." It is akin, he explains, to the ideas of the Christian "Mystics," that is, "people of secrets," and the "teaching that is transmitted by the scholars known in Islam as Sufis."[120] In other words, not only are all three religions related in their shared reverence for the same ancient prophets, but they have also experienced comparable religious movements through the course of their parallel histories (even if the rationalistically inclined Moyal was not particularly sympathetic to such mystical movements).[121]

[116] Mūyāl, *at-Talmūd*, 10.

[117] Ibid., 18.

[118] For a discussion of this passage of Moyal's *at-Talmūd*, see Levy, "Jewish Writers in the Arab East," 210–12.

[119] It seems likely that Moyal was informed here by the scholarship of the nineteenth-century Jewish historian Heinrich Graetz, whether by actually reading Graetz's writings or by learning of his conclusions indirectly. Graetz argued that the thirteenth-century Moses de Leon "forged" the Zohar, claiming that it was the work of Shimon bar Yoḥai. See Graetz, *History of the Jews*, 4:11ff. On the influence of Graetz's scholarship on the Jews of the Middle East, especially via curriculum of the Alliance Israélite Universelle schools, see Rodrigue, *French Jews, Turkish Jews*, 83; Rodrigue, *Jews and Muslims*, 110.

[120] Mūyāl, *at-Talmūd*, 119.

[121] On Moyal as a rationalist and participant in Enlightenment discourse, see Levy, "Jewish Writers in the Arab East," especially 210–12.

Moyal's Nationalist Reading of Jewish History and Its Ottoman Implications

Even as he works to present Judaism as favorably and familiarly as possible to Christian and Muslim Arabs, Moyal nonetheless writes of Jewish history in distinctly nationalist terms. While seeking to remove, as much as possible, elements of religious difference between Jews and their Christian and Muslim neighbors in the Middle East, he makes no effort to conceal what he perceives to be the Jews' history of nationalism and their defiant will for political independence. Indeed, he translates Jewish history and concepts not only into Christian and Islamic terms but also into the still-developing language of late nineteenth- and early twentieth-century nationalism in the Arab world, language that pervades *at-Talmūd.*

Consider, for instance, the way Moyal describes the biblical prophet Isaiah and the leaders Ezra and Nehemia. Of Isaiah, Moyal writes that "this prophet was sharp-tongued and bitter in speech, but he was extremely patriotic [*kāna waṭaniyyan shadīd al-waṭaniyya*], as is obvious to anyone who looks closely at his wonderfully eloquent sayings."[122] Here Moyal uses the term *waṭaniyya*, derived from homeland, *waṭan.*[123] In reference to the biblical figures Ezra and Nehemia, the leaders of the Israelite return to the Holy Land from the Babylonian Exile, he generally uses a word even more analogous to the then-current concept of nationalism, *qawmiyya*, from the word that was beginning to be used for the modern sense of "nation," *qawm.*[124] Moyal writes that Ezra and Nehemia were in the "vanguard of the Israelite national awakening [*muqaddimat tilka an-nahḍa al-qawmiyya al-isrāʾīliyya*] that brought about the rebuilding of the Temple and the walls of Jerusalem and the return of the ancient people [*ash-shaʿb al-qadīm*] to its land to govern itself by itself under the protectorate of King Cyrus."[125] Patriotism and nationalism, in Moyal's view, are not new sentiments for Jews; rather, they are of antique vintage, central to Jews' views and goals over two millennia earlier.

Moyal's particular presentation of the Jewish national past may reveal elements of the hopes he had for the contemporary Jewish national project in Palestine. Discerning the precise nature of these hopes

[122] Mūyāl, *at-Talmūd*, 21.

[123] The Egyptian *al-ḥizb al-waṭanī* was founded in 1879. See Ayalon, *Language and Change in the Arab Middle East*, 125–26.

[124] Although here I distinguish between *waṭaniyya* and *qawmiyya*, Eliezer Tauber has argued that, in the fin de siècle, there was not a "conceptual division of *qawmiyya* versus *waṭaniyya*." See Tauber, *The Emergence of the Arab Movements*, 245.

[125] Mūyāl, *at-Talmūd*, 25.

from a text of this genre is difficult, not least because Moyal's historical reconstructions suggest more than one model for Jewish independence. Given the Ottomanist political philosophy with which Moyal is associated in recent historiography,[126] especially because of lines like the one cited above in which he wrote of the compatibility of Zionist ambitions and those of "the Ottoman nation under whose shadow we stand,"[127] we may interpret his view of an Israelite awakening (nahḍa) "under the protectorate of King Cyrus" as his precursory model for a contemporary Jewish renaissance under the Ottoman sultan. Indeed, Moyal describes the period of the Second Temple as one of "partial independence [*baʿḍ al-istiqlāl*] under the rule of an Israelite governor appointed by the decree of the Persian king."[128] In his account of Alexander the Great's conquest of Judea, Moyal uses a more specific phrase, describing the Greek ruler's decision to preserve Judea's "internal (or domestic) independence [*istiqlālahā ad-dākhilī*]."[129] Employing the central terms of the modern Arabic political-ideological lexicon[130]—*waṭaniyya, qawmiyya, shaʿb, nahḍa, istiqlāl*—Moyal projects them onto the distant Jewish past, implying, perhaps, that such a national awakening, *nahḍa qawmiyya*, is possible again. This may well have been how Moyal was able to unite his Zionism with his Ottomanism, how his newspaper *Ṣawt al-ʿuthmāniyya* (The Voice of Ottomanism) could serve to defend Zionism. Just as the Israelites returned to their land with "partial independence" (*baʿḍ al-istiqlāl*) as a Persian protectorate in the Second Temple period, or with "internal independence" (*al-istiqlāl ad-dākhilī*) under Alexander's Greek regime,[131] so too in Moyal's own day the Jews might return to Palestine and live there, this time as an *Ottoman* protectorate. Moyal's particular vision of Zionism, then, could be perfectly consistent with his commitment to the Ottoman Empire.

However, this interpretation of Moyal's reading of Jewish history is complicated by other aspects of his presentation of Jewish history. For instance, he also writes admiringly about the Maccabees, during whose rule "the Israelite nation achieved complete independence [*tamām al-istiqlāl*] and power." Indeed, "the neighboring nations feared its [the Hasmonean state's] might."[132] Such a description could hardly have been intended to relax the anxieties of those Arabs who saw a threat in Zionist ambitions. If the precedent of the Jews under Cyrus or Alexan-

[126] See, e.g., Campos, *Ottoman Brothers*.
[127] *ha-Ḥerut* 4:70 (February 2, 1912), 3.
[128] Mūyāl, *at-Talmūd*, 25.
[129] Ibid., 66.
[130] See Ayalon, *Language and Change in the Arab Middle East*.
[131] Mūyāl, *at-Talmūd*, 66.
[132] Ibid., 31.

der could be understood to imply, in modern times, a semiautonomous Jewish community under the Ottomans, the precedent of the Maccabees would suggest something quite different and, from the Arab reader's perspective, far more insidious.

Moyal is even more explicit in his admiration of yet another historical advocate of the "full independence" of the "Israelite nation," namely, Bar Kokhba. In his introductory rendition of the transmission of the Jewish Oral Law and of Israelite history, Moyal ultimately reaches Rabban Gamaliel. Among the "famous contemporaries" of Rabban Gamaliel was

> Rabbi Akiba, the great teacher, leader of the famous nationalist party [*al-ḥizb al-waṭanī ash-shahīr*], who had twenty-four thousand rebels [under his control]. He created an army with them and placed them under the leadership of Bar Kokhba, whom Josephus, the biased historian [*al-muʾarrikh al-muḥābī*], names Bar Koziba, that is, the son of the liar. This was a shameful appellation from which the truth exonerates him. This Bar Kokhba was among the greatest leaders. . . . He rose up against the Roman conquerors who had subjugated Judea after they conquered Jerusalem and burned the Temple.[133]

This passage is one in which Moyal's voice (or, perhaps, that of an unnamed text on which he chose to rely) is most clearly discernible in the course of his historical exposition. Here Moyal unequivocally affirms his respect for Bar Kokhba and his efforts to achieve Israelite independence. Moyal further describes "Bar Kokhba and his brave men [*rijāluhu ash-shujʿān*]" who fought the Roman armies in "heroic wars" in which they attempted "to restore the independence of their nation [*ummatihim*], emulating the Maccabees who preceded them."[134] Such overt approval for Bar Kokhba, imagined as a militant nationalist hero, is more difficult to mesh with a model of internal autonomy in an Ottoman framework.

However, in his approval of Rabbi Akiba's national party, Moyal may have had a more recent example in mind, suggesting a far more positive approach to the Ottoman Empire. Rabbi Akiba, according to Moyal, was the leader of the national (or nationalist)[135] party (*al-ḥizb al-waṭanī*) of the Israelites. Having spent many years in Egypt, Moyal could not have written these words without thinking of political parties

[133] Ibid., 36.

[134] Ibid., 36

[135] Again, it is difficult to translate this term precisely. It may also be taken as "patriotic." See Tauber, *The Emergence of the Arab Movements*, 124.

with this very name in contemporary Egypt. In the three decades preceding the 1909 publication of *at-Talmūd*, there had already been two incarnations of parties named al-Ḥizb al-waṭanī.[136] The first such National Party was founded in 1879 and had some role in the ʿUrabi movement against European domination in Egypt (known by the slogan "Egypt for the Egyptians").[137] "The leaders of the ʿUrabi movement," write historians Israel Gershoni and James Jankowski, "repeatedly expressed their loyalty to the Ottoman Sultan, 'the Sultan of the Islamic Milla,' [and] emphasized their desire to see 'Islamic-Ottoman Egypt' continue under formal Ottoman sovereignty." After the British invasion of Egypt in 1882, this National Party disintegrated.

A decade later, in 1893, this party (or one with the same name, in any case) was revived, first as a secret society, and eventually as an open party. Importantly, this second incarnation of al-Ḥizb al-waṭanī had strong ties to the Ottoman government; its leader, Mustafa Kamil, was a firm proponent of Egyptian solidarity with the Ottoman Empire. The members of al-Ḥizb al-waṭanī, explain Gershoni and Jankowski, "were consistent advocates of Egyptian political collaboration with the Ottoman Empire."[138] This position concerning the Ottoman Empire was certainly not unanimous among Egyptian political movements in the first decade of the twentieth century. A rival party, Ḥizb al-umma (the People's Party[139]), "unambiguously rejected the idea of a continuing Egyptian political bond with the Ottoman Empire."[140] It would seem to be of some importance that Moyal chose to label Bar Kokhba's movement, which he described in the most laudatory language, not as Ḥizb al-umma but as al-Ḥizb al-waṭanī. This terminology might suggest that Moyal did not, ultimately, wish to have Bar Kokhba's "full independence" movement seen as a paradigm that would demand a complete separation from the Ottoman Empire.

Regardless of Moyal's precise political intentions, he wrote about the Jews and Jewish history in unmistakably nationalist terms. In this sense, *at-Talmūd* can be read not only as a religious apologetic-polemic but also as a subtle argument for the historical antiquity of Jewish

[136] Moyal was clearly not thinking of Palestine's *al-ḥizb al-waṭanī al-uthmānī*, which was formed in 1910—that is, after the publication of *at-Talmūd*. See Muslih, *The Origins of Palestinian Nationalism*, 82.

[137] On the ʿUrabi movement, see Schölch, *Egypt for the Egyptians!* On the development of nationalism in Egypt more generally, see Gershoni and Jankowski, *Egypt, Islam, and the Arabs*

[138] Gershoni and Jankowski, *Egypt, Islam, and the Arabs*, 5–7.

[139] As *umma* may also be rendered "nation," the name of this party might also be understood as the Party of the Nation.

[140] Ibid., 8.

nationalism in its various forms. The phenomenon that his Arab readers were witnessing in Palestine, Moyal may have been suggesting, was not wholly modern or novel; rather, it was one with historical precedents extending back nearly two millennia. It remains unclear, however, if Moyal believed that knowledge of the precedents might allay Arab fears about the Zionist movement in the present. The goal of Moyal's religious apologetic project is, in the end, much clearer than is the political vision driving his translation of Jewish history into Arab nationalist terminology.

However tempting it may be to see Moyal's political views as the ignored and forgotten key to Arab-Zionist cooperation and amity, the picture Moyal paints of ancient Jewish nationalism does not offer a model for anything less than "internal independence." To the extent that we may infer a political stance from his presentation of Jewish history, Moyal advocated neither binationalism nor the sublimation of Jewish nationalism for the sake of coexistence with Palestine's non-Jewish residents. For Moyal, Jewish sovereignty in ancient Palestine was limited only to the extent that the ruling empire was too powerful to be overthrown; the presence of non-Jews in the land did not represent an obstacle to the Jews' political independence. In other words, this was a vision that may well have been articulated to be consistent with loyalty to the Ottoman Empire, but it could hardly have been designed to promote sacrificing particularist Jewish nationalism on the altar of peace with Palestine's Arabs. Perhaps this was because Moyal, like many of his Jewish and non-Jewish contemporaries in Palestine, considered Zionism's relationship to the Ottoman Empire (rather than to Palestine's Arabs) to be the truly pressing concern in the minds of the empire's Arabs.

And yet Moyal had the linguistic tools, cultural knowledge, and political interest to reach out directly to his Christian and Muslim neighbors and present them with an apology for Judaism sensitive to their particular religious traditions and sensibilities, even as he subtly made the case for Jewish nationalism. It is this combination of capabilities and concerns that made Moyal and his fellow Sephardic Zionists a critical community for the broader Zionist efforts to understand and to instruct the non-Jewish natives of Late Ottoman Palestine.

Nissim Malul's *Secrets of the Jews*

Whereas discerning Moyal's particular intentions is challenging owing to the subtlety of his presentation, such subtlety is not a characteristic of the work of Moyal's younger colleague, Nissim Malul. Just two years after Moyal published *at-Talmūd*, Malul published his own short Arabic book aimed at answering contemporary Arab concerns about Jews and Judaism. Compared to Moyal's book, Malul's 1911 *Kitāb asrār al-yahūd* (The Book of the Secrets of the Jews) is more explicitly a work of apologetics. Through his sixty-four-page text, Malul tried to show that Judaism is not the foreign, insidious phenomenon that many Arabs believed it to be. Malul's book uses both philosophical discussion and historical analysis to set forth a sustained, if somewhat meandering, argument about the essential sameness of all religions, especially the monotheistic faiths of Judaism, Christianity, and Islam. Given the shared values and goals of these religions, Malul sets out to explain the hatred and violence that nonetheless developed between the various religious communities. The cause, Malul contends, has little to do with the religions' beliefs and principles; rather, it is *economic* jealousy that produces hostility between religious groups. While Malul's focus on financial competition may strike the reader as simplistic, it is, I argue, essential to understanding Malul's interpretation of Arab opposition to Zionism.

Before analyzing the text itself, it is instructive to consider the title Malul chose for it: *Secrets of the Jews*.[141] In 1893 in Beirut, Najib al-Hajj published *Fī az-zawāyā khabāyā aw kashf asrār al-yahūd* (Clandestine Things in the Corners, or Unveiling the Secrets of the Jews). This antisemitic book is an Arabic adaptation of Georges Corneilhan's 1889 *Juifs et opportunistes: Le judaisme en Egypte et Syrie*.[142] Because Malul knew of al-Hajj's book—he mentions it, though not by its title, in *Asrār al-yahūd*[143]—one suspects that he wished to have his own book understood as, at least in part, a rebuttal of al-Hajj's. Al-Hajj, he implies, failed to reveal truly the Jews' secrets; to understand the Jews properly, rather, one must read Malul's book.

After the book's dedication to his father, Malul immediately begins his broadside against critics of the Jews and Judaism. He contends that there are three types of knowledge-seekers: those who seek it without regard to its consequences; those who seek it in order to improve human society;[144] and those who seek it to satisfy their own ambition. It is people of the third category—a type Malul detests and regards

[141] While the phrase *asrār al-yahūd* is reminiscent of the Islamic notion of *asrār al-qurʾān*, the "secret meaning of the Qurʾan," Malul, I presume, had more recent anti-Jewish polemics in mind. On the concept of the Qurʾan's secret meanings, see Shigeru Kamada, "Secrets," EQ.

[142] See Norman A. Stillman, "Arab Antisemitic Literature," in Levy, *Antisemitism*. See also Haim, "Arabic Antisemitic Literature," 307–8.

[143] Malūl, *Kitāb asrār al-yahūd*, 1:19.

[144] Malul affiliates himself with this second category. Ibid., 8.

as "the root of the misfortune of humanity and the cause of human atrocities"—who

> recently rallied their forces and energies and published books the purpose of which was to oppress the Jews. Some claimed that the Talmud commands them [Jews] to offer human sacrifices each Passover. Others went so far as to say that the Israelites devote all of their interest now to the restoration of sovereignty [*al-mulk*] to Israel. Their proof of this is their [Jews'] colonization of Palestine. Some of the primary, ignoble leaders of this group do not refrain from publishing newspapers and despicable leaflets to popularize their beliefs among the classes of the people in order to attain their wicked goals.[145]

Though al-Hajj's book may have informed Malul's title, it was an article written in the widely circulated Cairo newspaper *al-Muʾayyad* that was, according to Malul, the primary impetus for penning this book.[146] This article, which was reprinted in the Beirut-based newspaper *al-Ḥaqīqa*, claimed "that the Israelites are trying to engage in agriculture and manufacture in Palestine because they aim to restore sovereignty to Israel and they rebel against the countries to which they belong." This article's author, Malul reports, warned "the government to look at them [the Jews] with a cautious and watchful eye."[147] Malul's response to this article was published in *al-Ḥaqīqa* itself, but he determined that a more sustained and vigorous rejoinder was necessary. "We wrote this book," he explains, "in order to disprove those accusations and to respond to the lies hurled at the Israelite nation by those ignoramuses and their ilk."[148]

If Malul was troubled by the allegations he read concerning Zionism's aims in Palestine, he chose to leave specific refutation of these matters to a planned subsequent volume of *Asrār al-yahūd*, which was meant to be a three-volume series. The second volume was conceived as an evaluation of the true—and, in Malul's mind, decidedly inoffensive and unthreatening—goals of Jewish immigration and settlement in Palestine,[149] while the third volume would have addressed

[145] Ibid., 7

[146] On *al-Muʾayyad*, see Ayalon, *The Press in the Arab Middle East*, 57–59.

[147] Malūl, *Kitāb asrār al-yahūd*, 7.

[148] Ibid., 8.

[149] In June 1913 Malul insisted in *ha-Ḥerut* that the Jews who immigrated to Palestine "came here to build a new nation." Cited in Behar and Ben-Dor Benite, eds., *Modern Middle Eastern Jewish Thought*. Apparently Malul believed that this motivation, if properly understood by Arabs, would be recognized as unproblematic.

the accusation that the Talmud prescribes human sacrifice, that is, the problem of the blood libel.[150]

In the end, Malul published only the first volume, which offered more general observations on the nature of religion, the characteristics of monotheistic religions, and the history of religious persecution. As he begins his discussion of religion, he acknowledges the perils of the task. "Religion is among the most difficult subjects of study," he asserts, "and the most dangerous."[151] Undeterred, however, Malul engages the subject directly. With an apparent penchant for categorization, he divides humanity first into those who "believe in the existence of a creator," including "Jews, Christians, Muslims, Magi, Confucians, Buddhists, and Brahmins," and those who do not believe.[152] He then further separates the first group into the monotheists, namely Jews, Christians, and Muslims, and the remaining polytheistic peoples [*al-mushrikūn*]. Arguing for the superiority of the monotheists, Malul claims that "if we look at human society in terms of [level of] civilization and progress, we see that the monotheists are ahead."[153]

"All Religions Have the Same Goal"

Despite these divisions, Malul insists early in his text that "all religions have the same goal, to order what is right and to forbid what is wrong (*al-amr bi-l-maʿarūf wa-n-nahy ʿan al-munkar*)," a phrase he repeats often throughout the book.[154] This refrain, significantly, is borrowed from the Qurʾan. It is used to describe the believers' moral mission. "You are the best community singled out for people," God tells believers in Q. 3:110, "you order what is right [and] forbid what is wrong" (*taʾmurūn bi-l-maʿrūf wa-tanhawn ʿan al-munkar*). This verse concludes by contrasting the believers with (most of) the People of the Book. "If the People of the Book had also believed, it would have been better for them. For although some of them do believe, most of them are lawbreakers." The Qurʾan, in this sura, highlights that segments of the People of the Book are considered to be among the believers.[155] "They

[150] Malūl, *Kitāb asrār al-yahūd*, 8.

[151] Ibid., 9–10.

[152] Ibid., 10.

[153] Ibid., 13.

[154] See, e.g., ibid.

[155] On the different groups associated with this quality, see Cook, *Commanding Right and Forbidding Wrong in Islamic Thought*, especially 13–14, 14n.5. On the relationship between Muhammad and those referred to in the Qurʾan as "the believers," see Donner, *Muhammad and the Believers*.

are not all alike," continues Sura 3, as "there are some among the People of the Book who are upright," who "believe in God and the Last Day, who order what is right and forbid what is wrong" (Q. 3:113–14). Malul boldly expands this Qurʾanic description to all monotheists, not merely to Muslims or a subgroup of the People of the Book.

In his book, Malul appears to be arguing not only against critics of the Jews but also against those who would delegitimize religion altogether. "Religion," he declares, "is the foundation of human society because it demands moral excellence and beneficence. It is the source of justice and integrity." Given religion's vital role, Malul contends that one must not abandon religion just because of the existence of "religious superstitions" or even the fact that religion "causes its radicals and extremists to use violence and force against those who disagree."[156] Because he devotes a great deal of attention in the book to acts of violence and persecution carried out in the name of religion, Malul is keen not to be misperceived as an opponent of religion broadly. Aiming to allay the concerns of both Muslim and Christian Arabs about the Jews and Judaism, Malul apparently recognized that he would have little effect were he to be perceived as harboring a bias against religion more generally.

Malul next presents his readers with brief descriptions of the three monotheistic religions (*diyānāt al-muwaḥḥidīn*), "in the order of their appearance" historically.[157] Beginning with "the Israelite religion," the term he generally uses for Judaism, Malul claims that this was "the first religion to be based on [the principle of] monotheism [*at-tawḥīd*]."[158] This religion's scripture, "the Torah," he elaborates, was "the first religious book in which the rules and duties of religion are written." Interestingly, in noting the diversity of Jewry, and particularly the distinction between Rabbanites and Karaites, Malul cites a medieval Islamic source, *al-Milal wa-n-niḥal*, the work of the eleventh- to twelfth-century Muslim author ash-Shahrastani (the same scholar whom al-Khalidi cited, as we saw in chapter 2).[159] Currently, Malul explains, "the Israelites are scattered throughout the world" as a result of "the Babylonian exile and the expansion of their dispersion by Titus the Emperor of Rome, who destroyed the Temple and demolished Jerusalem." Malul's account of Judaism concludes with the demographic

[156] Malūl, *Kitāb asrār al-yahūd*, 12.
[157] Ibid., 12.
[158] Ibid., 13.
[159] Ibid., 14.

estimate that the Jews of his day numbered "about ten million people around the world."[160]

Malul's concise presentation of "the Israelite religion" aims, in a number of ways, to prove that Judaism and Jews are not to be feared by Arabs. First of all, Jews are monotheists, just like Christians and Muslims; indeed, theirs was the very first monotheistic religion. The Jews, moreover, are a People of the Book, an *ahl al-kitāb*, and their Bible, the first scripture of its kind, guides their actions. Malul's appeal to ash-Shahrastani is certainly curious. While it highlights Malul's familiarity with certain medieval Islamic literature, it also may be part of his argument that Jews have been known to Muslims for centuries, and their religion was generally not viewed as any sort of threat. Finally, Malul at once acknowledges the Jews' history in Palestine but also emphasizes both their dispersion and their relatively small population. Especially when compared to the demographic estimates Malul offers later for Christians and Muslims, the implication may well be that Jews hardly merit anxiety.

Malul then moves from the relatively secure terrain of Judaism to the more sensitive topics (for a Jewish author) of Christianity and Islam. In his presentation of Christianity, Malul is keen from the first line to show the religion's close relationship to Judaism, an eagerness similar to that of Moyal in *at-Talmūd*. "The Christian religion," Malul writes, "was founded from the Israelite and it spread initially among the Jews and then among the rest of the nations." The primary principle of Christianity, he explains, is "that people are brothers and God is the father of all humanity." Like the other religions, Christianity demands that the faithful act kindly and it prohibits evil. In obvious parallel to his presentation of Judaism's holy texts and its factions, Malul explains that "the rules and teachings of this religion are based on the Four Gospels, the Book of Acts, and the Epistles," and that "Christianity is broadly divided into two churches: the eastern and the western." Finally, he notes that the Christians are at present "about five hundred million" in number.[161]

Entering the more precarious territory of Islam—given Muslims' political power and the fact that Muslims constituted the majority of the population in the societies in which this text would be read—Malul begins his presentation gingerly with a literal definition of the word Islam: " 'docility,' 'submission,' 'obedience' to the commands and prohibitions of the commander without objection." Again, in parallel to

[160] Ibid.
[161] Ibid., 14–15.

his presentations of Judaism and Christianity, Malul notes that Islam is also based on a scripture, namely, "the Qurʾan and the Sunna," and it "demands complete monotheism [*tawḥīd*]," a concept he already linked to Judaism. As he did with Judaism, Malul again cites the medieval Muslim author ash-Shahrastani as he explains the internal but, in his view, fairly insignificant sectarian divisions within Islam. He then lists the five pillars of Islam and concludes with a demographic estimate of about three hundred million Muslims worldwide.[162]

The precisely parallel form in which Malul presents these three brief descriptions matches the content of his ultimate claim, namely, that these religions are, in essence, identical.[163] Judaism, Christianity, and Islam, he argues, share much common ground, and are in harmony in the most important respects. "Broadly," Malul concludes, "the monotheistic religions mentioned above declare the unity of the Creator, that He is the creator of existence and engineer of reality.[164] The people of these religions and their adherents believe in the afterlife, resurrection, doomsday, and the Final Day, and that there is punishment for evil and reward for goodness."[165] Especially in light of our analysis of al-Khalidi's manuscript and its understanding of the grave implications for Palestine of the lack of a Jewish belief in the afterlife, Malul's insistence that Judaism shares these beliefs with Christianity and Islam is especially significant.

The question necessarily arises: if these religions are so patently in unison, why is there so much discord between them? It is in anticipation of this issue that Malul highlights the internal divisions within each religion:

> If you find that members of the same religion divide themselves due to selfishness, self-love, egotism, and politics (such as the division of the eastern and western churches in Christianity, and the divisions that arose since the illness of Islam's prophet in Islam, and the divisions of the tribes of the children of Israel in Israelitism [Judaism]), it is no surprise that one finds divisions between different religions.[166]

[162] Ibid., 15–16.

[163] Compare Malul's attempt to harmonize Judaism, Christianity, and Islam with Jurji Zaydan's contemporaneous attempt, "when dealing with the relationship between Islam and Christianity," to "play down any tension between both religions" and, as Umar Ryad puts it, to "show that Christians during most of history lived in harmony with their Muslim compatriots." Ryad, *Islamic Reformism and Christianity*, 77.

[164] Alternatively: "the universe."

[165] Malūl, *Kitāb asrār al-yahūd*, 16.

[166] Ibid., 16–17.

In other words, the tensions *between* religions are the result of "selfishness, self-love, egotism, and politics," no different from the tensions among members of the same religion. The tensions are decidedly *not* the consequence of essential differences between the religions or between religious beliefs.

Translation and the "Microbe" of Antisemitism

Malul now turns again specifically to the case of antisemitism in a section of the book entitled "Those Who Rise Up against the Jews." Here he sets out to identify the roots of antisemitism in the contemporary Middle East. Malul cites a number of recent, late nineteenth-century European antisemitic works, including Edouard Drumont's *La France Juive* (1886), Kalixt de Wolski's *La Russie Juive* (1887), Georges Corneilhan's *Juifs et opportunistes* (1889, mentioned above), along with the classic antitalmudic, anti-Jewish polemic *Entdecktes Judenthum* (1700) by Johann Andreas Eisenmenger.[167] Malul blames these European antisemites for the advent of antisemitism in the modern Middle East, tracing the phenomenon to Arabic translations of these types of works. "This microbe" of antisemitism, carried by "the wind of the sandstorm to some of the children of the East," ultimately "entered their veins and mixed with their blood."[168] Antisemitism, in Malul's view, is a foreign, European import to the Middle East, a disease that has regrettably infected the consciousness and sensibility of many Arabs. Importantly, Malul refers to the source of the phenomenon as "European," not "Christian," highlighting the regional or cultural origins, but not the *religion*, of its practitioners. Antisemitism is a disease in Malul's rendering,[169] unrelated to theological or religious principles. Particularly relevant for our discussion in this chapter, antisemitism is a disease that has spread through *translation*.

In one paragraph of his rendition of Jewish history, Malul seeks to explain two aspects of the Jewish experience that he believes are widely misunderstood. The first concerned Jews' loyalty to the governments of the lands in which they lived; the second related to the perception that Jews were exceedingly wealthy and obsessed with money.

[167] Malul renders Eisenmenger as "Armenger."

[168] Ibid., 19.

[169] It is unclear whether Malul had in mind here Leon Pinsker's 1882 *Autoemancipation*, in which the idea of antisemitism as a disease was a centerpiece of the author's proto-Zionist theory.

Both matters were obviously of great consequence to Malul as they represent two of the central rationalizations for hatred of the Jews.

> After the second destruction of Jerusalem, by Titus, the Jews were scattered throughout the world. They all came to belong to the authority [*sulṭa*] to which the land that they settled submitted. The lesson that the Israelites learned from the destruction and time, which is the best teacher, is that their destruction and the fall of the crown of their kingdom happened in order to spread their word. They also saw from the differences of the peoples, nations, and tribes in the Dark Ages that there was no better path to follow than to amass money in order to preserve their existence among those peoples.

Here Malul insists not only that Jews have consistently submitted to the authority of their host governments, but also that their loss of their own sovereignty and their subsequent dispersion served a positive function: "to spread their word." In his inversion of the traditional Jewish perspective on the exile as an unmitigated evil, a punishment for the Jews' sins, it is not clear to what extent Malul had in mind the nineteenth-century Reform movement's concept of the "Jewish mission" in the Diaspora, a concept that informed Reform's later rejection of Jewish nationalism and Zionism. The similarity of Moyal's view to classical Reform's transvaluation of the Diaspora view strikes the reader as markedly non- or even anti-Zionist.[170] But this book was published the very year Malul returned to Palestine and became an employee of the Zionist Organization. It is thus difficult to determine precisely where Malul stood on the matter. Did he believe that there was a value in the dissemination of Jewish ideas that resulted from Jewish dispersion, but that now that this had occurred, a Jewish return to Palestine was appropriate? Or did Malul, like many except the most radical Zionists of the time, see no contradiction between the perpetuation of Diasporic Jewish communities, on the one hand, and the growth of a Jewish community in Palestine, on the other? The explanation of the apparent discrepancy notwithstanding, there is no ambiguity or ambivalence with regard to the latter part of the paragraph. In the Diaspora, Malul contends, the Jews recognized that the only means of combating the existential threat posed by dispersion was to attain wealth and, with it, power.

[170] Cf. the nineteenth-century neo-Orthodox position of Samson Raphael Hirsch on the mission of Israel in exile: "Israel accomplished its task better in exile than in the full possession of good fortune. Indeed, improvement and correction were the chief purposes of the *Galuth*—exile." See Hirsch, *The Nineteen Letters of Ben Uziel*, 82.

Economics, Anti-Jewish Persecution, and Anti-Zionism

Though the acquisition of wealth helped to preserve the Diasporic Jewish communities, it also set the stage for the rise of antisemitism. The Jews, Malul writes:

> mostly worked in commerce and manufacture, but many paid attention to agriculture as well, aside from those who went to the sciences and the arts where they advanced ahead of their contemporaries. This caused envy among their contemporaries, who exerted effort to attack them and to plant the seeds of slander and groundless fabrications defaming them and their religion.[171]

In these lines, Malul at once impugns antisemitism and anti-Judaism as being driven by nothing more than base envy, while he also implicitly defends the Jews against the accusation that they exclusively engage in "unproductive" economic activities. The Jews are not involved merely in commerce; they participate in manufacture, agriculture, sciences, and arts as well. Indeed, as Malul sees it, it was particularly in the arts and sciences that the Jews distinguished themselves (in other words, not in commerce or banking).

In his text, Malul seeks to expose religious bigotry and persecution of varied sorts and in numerous contexts. He focuses heavily on religious persecution committed by Christians. In fact, he devotes fifteen of the book's sixty-four pages to enumerating the anti-Jewish policies of the Spanish Inquisition, a period in which he was interested owing in large measure, no doubt, to his own Sephardic heritage.[172] Though he concentrates most on the persecution suffered by Jews, Malul also highlights periods in which Christians persecuted Muslims. In his discussion of the Crusades, for instance, he cites the alleged slaughter of ten thousand Muslims perpetrated by Christians in Jerusalem.[173] However, he does not limit his discussion to discrimination carried out by Christians; he refers as well to the taxes levied on non-Muslims in the Muslim Umayyad state (the *jizya* and the *kharāj*). Moreover, even in his passages about the violence perpetrated by Christians in the course of the Crusades, Malul emphasizes that this "fanaticism" was driven by the fact that the "Christians remembered the advance of the Muslims and their oppression of them."[174] In his conclusion,

[171] Ibid., 26.
[172] See ibid., 27–41.
[173] Ibid., 49.
[174] Malul contends this twice. See ibid., 44, 46.

Malul insists that "Muslims and Jews are beaten in Christian countries, while Christians and Jews are humiliated in Muslim or Arab countries."[175] Religious persecution, in other words, is not the monopoly of any one religion; Jews, though, are conspicuously absent from the series of aggressors.

Malul returns one last time to his thesis as he brings his book to a close. "The biggest reason for these oppressions is money." This was the case, he repeats, with the persecution enacted by, among others, the Umayyads, the Abbasids, and the Crusaders. Indeed, Malul contends, "what the Arabs did to the Jews of Yathrib [Madina] was also for money, due to jealousy and envy. And this is the main impetus for the Russian Revolution that took place a few years ago."[176] For Malul, the motivation for intercommunal persecution is universal and timeless, the same at the founding moment of Islam in the medieval Arabian Peninsula as in the contemporary Russian Revolution. Neither the Muslims of seventh-century Yathrib nor the Christians of nineteenth-century Russia had reason to hate the Jews other than financial envy and resentment.

Malul applied this argument to his interpretation of Arab opposition to Zionism in his own time. Like all other cases of anti-Jewish harassment and discrimination in history, anti-Zionism, Malul contended, could also be explained by the economic interests of the Zionist movement's most outspoken critics. In his extended analytical review of "The Arabic Press," which he published in the Odessa-based Hebrew journal *ha-Shiloaḥ* in 1914, Malul wrote about the rise of the anti-Zionist press in Palestine. He attributed the inception of this press (in the form of the newspaper *al-Karmil*) to an incident about five years earlier involving "a Christian man named Najib Nassar who dealt in real estate in Tiberias." Malul explains that Nassar—the same Nassar who would later translate Gottheil's *Jewish Encyclopedia* article on Zionism—served as an agent in the sale of "hundreds of dunams of land" to the Jewish Colonization Association (JCA) settlement company. "One time," Malul alleges, Nassar:

> came to an official of this company and requested his commission for a sale, claiming that he had previously told this official about the availability of these lands, so he deserves a commission even though the sale had been completed without his involvement. Of course, the JCA official did not want to treat the company's money as one would treat his own and so he did not want to

[175] Ibid., 54.
[176] Ibid., 57.

> pay him [Nassar] anything given that this [Nassar's claim] was a fabrication, on the one hand. On the other hand, if the sum that the man requested had been small, perhaps he would have given up some of the rights of the company. But the sum was not small at all, so it was impossible to fulfill this strange demand. When Nassar saw that his hope was disappointed, he went and joined with a well-known author (Rashid Haddad, who is the editor of one of the large newspapers in Beirut) in Haifa, and together they produced the newspaper *al-Karmil.* Nassar's sole purpose was to write against the Hebrew settlement in the Land of Israel, so that Arabs would no longer sell land to Jews.[177]

Nassar's anti-Zionism, in Malul's interpretation, had nothing to do with his Christianity nor with his beliefs about the future of Palestine. Rather, "Nassar began writing harsh articles against 'the Zionists' and thought that the Jews would be frightened of him and fulfill his [monetary] demands." When he discovered that he was unsuccessful and that the Zionists were not taking him seriously, "he continued his war, and so he is fighting against the Yishuv until today."[178] According to Malul, Nassar, "the known hater of Israel" who stood at the center of the anti-Zionist Arabic press that *ha-Ḥerut*'s editors and writers regularly railed against as the "Great Danger," was simply a self-interested man seeking financial gain. Had he continued to profit from the Zionist movement, Malul implies, Nassar would have happily supported Jewish immigration, and the entire phenomenon of the anti-Zionist Arabic press might not have evolved. If certain Arabs considered the Jews to be obsessed with the pursuit of money, the feeling, for Jews like Malul, was mutual.

The Influence and Persistence of the Economic View of Anti-Zionism

In this chapter we have encountered a variety of ways in which influential Zionists of Late Ottoman Palestine sought to understand how they were perceived by their Arab neighbors and to influence those perceptions. We found that the Zionists were particularly interested in the Arabic press, viewing it as both a gauge and a generator of Arab public opinion. Moreover, we noted the multiple roles of translation in this encounter—in defending against anti-Zionism and in promoting

[177] *ha-Shiloaḥ* 31 (July–December 1914), 446.
[178] Ibid.

a more sympathetic view of Judaism and Jewish history (to combat antisemitism that was, itself, spread through translation).

In concluding this chapter, I should note a revealing irony that has emerged, especially in the study of the figure of Nissim Malul. Malul, to be sure, was not a political leader of the Zionist movement, neither in Palestine nor elsewhere. He was, however, highly influential in shaping the views of Zionists—both the leadership and the broader readership of Zionist periodicals—as regards their understanding of Arabs' perceptions of them.[179] Whether through his writing for *ha-Ḥerut* in Palestine and *ha-Shiloaḥ* in Odessa or his press reports for the Zionist officials in Jaffa, Constantinople, and Berlin, Malul's assessment of Arab views of Zionism in the Late Ottoman period was broadcast throughout the Zionist world. Given his central role in informing Zionists of how they were viewed by Arabs (or, more precisely, how he *thought* Zionists were viewed by Arabs), we should consider how Malul's assessment of Arab perceptions of Zionists accords with the argument of this book about religion and race. Concerning race, Malul says little, though in his call for Zionists to embrace the Arabic language as a basis for developing the Hebrew language and "a real Hebrew culture," he refers to the Jews as a "semitic nation" (*leʾum shemi*) that, through Arabic, can reinforce its "semitic nationhood" (*leʾumiyuteinu ha-shemi*).[180] This, however, concerns his understanding of the Jews, not how he believed they were viewed by Arabs.

The question is still more complex concerning religion. On the one hand, Malul would seem to have recognized the importance of religion in how Arabs viewed Jews and Zionism; after all, he wrote a book about *religion* in his effort to defend them. On the other hand, in his own book about intercommunal tension and persecution ostensibly motivated by religion, he insists that religion is never the "true" motivator behind the hostility and that what is really underlying the intolerance and violence is economic jealousy. For Malul, as for Moyal, religion—when "properly" understood—would naturally unite people within individual religions as well as across different religions. Problems arise only when religion is misunderstood. That actual substantive differences between religions could themselves cause hostility between practitioners of the respective religions was unfathomable. For some Zionists—then and since—it was perhaps easier to imagine a

[179] Cf. Yoav Gelber's dismissal of Rashid Khalidi's reference to Malul as having "played an important role in the Zionist movement." See Khalidi, *The Iron Cage*, 103; Gelber, "The Iron Cage."

[180] *ha-Ḥerut* (June 19, 1913), 2. See also Behar and Ben-Dor Benite, *Modern Middle Eastern Jewish Thought*, 69.

resolution to the tensions if economics, rather than religion, were seen to be at the heart of Arab opposition to Zionism. How and why both Zionists and Arabs tended to move away from the perception of religion and race at the core of their encounter in Palestine are questions I will address in the conclusion.

Conclusion

Ultimately this book has explored the ways in which the categories of religion and race functioned within a complex of categories used by Zionists and Arabs to define one another in the increasingly nationalizing environment of Late Ottoman Palestine and the broader region. I have argued that while there were deep concerns about land in the encounter between these communities, the parties related to one another not as perfect strangers competing for territory, but rather as groups with intertwined histories, cultures, beliefs, even blood. These points of intersection and commonality could at times produce a sense of shared interests while at other times they could generate hostility and fear.

"Enemies of the Crescent and the Cross": Religion and Palestinian Identity

My argument—that religion and race were central modes of perception and identification of others in the Arab-Zionist encounter—has a number of important implications for our understanding of the emergence of nationalisms in Palestine. First, it is worth highlighting the way in which the use of Judaism as a counterpoint facilitated the construction of a Palestinian Arab national identity that unites Christians and Muslims on religious/textual grounds. In my analysis of al-Khalidi's discussion of the absence of the afterlife in Judaism, I noted how al-Khalidi linked the New Testament and the Qurʾan, in contrast to the Jews' Torah. This association of Christianity and Islam, in explicit contradistinction to Judaism, is a phenomenon that developed further in the years immediately following the Great War. This was evidenced by, inter alia, the rise of groups called Muslim-Christian Associations in Palestine.[1] For instance, at an anti-Zionist rally in February 1920,

[1] This organization "first appeared in Jaffa early in November 1918, then spread to Jerusalem later in the same month." See Muslih, *The Origins of Palestinian Nationalism*, 158. On the MCA's origins and its emergence as the dominant nationalist organization among Palestinian Arabs in the years immediately following the Great War, see Porath, *The Emergence of the Palestinian-Arab National Movement 1918–1929*, 32–34, 105–8.

one of the Muslim-Christian Association movement's leaders, Maronite vicar Paul ʿAbboud, reminded his audience that Palestine, "this blessed land," is the "sanctuary [*mazār*] of Christianity and the direction of prayer [*qibla*] for Islam."[2] In perhaps the most evocative line in his speech, ʿAbboud beseeched his audience: "Do you want our holy places of worship, our noble sanctuaries, our glorious antiquities to be at the mercy of those enemies of the cross and the crescent?"[3] The designation of the Jews as "enemies of the cross and the crescent," if not unprecedented, is surely a rarity,[4] and its appearance here is indicative of a transformation in relations between Muslims and Christians in Palestine, and between those two groups and the Jews as the political situation transformed after the rise of Zionism and, still more, after the Balfour Declaration and the establishment of the British Mandate.[5]

ʿAbboud's rhetoric goes even further, linguistically fashioning a *single religious community* that unites Palestinian Christians and Muslims, and this is consistently done in relation and contrast to the Jews. In a speech to Muslims and Christians, ʿAbboud warned that "the goal of the Jews is dangerous for our religious-communal existence [*kayānunā al-millī*] and our national life [*ḥayātunā al-qawmiyya*]."[6] Speaking in Arabic, a language with a grammatical dual form, ʿAbboud nonetheless chooses the *singular* (rather than the dual) in the phrase "our religious-communal existence," suggesting that the Muslims and Christians of Palestine share not merely a "national life" but also a "religious-communal existence." In a later speech, also to a mixed crowd of Christians and Muslims, ʿAbboud appealed not only to their "Arab pride" in their common "nation" and "race" but also to their common language, "our noble Arabic language, the Sultaness of the Semitic languages,"[7] yet another mark of identity implicitly contrasted with the Jews and their less exalted Semitic language. This is not to say, though, that particularistic Christian language is wholly absent from this speech. In the text's conclusion, those who argue that the battle against Zionism is already lost

[2] According to Muslim tradition, Jerusalem was the first of the two directions of Islamic prayer [*ūlā al-qiblatain*] but had been replaced by Mecca in the second year of the Hijrah. See A. J. Wensinck, "Ḳibla," *Encyclopaedia of Islam*; and "Qibla," *Encyclopaedia of the Qur'ān*. ʿAbboud, *al-Arḍ al-muqaddasa wa-ṣ-ṣahyūniyya*, 11.

[3] ʿAbboud, *al-Arḍ al-muqaddasa wa-ṣ-ṣahyūniyya*, 13.

[4] I know of no earlier use of this phrase and, in personal correspondence, Mark Cohen confirmed that he, too, had not seen this phrase used previously. See Cohen, *Under Crescent and Cross*.

[5] On the role of Christians in the development of mandate-era Palestinian nationalism, see Haiduc-Dale, *Arab Christians in British Mandate Palestine*; Robson, *Colonialism and Christianity in Mandate Palestine*.

[6] ʿAbboud, *al-Arḍ al-muqaddasa wa-ṣ-ṣahyūniyya*, 7.

[7] Ibid., 13.

are reminded of "the formal and repeated protestations of his holiness the Pope."[8] Did not the Pope "make clear," asks the editor of the published speech rhetorically, "that it is forbidden for Jews to rule in the homeland of Christ [*waṭan al-masīḥ*] and for other religions and races to be subjugated in it on account of Jewish domination?"[9] Even with this powerful reference to Palestine as "Christ's homeland," though, this is a defense of all "other," i.e., non-Jewish, "religions and races." My book provides some of the necessary context to understand this intermixing of religious and racial language in the development of a national identity.

Race as a Tool of Inclusion or Annexation

Second, it is worth emphasizing the way in which the racial perspective of Zionists like Ben-Zvi informed their perceptions of nationalism. In contrast to Europe, where race in the fin de siècle was generally a language and tool of *national differentiation*, in the sphere of Palestine, racial discourse was able to serve an entirely opposite end. As we saw in chapter 3, Ben-Zvi imagined that Palestine's fellahin, who were in his view racially Jewish, "might become a distinct nation, or they might be dragged toward one of the nations that is established in Palestine in the process of national differentiation that has begun in our time."[10] In other words, in the context of Palestine, race permitted, in the minds of some, a marked flexibility in the boundaries of nationhood. The concept of race could be employed by nationalists not merely to divide communities and to legitimate that division as primordial and scientific; it could also be employed by nationalists to unite apparently disparate communities, for no less national ends.

Religion and Race in the Age of the Mandate

If religion and race were among the dominant categories in the Late Ottoman period, what came of these categories in the subsequent years of the British Mandate? The encounter that these later decades witnessed is typically viewed as a textbook case of *nationalist* conflict, that is, as

[8] This reference is presumably to Pope Benedict XV (served from 1914 to 1922), who had expressed his opposition to Zionism. See Minerbi, *The Vatican and Zionism*; Kreutz, *Vatican Policy on the Palestinian-Israeli Conflict*. The previous pope, Pius X, had also famously opposed Zionism in his meeting with Theodor Herzl. See Canepa, "Pius X and the Jews."

[9] ʿAbboud, *al-Arḍ al-muqaddasa wa-ṣ-ṣahyūniyya*, 29.

[10] Ben-Ẓevi, *ha-Tenuʿah ha-ʿarvit*, 20–21.

a conflict between groups that perceive themselves and their counterparts in national terms. Did religious and racial modes of perception and identification morph into national ones, and if so, through what process? In part, ʿAbboud's simultaneous use of religious, racial, and national language discussed above alludes to the fluidity between these categories and the ways in which one might be employed in the service of another. Methodologically, however, it is difficult to discern which is the most significant, motivating category and which others are simply serving it. Were speeches such as ʿAbboud's "truly" nationalist arguments expressed in a language that had not yet fully evolved for the purposes of nationalism and that still depended on older forms of categorization? Were the elites of each community "really" thinking in national terms but employing other terminology and logic to appeal to the masses? Or did all these categories simply continue meaningfully to be used simultaneously, as they had in the Late Ottoman period? I do not propose to answer these questions here—they obviously demand considerable research on the post-Ottoman period. I do, however, offer some suggestive reflections on the years that followed based on the Late Ottoman background that I have presented in this book.

It seems reasonable to expect that modes of categorization and perception might have changed after the fall of the Islamic Ottoman Empire and the imposition of a League of Nations mandatory regime led by a European (majority Christian) government that was charged with helping to forge a "national home for the Jewish people."[11] But to the extent that mutual perceptions in Palestine were informed by the legal structures of the governing regime, matters in this regard did not change quite as radically with the arrival of the British conquerors as one might suspect. The British left in place much of the Ottoman millet system. In Article 83 of the 1922 Palestine Order in Council, the British declared that "each Religious Community recognized by the Government shall enjoy autonomy for the internal affairs of the Community, subject to the provisions of any Ordinance or Order issued by the High Commissioner." Four years later, in 1926, the British issued the Religious Communities Organization Ordinance, establishing the process by which a "Religious Community" would apply to the high commissioner to make "regulations for its organization as a religious community and its recognition as such by the Government of Palestine."[12] Assaf Likhovski explains that the British may have left the millet

[11] As per the Balfour Declaration, the language of which was adopted in the League of Nations Mandate for Palestine.

[12] "Palestine Communities Ordinance: Text," *Jewish Telegraphic Agency Mail Service*, Jerusalem, February 16, 1926 (March 12, 1926).

structure in place "to prevent or at least retard the rise of a nationalist nonsectarian notion of Arab identity." Indeed, the British treated Palestine's population as three separate groups differentiated by religious affiliation—not merely in matters clearly related to religion—such that the mandatory administration envisioned three separate electoral colleges of Muslims, Christians, and Jews that would elect members of a proposed legislative council. It was only in the 1930s that the British began to include "race" or "nationality" (not as a replacement for but simply an addition to "religion") as a category of classification of the population in their census.[13]

The British did not merely maintain the Ottoman millet system; in certain respects, they actually expanded the Ottoman focus on religion in defining groups in Palestine. As Rashid Khalidi has stressed, the British actually *invented* "Islamic" institutions that lacked precedent either in Palestine or elsewhere in the Islamic world. These inventions included the Supreme Muslim Council (al-Majlis al-islāmī al-aʿlā), which was granted extensive powers including control over the revenues of the country's public *awqāf*[14] as well as over appointments of a wide variety of religious bureaucrats and other officials.[15] The British also significantly refashioned other religious institutions, especially the position the British named the grand mufti of Palestine (muftī filasṭīn al-akbar), vastly expanding the authority of the former position of Jerusalem's mufti for the Hanafi rite.[16] In other words, far from muting or limiting the place of religion in public life, the British in Palestine consolidated and fortified Islamic religious institutions and positions (even if for ends entirely their own). Thus, despite the fall of the Islamic Ottoman Empire and the advent of the British Mandate, even if one considers simply the legal, public frameworks of Palestinian society, there is ample reason to suspect that religion would have persisted as a primary lens of mutual perception.

And evidence suggests that religion remained at the center of the encounter, indicated not least by the fact that the moments of greatest conflict in the mandate period were generally associated with religious festivals or locations with strong religious valences.[17] Consider the riots of 1920 at the time of the Nabī Mūsā pilgrimage to a location where the biblical Moses was believed to have been buried; or the calls "to protect al-Aqsā from Jewish attacks" in the wake of the incidents at

[13] Likhovski, *Law and Identity in Mandate Palestine*, 37–38.

[14] Plural of *waqf*, an Islamic legal endowment.

[15] On the Supreme Muslim Council, see Kupferschmidt, *The Supreme Muslim Council*.

[16] Khalidi, *The Iron Cage*, 55–56. See also Kupferschmidt, *The Supreme Muslim Council*, 17–20.

[17] On this pattern, see Wasserstein, "Patterns of Communal Conflict in Palestine."

and around al-Ḥaram ash-Sharīf, the Temple Mount, around the Jewish holidays of Yom Kippur 1928 and Tishʿah be-Av 1929; or the so-called Great Revolt of 1936 through 1939, after the funeral of the Muslim preacher ʿIzz ad-Din al-Qassam, who was eulogized popularly as "Islam's ideal soldier."[18] In each of these cases, religion should not be considered the *sole* factor in either creating or sustaining the hostility felt between the various communities of Palestine, but it was certainly *a* factor, and an important one, that informed (and sometimes *mis*informed) the groups' perceptions of one another, even as the language and logic of nationalism became more deeply ingrained on all sides.

The language of race and the notion of a racial link between Jews and Arabs also continued to play a role in the years immediately following the Great War. In January 1919, in the context of the postwar peace conference in Paris, the Zionist leader Chaim Weizmann met with Faisal Hussein, who had led the wartime Arab Revolt against the Ottomans and then proclaimed himself king of Syria. Weizmann and Faisal produced an agreement that stressed race as a point of commonality: "His Royal Highness the Amir Faisal, representing and acting on behalf of the Arab Kingdom of Hejaz and Dr. Chaim Weizmann, representing and acting on behalf of the Zionist Organization, mindful of the racial kinship and ancient bond existing between the Arabs and the Jewish people."[19] In the subsequent months in Paris, Faisal continued to use this language in expressing his sense of connection to the Jews and even his sympathy for the Zionist enterprise. In a March 1919 letter to the Viennese-born American Zionist leader (and future US Supreme Court justice) Felix Frankfurter, Faisal wrote of his belief that "the Arabs and Jews are cousins in race." As such, he continued, "we Arabs, especially the educated among us, look with the deepest sympathy on the Zionist movement." Indeed, deeming the Zionist proposals submitted to the peace conference as "moderate and proper," Faisal offered to support them. Upon the success of the Zionist project, Faisal assured Frankfurter that he and his fellow Arabs "will wish the Jews a most hearty welcome home."[20] In emphasizing the connection between Jews and Arabs, Faisal was obviously seeking Jewish support for his political ambitions in Syria and the broader Arab world. However, regardless of the sincerity of his expressions of commonality with and support for the Jews and Zionism, that he framed these expressions through the language and logic of race is significant.

[18] Cited in Johnson, *Islam and the Politics of Meaning in Palestinian Nationalism*, 45.

[19] Feisal-Weizmann Agreement, January 1919.

[20] Emir Feisal and Felix Frankfurter Correspondence (March 3–5, 1919) in Laqueur and Rubin, eds., *The Israel-Arab Reader*, 19–20.

"Irrespective of Race and Religion": A New Discourse of Difference in the Global Sphere

If, despite their persistent presence, the language and categories of race and religion were less pronounced during the British Mandate than under the Ottomans, the official terms of the mandate likely played a key role in this process. The League of Nations famously incorporated the Balfour Declaration into the preamble of its 1922 Mandate for Palestine, condemning the British (apparently on their own insistence and against the objections of other league members[21]) to follow through on their dual commitments to promote "the establishment in Palestine of a national home for the Jewish people" while somehow also doing nothing "which might prejudice the civil and religious rights of existing non-Jewish communities in Palestine." Article 2 of the Palestine Mandate restates the Balfour commitment in new and highly revealing terms:

> The Mandatory [i.e., the British] shall be responsible for placing the country under such political, administrative, and economic conditions as will secure the establishment of the Jewish national home, as laid down in the preamble, and the development of self-governing institutions, and also for safeguarding the civil and religious rights of all the inhabitants of Palestine, *irrespective of race and religion.*[22]

Whereas in the Balfour Declaration, Palestine's Muslim and Christian Arabs were referred to as "existing non-Jewish communities," half a decade later, in 1922, they were now regarded as "inhabitants" (though the categories of rights they could expect to be safeguarded remained the same, still ambiguous "civil and religious"). For our purposes, however, the more significant and consequential change from Balfour's language was the addition of the phrase "irrespective of race and religion." The League of Nations demanded that there be no discrimination in civil and religious rights on the basis of the categories of race and religion, those very categories that I have highlighted throughout this book.[23]

[21] See Pedersen, "The Impact of League Oversight on British Policy in Palestine," 42.

[22] Article 2, League of Nations Mandate for Palestine, 1922.

[23] It is worth noting that in the White Paper issued in 1922 by the British just before the official ratification of the mandate by the League of the Nations, Colonial Secretary Winston Churchill explained that by "the development of the Jewish National Home in Palestine," the Balfour Declaration meant "the further development of the existing Jewish community, with the assistance of Jews in other parts of the world, in order that it may become "a centre in which the Jewish people as a whole may take, on the grounds

To understand the significance of the decisions by the authors of the mandate to make explicit reference to race and religion, to pair the two, and to insist that these were illegitimate categories of legal or political distinction, we must widen our historical lens far beyond Palestine and even outside the Middle East. The Palestine Mandate document emerged in the context of a series of postwar agreements and mandates imposed by the victorious Allies. As Eric Weitz has argued, the "Paris system," represented in the fateful decisions that emerged from the Paris Peace Conference at the conclusion of the First World War, stressed "population politics." By "population politics," Weitz denotes the Allies' vision of the political problems "naturally" posed by "essential" differences among populations within individual states.[24] From the perspective of the Allies, there were two primary solutions to the problem of heterogeneity in the regions they had conquered during the war. One option was population transfer—whether voluntary or compulsory—that would create demographic homogeneity where it did not exist. The other solution was to permit heterogeneity within a state but to insist that minorities, per se, be granted special rights and protections from the tyranny of the majority.

In identifying the problematic demographic differences within a single territory that would warrant population transfer or exchange, the league generally pointed to "race" (or otherwise "race" and "language"). For instance, in the 1920 Treaty of Sevres, dealing with former Ottoman territories, the Allies insisted that adults

> habitually resident in territories detached from Turkey in accordance with the present Treaty and differing in race from the majority of the population of such territory shall . . . be entitled to opt for Armenia, Azerbaijan, Georgia, Greece, the Hedjaz, Mesopotamia, Syria, Bulgaria or Turkey, if the majority of the population of the State selected is of the same race as the person exercising the right to opt.[25]

Turkey and Greece were to permit "reciprocal and voluntary emigration of the populations of Turkish and Greek race in the territories transferred to Greece and remaining Turkish respectively."[26] In the 1920 Treaty of Trianon, concerning territories of the former Austro-Hungarian Empire, the Allies granted "the right to opt" to migrate to

of *religion and race*, an interest and a pride." Italics mine. Winston Churchill, "The Churchill White Paper (June 1922)," in Laqueur and Rubin, *The Israel-Arab Reader*, 27.

[24] See Weitz, "From the Vienna to the Paris System."

[25] Article 125, Treaty of Sevres, 1920.

[26] Article 143, Treaty of Sevres, 1920.

a region in which one would be among the majority to those who differed from the majority in "race and language."[27] Difference in race, or in race and language, constituted a reason to leave, in the minds of the drafters of these treaties, though, as we have recognized in other contexts in this book, it is far from clear what precisely was meant by "race"—an ambiguity accentuated by the Treaty of Sevres' references to "non-Moslem races."[28] In cases in which population exchange was deemed undesirable or impracticable, "minority rights" were proposed. For these, the Paris system identified three categories of difference—race, language, and religion. At Versailles in 1919, for instance, the new Czecho-Slovak state and Poland were ordered "to protect the interests of inhabitants of that State who differ from the majority of the population in race, language, or religion."[29]

It was in this political, ideological, and terminological environment that the Palestine Mandate was composed. As we have seen, during the Late Ottoman period, for Jews and Arabs in Palestine, religion and race were at once fundamental marks of distinction *and* sources of intercommunal commonality. Now, however, in the post–Great War moment, these same categories were redefined by a new dominant international system (the League of Nations) and ruling power (the British Mandate). The insistence that governments treat their residents and citizens equally, "irrespective of race and religion," implied that, above all, these two frames of identity and status were dangerous sources of difference and potential conflict. These categories were at once acknowledged and, at the same time, relegated to the unspeakable and politically irrelevant.

The Paris system continued to recognize intercommunal difference, of course, but the main form of difference that it repeatedly legitimated was that of the "nation" (after all, this system created the League of *Nations*). There were cases in which the league deemed even "nationality" to be an illegitimate basis for discrimination—requiring, in various treaties, Bulgaria, Hungary, and Turkey "to assure full and complete protection of life and liberty to all inhabitants of Bulgaria without distinction of birth, nationality, language, race or religion." Tellingly, however, the authors of the Palestine Mandate do not mention birth and nationality.

27 Article 64, Treaty of Trianon, 1920.

28 See, e.g., Article 149, Treaty of Sevres, 1920.

29 Articles 86 and 93, Treaty of Versailles, 1919. The same was demanded in 1920 of the Serb-Croat Slovene state, Roumania, and Hungary at Trianon, and of Greece and Armenia at Sevres. Articles 44, 47, 58, Treaty of Trianon, 1920; Articles 86, 93, Treaty of Sevres, 1920.

In identifying race, religion, and language as categories the mandatory power must ignore in relating to the local population, the Palestine Mandate reflected the Allies' sense that these were the fundamental differences between the communities in Palestine. Beyond merely reflecting the Allies' assessment, the mandate document also had prescriptive implications. By not naming "nationality" as an illegitimate category of legal distinction (and by following Balfour's language of "a *national* home for the Jewish people"), the mandate effectively permitted distinction and advocacy of distinction based on this category. This would help to shape claims and tensions around the category of nation—one that, incidentally, for many Jews and Arabs seemed to fuse religion and race—in the years to come.

All parties appealed to the terms of the mandate throughout the years of British rule in Palestine; indeed, the language of the mandate document became the subject of intensive exegesis. In explaining, defending, or, as they often did, modifying or reversing their policies, the British would regularly cite their responsibilities as dictated by the text of the mandate. Thus, for instance, in 1931, British prime minister Ramsay MacDonald aimed to clarify the meaning of Article 2 of the mandate, particularly the phrase "safeguarding the civil and religious rights of all inhabitants of Palestine *irrespective of race and religion*." MacDonald insisted that "the key to the true purpose and meaning of the sentence is to be found in these concluding words of the article." This "protective provision applies equally to Jews, Arabs, and all sections of the population," MacDonald insisted, implying again that these communities were defined and distinguished by these two categories.[30] Similarly, the phrase "irrespective of race and religion" was quoted and highlighted in the 1939 White Paper's restatement of the primary obligations of the mandate.[31] Given the persistent British appeal to this phrase, it is perhaps unsurprising that the parties themselves also cited it in seeking to legitimize their own positions and to challenge the legitimacy of their antagonists' demands. For example, as late as 1946, in its statement to the Anglo-American Committee of Inquiry, the Arab Office called for a representative government in Palestine that "should be based upon the principle of absolute equality of all citizens irrespective of race and religion."[32] Using the terminology of

[30] British Prime Minister Ramsay MacDonald: The MacDonald Letter (February 13, 1931), in Laqueur and Rubin, *The Israel-Arab Reader*, 38.

[31] The British Government: The White Paper (May 17, 1939), in ibid., 44.

[32] The Arab Office: The Arab Case for Palestine (March 1946), in ibid., 60. For a discussion of this meeting and for the text of Albert Hourani's testimony to the committee, see Khalidi, "On Albert Hourani, the Arab Office, and the Anglo-American Committee of 1946"; Hourani, "The Case against a Jewish State in Palestine."

the mandate, the Arab Office called on the Western powers to comply with their own ostensible values, and thus insisted that communities should not be treated differently based on the categories of race and religion. Throughout the years of the mandate, distinctions based on religion and race were delegitimized, requiring the parties—at least rhetorically—to stress other categories of difference. In this interwar political-ideological context, nationalism seems to have replaced religion and race as the category of legitimate intercommunal distinction.

Religion, Race, and the Contemporary Israeli-Palestinian Encounter

In the years after the 1948 war, ostensibly secular nationalism emerged as the dominant language on both sides of the Israeli-Palestinian conflict.[33] Secularists among Israelis and Palestinians, representing the political elites in both societies, sought to define their respective movements as national struggles to restore a nation to its homeland. And yet any observer of the contemporary, early twenty-first-century conflict recognizes the central role religion plays in each society as well as in

[33] If from 1922 to 1946 the terms of the League of Nations mandate set the tone and fixed the boundaries of the discourse on difference—removing the race-religion-language triad from the realm of legitimacy—United Nations General Assembly Resolution 181 in 1947 on the partition of Palestine delegitimized an additional fourth term, namely, sex. The resolution read: "no discrimination of any kind shall be made between inhabitants on the ground of race, religion, language or sex." The inclusion of sex in this list is, of course, a consequence of significant changes in the realm of gender equality in the West. As in the case of the mandate, this resolution set the terms that all parties would have to consider in articulating their own positions. In the 1948 Israeli proclamation of independence, the state's founders were willing to agree to "complete equality of social and political rights to all its inhabitants irrespective of religion [*dat*], race [*gezaʿ*], or sex." Language, however, is notably absent from the list, a sign of the sensitivity of the issue of language in the Zionist enterprise. (The proclamation nonetheless ensures freedom of language.) In contrast, the Palestinian National Charter, drafted in 1964 and approved in 1968, insists that with "the liberation of Palestine," freedoms of worship and visit would be extended "to all, without discrimination of race [*al-ʿunṣur*], color [*al-lawn*], language, or religion [*ad-dīn*]." The absence of "sex" in this list may reflect different gender concerns in the Palestinian national movement of the mid-twentieth century; the inclusion, instead, of "color" was meant to ally the Palestinian cause with other anticolonial, anti-imperialist, and antiracist movements of the period. Whatever ambivalences may be discerned concerning sex discrimination in 1968 appear to have been overcome within two decades. The Palestine National Council's Declaration of Independence of November 1988 ensures that "governance will be based on principles of social justice, equality, and non-discrimination in public rights of men or women, on grounds of race, religion, color or sex." The texts of the documents cited here are found in Laqueur and Rubin, *The Israel-Arab Reader*, 75, 82–83, 119, 356.

each side's conception of its counterpart. Israel's rapidly growing ultra-Orthodox community wields immense power in domestic and budgetary politics (evidenced, not least, by the popularity of political parties formed for hardly another purpose than to rein in this power), and the religious nationalist settler movement exercises its muscle in the state's policies in the West Bank. At the same time, that Hamas—the Islamic Resistance Movement, which, according to its charter, "owes its loyalty to God, derives from Islam its way of life and strives to raise the banner of God over every inch of Palestine"—won the Palestinian parliamentary elections in 2006 and retains control of the Gaza Strip is indicative of the prominent place of Islam in today's Palestinian politics. As important, each side *perceives* religion as a central, guiding force in *the other's* actions. Many contemporary Israelis believe that the Palestinians are all—or are dominated by—Islamist extremists whose religious requirement of jihād ensures that they will continue to fight Israel until they have removed the Jewish infidels from Palestine. That mass violence erupted when Israeli prime minister Ariel Sharon visited the Temple Mount/Noble Sanctuary in September 2000, and that the half-decade of bloodletting that followed quickly became known as the al-Aqsa Intifada (after the mosque that sits atop the mount), reveal not only the enduring importance of religious symbols in the conflict but also the sense among many Palestinians that, notwithstanding their protestations of secularism, Israelis actually have a religious agenda that seeks to undermine Islam's (literal and figurative) foundations in Palestine. While we must not draw a straight line from this book's conclusions about the Ottoman period to the contemporary conflict in the twenty-first century, the prominence of religion in today's mutual perceptions should be recognized not as a historic aberration but rather as the latest stage in the story of evolving ideas and perspectives about religion in this encounter that began more than a century earlier.

If religion remains, or has again become, central in today's mutual perceptions among Israelis and Palestinians, what may be said of the present status of ideas of race? To be sure, explicitly racial discourse has largely fallen out of favor,[34] especially in light of the widespread perception of the horrific potential of racial thinking as articulated by Nazism and as evidenced in the Holocaust. Yet, at least in the minds of each side, its antagonist tenaciously employs racial, indeed racist, ideology. This accusation was made most famously in United Nations General Assembly Resolution 3379, adopted in 1975, which declared

[34] A recent Israeli exception can be seen in the case of Upper Nazareth mayor Shimon Gaspo. See "If you think I'm a racist, then Israel is a racist state," Haaretz, August 7, 2013, http://www.haaretz.com/opinion/1.540278.

that "zionism is a form of racism and racial discrimination." This alleged link between Zionism and racism had already been made the previous decade in the Palestinian National Charter, in which the Palestine National Council declared that Zionism "is racist [*ʿunṣuriyya*] and fanatic in its nature, aggressive, expansionist, and colonial in its aims, and fascist in its methods."[35] Even after the UN's revocation of Resolution 3379 in 1991, the indictment of Zionism as a form of racism and of Israeli policies as racist remains prevalent. Palestinian president Mahmoud Abbas's reference, in his 2011 speech before the UN General Assembly, to Israel's "settlement and apartheid policies and its construction of the racist annexation wall" is characteristic of contemporary Palestinians' association of Israel with racism in general and with South African apartheid in particular.[36] On the Israeli side, a popular focus on the mandate-period Palestinian leader Hajj Amin al-Husseini and his wartime relationship with Adolf Hitler reinforces the sense among Israelis that their Palestinian antagonists are, like the Nazis, motivated not by legitimate claims but by irrational racism.[37] Israelis point to Hamas's embrace of conspiracy theories historically linked to racist antisemitism, most notably the Hamas Charter's claim that "their scheme has been laid out in the Protocols of the Elders of Zion," as evidence that Hajj Amin's legacy lives on.[38] Notions of race clearly remain part of the contemporary Israeli-Palestinian discourse, even as these racial ideas are now generally relegated to condemnations of the other side's motivations and bigotry. Both sides, it would seem, are at least partially correct in their perceptions of the other, and, as such, both also project their own prejudices onto the other.

I close with a statement of hope that emerges from this research: the ways in which people perceive and understand one another are not fixed or immutable. Given later events, I was surprised by much of what I discovered in this study; Zionists and Arabs imagined one another in very different terms in the Late Ottoman period from the ways their descendants look at one another today. The perceptions have changed, if generally not for the better. Just as perceptions can worsen, however, it stands to reason that they can improve as well.

[35] Article 22, Palestinian National Charter, in Laqueur and Rubin, *The Israel-Arab Reader*, 119.

[36] "Full transcript of Abbas's speech at UN General Assembly," http://www.haaretz.com/news/diplomacy-defense/full-transcript-of-abbas-speech-at-un-general-assembly-1.386385.

[37] On this subject, see Penslar, "The Hands of Others." This is a review of Achcar, *The Arabs and the Holocaust.*

[38] Hamas Charter in Laqueur and Rubin, *The Israel-Arab Reader*, 347.

Bibliography

Archives

CAHJP	Central Archives for the History of the Jewish People, Jerusalem
CZA	Central Zionist Archives, Jerusalem
HMA	Haifa Municipal Archive, Haifa
ISA	Israel State Archives, Jerusalem
JMA	Jerusalem Municipal Archive, Jerusalem
LLA	Lavon Labor Archive, Tel Aviv
RZA	Rishon le-Zion Archive, Rishon le-Zion

Libraries

al-Ansari Library
al-Aqsa Library
al-Khalidiyya Library

Newspapers and Journals

ha-Aḥdut
ha-Ḥerut
al-Hilāl
al-Manār
al-Muqtaṭaf
ha-Or / ha-Ẓevi
ha-Shiloaḥ

Dictionaries and Encyclopedias

EḤY — Tidhar, David. *Enẓayklopidiyah la-ḥaluẓei ha-yishuv u-vonav.* Tel Aviv: Sifriyat Rishonim, 1947–1971.

EI[2] — *Encyclopedia of Islam,* edited by P. Bearman, Th. Bianquis, C. E. Bosworth, E. van Donzel, and W. P. Heinrichs. 2nd ed. Leiden: E. J. Brill, 1960–2005.

EI[3] — *Encyclopedia of Islam,* edited by Kate Fleet, Gudrun Krämer, Denis Matringe, John Nawas, and Everett Rowson. 3rd ed. Leiden: E. J. Brill, 2007.

EJ[2] *Encyclopaedia Judaica*, edited by Michael Berenbaum and Fred Skolnik. 2nd ed. Detroit: Macmillan Reference USA, 2007.

EQ *Encyclopedia of the Qur'an*, edited by Jane Dammen McAuliffe. Leiden: E. J. Brill, 2001–2006.

JE *The Jewish Encyclopedia*, edited by Isidore Singer et al. New York: Funk and Wagnalls, 1901–1906.

MBY Ben-Yehuda, Eliezer, M. H. Segal, and Naphtali H. Tur-Sinai. *Milon ha-lashon ha-ʿivrit ha-yeshanah ve-ha-ḥadashah*. Jerusalem: Hoẓa'at Makor, 1980.

MTAY Blau, Joshua. *Milon le-tekstim ʿarviyim-yehudiyim mi-mei ha-benayim*. Jerusalem: ha-Akademiyah la-lashon ha-ʿivrit, 2006.

NEI Glassé, Cyril. *The New Encyclopedia of Islam*. Rev. ed. Walnut Creek, CA: AltaMira Press, 2001.

OEMIW *Oxford Encyclopedia of the Modern Islamic World*, edited by John L. Esposito. New York: Oxford University Press, 2001.

ARTICLES, BOOKS, AND MANUSCRIPTS

Abassi, Mustafa. "Temurot ba-ukhlusiyah ha-muslimit bi-rushalayim 1840–1914." In *Sefer yerushalayim: Be-shilhei ha-tekufah ha-ʿot'manit, 1800–1917*, edited by Israel Bartal and H. Goren, 127–40. Jerusalem: Yad Yiẓḥak Ben-Ẓevi, 2010.

ʿAbboud, Boulos [ʿAbūd, Bawlus]. *al-Arḍ al-muqaddasa wa-ṣ-ṣahyūniyya*. Khalidiyya Library. Jaffa: n.p., 1920.

Abdel Haleem, M.A.S. *The Qur'an*. New York: Oxford University Press, 2005.

Abu Sway, Mustafa. "The Holy Land, Jerusalem and Al-Aqsa Mosque in the Qur'an, Sunnah and Other Islamic Literary Sources." In *The Meeting of Civilizations: Muslim, Christian, and Jewish*, edited by Moshe Ma'oz. Portland, OR: Sussex Academic Press, 2009.

Abu-Manneh, Butrus. "Arab-Ottomanists' Reactions to the Young Turk Revolution." In *Late Ottoman Palestine: The Period of Young Turk Rule*, edited by Yuval Ben-Bassat and Eyal Ginio, 145–64. New York: I. B. Tauris, 2011.

———. "The Rise of the Sanjak of Jerusalem in the Late Nineteenth Century." In *The Israel/Palestine Question: A Reader*, edited by Ilan Pappé. 2nd ed. New York: Routledge, 2007.

Achcar, Gilbert. *The Arabs and the Holocaust: The Arab-Israeli War of Narratives*. New York: Metropolitan Books, 2010.

Ackerman-Lieberman, Phillip. "Comparison between the Halakha and Shariʿa." In *A History of Jewish-Muslim Relations: From the Origins to the Present Day*, edited by Abdelwahab Meddeb and Benjamin Stora, translated by Jane Marie Todd and Michael B. Smith, 683–93. Princeton: Princeton University Press, 2013.

Adams, Charles C. *Islam and Modernism: A Study of the Modern Reform Movement Inaugurated by Muḥammad ʿAbduh*. London: Oxford University Press, 1933.

Agmon, Iris. *Family & Court: Legal Culture and Modernity in Late Ottoman Palestine*. Syracuse, NY: Syracuse University Press, 2006.

Akarlı, Engin Deniz. *The Long Peace: Ottoman Lebanon, 1861–1920*. Berkeley: University of California Press, 1993.

Almog, Shmuel. "The Role of Religious Values in the Second Aliyah." In *Zionism and Religion*, edited by Shmuel Almog, Jehuda Reinharz, and Anita Shapira, 237–50. Hanover, MA: University Press of New England, 1998.

Alroey, Gur. *Imigrantim: ha-Hagirah ha-yehudit le-ereẓ-yisraʾel be-reshit ha-meʾah ha-ʿesrim*. Jerusalem: Yad Yiẓḥak Ben-Ẓevi, 2004.

———. "Journey to Early-Twentieth-Century Palestine as a Jewish Immigrant Experience." *Jewish Social Studies* 9, no. 2 (2003): 28–64.

Anderson, Benedict R. *Imagined Communities: Reflections on the Origin and Spread of Nationalism*. Rev. ed. New York: Verso, 2006.

Angel, Marc D. "The Responsa Literature in the Ottoman Empire as a Source for the Study of Ottoman Jewry." In *The Jews of the Ottoman Empire*, edited by Avigdor Levy, 669–86. Princeton: Darwin Press, 1994.

Anidjar, Gil. *Semites: Race, Religion, Literature*. Stanford: Stanford University Press, 2008.

Asad, Nāṣir ad-Dīn. *Muḥammad Rūḥī al-Khālidī rāʾid al-baḥth at-tārīkhī al-ḥadīth fī filasṭīn, muḥāḍarāt alqāhā Nāṣir ad-Dīn al-Asad ʿalā ṭalabat qism ad-dirāsāt al-adabiyya wa-l-lughawiyya*. Cairo: Maʿhad al-Buḥūth wa-d-Dirāsāt al-ʿArabiyya, 1970.

Asaf, Mikhael. *ha-Yeḥasim beyn ʿarvim vi-hudim be-ereẓ-yisraʾel 1860–1948*. Tel Aviv: Tarbut ve-ḥinukh, 1970.

Augstein, Hannah Franziska. *Race: The Origins of an Idea, 1760–1850*. Bristol, England: Thoemmes Press, 1996.

Avishur, Yiẓḥak. "ha-Markiv ha-ʿarvi ba-lashon ha-ʿivrit bat zemanenu u-visifrutah me-Eliʿezer Ben-Yehuda ʿad Netivah Ben-Yehuda (ve-Dan Ben-Amoẓ)." *ha-ʿIvrit va-aḥiyoteha* 2–3 (2002–2003): 9.

Ayalon, Ami. *Language and Change in the Arab Middle East*. New York: Oxford University Press, 1987.

———. *The Press in the Arab Middle East: A History*. New York: Oxford University Press, 1995.

———. *Reading Palestine: Printing and Literacy, 1900–1948*. Austin: University of Texas Press, 2004.

Bakhos, Carol. *Ishmael on the Border: Rabbinic Portrayals of the First Arab*. Albany: State University of New York Press, 2006.

Banton, Michael. *Racial Theories*. New York: Cambridge University Press, 1987.

Barnai, Yaʿakov. *Historiyografiyah u-leʾumiyut: Megamot be-ḥeker ereẓ-yisraʾel vishuvah ha-yehudi, 634–1881*. Jerusalem: Magnes, 1995.

Bartal, Israel [Yisraʾel]. " 'ʿAm' ve-'Areẓ' ba-historiyografiyah ha-ẓiyonit." In *Kozak ve-bedvi: "ʿAm" ve-"Areẓ" ba-leʾumiyut ha-yehudit*, 122–32. Tel Aviv: ʿAm ʿoved, 2007.

———. "Du-kiyum nikhsaf: Eliyahu Eliachar ʿal yeḥasei yehudim ve-ʿarvim." In *Liḥyot ʿim palestinim*, edited by Elie Eliachar, 9–20. Jerusalem: Misgav Yerushalayim, 1997.

Bartal, Israel [Yisra᾽el]. *Galut ba-areẓ: Yishuv ereẓ-yisra᾽el be-terem ẓiyonut: Koveẓ masot u-meḥkarim*. Jerusalem: ha-Sifriyah ha-ẓiyonit, 1994.

———. "Me-'ereẓ kodesh' le-ereẓ historit—'Otonomizm' ẓiyoni be-reshit ha-me᾽ah ha-esrim." In *Kozak ve-bedvi: "ʿAm" ve-"Areẓ" ba-le᾽umiyut ha-yehudit*, 152–69. Tel Aviv: ʿAm ʿoved, 2007.

———. " 'Old Yishuv' and 'New Yishuv': Image and Reality." In *The Jerusalem Cathedra: Studies in the History, Archaeology, Geography, and Ethnography of the Land of Israel*, edited by Lee I. Levine, 1:215–31. Jerusalem: Wayne State University Press, 1981.

Bartal, Israel, Yehoshua Kaniel, and Zeev Ẓaḥor, eds. *ha-ʿAliyah ha-sheniyah: Ishim*. Jerusalem: Yad Yiẓḥak Ben-Ẓevi, 1997.

Barzilay, Isaac E. "Smolenskin's Polemic against Mendelssohn in Historical Perspective." *Proceedings of the American Academy for Jewish Research* 53 (1986): 11–48.

Bashkin, Orit. *New Babylonians: A History of Jews in Modern Iraq*. Stanford: Stanford University Press, 2012.

Batnitzky, Leora Faye. *How Judaism Became a Religion: An Introduction to Modern Jewish Thought*. Princeton: Princeton University Press, 2011.

Be᾽eri, Eliʿezer. *Reshit ha-sikhsukh yisra᾽el-ʿarav, 1882–1911*. Tel Aviv: Sifriyat poʿalim, 1985.

Behar, Moshe, and Zvi Ben-Dor Benite, eds. *Modern Middle Eastern Jewish Thought: Writings on Identity, Politics, and Culture, 1893–1958*. Waltham, MA: Brandeis University Press, 2013.

Beinin, Joel. *The Dispersion of Egyptian Jewry: Culture, Politics, and the Formation of the Modern Diaspora*. Berkeley: University of California Press, 1998.

Belkind, Yisrael and David Ben-Gurion. *ha-ʿArvim asher be-ereẓ-yisra᾽el: Le-verur moẓa ha-falaḥim*. Tel Aviv: Ḥermon, 1969.

Ben-Arieh, Yehoshua. *Jerusalem in the 19th Century—the Old City*. New York: St. Martin's Press, 1984.

———. *Jerusalem in the Nineteenth Century*. Tel Aviv: MOD Books, 1989.

———. *Jerusalem in the Nineteenth Century: Emergence of the New City*. New York: St. Martin's Press, 1986.

Ben-Arieh, Yehoshua, and Yisrael Bartal. *Shilhei ha-tekufah ha-ʿot'omanit (1799–1917). ha-Historiyah shel ereẓ yisra᾽el*. Vol. 8. Jerusalem: Keter, 1983.

Ben-Bassat, Yuval. "Beyond National Historiographies: Reflections on the Ottoman Background of Proto-Zionist-Arab Encounters in *Fin De Siècle* Nineteenth-Century Palestine." In *Ottoman Legacies in the Contemporary Mediterranean: The Balkans and the Middle East Compared*, edited by Eyal Ginio and Karl Kasr, 93–118. Jerusalem: European Forum at the Hebrew University, 2013.

———. "Rural Reactions to Zionist Activity in Palestine before and after the Young Turk Revolution of 1908 as Reflected in Petitions to Istanbul." *Middle Eastern Studies* 49, no. 3 (2013): 349–63.

Ben-Bassat, Yuval, and Eyal Ginio. *Late Ottoman Palestine: The Period of Young Turk Rule*. New York: I. B. Tauris, 2011.

Ben-Gurion, David. *Ben-Gurion Looks at the Bible*, translated by Jonathan Kolatch. Middle Village, NY: Jonathan David Publishers, 1972.

Ben-Gurion, David, and Yiẓḥak Ben-Ẓevi. *Erets Yisroel in Fergangenhayt un Gegenvart: Geografie, Geshikhte Rekhtilikhe Ferheltnise, Befelkerung, Landvirtshaft, Handel un Industrye*. New York: Poale-Tsiyon Palestine Komitet, 1918.

Ben-Ze'ev, Yisra'el. "ha-ʿItona'i ve-ha-ʿaskan d"r Nissim Malul z"l." *Maḥberet* 8, no. 12 (5719): 146–48.

Ben-Ẓevi, Yiẓḥak. *ha-Tenuʿah ha-ʿarvit*, edited by Z. Ben-Kohen. Vol. 1. Jaffa: Hoẓa'at ʿAvodah, 1921.

Berg, Emmanuel van den. *Petite histoire ancienne des peuples de l'Orient: Égyptiens, Assyriens et Babyloniens, Mèdes et Perses, Phéniciens*. Paris: Librairie Hachette, 1878.

Bergounioux, Gabriel. "Semitism: From a Linguistic Concept to a Racist Argument." In *A History of Jewish-Muslim Relations: From the Origins to the Present Day*, edited by Abdelwahab Meddeb and Benjamin Stora, translated by Jane Marie Todd and Michael B. Smith, 676–82. Princeton: Princeton University Press, 2013.

Bernasconi, Robert, and Tommy Lee Lott. *The Idea of Race*. Indianapolis: Hackett, 2000.

Bettany, George Thomas. *The World's Inhabitants, or Mankind, Animals, and Plants: Being a Popular Account of the Races and Nations of Mankind, Past and Present, and the Animals and Plants Inhabiting the Great Continents and Principal Islands*. London: Ward, Lock, 1892.

———. *The World's Religions: A Popular Account of Religions Ancient and Modern, Including Those of Uncivilised Races, Chaldaeans, Greeks, Egyptions, Romans; Confucianism, Taoism, Hinduism, Buddhism, Zoroastrianism, Mohammedanism, and a Sketch of the History of Judaism and Christianity*. London: Ward, Lock, 1890.

Beẓal'el, Yiẓḥak. "ʿAl yiḥudo shel '*ha-Ḥerut*' (1909–1917) ve-ʿal Ḥayim Ben-ʿAtar ke-ʿorkho." *Peʿamim* 40 (1989): 121–45.

———. *Noladetem ẓiyonim: ha-Sefaradim be-ereẓ-yisra'el ba-ẓiyonut u-va-teḥiyah ha-ʿivrit ba-tekufah ha-ʿot'manit*. Jerusalem: Yad Yiẓḥak Ben-Ẓevi, 2007.

Bickerton, Ian J., and Carla L. Klausner. *A Concise History of the Arab-Israeli Conflict*. Englewood Cliffs, NJ: Prentice Hall, 1991.

Braude, Benjamin. "Foundation Myths of the *Millet* System." In *Christians and Jews in the Ottoman Empire: The Functioning of a Plural Society*, edited by Benjamin Braude and Bernard Lewis, 1:69–88. New York: Holmes & Meier, 1982.

Braude, Benjamin, and Bernard Lewis. *Christians and Jews in the Ottoman Empire: The Functioning of a Plural Society*. 2 vols. New York: Holmes & Meier, 1982.

Brody, Robert. *The Geonim of Babylonia and the Shaping of Medieval Jewish Culture*. New Haven: Yale University Press, 1998.

Brugman, J. *An Introduction to the History of Modern Arabic Literature in Egypt*. Leiden: E. J. Brill, 1984.

Campos, Michelle U. *Ottoman Brothers: Muslims, Christians, and Jews in Early Twentieth-Century Palestine*. Stanford: Stanford University Press, 2011.

———. "A 'Shared Homeland' and Its Boundaries: Empire, Citizenship and the Origins of Sectarianism in Late Ottoman Palestine, 1908–1913." PhD dissertation, Stanford University, 2003.

Canepa, Andrew M. "Pius X and the Jews: A Reappraisal." *Church History* 61, no. 3 (September 1992): 362–72.

Casanova, José. *Public Religions in the Modern World*. Chicago: University of Chicago Press, 1994.

Chelouche, Yosef Eliyahu. *Parashat ḥayai 1870–1930*. Tel Aviv: Bavel, 2005.

Clarke, Adam. *The Holy Bible, Containing the Old and New Testaments: The Text Carefully Printed from the Most Correct Copies of the Present Authorized Translation. Including the Marginal Readings and Parallel Texts. with a Commentary and Critical Notes, Designed as a Help to a Better Understanding of the Sacred Writings*. New York: Ezra Sargeant, 1811.

Cleveland, William L. *A History of the Modern Middle East*. 3rd ed. Boulder: Westview Press, 2004.

Cohen Albert, Phyllis. "Israelite and Jew: How did Nineteenth-Century French Jews Understand Assimilation?" In *Assimilation and Community: The Jews in Nineteenth-Century Europe*, edited by Jonathan Frankel and Steven J. Zipperstein, 88–109. New York: Cambridge University Press, 1992.

Cohen, Julia Phillips. "Fashioning Imperial Citizens: Sephardi Jews and the Ottoman State, 1856–1912." PhD dissertation, Stanford University, 2008.

Cohen, Mark R. "Muslim Anti-Semitism: Old or New?" In *A History of Jewish-Muslim Relations: From the Origins to the Present Day*, edited by Abdelwahab Meddeb and Benjamin Stora, translated by Jane Marie Todd and Michael B. Smith, 546–53. Princeton: Princeton University Press, 2013.

———. *Under Crescent and Cross: The Jews in the Middle Ages*. Princeton: Princeton University Press, 1994.

Cohen, Yiẓḥak, ed. *Ẓiyonut ve-ha-she'elah ha-ʿarvit: Koveẓ ma'amarim*. Jerusalem: Merkaz Zalman Shazar, 1979.

Commins, David Dean. *Islamic Reform: Politics and Social Change in Late Ottoman Syria*. New York: Oxford University Press, 1990.

Conrad, Lawrence I. "Ignaz Goldziher on Ernest Renan: From Orientalist Philology to the Study of Islam." In *The Jewish Discovery of Islam: Studies in Honor of Bernard Lewis*, edited by Bernard Lewis and Martin S. Kramer, 137–80. Tel Aviv: Moshe Dayan Center for Middle Eastern and African Studies, Tel Aviv University, 1999.

———. "The Khalidi Library." In *Ottoman Jerusalem: The Living City, 1517–1917*, edited by Sylvia Auld, Robert Hillenbrand, and Yusuf Said Natsheh, 1:191–209. London: Altajir World of Islam Trust, 2000.

Cook, Michael. *Commanding Right and Forbidding Wrong in Islamic Thought*. New York: Cambridge University Press, 2000.

Coulson, Noel J. *A History of Islamic Law*. Edinburgh: University Press, 1964.

Davison, Roderic H. *Reform in the Ottoman Empire, 1856–1876*. Princeton: Princeton University Press, 1963.

Dawood, N.J. *The Koran*. New York: Penguin Books, 2006.
Der Matossian, Bedross. "Administrating the Non-Muslims and the 'Question of Jerusalem' after the Young Turk Revolution." In *Late Ottoman Palestine: The Period of Young Turk Rule*, edited by Yuval Ben-Bassat and Eyal Ginio, 211–39. New York: I. B. Tauris, 2011.
Disraeli, Benjamin. *Tancred: Or, the New Crusade*. Leipzig: B. Tauchnitz, 1847.
Donner, Fred M. *Muhammad and the Believers: At the Origins of Islam*. Cambridge, MA: Belknap Press of Harvard University Press, 2010.
Doumani, Beshara. *Rediscovering Palestine: Merchants and Peasants in Jabal Nablus, 1700–1900*. Berkeley: University of California Press, 1995.
Dowty, Alan. " 'A Question That Outweighs All Others': Yitzhak Epstein and Zionist Recognition of the Arab Issue." *Israel Studies* 6, no. 1 (2001): 34–54.
———. *Israel/Palestine*. Hot Spots in Global Politics. Cambridge: Polity, 2005.
Drews, Arthur. *Die Christusmythe*. Jena: E. Diederichs, 1910.
Drews, Arthur, and Cecil Delisle Burns. *The Christ Myth*. London: T. F. Unwin, 1910.
Drews, Arthur, and Friedrich Loofs. *Hat Jesus gelebt?: Reden gehalten auf dem Berliner Religionsgespräch des Deutschen Monistenbundes am 31. Januar und 1. Februar 1910 im Zoologischen Garten über "Die Christusmythe" von Arthur Drews*. Berlin: Verlag des Deutschen Monistenbundes, 1910.
Druyan, Nitza. "ʿAliyatam ve-hitʿarutam shel yehudei teiman ba-ʿaliyah ha-rishonah." In *Sefer ha-ʿaliyah ha-rishonah*, edited by Mordechai Eliav, Yemima Rosenthal, and Chaya Har-El, 1:207–24. Jerusalem: Yad Yiẓḥak Ben-Ẓevi, 1981.
———. *Be-ein "marvad-kesamim": ʿOlei-teiman be-ereẓ-yisraʾel, 642–674, 1881–1914*. Jerusalem: Mekhon Ben-Ẓevi le-ḥeker kehilot yisraʾel ba-mizraḥ, 1981.
Efron, John M. *Defenders of the Race: Jewish Doctors and Race Science in Fin-de-Siècle Europe*. New Haven: Yale University Press, 1994.
Eliav, Mordechai. *Ereẓ yisraʾel vi-shuvah ba-meʾah ha-19: 1777–1917*. Jerusalem: Keter, 1978.
Elmaleh, Abraham. *ha-Rishonim le-ẓiyon: Toldoteihem u-peʿulotam*. Jerusalem: R. Mas, 1970.
Elshakry, Marwa S. "Darwin's Legacy in the Arab East: Science, Religion and Politics, 1870–1914." PhD dissertation, Princeton University, 2003.
———. "Global Darwin: Eastern Enchantment." *Nature* 461, no. 7268 (October 29, 2009): 1200.
———. "The Gospel of Science and American Evangelism in Late Ottoman Beirut." *Past & Present* no. 196 (August 2007): 173.
Engel, David. *Zionism*. New York: Pearson/Longman, 2009.
Ervine, Roberta. "Yerushalayim ha-armanit." In *Sefer yerushalayim: Be-shilhei ha-tekufah ha-ʿot'manit, 1800–1917*, edited by Yisrael Bartal and H. Goren, 165–78. Jerusalem: Yad Yiẓḥak Ben-Ẓevi, 2010.
Falah, Salman. "A History of the Druze Settlements in Palestine during the Ottoman Period." In *Studies on Palestine during the Ottoman Period*, edited by Moshe Ma'oz, 31–48. Jerusalem: Magnes Press, 1975.

Falk, Raphael. "Zionism and the Biology of the Jews." *Science in Context* 11, no. 3–4 (1998): 587–607.

Farag, Nadia. "The Lewis Affair and the Fortunes of al-Muqtataf." *Middle Eastern Studies* 8, no. 1 (January 1972): 73–83.

Fāris, Ḥabīb. *adh-Dhabāʾiḥ al-bashariyya at-talmūdiyya*, edited by ʿAbd al-ʿĀṭī Jalāl. Cairo: ad-Dār al-Qawmīyah liṭ-Ṭibāʿah wa-an-Nashr, 1962.

Fenton, Paul B. "The Literary Legacy of David Ben Joshua, Last of the Maimonidean Negidim." *Jewish Quarterly Review* 75, no. 1 (1984): 1–56.

Finkel, Sam. *Rebels in the Holy Land: Mazkeret Batya, an Early Battleground for the Soul of Israel*. Nanuet, NY: Feldheim, 2012.

Firestone, Reuven. *Holy War in Judaism: The Fall and Rise of a Controversial Idea*. New York: Oxford University Press, 2012.

———. "Rituals: Similarities, Influence, and Processes of Differentiation." In *A History of Jewish-Muslim Relations: From the Origins to the Present Day*, edited by Abdelwahab Meddeb and Benjamin Stora, translated by Jane Marie Todd and Michael B. Smith, 701–11. Princeton: Princeton University Press, 2013.

Fishman, Louis Andrew. "Palestine Revisited: Reassessing the Jewish and Arab National Movements, 1908–1914." PhD dissertation, University of Chicago, 2007.

Fishman, Talya. "Guarding Oral Transmission: Within and between Cultures." *Oral Traditions* 25, no. 1 (2010).

Frankel, Jonathan. *The Damascus Affair: "Ritual Murder," Politics, and the Jews in 1840*. New York: Cambridge University Press, 1997.

Friedman, Isaiah. "The System of Capitulations and Its Effects on Turco-Jewish Relations in Palestine, 1856–1897." In *Palestine in the Late Ottoman Period: Political, Social, and Economic Transformation*, edited by David Kushner, 280–93. Jerusalem: Yad Izhak Ben-Zvi, 1986.

Frisch, Hillel. "The Druze Minority in the Israeli Military: Traditionalizing an Ethnic Policing Role." *Armed Forces and Society* 20, no. 1 (1993): 51–67.

Frumkin, Gad. *Derekh shofet bi-rushalayim*. Tel Aviv: Devir, 1954.

Gätje, Helmut. *The Qurʾān and Its Exegesis*. Oxford: Oneworld Publications, 1996.

Gelber, Yoav. "Antecedents of the Jewish-Druze Alliance in Palestine." *Middle Eastern Studies* 28, no. 2 (1992): 352–73.

———. "The Iron Cage: The Story of the Palestinian Struggle for Statehood (Review)." *Israel Studies* 12, no. 2 (2007): 164–70.

Gelvin, James L. *The Israel-Palestine Conflict: One Hundred Years of War*. New York: Cambridge University Press, 2005.

———. *The Israel-Palestine Conflict: One Hundred Years of War*. 2nd ed. New York: Cambridge University Press, 2007.

———. "Secularism and Religion in the Arab Middle East: Reinventing Islam in a World of Nation-States." In *The Invention of Religion: Rethinking Belief in Politics and History*, edited by Derek R. Peterson and Darren R. Walhof, 115–30. New Brunswick, NJ: Rutgers University Press, 2002.

George, Alan. " 'Making the Desert Bloom': A Myth Examined." *Journal of Palestine Studies* 8, no. 2 (1979): 88–100.

Gerber, Haim. *Ottoman Rule in Jerusalem, 1890–1914*. Islamkundliche Untersuchungen. Berlin: K. Schwarz, 1985.

———. *State and Society in the Ottoman Empire*. Farnham: Ashgate/Variorum, 2010.

Gershoni, Israel, and James P. Jankowski. *Egypt, Islam, and the Arabs: The Search for Egyptian Nationhood, 1900–1930*. New York: Oxford University Press, 1987.

Gidney, William Thomas. *The History of the London Society for Promoting Christianity amongst the Jews: From 1809 to 1908*. London: London Society for Promoting Christianity amongst the Jews, 1908.

Goitein, S. D. *A Mediterranean Society; the Jewish Communities of the Arab World as Portrayed in the Documents of the Cairo Geniza*. Vol. 2: *The Community*. Berkeley: University of California Press, 1967.

Goldenberg, David M. " 'It Is Permitted to Marry a Kushite.' " *AJS Review* 37, no. 1 (2013): 29–49.

Goldschmidt, Arthur, and Robert Johnston. *Historical Dictionary of Egypt*. Lanham, MD: Scarecrow Press, 2003.

Goldschmidt, Henry, and Elizabeth A. McAlister. *Race, Nation, and Religion in the Americas*. New York: Oxford University Press, 2004.

Goldstein, Eric L. *The Price of Whiteness: Jews, Race, and American Identity*. Princeton: Princeton University Press, 2006.

———. "The Unstable Other: Locating the Jew in Progressive-Era American Racial Discourse." *American Jewish History* 89, no. 4 (2001): 383–409.

Gorni, Yosef. *Zionism and the Arabs 1882–1948: A Study of Ideology*. Oxford: Clarendon Press, 1987.

Gottheil, Richard J. H. *Zionism*. Philadelphia: Jewish Publication Society of America, 1914.

Gottreich, Emily Benichou. "Historicizing the Concept of Arab Jews in the Maghrib." *Jewish Quarterly Review* 98, no. 4 (2008): 433–51.

Govrin, Nurit. *"Me'ora' Brener": ha-Ma'avak 'al ḥofesh ha-bitui*. Jerusalem: Yad Yiẓḥak Ben-Ẓevi, 1985.

Graetz, Heinrich, *History of the Jews*, translated and edited by Bella Löwy. 6 vols. Philadelphia: Jewish Publication Society of America, 1891–1898.

Gribetz, Jonathan Marc. "An Arabic-Zionist Talmud: Shimon Moyal's at-Talmud." *Jewish Social Studies* 17, no. 1 (Fall 2010): 1–30.

———. "The Question of Palestine before the International Community, 1924: A Methodological Inquiry into the Charge of 'Bias." *Israel Studies* 17, no. 1 (Spring 2012): 50–77.

———. " 'Their Blood Is Eastern': Shahin Makaryus and *Fin de Siècle* Arab Pride in the Jewish 'Race.' " *Middle Eastern Studies* 49, no. 2 (2013): 143–61.

Griffith, Sidney H. *The Bible in Arabic: The Scriptures of the "Peiople of the Book" in the Language of Islam*. Princeton: Princeton University Press, 2013.

Haiduc-Dale, Noah. *Arab Christians in British Mandate Palestine: Communalism and Nationalism, 1917–1948*. Edinburgh: Edinburgh University Press, 2013.

Haim, Abraham, and Elie Eliachar. *Teʿudot min ha-osef shel Eliyahu Elyashar: Seker*. Jerusalem: Karta, 1971.

Haim, Sylvia G., ed. *Arab Nationalism: An Anthology*. Berkeley: University of California Press, 1962.

———. "Arabic Antisemitic Literature: Some Preliminary Notes." *Jewish Social Studies* 17, no. 4 (1955): 307–12.

———. "Islamic Anti-Zionism." *Jewish Quarterly* 31, no. 2 (1984): 48–51.

Hall, Bruce S. *A History of Race in Muslim West Africa, 1600–1960*. New York: Cambridge University Press, 2011.

Hallaq, Wael B. *A History of Islamic Legal Theories: An Introduction to Sunnī uṣul al-fiqh*. New York: Cambridge University Press, 1997.

Halper, Jeff. *Between Redemption and Revival: The Jewish Yishuv of Jerusalem in the Nineteenth Century*. Boulder: Westview Press, 1991.

Halperin, Liora. "Orienting Language: Reflections on the Study of Arabic in the Yishuv." *Jewish Quarterly Review* 96, no. 4 (2006): 481–89.

el Hamel, Chouki. " 'Race,' Slavery and Islam in Maghribi Mediterranean Thought: The Question of the Haratin in Morocco." *Journal of North African Studies* 7, no. 3 (2002): 29–52.

Hanioğlu, M. Şükrü. *A Brief History of the Late Ottoman Empire*. Princeton: Princeton University Press, 2008.

———. *Preparation for a Revolution: The Young Turks, 1902–1908*. New York: Oxford University Press, 2001.

Hanssen, Jens. *Fin de Siècle Beirut: The Making of an Ottoman Provincial Capital*. Oxford: Oxford University Press, 2005.

Harani, Yisca. "ha-ʿEdot ha-noẓriyot: ha-Kenesiyot ha-mizraḥiyot." In *Sefer yerushalayim: Be-shilhei ha-tekufah ha-ʿot'manit, 1800–1917*, edited by Yisrael Bartal and H. Goren, 147–63. Jerusalem: Yad Yiẓḥak Ben-Ẓevi, 2010.

Hart, Mitchell Bryan, ed. *Jews and Race: Writings on Identity and Difference, 1880–1940*. Waltham, MA: Brandeis University Press, 2011.

Havrelock, Rachel. *River Jordan: The Mythology of a Dividing Line*. Chicago: The University of Chicago Press, 2011.

Hayes, Carlton J. H. *Nationalism: A Religion*. New York: Macmillan, 1960.

Hertzberg, Arthur, ed. *The Zionist Idea: A Historical Analysis and Reader*. Philadelphia: Jewish Publication Society, 1997.

Herzl, Theodor. *Complete Diaries*, edited by Raphael Patai, translated by Harry Zohn. Vol. 2. New York: Herzl Press, 1960.

———. *The Jewish State*. New York: Dover Publications, 1988.

Hirsch, Samson Raphael. *The Nineteen Letters of Ben Uziel: Being a Spiritual Presentation of the Principles of Judaism*, translated by Bernard Drachman. New York: Funk and Wagnalls, 1899.

Hofstadter, Richard. *Social Darwinism in American Thought*. Boston: Beacon Press, 1944.

Hourani, Albert Habib. *Arabic Thought in the Liberal Age, 1798–1939*. New York: Cambridge University Press, 1983.

———. "The Case against a Jewish State in Palestine: Albert Hourani's Statement to the Anglo-American Committee of Enquiry of 1946." *Journal of Palestine Studies* 35, no. 1 (Autumn 2005): 80–90.

Hourani, George F. "The Basis of Authority of Consensus in Sunnite Islam." *Studia Islamica* no. 21 (1964): 13–60.

Hyman, Paula. *The Jews of Modern France*. Berkeley: University of California Press, 1998.

Jacobson, Abigail. *From Empire to Empire: Jerusalem between Ottoman and British Rule*. Syracuse: Syracuse University Press, 2011.

———. "From Empire to Empire: Jerusalem in the Transition between Ottoman and British Rule, 1912–1920." PhD dissertation, University of Chicago, 2006.

———. "Jews Writing in Arabic: Shimon Moyal, Nissim Malul and the Mixed Palestinian/Eretz Israeli Locale." In *Late Ottoman Palestine: The Period of Young Turk Rule*, edited by Yuval Ben-Bassat and Eyal Ginio, 165–82. New York: I. B. Tauris, 2011.

———. "The Sephardi Community in Pre–World War I Palestine." *Jerusalem Quarterly File* 14 (Autumn 2001): 23–34.

———. "Sephardim, Ashkenazim and the 'Arab Question' in Pre–First World War Palestine: A Reading of Three Zionist Newspapers." *Middle Eastern Studies* 39, no. 2 (April, 2003): 105–30.

Jeha, Shafik. *Darwin and the Crisis of 1882 in the Medical Department: And the First Student Protest in the Arab World in the Syrian Protestant College (Now the American University of Beirut)*, translated by Helen Khal. Beirut: American University of Beirut Press, 2004.

Kalmar, Ivan Davidson. "Benjamin Disraeli, Romantic Orientalist." *Comparative Studies in Society and History* 47, no. 2 (2005): 348–71.

Kaniel, Yehoshua. "Anshei ha-ʿaliyah ha-sheniyah u-venei ha-ʿedah ha-sefaradit." In *ha-ʿAliyah ha-sheniyah: Meḥkarim*, edited by Yisrael Bartal, 307–19. Jerusalem: Yad Yiẓḥak Ben Ẓevi, 1997.

———. "The Terms 'Old Yishuv' and 'New Yishuv': Problems of Definition." In *The Jerusalem Cathedra: Studies in the History, Archaeology, Geography and Ethnography of the Land of Israel*, edited by Lee I. Levine, 1:232–45. Jerusalem: Wayne State University Press, 1981.

Kaplan, Eran, and Derek Jonathan Penslar, eds. *The Origins of Israel, 1882–1948: A Documentary History*. Madison: University of Wisconsin Press, 2011.

Kasmieh, Khairieh. "Ruhi Al-Khalidi 1864–1913: A Symbol of the Cultural Movement in Palestine towards the End of Ottoman Rule." In *The Syrian Land in the 18th and 19th Century: The Common and the Specific in the Historical Experience*, edited by Thomas Philipp, 123–46. Stuttgart: F. Steiner, 1992.

Kaufman, Asher S. *Reviving Phoenicia: In Search of Identity in Lebanon*. New York: I. B. Tauris, 2004.

Keane, Augustus Henry. *The World's Peoples: A Popular Account of Their Bodily & Mental Characters, Beliefs, Traditions, Political and Social Institutions*. New York: G. P. Putnam's Sons, 1908.

Kedourie, Elie. "Young Turks, Freemasons and Jews." *Middle Eastern Studies* 7, no. 1 (1971): 89–104.
al-Khālidī, Muḥammad Ruḥi. *al-Kīmiyāʾ ʿind al-ʿarab*. Cairo: Dar al-Maʿarif, 1953.
———. *al-Muqaddima fī al-masʾala ash-sharqiyya: Mundhu nashʾatihā al-ūlā ilā ar-rubʿ ath-thānī min al-qarn ath-thāmin ʿashar*. Jerusalem: Maṭbaʿat Madrasat al-Aytām al-Islāmiyya bi-l-Quds, n.d. [1920].
———. "as-Sayūnīzm, ay al-masʾala aṣ-ṣahyūniyya" [author's version]. al-Khalidiyya Library, c. 1913.
———. "as-Sayūnīzm, ay al-masʾala aṣ-ṣahyūniyya" [copyist version]. al-Khalidiyya Library, c. 1913.
———[el Khalidy, Rouhi]. "Statistique de l'Univers Musulman." *Revue de l'Islam* 21 (1897): 113–16.
———. *Tārīkh ʿilm al-adab ʿind al-ifranj wa-l-ʿarab wa-Fīktūr Hūgū: wa-huwa yashtamil ʿalā muqaddimāt tārīkhiyya wa-ijtimāʿiyya fī ʿilm al-adab ʿind al-ifranj wa-mā yuqābiluhū min dhālika ʿind al-ʿarab wa-mā iqtabasahū al-ifranj ʿanhum wa-khuṣūṣan ʿalā yad Fīktūr Hūgū*. Cairo: Maṭbaʿat al-Hilāl, 1904.
Khalidi, Rashid. "Intellectual Life in Late Ottoman Jerusalem." In *Ottoman Jerusalem: The Living City, 1517–1917*, edited by Sylvia Auld, Robert Hillenbrand, and Yusuf Said Natsheh, 1:221–28. London: Altajir World of Islam Trust, 2000.
———. *The Iron Cage: The Story of the Palestinian Struggle for Statehood*. Boston: Beacon Press, 2006.
———. *Palestinian Identity: The Construction of Modern National Consciousness*. New York: Columbia University Press, 1997.
al-Khālidī, Walīd. "Kitāb as-sayūnīzm aw al-masʾala aṣ-ṣahyūniyya li-Muḥammad Rūḥī al-Khālidī al-mutawaffā sanat 1913." In *Dirāsāt Filasṭīniyya: Majmūʿat abḥāth wuḍiʿat takrīman li-d-Duktūr Qusṭanṭīn Zurayq*, edited by Hisham Nashshabah. Beirut: Muʾassasat ad-Dirāsāt al-Filasṭīniyya, 1988.
———. "On Albert Hourani, the Arab Office, and the Anglo-American Committee of 1946." *Journal of Palestine Studies* 35, no. 1 (Autumn 2005): 60–79.
al-Khateeb, H. "Ruhi Al-Khalidi: A Pioneer of Comparative Literature in Arabic." *Journal of Arabic Literature* 18 (1987): 81–87.
Kimmerling, Baruch, and Joel S. Migdal. *The Palestinian People: A History*. Cambridge, MA: Harvard University Press, 2003.
Knaʿani, David. *ha-ʿAliyah ha-sheniyah ha-ʿovedet ve-yaḥasah la-dat ve-la-masoret*. Tel Aviv: Sifriyat poʿalim, 1976.
Knoppers, Gary N. *Jews and Samaritans: The Origins and History of Their Early Relations*. New York: Oxford University Press, 2013.
Kolsky, Thomas A. *Jews against Zionism: The American Council for Judaism, 1942–1948*. Philadelphia: Temple University Press, 1990.
Korn, Eugene. "Gentiles, the World to Come, and Judaism: The Odyssey of a Rabbinic Text." *Modern Judaism* 14, no. 3 (1994): 265–87.

Krämer, Gudrun. *A History of Palestine: From the Ottoman Conquest to the Founding of the State of Israel*. Princeton: Princeton University Press, 2008.
———. *The Jews in Modern Egypt, 1914–1952*. Seattle: University of Washington Press, 1989.
Kressel, Getzel. *Toldot ha-ʿitonut ha-ʿivrit be-ereẓ yisraʾel*. Jerusalem: ha-Sifriyah ha-Ẓiyonit, 1964.
Kreutz, Andrej. *Vatican Policy on the Palestinian-Israeli Conflict: The Struggle for the Holy Land*. New York: Greenwood Press, 1990.
Kupferschmidt, Uri M. *The Supreme Muslim Council: Islam under the British Mandate for Palestine*. New York: E. J. Brill, 1987.
Kushner, David, ed. *Palestine in the Late Ottoman Period: Political, Social, and Economic Transformation*. Jerusalem: Yad Izhak Ben-Zvi, 1986.
———. *The Rise of Turkish Nationalism, 1876–1908*. London: Cass, 1977.
———. *To Be Governor of Jerusalem: The City and District during the Time of Ali Ekrem Bey, 1906–1908*. Istanbul: Isis Press, 2005.
La Guardia, Anton. *War without End: Israelis, Palestinians, and the Struggle for a Promised Land*. New York: Thomas Dunne Books, 2002.
Lakoff, George, and Mark Johnson. *Metaphors We Live By*. Chicago: University of Chicago Press, 1980.
Landau, Jacob. "ʿAlilot dam u-redifot yehudim be-miẓrayim be-meʾah ha-teshaʿ ʿesreh." *Sefunot: Sefer shana le-ḥeker kehilot yisraʾel ba-mizraḥ* 5 (1961): 415–60.
———. *ha-Yehudim be-miẓrayim ba-meʾah ha-teshaʿ-ʿesreh*. Jerusalem: Mekhon Ben-Ẓevi ba-universitah ha-ʿivrit, 1967.
———. *Jews in Nineteenth-Century Egypt*. New York: New York University Press, 1969.
Lang, Yoseph. *Daber ʿivrit! Ḥayei Eliʿezer Ben-Yehuda*. 2 vols. Jerusalem: Yad Yiẓḥak Ben-Ẓevi, 2008.
Laqueur, Walter, and Barry M. Rubin, eds. *The Israel-Arab Reader: A Documentary History of the Middle East Conflict*. 6th ed. New York: Penguin Books, 2001.
Lasker, Daniel J. "The Jewish Critique of Christianity under Islam in the Middle Ages." *Proceedings of the American Academy for Jewish Research* 57 (1990): 121–53.
Laurent, Achille. *Relation historique des affaires de Syrie depuis 1840 jusqu'en 1842*. 2 vols. Paris: Gaume Frères, 1846.
Lauzière, Henri. "The Construction of *Salafiyya:* Reconsidering Salafism from the Perspective of Conceptual History." *International Journal of Middle East Studies* 42, no. 3 (2010): 369–89.
LeBor, Adam. *City of Oranges: Arabs and Jews in Jaffa*. London: Bloomsbury, 2006.
Levy, Avigdor. *The Sephardim in the Ottoman Empire*. Princeton, NJ: Darwin Press, 1992.
Levy, Lisa Lital. "Historicizing the Concept of Arab Jews in the Mashriq." *Jewish Quarterly Review* 98, no. 4 (2008): 452–69.

Levy, Lisa Lital. "Jewish Writers in the Arab East: Literature, History, and the Politics of Enlightenment, 1863–1914." PhD dissertation, University of California, Berkeley, 2007.

Levy, Richard S. *Antisemitism: A Historical Encyclopedia of Prejudice and Persecution*. Santa Barbara: ABC-CLIO, 2005.

Lewis, Bernard. *The Political Language of Islam*. Chicago: University of Chicago Press, 1988.

———. *Race and Slavery in the Middle East: An Historical Enquiry*. New York: Oxford University Press, 1990.

———. *Semites and Anti-Semites: An Inquiry into Conflict and Prejudice*. New York: Norton, 1999.

Libson, Gideon. "Halakhah and Reality in the Gaonic Period: Taqqanah, Minhag, Tradition and Consensus: Some Observations." In *The Jews of Medieval Islam: Community, Society, and Identity*, edited by Daniel Frank, 67–99. New York: E. J. Brill, 1995.

———. *Jewish and Islamic Law: A Comparative Study of Custom during the Geonic Period*. Cambridge, MA: Harvard University Press, 2003.

Likhovski, Assaf. *Law and Identity in Mandate Palestine*. Studies in Legal History. Chapel Hill: University of North Carolina Press, 2006.

Lockman, Zachary. *Comrades and Enemies: Arab and Jewish Workers in Palestine, 1906–1948*. Berkeley: University of California Press, 1996.

———. *Contending Visions of the Middle East: The History and Politics of Orientalism*. New York: Cambridge University Press, 2004.

Maccoby, Hyam, ed. *Judaism on Trial: Jewish-Christian Disputations in the Middle Ages*. Rutherford, NJ: Fairleigh Dickinson University Press, 1982.

Maimonides, Moses. *Sefer mishneh torah*, edited by Yosef Kafaḥ, vol. 1. Jerusalem: Mekhon mishnat ha-Rambam, 1983.

———. *Zeraʿim. Mishnah: ʿim perush Rabeinu Mosheh Ben Maimon*, edited by Yosef. Kafaḥ. Jerusalem: Hoẓaʾat mosad ha-Rav Kook, 1963.

Maimuni, David ben Abraham. *Pirkei avot: ʿim perusho shel Rabeinu Dayid ha-Nagid, zaẓal, nekhed ha-Rambam, zaẓal, Midrash David*, edited by Ben Ẓiyon ben Yeshʿayah Krinfis. Jerusalem: Mekhon ha-ketav, 1991.

Makaryus, Shahin. *Tārīkh al-isrāʾīliyyīn*. Cairo: al-Muqtaṭaf, 1904.

Makdisi, Ussama Samir. *Artillery of Heaven: American Missionaries and the Failed Conversion of the Middle East*. Ithaca: Cornell University Press, 2008.

———. *The Culture of Sectarianism: Community, History, and Violence in Nineteenth-Century Ottoman Lebanon*. Berkeley: University of California Press, 2000.

Malūl, Nisīm. *Kitāb asrār al-yahūd*. Vol. 1. N.p., 1911.

Mandel, Neville J. *The Arabs and Zionism before World War I*. Berkeley: University of California Press, 1976.

———. "Ottoman Policy and Restrictions on Jewish Settlement in Palestine: 1881–1908: Part I." *Middle Eastern Studies* 10, no. 3 (1974): 312–32.

———. "Ottoman Practice as Regards Jewish Settlement in Palestine: 1881–1908." *Middle Eastern Studies* 11, no. 1 (1975): 33–46.

Mannāʿ, ʿAdil. *Aʿlām filasṭīn fī awākhir al-ʿahd al-ʿuthmānī (1800–1918)*. 2nd ed. Beirut: Muʾassasat ad-Dirāsāt al-Filasṭīniyya, 1995.

———. "ha-Ukhlusiyah ha-ʿarvit: Ḥevrah, kalkalah ve-irgun." In *ha-Historiyah shel ereẓ yisraʾel: Shilhei ha-tekufah ha-ʿot'omanit (1799–1917)*, edited by Yehoshua Ben-Arieh and Yisrael Bartal, 8:162–77. Jerusalem: Yad Yiẓḥak Ben-Ẓevi, 1983.

Marcus, Amy Dockser. *Jerusalem 1913: The Origins of the Arab-Israeli Conflict*. New York: Viking, 2007.

Margoliouth, D. S., and W.S.S. Tyrwhitt. *Cairo, Jerusalem, and Damascus, Three Chief Cities of the Egyptian Sultans*. New York: Dodd, Mead, 1907.

Masterman, E.W.G. "Palestine: Its Resources and Suitability for Colonization." *The Geographical Journal* 50, no. 1 (1917): 12–26.

Masters, Bruce Alan. *The Arabs of the Ottoman Empire, 1516–1918: A Social and Cultural History*. New York: Cambridge University Press, 2013.

McCarthy, Justin. *The Population of Palestine: Population History and Statistics of the Late Ottoman Period and the Mandate*. New York: Columbia University Press, 1990.

McCullagh, Francis. *The Fall of Abd-Ul-Hamid*. London: Methuen, 1910.

Mendelssohn, Moses. *Jerusalem, Or, on Religious Power and Judaism*, translated by Alexander Altmann, edited by Allan Arkush. Hanover, MA: Brandeis University Press, 1983.

Mendes-Flohr, Paul R., and Jehuda Reinharz, eds. *The Jew in the Modern World: A Documentary History*. 2nd ed. New York: Oxford University Press, 1995.

Meyer, Michael A. *Response to Modernity: A History of the Reform Movement in Judaism*. New York: Oxford University Press, 1988.

Minerbi, Sergio I. *The Vatican and Zionism: Conflict in the Holy Land, 1895–1925*. New York: Oxford University Press, 1990.

Mintz, Matityahu. "Beyn David Ben-Gurion le-Yiẓḥak Ben-Ẓevi: ʿAl mikbaẓ eḥad shel mikhtavei Ben-Gurion be-galut amerika (1915–1916)." *Katedra* 44 (1987): 81–96.

Moncrieff, A. R. Hope. *The World of to-Day: A Survey of the Lands and Peoples of the Globe as Seen in Travel and Commerce*. 6 vols. London: Gresham, 1907.

Morris, Benny. *Righteous Victims: A History of the Zionist-Arab Conflict, 1881–2001*. New York: Vintage Books, 2001.

Mūyāl, Shimʿūn Yūsuf. *at-Talmūd: Aṣluhu wa-tasalsuluhu wa-ādābuhu*. Maṭbaʿat al-ʿArab, 1909.

Muslih, Muhammad Y. *The Origins of Palestinian Nationalism*. New York: Columbia University Press, 1988.

Myers, David N. *Re-Inventing the Jewish Past: European Jewish Intellectuals and the Zionist Return to History*. New York: Oxford University Press, 1995.

———. *Resisting History: Historicism and Its Discontents in German-Jewish Thought*. Princeton: Princeton University Press, 2003.

Nadolski, Dora Glidewell. "Ottoman and Secular Civil Law." *International Journal of Middle East Studies* 8, no. 4 (October 1977): 517–43.

Naṣṣār, Najīb al-Khūrī. *aṣ-Ṣahyūniyya: Tārīkhuhu gharaḍuhu ahammiyyatuhu (mulakhkhaṣan ʿan al-insaykulūbīdiyya al-yahūdiyya)*. Haifa: al-Karmil, 1911.

Naṣṣār, Sihām. Mawqif aṣ-ṣiḥāfa al-miṣriyya min aṣ-ṣahyūniyya khilāl al-fatra min 1897–1917: Dirāsa taḥlīliyya li-ṣuḥuf al-ahrām, al-muqaṭṭam wa-l-mu'ayyad wa-l-liwā' wa-l-jarīda wa-l-ahālī. [Cairo]: al-Hay'a al-Miṣriyya al-ʿĀmma li-l-Kitāb, 1993.

Nehorai, Michael Zvi. "Ḥasidei umot ha-ʿolam yesh la-hem ḥelek le-ʿolam ha-ba." *Tarbiẓ* 61, no. 3–4 (1992): 465–88.

Neusner, Jacob, and Tamara Sonn. *Comparing Religions through Law: Judaism and Islam*. New York: Routledge, 1999.

Neusner, Jacob, Tamara Sonn, and Jonathan E. Brockopp. *Judaism and Islam in Practice: A Sourcebook*. New York: Routledge, 2000.

Newby, Gordon Darnell. *A History of the Jews of Arabia: From Ancient Times to Their Eclipse under Islam*. Columbia: University of South Carolina Press, 1988.

Nongbri, Brent. *Before Religion: A History of a Modern Concept*. New Haven: Yale University Press, 2013.

Nordau, Max. *Zionism: Its History and its Aims*, translated by Israel Cohen. London: English Zionist Federation, 1905.

Oren-Nordheim, Michal. "ha-Merkhav ha-kafri bi-svivot yerushalayim be-shilhei ha-tekufah ha-ʿot'manit." In *Sefer yerushalayim: Be-shilhei ha-tekufah ha-ʿot'manit, 1800–1917*, edited by Yisrael Bartal and H. Goren, 211–21. Jerusalem: Yad Yiẓḥak Ben-Ẓevi, 2010.

Parsons, Laila. "The Druze and the Birth of Israel." In *The War for Palestine: Rewriting the History of 1948*, edited by Eugene L. Rogan and Avi Shlaim, 60–78. 2nd ed. New York: Cambridge University Press, 2007.

Pedersen, Susan. "The Impact of League Oversight on British Policy in Palestine." In *Britain, Palestine, and Empire: The Mandate Years*, edited by Rory Miller, 39–66. Burlington, VT: Ashgate, 2010.

Penslar, Derek Jonathan. "The Hands of Others." *Jewish Review of Books* 5 (Spring 2011): 25–27.

———. *Jews and the Military: A History*. Princeton: Princeton University Press, 2013.

———. *Shylock's Children: Economics and Jewish Identity in Modern Europe*. Berkeley: University of California Press, 2001.

———. *Zionism and Technocracy: The Engineering of Jewish Settlement in Palestine, 1870–1918*. Bloomington: Indiana University Press, 1991.

Perlmann, Moshe. "The Medieval Polemics between Islam and Judaism." In *Religion in a Religious Age*, edited by S. D. Goitein, Cambridge, MA: Association for Jewish Studies, 1974.

———, ed. "Samau'al al-Maghribī: Ifḥām al-yahūd: Silencing the Jews." *Proceedings of the American Academy for Jewish Research* 32 (1964).

Perry, Yaron. *British Mission to the Jews in Nineteenth-Century Palestine*. London: Frank Cass, 2003.

———. "ha-Naẓrut ha-maʿaravit: Protastantim." In *Sefer yerushalayim: Be-shilhei ha-tekufah ha-ʿot'manit, 1800–1917*, edited by Yisrael Bartal and H. Goren, 141–45. Jerusalem: Yad Yiẓḥak Ben-Ẓevi, 2010.

Perry, Yaron, and Efraim Lev. *Modern Medicine in the Holy Land: Pioneering British Medical Services in Late Ottoman Palestine*. London: Tauris Academic Studies, 2007.

Peters, F. E. *The Children of Abraham: Judaism, Christianity, Islam*. New edition. Princeton: Princeton University Press, 2004.

Peters, Joan. *From Time Immemorial: The Origins of the Arab-Jewish Conflict over Palestine*. New York: Harper & Row, 1984.

Petrie, W. M. Flinders, and C. T. Currelly. *Researches in Sinai*. New York: E. P. Dutton, 1906.

Philipp, Alfred. *Die Juden und das Wirtschaftsleben. Eine antikritisch-bibliographische Studie zu Werner Sombart: Die Juden und das Wirtschaftsleben*. Strasbourg: Heitz, 1929.

Philipp, Thomas. *Acre: The Rise and Fall of a Palestinian City, 1730–1831*. New York: Columbia University Press, 2001.

Philipp, Thomas, and Jirjī Zaydān. *Ǧurǧī Zaidān, His Life and Thought*. Beiruter Texte und Studien. Beirut: Orient-Inst. d. Dt. Morgenländ. Ges., 1979.

Porath, Yehoshua. *The Emergence of the Palestinian-Arab National Movement 1918–1929*. London: Frank Cass, 1974.

Portnoy, Edward A. "The Creation of a Jewish Cartoon Space in the New York and Warsaw Yiddish Press, 1884–1939." PhD dissertation, Jewish Theological Seminary of America, 2008.

Powell, Eve Troutt. *A Different Shade of Colonialism: Egypt, Great Britain, and the Mastery of the Sudan*. Berkeley: University of California Press, 2003.

Prätor, Sabine. *Der Arabische Faktor in der Jungtürkischen Politik: Eine Studie zum osmanischen Parlament der II. Konstitution (1908–1918)*. Berlin: Klaus Schwarz, 1993.

Quataert, Donald. *The Ottoman Empire, 1700–1922*. 2nd ed. New York: Cambridge University Press, 2005.

Rabinovitch, Simon, ed. *Jews and Diaspora Nationalism: Writings on Jewish Peoplehood in Europe and the United States*. Waltham, MA: Brandeis University Press, 2012.

Reichman, Shalom, Yossi Katz, and Yair Paz. "The Absorptive Capacity of Palestine, 1882–1948." *Middle Eastern Studies* 33, no. 2 (1997): 338–61.

Reinkowski, Maurus. "Late Ottoman Rule over Palestine: Its Evaluation in Arab, Turkish and Israeli Histories, 1970–90." *Middle Eastern Studies* 35, no. 1 (1999): 66–97.

Robson, Laura. *Colonialism and Christianity in Mandate Palestine*. Austin: University of Texas Press, 2011.

Rodinson, Maxime. *Europe and the Mystique of Islam*. Seattle: University of Washington Press, 1987.

———. *Israel and the Arabs*. 2nd ed. New York: Penguin, 1982.

Rodrigue, Aron. *French Jews, Turkish Jews: The Alliance Israélite Universelle and the Politics of Jewish Schooling in Turkey, 1860–1925*. Bloomington: Indiana University Press, 1990.

———. *Jews and Muslims: Images of Sephardi and Eastern Jewries in Modern Times*. Seattle: University of Washington Press, 2003.

Rohling, August. *al-Kanz al-marṣūd fī qawāʿid at-talmūd*, edited by Yusuf Nasr Allah. Cairo: Maṭbaʿat al-Maʿārif, 1899.

Roʾi, Yaacov [Yaʿakov]. "Nisyonoteihem shel ha-mosadot ha-ẓiyonim lehashpiʿa ʿal ha-ʿitonut ha-ʿarvit be-ereẓ yisraʾel ba-shanim 1908–1914." *Ẓion* 32, no. 3–4 (1967): 201–27.

———. "The Relationship of the Yishuv to the Arabs." MA thesis, Hebrew University, 1964.

———. "Yeḥasei yehudim-ʿarvim be-moshavot ha-ʿaliyah ha-rishonah." In *Sefer ha-ʿaliyah ha-rishonah*, edited by Mordechai Eliav, Yemima Rosenthal, and Chaya Har-El, vol. 1, 245–68. Jerusalem: Yad Yiẓḥak Ben-Ẓevi, 1981.

———. "The Zionist Attitude to the Arabs 1908–1914." *Middle Eastern Studies* 4, no. 3 (April 1968): 198–242.

Ryad, Umar. *Islamic Reformism and Christianity: A Critical Reading of the Works of Muḥammad Rashīd Riḍā and His Associates (1898–1935)*. Boston: E. J. Brill, 2009.

Said, Edward W., and Christopher Hitchens, eds. *Blaming the Victims: Spurious Scholarship and the Palestinian Question*. London: Verso, 2001.

Salmon, Yosef. "ha-Yishuv ha-ashkenazi ha-ʿironi be-ereẓ yisraʾel (1880–1903)." In *Toldot ha-yishuv ha-yehudi be-ereẓ-yisraʾel: Me-az ha-ʿaliyah ha-rishonah: ha-tekufah ha-ʿotomanit*, edited by Moshe Lissak, Gavriel Cohen, and Israel Kolatt, 1:539–619. Jerusalem: Mosad Byalik, 1999.

Sand, Shlomo. *The Invention of the Jewish People*, translated by Yael Lotan. New York: Verso, 2009.

———. *The Invention of the Land of Israel: From Holy Land to Homeland*, translated by Geremy Forman. New York: Verso Books, 2012.

Saposnik, Arieh Bruce. *Becoming Hebrew: The Creation of a Jewish National Culture in Ottoman Palestine*. New York: Oxford University Press, 2008.

Schäfer, Peter. *Jesus in the Talmud*. Princeton: Princeton University Press, 2007.

Schidorsky, Dov. "Libraries in Late Ottoman Palestine between the Orient and the Occident." *Libraries and Culture* 33, no. 3 (1998): 260–76.

Schölch, Alexander. *Egypt for the Egyptians!: The Socio-Political Crisis in Egypt, 1878–1882*. London: Ithaca Press, 1981.

———. *Palestine in Transformation, 1856–1882: Studies in Social, Economic, and Political Development*. Washington, DC: Institute for Palestine Studies, 1993.

Schreier, Joshua. *Arabs of the Jewish Faith: The Civilizing Mission in Colonial Algeria*. New Brunswick, NJ: Rutgers University Press, 2010.

Schwartz, Shuly Rubin. *The Emergence of Jewish Scholarship in America: The Publication of the Jewish Encyclopedia*. Cincinnati: Hebrew Union College Press, 1991.

Sedgwick, Mark J. *Muhammad Abduh*. New York: Oneworld, 2010.

Sehayik, Shaʾul. "Demut ha-yehudi bi-reʾi ʿitonut ʿarvit beyn ha-shanim 1858–1908." PhD dissertation, Hebrew University of Jerusalem, 1991.

Seidman, Naomi. *Faithful Renderings: Jewish-Christian Difference and the Politics of Translation*. Chicago: University of Chicago Press, 2006.

Shafir, Gershon. *Land, Labor, and the Origins of the Israeli-Palestinian Conflict, 1882–1914*. Updated ed. Berkeley: University of California Press, 1996.

El Shakry, Omnia S. *The Great Social Laboratory: Subjects of Knowledge in Colonial and Postcolonial Egypt*. Stanford: Stanford University Press, 2007.

Shavit, Jacob. *The New Hebrew Nation: A Study in Israeli Heresy and Fantasy*. London: Frank Cass, 1987.

Shelef, Nadav G. *Evolving Nationalism: Homeland, Identity, and Religion in Israel, 1925–2005*. Ithaca: Cornell University Press, 2010.

Shenhav, Yehouda A. *The Arab Jews: A Postcolonial Reading of Nationalism, Religion, and Ethnicity*. Stanford: Stanford University Press, 2006.

Shimoni, Gideon. *The Zionist Ideology*. Hanover, MA: Brandeis University Press, 1995.

Silberstein, Laurence. "Religion, Ethnicity, and Jewish History: The Contribution of Yehezkel Kaufmann." *Journal of the American Academy of Religion* 42, no. 3 (September 1974): 516–31.

Simon, Reeva S., Michael M. Laskier, and Sara Reguer. *The Jews of the Middle East and North Africa in Modern Times*. New York: Columbia University Press, 2003.

Smith, Anthony D. *Chosen Peoples*. New York: Oxford University Press, 2003.

———. *The Ethnic Origins of Nations*. New York: Blackwell, 1987.

Snir, Reuven. "Arabness, Egyptianness, Zionism, and Cosmopolitanism: The Arabic Cultural and Journalistic Activities of Egyptian Jews in the 19th and 20th Centuries." *Orientalia Suecana* 55 (2006): 133–64.

Somekh, Sasson. *Baghdad, Yesterday: The Making of an Arab Jew*. Jerusalem: Ibis Editions, 2007.

Spinoza, Benedictus de. *Theological-Political Treatise*, edited by Jonathan I. Israel. New York: Cambridge University Press, 2007.

Stanislawski, Michael. *Autobiographical Jews: Essays in Jewish Self-Fashioning*. Seattle: University of Washington Press, 2004.

Stav, Arie. *Peace: The Arabian Caricature: A Study of Anti-Semitic Imagery*. New York: Gefen, 1999.

Sternhell, Zeev. *The Founding Myths of Israel: Nationalism, Socialism, and the Making of the Jewish State*. Princeton: Princeton University Press, 1998.

Stillman, Norman A. *The Jews of Arab Lands in Modern Times*. Philadelphia: Jewish Publication Society, 1991.

Stolz, Daniel A. " 'By Virtue of Your Knowledge': Scientific Materialism and the Fatwās of Rashīd Riḍā." *Bulletin of the School of Oriental and African Studies* 75, no. 2 (2012): 223–47.

Tamari, Salim. *Mountain against the Sea: Essays on Palestinian Society and Culture*. Berkeley: University of California Press, 2009.

Tauber, Eliezer. *The Emergence of the Arab Movements*. London: F. Cass, 1993.

———. "Jewish–non-Palestinian-Arab Negotiations: The First Phase." *Israel Affairs* 6, no. 3–4 (2000): 159–76.

Taylor, Charles. *A Secular Age*. Cambridge, MA: Belknap Press of Harvard University Press, 2007.

Townsend, Philippa. "Who Were the First Christians? Jews, Gentiles, and the *Christinoi*." In *Heresy and Identity in Late Antiquity*, edited by Eduard Iricinschi and Holger M. Zellentin, 212–30. Tubingen: Mohr Siebeck, 2008.

Tylor, Edward B. *Anthropology: An Introduction to the Study of Man and Civilization*. London: Macmillan, 1890.

Venuti, Lawrence. "Translation, Community, Utopia." In *The Translation Studies Reader*, edited by Lawrence Venuti. 2nd ed. New York: Routledge, 2004.

Waardenburg, Jean Jacques. *Muslim Perceptions of Other Religions: A Historical Survey*. New York: Oxford University Press, 1999.

Wasserstein, Bernard. "Patterns of Communal Conflict in Palestine." In *Essential Papers on Zionism*, edited by Jehuda Reinharz and Anita Shapira, 671–88. New York: New York University Press, 1996.

Wegner, Judith Romney. "Islamic and Talmudic Jurisprudence: The Four Roots of Islamic Law and Their Talmudic Counterparts." *The American Journal of Legal History* 26 (1982): 25–71.

Weitz, Eric D. *A Century of Genocide: Utopias of Race and Nation*. Princeton: Princeton University Press, 2003.

———. "From the Vienna to the Paris System: International Politics and the Entangled Histories of Human Rights, Forced Deportations, and Civilizing Missions." *American Historical Review* 113, no. 5 (December 2008): 1313–43.

Wood, Simon A. *Christian Criticisms, Islamic Proofs: Rashīd Riḍā's Modernist Defense of Islam*. Oxford: Oneworld, 2008.

Yehoshuʿa, Yaʿqūb. *Tārīkh aṣ-ṣiḥāfa al-ʿarabiyya fī filasṭīn fī al-ʿahd al-ʿuthmānī, 1908–1918*. Jerusalem: al-Muʿārif, 1974.

Yehoshuʿa, Yaʿqūb [Yaʿakov], and Avraham B. Yehoshua. *Yerushalayim ha-yeshanah ba-ʿayin u-va-lev: Mivḥar ketavim*. Jerusalem: Keter, 1988.

Yerushalmi, Yosef Hayim. *Zakhor: Jewish History and Jewish Memory*. Seattle: University of Washington Press, 1982.

Yūsuf ʿAlī, ʿAbdullah. *The Meaning of the Holy Qurʾān*. 11th ed. Beltsville, MD: Amana Publications, 2009.

Yuval, Israel Jacob. *Two Nations in Your Womb: Perceptions of Jews and Christians in Late Antiquity and the Middle Ages*. Berkeley: University of California Press, 2006.

Zaman, Muhammad Qasim. *Modern Islamic Thought in a Radical Age: Religious Authority and Internal Criticism*. New York: Cambridge University Press, 2012.

Zaydān, Jirjī. *Ṭabaqāt al-umam aw as-salāʾil al-bashariyya*. Cairo: Maṭbaʿat al-Hilāl, 1912.

Zerubavel, Eviatar. *Ancestors and Relatives: Genealogy, Identity and Community*. New York: Oxford University Press, 2012.

Zerubavel, Yael. "Memory, the Rebirth of the Native, and the 'Hebrew Bedouin' Identity." *Social Research* 75, no. 1 (Spring 2008): 315–52.

Zürcher, Eric-Jan. "The Ottoman Conscription System, 1844–1914." *International Review of Social History* 43 (1998): 437–49.

Index

Aaron, 204
Abbas, Mahmoud, 247
Abbasids, 156, 231
ʿAbboud, Paul, 236–37, 238
ʿAbduh, Muhammad, 65, 161, 164; *al-Islām wa-n-naṣrāniyya maʿ al-ʿilm wa-l-madaniyya*, 74; *al-ʿUrwa al-wuthqā*, 83n155
Abdul Hamid (Abdülhamid) II, Sultan, 24–25, 39
Abraham, 144–45, 168
Abu al-Faraj al-Iṣfahānī (al-Iṣbahānī): *Kitāb al-aghānī*, 144
Abu al-Fidaʾ, 71n113, 72
Acre, 16, 17
al-Afghani, Jamal ad-Din, 83n155
agriculture: and Ben-Zvi, 124; and First vs. Second Aliyah, 34; and *ha-Ḥerut*, 97; and M. R. al-Khalidi, 82, 84; and Malul, 223, 230; and Rida, 163, 167; and Zaydan, 143; Zionist colonies for, 33, 76
Agudat ha-Magen (Shield Society), 194
ha-Aḥdut, 96, 120–22; attitude toward Arabs, 126–28; and Ben-Zvi, 123; religion in, 101
al-Ahrām, 194
Akçura, Yusuf, 25
Akiba, Rabbi, 79n141, 219–20
Aleppo, 202
Alexander the Great, 80–81, 218–19
Alexandria, 26, 131; ancient Israelite synagogue in, 199
Alexandria, ancient, 81, 208–10
Ali Ekrem Bey, 24
Alliance Israélite Universelle (AIU) school, 44
Allies, 242–43, 244
Amalekites, 144
American Jewish press, 118
American School of Archaeology, 47
Andalusia, 156, 165
Anderson, Benedict, 5n6
Anglo-American Committee of Inquiry, 244
Antioch, 202
antisemitism: blame for, 71; causes of, 133; and Christian Arabic press, 120; Christian element of European economic, 88n167; and Christianity, 228; and Drews, 116; and economy, 71; and Europeans, 228; and Jewish wealth, 156–57, 230; and M. R. al-Khalidi, 43, 70, 82–85, 92; and N. Malul, 222–23, 228–29, 230; and Mendes, 173; and Rida, 153–54, 156, 157; as self-inflicted, 84; and translation, 233; and E. Zaydan, 180, 182; J. Zaydan's defense of Jews against, 182. *See also* Jews
anti-Zionism: and Arabic press, 9, 106, 127–28, 129, 187, 190, 192, 231–32; and Arabs, 222, 231, 234; of Christian Arabic press, 122; economic view of, 232–34; and *ha-Ḥerut*, 106; and Mendelssohn, 59–60n74, 61. *See also* Zionism
apologetics: and N. Malul, 10, 222; and Moyal, 10, 199, 203–5, 209, 212, 220, 221
al-Aqsa Intifada, 246
al-Aqsa Library, 136
al-Aqsa Mosque, 43, 52, 53, 166, 168–69, 239–40
Arab conquest, 40
Arab Episcopalians, 33

Arab Hebrews, 111–12. *See also* Arab Jews
Arabic: and Islamic religious terminology, 211; knowledge of among Jews, 36–38, 50, 103, 187–90, 200; literacy in, 49, 193; and N. Malul, 233; as mark of identity vs. Hebrew, 236; and military conscription, 107, 108; and Sephardic Zionists, 9; and Sephardim vs. Ashkenazim, 127; Zionist literacy in, 187–90; and Zionists, 233
Arabic journals, 9, 12, 26–28. See also *al-Hilāl* (The Crescent); *al-Manār* (The Beacon); *al-Muqtaṭaf* (The Digest)
Arabic press, 187, 232; as anti-Zionist, 9, 106, 127–28, 129, 187, 190, 192, 231–32; Christian-edited, 6n11; letters to editors by Zionists in, 194; and N. Malul, 231–32; and Nassar, 231, 232; and Ottoman ethnic and religious communities, 196; Zionist attempts to influence, 9, 10, 11, 186–87, 191–95
Arabic readers/speakers, 12, 188; and Arabic journals, 135; Christian, 35, 210; Greek Orthodox, 33; Jewish, 36–38, 50, 103, 187–90, 200; Karaites as, 112, 113; and M. R. al-Khalidi, 7, 49–50; and Moyal, 77, 200, 210; Muslim, 32, 35, 210–15; *mustaʿribūn*, 36; Sephardic, 9, 188–89, 192; Zionist attempts to influence, 10, 197
Arab Jews, 36–38. *See also* Arab Hebrews
Arab Office, 244–45
Arab Revolt, 240
Arabs, 75, 92; benefit of Jewish immigration for, 128; and Ben-Zvi, 123–25; borders of identity of, 111–12; conquest by, 15, 40, 124; and fear of Jews, 184; and fellahin, 124–25; in *ha-Ḥerut*, 102, 103; and historically good relations with Jews, 149–50; inexpensive labor of, 76; and intellectual interchange with Jews, 46; Ishmael as ancestor of, 145; Jews as living among, 144; Jews as proof of potential of, 146–49; Jews in land of before Islam, 149, 150; and Jews of Yathrib, 231; Jews tolerated by, 158; Jews under rule of, 149–50, 158; and M. R. al-Khalidi, 40; and Kremer, 105; and language and translation, 185, 186; loyalty of, 35; and N. Malul, 222; and Mandate for Palestine, 244; medieval, 143; and Middle Eastern-born Jews, 114; and nationalism, 3; nationalist nonsectarian notion of identity of, 239; Palestinian identity among, 3, 7, 18, 35, 75, 235–37; population of, 32; and race, 13, 140, 141; as racially linked with Jews, 6, 133, 143–50, 240; and Radler-Feldmann, 93; Sephardic vs. Ashkenazic attitudes toward, 126–30; tolerance as quality of, 158, 159; views of Zionism of (*see under* Zionism); as workers, 122; in *ha-Ẓevi/ha-Or*, 102–3. *See also* Christian Arabs; Muslim Arabs; Palestinians (Palestinian Arabs)
Arafat, Yasser, 50n40
Argentina, 90, 91–92, 143
al-Arish, 90
Armenia, 242
Armenian Orthodox, 33
Armenians, 20
Arslan, Muhammad, 109n62
Aryans, 141
Ashkenazim, 34, 36, 37, 103; and Arabic literacy, 188; attitude toward Arabs, 126–30; and Christian intolerance, 120; and creation of Arabic newspaper, 197–98; First Aliyah, 95, 96, 100; and *ha-Ḥerut*, 97–98, 105; and literacy in Arabic, 193; Second Aliyah, 96; and Sephardim, 100, 105, 195; and Zionists' self-conceptions, 94. *See also* Jews
asqāmah, 60–64, 66, 69, 70, 91
Assembly of Notables, 62
assimilationism, 195–96, 197
Auerbach, Elias, 139n26
Austria, 29, 183
Austro-Hungarian Empire, 242–43
Ayalon, Ami, 135

Babylonia, 82
Babylonian exile, 164, 225

Balfour Declaration, 45, 66, 179, 236, 241, 244
Balkan wars, 120n101
Banton, Michael, 5n7
Bar Giora, 123
Bar Kokhba, 53, 70, 219, 220
Barzilay, Isaac, 56n63
Bashkin, Orit, 37n80
Batnitzky, Leora, 56
bedel-i askeri, 23
Bedouin, 31, 123, 124
Beer Sheba, 88
Beirut, 17, 26–29, 43, 202
Beisan Valley, 88
Belgium, 29, 183
Ben-Attar, Hayyim, 129n129
Ben-Bassat, Yuval, 19n13
Benedict XV, 237n8
Ben-Gurion, David, 96, 123; and Ben-Zvi, 123; "Clarifying Our Political Situation," 120–22; *Erets yisroel in fargangenheit un gegenvart*, 123, 124, 126
Ben-Yehuda, Eliezer (Perelman), 24, 118; anniversary celebration of, 129; and Arabic literacy, 188; Arabs in newspapers of, 102, 103; attitude toward Arabs, 127; background of, 1; and borders of identity, 112; and Christians as non-Arabs, 107–8; and de Boton, 100; and distinctions between groups, 111; and Europe, 29; and *haskamah*, 67–68; and Hebrew, 99, 100; and M. R. al-Khalidi, 1, 10, 15, 19, 39; library of, 46n26; and Mendelssohn, 61n83; and Muslims as enemies of Christians, 109; and Nahḍa, 29; and nationalism, 35n74; and religion in newspapers, 99, 100; as representative of Jewish community, 4; and *ha-Ẓevi*, 96
Ben-Yehuda, Hemda, 108n53
Ben-Yehuda, Itamar Ben-Avi, 108n53
Ben-Zvi, Rachel Yanaʾit, 96, 123
Ben-Zvi, Yitzhak, 96, 123–26, 237; *Erets yisroel in fargangenheit un gegenvart*, 123, 124, 126; *ha-Tenuʿah ha-ʿarvit* (The Arab Movement), 123
Berakhot, 203
Bernasconi, Robert, 27
Bezalel, Yitzhak, 97, 98
Bibas, Rahamim, 112, 113
Bible, Christian: and M. R. al-Khalidi, 235; and Moyal, 206–8, 209; and Septuagint, 212
Bible, Christian, books of: Gospel of John, 206; New Testament (*al-injīl*), 71, 73, 75, 88n167, 205, 206–8, 209, 235; Romans, 206n79
Bible, Hebrew, 18; and Amalekites, 144; and archaeology, 169–72; basis of Zionism in, 76; European criticism of, 164; European research on, 172; European scholarship on, 161, 162; in *al-Hilāl*, 169, 170, 171; historicity of, 169–72; and M. R. al-Khalidi, 43, 46, 51–52, 71, 75, 76n129, 77–80, 84; Makaryus on, 173; and N. Malul, 226; and Moyal, 201, 202, 212; in *al-Muqtaṭaf*, 169–72; Muslims on corruption of, 212; origins and historicity of, 133; and prophecy, 77–80; prophets of, 70; and racial link between Arabs and Jews, 144–45; and Rida, 152; Septuagint, 210, 211–12; and E. Zaydan, 132, 180; and Zionism, 132. *See also* Torah
Bible, Hebrew, books of: Daniel, 71; Deuteronomy 6:4, 116; Ezekiel, 51, 52; Isaiah, 76, 84, 217; Lamentations, 51; Psalms, 51
Bilu movement, 35n74
Bliss, Daniel, 30n58
B'nai Brith, 46n26
Brenner, Yosef Hayim, 93n1
bribery, 87
British Palestine Society, 179
Brugman, J., 42n10
Brunswick Conference (1844), 62n88
Bulgaria, 242, 243
Bulgarians, 21
Byzantines, 40, 124

Cairo, 26–29, 112, 131
Capitulations, 21–22, 31; as term, 22n23

Carmilly-Weinberger, Moshe, 68n108
Casanova, José, *Public Religions in the Modern World*, 57
Catholics, 21, 33, 158, 159, 166. *See also* Christians
Christendom vs. Islamic countries, 120, 133, 150, 157, 159, 165
Christian Arabic press, 6n11, 106, 120, 122
Christian Arabic-speakers, 35, 210
Christian Arabs, 6n11, 8, 9; and Balfour Declaration vs. Mandate for Palestine, 241; in *ha-Ḥerut*, 106–7, 108; and Jewish ritual murder, 201, 202; and M. R. al-Khalidi, 50; and Moyal, 205; as not authentic Arabs, 107–8; tolerance as quality of, 158; and toleration vs. persecution of Jews, 159; in *ha-Ẓevi*, 108–9. *See also* Greek Catholics
Christian-edited newspapers, 196
Christianity: and antisemitism, 88n167, 228; divisions within, 227–28; and essential sameness of all religions, 222, 224; Hellenistic Jewish roots of, 209–10; and inauthentic form of Judaism, 210; and Islam, 50, 73–75, 151; Islam's close relationship to, 227; Jewish conversion to, 53; and Jewish philosophy, 150; Jewish sermons in support of, 118; Jews as unequal under, 53; and Judaism, 50, 75, 205–10, 215–16, 221; Judaism's close relationship to, 206, 226, 227; and Judaism vs. Islam, 235–36; and M. R. al-Khalidi, 50; and N. Malul, 222, 224, 226, 227; and Moyal, 199, 205–10, 215–16; and religion vs. nationality, 138–39; and Zionists, 8. *See also* Greek Orthodox faith; Jesus
Christian missionaries, 18, 29–30, 99–100, 116–18, 171n126
Christian Muslims, 112
Christians, 8, 21, 166, 235; and British Mandate period, 239; as category of interpretation, 3; compared to Muslims, 136–37; as enemies of Muslims, 109–11; European protection of, 22; and fellahin, 124; in *ha-Ḥerut*, 100; and Jewish ritual murder, 201; Jews as evicting, 167, 169; Jews as excluding from workforce, 167; Jews as persecuted by, 8, 119–20, 121, 150, 154, 156, 157, 158, 159, 165, 230–31; and M. R. al-Khalidi, 43; as less tolerant of Jews, 165, 236; and messiah, 163; and monotheism, 116n90, 222, 224, 225, 226, 227; and Moyal, 221; and Muslims, 94; Muslims as persecuted by, 230–31; Muslims in shared religious-communal existence with, 236; as non-Arabs, 107–8; and Ottoman military draft, 22–23, 98, 107–8; population of, 32, 33; preaching to Jews by, 116–18; pro- vs. anti-Jewish views of, 136–37; and racial hatred for Jews, 106–7, 114; and redemption in Islam, 151–53; and religious hatred for Jews, 83–84, 106–7, 114–20, 121; and Septuagint, 212; socioeconomic status of, 115; and Tanzimat, 20; and toleration, 8, 119–20, 121, 157, 158, 159, 165; in *ha-Ẓevi* (*ha-Or*; *Hashkafah*), 99–100; Zionist category of, 95; Zionist views of, 94
Christians, Palestinian: characteristics shared with Jews, 98; in *ha-Ḥerut*, 98–99; and Muslim-Christian Association, 235–37
Christian Syrians, 26
Church Fathers, 209
Churchill, Winston, 241–42n23
circumcision, 74
Clarke, Adam, 164
Cohen, Julia Phillips, 119n99
Cohen, Mark R., 53n54, 150–51n67
Cohen, Mendel, 199
commerce, 81–82, 83n154, 84, 87, 146, 230
Committee of Union and Progress (CUP), 25
Conference of Rabbis, Frankfurt-am-Main, 62
Copts, 21, 33
Corneilhan, Georges, *Juifs et opportunistes*, 222, 228
Crusaders, 124, 231

Cyrus, 217, 218–19
Czecho-Slovak state, 243

Damascus, 16n5, 26, 53
Damascus Affair, 201, 202
Darwin, Charles: *The Descent of Man*, 27; *On the Origin of Species*, 27
Darwinism, 26–28, 139
David, 49, 168, 172
David ha-Nagid (David ben Abraham Maimun), 200, 207, 208
de Boton, David, 100
Deganiah, 33
Derenbourg, Hartwig, 44
Dhu Nuwas, 144
Disraeli, Benjamin, 148
Dome of the Rock, 41, 52–53
Drews, Arthur, 115–16
Dreyfus Affair, 92, 147
Drumont, Edouard, *La France Juive*, 228
Druze, 21, 32, 176n141

East Africa, 90, 91
East Central Africa, 143
Eastern Orthodox church, 33
Efron, John, 31, 139n26
Egypt, 88; British conquest and occupation of, 28; Fatimid state in, 156; and al-Ḥizb al-waṭanī (National Party), 220; and intellectual and cultural orbit of, 26; Israelite emigration to from Judea, 208–9; Jewish migration from Palestine to, 131–32, 138, 179; Jews in, 156, 177; and race, 28, 29; and Sudan, 28
Egypt, ancient, 71, 82, 171
Egyptian press. See *al-Hilāl* (The Crescent); *al-Manār* (The Beacon); *al-Muʾayyad*; *al-Muqaṭṭam*; *al-Muqtaṭaf* (The Digest)
Eisenmenger, Johann Andreas, *Entdecktes Judenthum*, 228
Elijah, 216
Elmaleh, Avraham, 97, 192
Ereẓ Yisraʾel, as term, 18
Essenes, 149
Europe: as imagined Other, 150; immigration of Spanish Jews to, 53; and Jerusalem, 29–31; Jewish acculturation in, 58; Jewish citizenship in, 31, 55–56; Jews in, 125, 146–47, 179; oppression of Jews in, 150, 151, 153, 156–57, 158, 159; religious intolerance in, 120–21; and representation of non-Muslims in Ottoman lands, 21. *See also* Capitulations
European Christian missionary activity, 18
European Christians: as residents of Palestine, 99–100
European consuls, 29
Europeans: and antisemitism, 228; anti-talmudic claims of, 11; biblical criticism of, 164; and Capitulations, 22; and claim of Eastern inferiority, 146, 147; and context of Jerusalem, 7; and Jewish ritual murder, 201; and Jews in Holy Land, 24; and M. R. al-Khalidi, 8, 43; and Moyal, 207; and Nahḍa, 145–46; protection of Christians by, 22; and race, 30, 139, 140, 146; and research on Bible, 172
Eusebius, 171
Exodus, biblical, 169–70
Ezra the Scribe, 78–80, 164, 217

Faisal Hussein, 240
Faris, Habib, *Ṣurākh al-barīʾ fī būq al-ḥuriyya*, 202, 203, 208
Fatimid state, 156
Federation of American Zionists, 48
Feldman, Yehoshua, 191n28
fellahin, 123, 124–26
Filasṭīn (Palestine), as term, 50. *See also* Palestine
finance, 82, 86, 87, 133, 146, 155, 157. *See also* money
First Aliyah, 34, 76, 95, 96, 100
Fleisher, Rabbi, 118
Four Holy Cities, 33
France, 21, 29, 147, 158, 166, 173, 182
Frankfurter, Felix, 240

Galilee, 33
Gamaliel, Rabban, 219
Gaspo, Shimon, 246n34
Gaza Strip, 16, 246
Gelvin, James, 22n26
gender equality, 245n33
Geonim, 66
Germany, 173, 183
Gershoni, Israel, 220
Gezer, 170
Glass, Cyril, 213n101
Goldziher, Ignaz, 47, 47n31
Gorni, Yosef, 197n52
Gospel of Barnabas, 163
Gottheil, Richard James Horatio: and M. R. al-Khalidi, 11, 40–41, 42, 43, 46–47, 48, 51–52, 53, 62, 71, 76, 77, 86n162, 90, 91, 185; and Makaryus, 11; and Moyal, 185, 186, 190; and Nassar, 90, 91, 106, 185, 190, 231; *Zionism*, 48n33; "Zionism" (*Jewish Encyclopedia*), 11, 40–41, 42, 43, 46–47, 48, 51–52, 53, 62, 71, 76, 77, 86n162, 90, 91, 106, 185, 186, 190, 231
Graetz, Heinrich, 216n119
Great Britain, 29, 143; conquest of Palestine by, 179; and Egypt, 26; and grand mufti of Palestine (muftī filasṭīn al-akbar), 239; and al-Ḥizb al-waṭanī (National Party), 220; Jews in, 183; and Mandate for Palestine, 12n16, 16, 45, 66, 236, 237–45; and millet system, 238–39; and national home for Jews, 238, 241; and representation of non-Muslims in Ottoman lands, 21; The White Paper (May 17, 1939), 244
Greater Syria, 26
Great Revolt of 1936–1939, 240
Great War, 2, 6, 7, 8, 16, 32, 35, 123, 178, 240; and Jews, 132, 179–80, 183; new political discourse after, 10; and Paris Peace Conference, 242
Greece, 29, 242
Greek Catholics, 33
Greek Orthodox faith, 20, 21, 33
Greeks, ancient, 209
Greek-speakers, 36
Griffith, Sidney H., *The Bible in Arabic*, 76n129
Groyser Kundes, Der (The Big Stick), 181, 182–83

Haddad, Rashid, 232
hahambaşi, 19, 36
Haim, Sylvia, 154n75, 161n92
al-Hajj, Najib, *Fī az-zawāyā khabāyā aw kashf asrār al-yahūd*, 222–23
Halevi, Judah, 53
Halevi, Solomon, 53
Hallaq, Wael, 63–64
Hama, 202
Hamas (Islamic Resistance Movement), 246, 247
Hammurabi's Code, 164
Ḥanafī *madhhab*, 32
Hanina, Rabbi, 206–7
Hanioğlu, M. Şükrü, 21, 23n30
al-Ḥaqīqa, 223
al-Ḥaram ash-Sharīf. *See* Temple Mount
al-Harizi, Judah ben Solomon, 200n56
Hasidic Jews, 1
haskamah/haskamot, 61, 66–68
Hayes, Carlton, 5n7
Hebrew, 55, 189, 191; Arabic as mark of identity vs., 236; and Ben-Yehuda, 99, 100, 108; learning of, 188; and N. Malul, 233
Hebrew press, 8–9, 11. See also *ha-Aḥdut*; *ha-Ḥerut*; *ha-Ẓevi* (*ha-Or*; *Hashkafah*)
Hebron, 33, 97
Herodotus, 171
ha-Ḥerut, 96, 185; anti-Christian polemics of, 117; and anti-Zionist Arabic press, 190; and Arabic press, 192; Arabs in, 102, 103, 126–30; and Ben-Gurion, 122; Christian Arabs in, 106–7, 108; and Christian religious intolerance, 119–20, 121; Christians in, 100; and Christians' religious hatred for Jews, 114–20, 121; "A Christian Stabs a Hebrew," 103; and creation of Arabic newspaper, 195; "The Enemies of Judah," 114; "The Great

Danger," 106–7; "Heresy or Incitement?," 116–18; "Jesus of Nazareth Never Existed," 115–16; and Jews in Christian countries vs. Muslim world, 119–20, 121; and Kremer, 104, 105; "The Libel of our Enemies," 129; and literacy in Arabic, 193; and N. Malul, 233; mission statement of, 97–98; Moyal's translations of Arabic press in, 191; Muslims in, 100; and Nassar, 232; as offended by criticism of Zionism, 128–30; religion in, 98–99, 100, 101–2, 103; and Sephardic Zionists, 97–98; and Zakka's *an-Nafīr*, 193

Herzl, Theodor, 35n74, 42n12, 50, 54, 62, 66, 84n157, 172–73; and Hirsch, 91; and Yusuf Diyaʾ al-Khalidi, 89; and Kremer, 104; and Makaryus, 175; and Nassar, 90; and Pius X, 237n8

Hibbat Zion, 35n74, 50n42, 197n52

al-Hilāl (The Crescent), 133, 134–35, 158, 184; agent in Jerusalem, 135–36; Bible in, 169, 170, 171; cartoon from, 181, 182–83; Christian vs. Muslim editors, contributors, and audience of, 136n19; defense of Judaism against defamation in, 159, 160–61; "The House of Rothschild," 154–57; "The Jews and the War," 131–32, 138–39, 179–84; "The Jews in the Lands of the Arabs," 143; and N. Malul, 11; and Moyal, 11; and pro- vs. anti-Jewish views, 136–37; and race, 9, 28; on Rothschild family, 174–75; and J. Zaydan, 141, 203

Hillel, 204–5, 214–15

al-Hindi, Rahmat Allah, 164

Hirsch, Maurice de, baron, 91–92

Histadrut ha-poʿalim ha-ẓeʿirim be-ereẓ yisraʾel (Organization of Young Workers in the Land of Israel), 127

Hitler, Adolf, 247

Ḥizb al-umma (People's Party), 220

al-Ḥizb al-waṭanī (National Party), 219, 220

Holland, 29

Holocaust, 246

Holy Land. *See* Palestine

Hourani, Albert Habib, 83n155, 153n74

Hourani, George, 65

Hugo, Victor, 51

Hungary, 243

al-Husseini, Hajj Amin, 247

Husseinis (family), 41

Ibn Gabirol, 53

Ibn Hazm, 79

Ibn Khaldun, 144

Ibn Yahya, Gedalia, *Shalshelet ha-kabbalah*, 200

ijmāʿ (consensus), 63–67, 69, 74, 213–14

Iraq, 156

Isaac, 145, 168

Ishmael, 145, 168

Ishmael, Rabbi, 214

Ishmaelites, 100, 101, 104, 105

Islam: and anti-Jewish polemic, 162; and Arabic, 211; as associated with Christianity vs. Judaism, 235–36; and Christianity, 50, 73–75, 120, 133, 150, 151, 157, 159, 165; Christianity's close relationship to, 227; divisions within, 227–28; as enemy of Jews, 236; and essential sameness of all religions, 222, 224; five pillars of, 214, 227; and Hamas, 246; Jewish experience of justice and equality under, 53; and Jewish financial houses, 156; and Jewish wealth, 82; Jews and middle ages of, 63n91, 64, 66–67; Jews and notion of *ijmāʿ* in, 64, 66–67; Jews in Arab lands before, 143–44, 149, 150; Jews tolerated in, 8, 53, 115, 118–20, 121, 149–50, 151–54, 156, 157, 158, 159, 165; Jews under rule of, 53, 133, 149–50, 156; and Judaism, 50, 68, 71–76, 210–16, 221, 227; and M. R. al-Khalidi, 8, 43–44, 45, 63, 64, 68, 69, 92; and Last Day, 162; and N. Malul, 222, 224–25, 226–27; medieval, 64, 66–67, 72, 74; and Moyal, 199, 210–16; and polemic, 164; polemic against, 118; redemption in, 151–53; and religion vs. nationality, 138–39;

Islam *(continued)*
and Salafis, 65; and Zionists, 8. *See also* Muslim Arabs; Muslims
Islamic-Jewish polemic, 43, 70
Islamic law, 63–69
Israel, 16, 245–47; proclamation of independence, 245n33; religious nationalist settler movement in, 246; ultra-Orthodox community of, 246
Israel, Leon (Lola), 182–83
Israeli-Palestinian conflict, 2, 3, 6, 31, 37, 245–46
Israelites, 143–44; Jews vs., 51; judges of, 201; and M. R. al-Khalidi, 51, 52, 56, 69, 76, 78, 79, 80, 81; kingdoms of, 51; and link to Jerusalem, 168; Makaryus on, 173; and Moyal, 77, 78, 79, 80–82, 200, 201, 204–10, 212, 215–19; national renaissance of, 78, 79; in Palestine, 172; Petrie on, 169–70; as term for ethical individuals, 205–6; as term in Arabic journals, 137; and E. Zaydan, 132; and J. Zaydan, 142–43. *See also* Jews; Judaism
Istanbul, 21, 112, 123; central authority in, 17; Karaites in, 112; and M. R. al-Khalidi, 1, 41, 44, 67, 71, 87; and millet system, 19; Ottoman Parliament in, 1; shaykh al-islām in, 32, 44; Young Turk Revolution in, 96
Italy, 29, 82, 86, 87, 158, 183

Jacobson, Abigail, 97n8, 120n101, 126–27, 128, 130
Jaffa, 88, 131, 188; immigrants in, 33; Jewish expulsions from, 131; and Malul, 233; and Moyal, 77, 186, 189, 194; reporting on, 99, 100, 102, 103, 108, 109; Zionists' Palestine Office in, 11
Jankowski, James, 220
Jephtah, 201
Jericho, 170–71
Jerusalem, 33, 49, 78, 112, 166–67, 170, 202; as administrative unit, 16–17; Bāb as-Silsila neighborhood of, 41; and Beirut and Cairo, 26–29; contexts of, 7, 15–38; and Damascus, 26; destruction of by Titus, 225, 229; and Europe, 29–31; and *ha-Ḥerut*, 97; and intercommunal difference, 23–25; and Islamic prayer, 236n2; Jewish connection to as limited, 171–72; Jewish immigration to, 33; Jews' historical link to, 50; and M. R. al-Khalidi, 43; and Makaryus, 174; and Mecca, 168; and Moyal, 217; and mufti for Hanafi rite, 239; as *mutasarriflik*, 17; and Nahḍa, 26; and Ottoman Empire, 15–17, 18–19; and Palestine and Holy Land, 15–18; sanjak of, 17
Jesus, 152; and Christian missionaries, 117; and economic antisemitism, 88n167; historic existence of as questioned, 115–16; and Israelite as term for ethical individual, 206; Jewish sermons in support of, 118; Jews as killers of, 83–84; and Mendelssohn, 57; and Moyal, 206–8; in Qurʾan, 73–74. *See also* Christianity
Jeunes Turcs, 87n163
Jewish Colonization Association (JCA), 176n141, 231–32
Jewish Diaspora, 53, 155, 174, 175, 225, 226, 229, 230
Jewish Encyclopedia, 11, 185; article on Mendelssohn, 59–60n74; "Ascama," 67; "Costume," 83n152; "Islam," 47, 62n89; and M. R. al-Khalidi, 46–47, 48, 50, 51; and Nassar, 90; "Zionism," 11, 40–42, 43, 46–47, 48, 51–52, 53, 62, 71, 76, 77, 86n162, 90, 91, 106, 185, 186, 190, 231
Jewish history: books in Arabic about, 198; and M. R. al-Khalidi, 8, 40, 42, 43, 46, 48, 50, 51–54, 69, 70, 80–81, 92, 168; Makaryus on, 173–74; and N. Malul, 225–26, 228; and Moyal, 199, 208–10, 217–21; in Palestine, 226; and toleration vs. persecution of Jews, 159; translated into Arabic, 69; and wealth, 155; and E. Zaydan, 132, 179
Jewish law, 201. See also *haskamah/ haskamot*

Jewish Legion, 123
Jewish medieval literature, 60
Jewish nationalism, 15; birth of modern, 3; and M. R. al-Khalidi, 8, 40, 61; and Yusuf Diyaʾal-Khalidi, 89; and Mendelssohn's theory, 54–56; and Moyal, 199; non-Palestinocentric, 89; rabinnic consensus about, 60–64, 66, 91; and Reform movement, 229. *See also* Zionism
Jewish nationality, 63, 64
Jewish National Library in Jerusalem, 46n26
Jewish Oral Law, 199, 203, 213–14, 216, 219
Jewish philosophy, 150
Jewish Reform movement, 59–60n74, 90–91
Jewish state, in antiquity, 168
Jewish territorialism, 89, 90, 91
Jews: antique national past of, 40, 199; Arab fear of, 184; in Arabian Peninsula, 156; in Arab lands before Islam, 149, 150; Arab-like, 114; in Arab medieval culture, 143; Arab potential proved by, 146–49; and Arab rule, 149–50, 158; Arabs as racially linked to, 6, 133, 143–50, 240; Arab toleration of, 158; as Arab tribe, 145; assimilation by western, 86–87; and biblical Israelites, 51; destitution of, 151, 162; Eastern European, 91; Eastern vs. western European, 86–89; and economy, 71; emancipation of, 58–59; envy of, 230, 231; and fellahin, 124–26; and fertility, 80, 85, 162; and First vs. Second Aliyah, 34; gentiles as exploited by, 84; and Greeks, 209; and happiness in Zion, 75, 80; homelessness of, 173–75, 182; and Karaites, 113; and Yusuf Diyaʾal-Khalidi, 89; *Landfresser* (landgrabber) myth of, 88n166; land purchases by, 24, 165, 167; laws on occupations of, 81–82; and loyalty to states, 58, 59, 228–29; and manufacture, 82, 146, 223, 230; and messiah, 59, 163; Middle Eastern-born, 10, 114, 188–89, 200; as monotheists, 119, 121, 222, 224, 225, 226, 227; as *mustaʿribūn*, 36; as nation, 66, 89, 91, 138–39; as nondiscriminatory against non-Jews, 204–5; and old vs. new yishuv, 33–34; and prophecy, 77–80; as race, 31, 138, 139–43; racial solidarity and religious bond of, 153, 154; as religion, 66, 89, 91, 138–39, 142, 155; and religious government, 165; return from Babylonian exile, 54; and ritual murder, 159–61, 201–3; in science and politics, 156; and sciences and arts, 146, 230; self-love of, 153–54, 156; and shame, 151, 162; and usury, 166; in Western countries, 183; workers for, 84; of Yathrib, 231; and Young Turk Revolution, 165; and J. Zaydan, 143–44. *See also* antisemitism; Arabic readers/speakers; Arab Jews; Ashkenazim; Christianity; Christians; Egypt; Islam; Israelites; Judaism; al-Khalidi, Muhammad Ruhi; Muslims; Ottoman Empire; Palestine; rabbis; Russia; Sephardim; Spain; Talmud; Torah; Zionism
jihād, 153, 214, 246
Johnson, Mark, 95
Jonah, 216
Jordan Valley, 88
Josephus, 171, 219
Joshua ben Perahiah, 207, 208
Judah ha-Nasi, 213
Judaism: and afterlife, 71–73, 75–76, 88–89, 162, 204, 205, 227, 235; in Arabian Peninsula, 144; in Arabic intellectual journals, 9; books in Arabic about, 198; and Christianity, 50, 75, 205–10, 215–16, 221, 226, 227, 235–36; and construction of Palestinian Arab national identity, 235; defense of against defamation, 159–61; and disentanglement from Jewish nationality, 55–56; and divine judgment, 71–73, 75–76; divisions within, 227–28; and essential sameness of all religions, 222, 224; Hellenized, 208–10; and human sacrifice, 201, 202, 223, 224; and

Judaism *(continued)*
Islam, 68, 71–76, 210–16, 221, 227; and Islam and Christianity, 50, 75, 235–36; and M. R. al-Khalidi, 8, 50, 54, 69, 162, 235; and Last Day, 162; and N. Malul, 222–33; and Moyal, 77–78, 79, 80–82, 198–221; as nondiscriminatory against non-Jews, 204–5; oral tradition in, 213; as outsider religion, 50; and polygyny, 214–15; rabbinic, 149; and reward and punishment, 72; as source of law and foundation of true religions, 160, 161
Judas, 88n167
Jund Filasṭīn, 15

Kabbalah, 216
Kahn, Zadoc, 50, 54
Kamil, Mustafa, 220
Karaites, 112–13, 225
al-Karmil, 90, 106, 129, 185, 190, 192, 196, 231, 232
Kaufman, Asher, 159n85
Keane, Augustus Henry, 28n49; *The World's Peoples*, 142, 143
Kennaway, John, 117
kevuẓot (collective settlements), 33
Kfar Saba, 88
al-Khalidi, Muhammad Ruhi, 1, 12, 24, 41, 45; and afterlife, 227, 235; and antisemitism, 43, 70, 82–85, 92, 153; and Arab journals, 136; audience of, 48–50; on Bāb as-Silsila Street, 53; and Ben-Yehuda, 1, 10, 15, 19; and Ben-Zvi, 123; and Bible, 43, 46, 51–52, 71, 75, 76n129, 77–80, 84, 161–62, 235; and École des Hautes Études of Sorbonne, 44; education of, 43–45, 64, 72, 92; and Europe, 29; and Gottheil, 11, 40–41, 42, 43, 46–47, 48, 51–52, 53, 62, 71, 76, 77, 86n162, 90, 91, 185; and Islam, 8, 43–44, 45, 63, 64, 68, 69, 92; in Istanbul, 44; and Jewish history, 8, 40, 42, 43, 46, 48, 50, 51–54, 69, 70, 80–81, 92, 168; and Jewish scholars, 47–48; and Jews, 12, 39, 162; and Jews' historical link to Palestine, 50–54; and Judaism, 8, 50, 54, 69, 162, 235; *al-Kīmiyāʾ ʿind al-ʿarab*, 41; and Mendelssohn's theory, 54–64, 66, 87, 91, 139; and Moyal, 11, 43, 77, 78, 79, 80–82, 186, 198; *al-Muqaddima fī al-masʾala ash-sharqiyya*, 42; and Nahḍa, 26, 29; as orientalist scholar, 44, 47, 72; as Ottoman consul general in Bordeaux, 62; and Ottoman Parliament, 4n4, 19, 41, 42n13, 92; in Paris, 44; and polemic, 43, 162; and pseudonym "al-Maqdisī," "the Jerusalemite," 136; and rabbis, 60–63; and religion, 8, 45, 80; and religious toleration, 153; as representative of Arab (or Muslim) communities, 4; "as-Sayūnīzm ay al-masʾala aṣ-ṣahyūniyya," 7–8, 42–43, 45–92; "Statistics from the Islamic World," 44, 47; and Talmud, 46, 52; *Tārīkh ʿilm al-adab ʿind al-ifranj wa-l-ʿarab wa-Fīktūr Hūgū*, 41–42; and Western education, 44; and E. Zaydan, 132; and Zionism, 7–8, 12, 42, 43, 45–92, 162, 166
Khalidi, Rashid, 35, 65n97, 159n85, 194n38, 239
Khalidi, Walid, 45, 46
al-Khalidi, Yasin, 43
al-Khalidi, Yusuf Diyaʾ, 50–51, 54, 89, 91
Khalidi Library, 45, 46, 65n97, 76, 136
Kohler, Kaufmann, 47, 47n31, 62n89
Kremer, Mendel, 100n25, 104–6, 118, 120; "The Enemies of Judah," 114

Ladino, 118, 189
Lakoff, George, 95
Land of Israel, as term, 15, 17, 29. *See also* Palestine
Lang, Yoseph, 104n37
Lassalle, Ferdinand, 183
Late Ottoman Palestine, as term, 16
Latin Catholics, 33
Laurent, Achille, 202
Lazarus-Yafeh, Hava, 212
League of Nations, 238; and Mandate for Palestine, 45, 241–45, 245n33
Lebanon, 32

Levy, Lisa Lital, 200n60
Lewis, Bernard, 19n14
Lewis, Edwin, 26–27
Likhovski, Assaf, 238–39
Lockman, Zachary, 35–36n76, 45n20
London Society for Promoting Christianity amongst the Jews, 29–30
Lott, Tommy, 27
Ludvipol, Abraham, 195–97
Luzzatti, Luigi, 183

Macalister, R. A. Stewart, 170
Maccabees, 218–19
MacDonald, Ramsay, 244
Maimonides, Moses, 66, 200, 204, 213n103
Makaryus, Shahin, 134, 135, 148; and *al-Muqtaṭaf*, 178; "The Origin and Lineage of the Jews," 139–40; Rida on, 177–78; and Suares, 146, 176–77; *Tārīkh al-isrā ʾīliyyīn* (History of the Israelites), 11, 139–40, 144–45, 173–78; and Zionism, 175–78, 179
Makdisi, Ussama, 22, 30n58
Malul, Moshe (Musa) Hayyim, 189–90
Malul, Nissim, 192, 194; on Arab culture as minor, 197–98; "The Arabic Press," 231; articles for Arabic press, 196; background of, 189–91; and Christianity, 222, 224, 226, 227; and creation of Arabic newspaper, 195, 197; and Islam, 222, 224–25, 226–27; and Jewish history, 225–26, 228; and Judaism, 222–33; *Kitāb asrār al-yahūd* (The Book of the Secrets of the Jews), 10, 11, 12, 221–32; and Ludvipol, 196; and religion, 10, 222, 224–28, 233–34; and Zionism, 222, 229, 231, 233
al-Manār (The Beacon), 133, 134–35, 157, 158, 159, 184; challenge to Judaism in, 161–62; as Islamic journal, 136n19; and pro- vs. anti-Jewish views, 136–37; and Qurʾan, 151, 154, 161, 162; race in, 9; and racial link between Jews and Arabs, 148–49; religious toleration in, 151–54; and Rida, 11. *See also* Rida, Muhammad Rashid
Mandate for Palestine, 12n16, 16, 45, 66, 236, 237–45
Mandel, Neville, 24n32, 90, 186n3, 193n37
al-Maqrizi, Ahmad ibn ʿAlī, 144
Margoliouth, David Samuel, *Cairo, Jerusalem, and Damascus*, 171–72
Maronites, 33
Marx, Karl, 183
Mary, 73, 74
Mashbek, Eftim Effendi, 136
Masie, Aaron Meir, 104
Masterman, E.W.G., 179
Mecca, 168
Mekteb-i Mülkiye (School of Civil Service), 44
Mendelssohn, Moses: *Jerusalem*, 56, 58; and Jewish religion vs. nationhood, 56–59; and M. R. al-Khalidi, 54–64, 66, 87, 91, 139; and Michaelis, 58–59
Mendes, Dr., 173
messiah, 52, 59, 69–70, 74, 163
Michaelis, Johann David, 58–59
Midrash Abravanel, 46n26
military service. *See* Ottoman Empire
millet system. *See* Ottoman Empire
mishnah, 199, 200, 203, 204, 207, 213
missionaries. *See* Christian missionaries
mizraḥim, 36
money, 166, 167; and *al-Hilāl*, 155–57, 175; and M. R. al-Khalidi, 76, 80–82, 84, 87–89; and Malul, 228, 230, 231; and Rida, 162, 163, 166. *See also* finance
Mongols, 15, 124
Moses, 78, 79n141, 152, 161, 163, 164, 239; authorship of, 170; and Jewish Oral Law, 203, 213–14; and Moyal, 199
moshavot (agricultural colonies), 33, 76
Moskovskie vedomosti, 110, 111
Mount Lebanon, 22
Mount of Olives, 170
Moyal, Esther al-Azhari, 189
Moyal, Shimon, 187, 191, 194–95; *at-Talmūd*, 10, 11, 12, 43, 77–78, 79, 80–82, 186, 198–221, 226; background of, 189;

Moyal, Shimon *(continued)*
and creation of Arabic newspaper, 195–97; and Jewish ritual murder, 201–3; and jihād, 214
al-Mu'ayyad, 223
muftis, 32
Muhammad, 65, 78, 152, 163, 164, 168, 227
Muhammad Ali, 18
mukhtār, 32
al-Muqaṭṭam, 190, 194
al-Muqtaṭaf (The Digest), 133, 134–35, 136n19, 184; Bible in, 169–72; "The Colonization of Palestine," 178; "The Country of Palestine," 179; and Darwinism, 26–28; defense of Judaism against defamation in, 159–60; "The Excavation of the Antiquities of Palestine," 170; "The Exodus and Number of the Children of Israel," 169–70; Felix Suares in, 146, 148; "The History of the Torah," 170; and Jewish return to Palestine, 173; "The Jews of France," 137, 147–48, 157–58; Jew vs. Israelite in, 137–38; and Lewis Affair, 27; and Makaryus, 11, 139, 178; "New York: Capital of the Nations," 138; "Philosophy among the Jews," 149; and Protestantism, 159; and pro- vs. anti-Jewish views, 136–37; race in, 9; and racial link between Jews and Arabs, 146–48; and Zionism, 178–79
Muslim Arabic-speakers, 32, 35, 210–15
Muslim Arabs, 8, 124; and Balfour Declaration vs. Mandate for Palestine, 241; in *ha-Ḥerut*, 106–7; as Jews, 94; and positive attitude toward Jews, 114, 115; tolerance of, 115, 158; in *ha-Ẓevi*, 108; Zionist views of, 94. *See also* Arabs; Islam; Muslims
Muslim-Christian Associations, 235–37
Muslim-Christian polemics, 73–74
Muslim-Jewish polemics, 72–73
Muslims, 8, 9, 235; and British Mandate period, 239; and Capitulations, 22; Christian persecution of, 230–31; and Christians, 94; as enemies of Christians, 109–11; and fellahin, 124–25; in *ha-Ḥerut*, 100; and *isnād* tradition for *ḥadīth* literature, 213; Jews as evicting, 167, 169; Jews as excluding from workforce, 167; Jews as racially linked to, 106, 107, 114; and M. R. al-Khalidi, 50; and millet system, 20; as monotheists, 119, 121, 222, 224, 225, 226, 227; and Moyal, 215–16, 221; and Ottoman military draft, 22–23, 107–8; population of, 32; pro- vs. anti-Jewish views of, 136–37; shared religious-communal existence with Christians, 236; Sunni, 1, 22, 25, 32, 63, 64, 213; and Tanzimat, 20; and taxes levied on non-Muslims, 230; tolerance of, 8; in *ha-Ẓevi* (*ha-Or*; *Hashkafah*), 100–101; Zionist category of, 95; Zionist views of, 94. *See also* Islam; Muslim Arabs
al-Mutallah, 176

Nabi Musa pilgrimage, 239
Nablus, 16, 17, 43
Nadolski, Glidewell, 21n20
an-Nafīr, 192–93
Nahḍa (Arab renaissance), 26, 29, 135, 145–46
Napoleon I, 62
naqīb/nuqabā al-ashrāf, 32
Nashashibis (family), 41
Nasrallah, Yusuf, *al-Kanz al-marṣūd fī qawā'id at-talmūd*, 202, 203, 208
Nassar, Najib, 196; as anti-Zionist, 190; *aṣ-Ṣahyūniyya*, 11, 52n47, 52n52, 90–91, 185, 186; and Great Danger, 106; and M. R. al-Khalidi, 50; and N. Malul, 231–32; "Zionism," 50
nationalism, 8n13; and 'Abboud, 238; and Arabs, 35; birth of modern Arab, 3; in British Mandate period, 237–38, 240; as category of interpretation, 3–7, 13; Hebrew, 197; and Israeli-Palestinian conflict, 245–46; and Moyal, 199, 217–21; and old vs. new yishuv, 34–35; and race, 6–7, 13, 237; and religion, 6–7,

13, 95. *See also* Palestinian Arab nationalism; Zionism
nationality: and British Mandate period, 239; and Paris system, 243; and religion, 138–39
National Party. *See* al-Ḥizb al-waṭanī (National Party)
Nazism, 246, 247
Nebuchadnezzar, 180
Nehemia, 78, 217
Nile Valley, 88
Nimr, Faris, 134
1948 war, 245
Nongbri, Brent, *Before Religion*, 5n6
Nordau, Max, *Zionism*, 59–60n74

ha-Or. See *ha-Ẓevi* (*ha-Or*; *Hashkafah*)
original sin, 74
Orthodox Church, 212
Orthodox Jews, 66
Ottoman Constitution, 25, 96
Ottoman Empire, 123; administrative units of, 16n6; and anti-Islamic polemic, 118; Arab Revolt against, 240; Ben-Gurion on, 121–22; and Capitulations, 22; censorship by, 118; and citizenship for Jews, 39; and *dhimmī*, 20; and *ecnebī*, 20; fall of, 12n16, 66, 238, 239; and *ha-Ḥerut*, 97; and al-Ḥizb al-waṭanī (National Party), 220; Islamic identity of, 122; Jerusalem under, 7, 15–17; Jewish immigration policy in, 23–24, 39–40; and Jewish land purchases in Palestine, 24n32, 165; and Jewish settlement of Palestine, 178; and Jews and military draft, 22–23, 31, 98, 107–8, 121, 122; and Jews and Tanzimat, 20; Jews as threat to, 165–66, 167; and M. R. al-Khalidi, 92; lands of former, 242; Law of Nationality of 1869, 20; and Middle Eastern Sephardim, 126; military service in, 22–23, 31, 98, 107–8, 121, 122; millet system in, 19–20, 22, 238–39; and Moyal, 207, 218, 219–20, 221; Palestine under, 15–17; and parliamentary system, 25; and poll tax, 23; press censorship by, 187; press freedoms in, 196; Red Slip policy of, 24, 85–86; and reforms of 1864, 16n6; religion in, 19–20; Sehayik on, 134n9; Spanish Jewish immigration to, 53; sultan of, 36, 165; and Tanzimat, 20–23, 24, 25; taxation in, 22, 23, 31; Turks in, 139; *ha-Ẓevi*'s criticism of, 118
Ottoman Parliament, 1, 4n4, 41, 42n13, 92, 96

Palestine, 18; ancient Jewish kingdoms in, 40, 51; Arab conquest of, 40; blended history of, 13; and Europe, 29; European Christians in, 99–100; and Herzl, 90; home for Jews in, 238, 241, 244; homeland for Jews other than, 182, 183; intellectual community and culture of, 135–36; Islamic conquest of, 124, 165; Israelites in, 172; Jerusalem in context of, 7; Jewish exploitation of population of, 76; Jewish historical link to, 50–54, 91, 92, 180, 226; Jewish settlement of, 173–75, 176, 178–79, 229; Jewish territorial projects outside of, 90; Jewish this-worldly possession of, 162; Jews' desire to return to, 51–53, 54, 58–59, 60, 69, 70, 87, 173–74, 229; Jews' desire to rule, 75, 162, 165–169, 173, 184, 223; and Yusuf Diyaʾal-Khalidi, 89; nationalisms in, 235; under Ottoman Empire, 15–17; and Ottoman Red Slip policy, 85–86; population of, 31–38; under Rome, 15; between Syria and Egypt, 26; as term, 18n11; and wealth of Jews, 87–89; and J. Zaydan, 143; Zionism as danger for, 90; Zionist colonies in, 87–88, 92. *See also* Mandate for Palestine
Palestine, Jewish immigration to, 187; after Spanish expulsion, 53–54; from Arabic-speaking lands, 188; as beneficial to Arabs, 128; and bribery, 193n37; from Egypt, 131–32, 138, 179; and M. R. al-Khalidi, 39–40, 41; mass nationalist, 39; and Nassar, 232; Ottoman policy on, 23–24, 39–40; from Russia, 193

Palestine Exploration Fund, 170
Palestine Liberation Organization, 62n89
Palestine National Council, 247; Declaration of Independence, 245n33
Palestine Office, 11
Palestine Order in Council, 238
Palestinian Arabic press. *See* Arabic press; *al-Karmil*; *an-Nafīr*
Palestinian Arab nationalism, 3, 7, 18, 35, 75, 235–37
Palestinian National Charter, 245n33, 247
Palestinian peasants, 125
Palestinians (Palestinian Arabs), 2, 148–49, 245–47; as Christians and Muslims distinguished from Jews, 236; and early opposition to Zionism, 39n2; and Hamas, 246; intellectuals among participating in broader Arab discourse, 135–36; and nationalism and national identity, 3, 7, 18, 35, 75, 235–37; origins of according to Ben-Zvi, 123–26; and parliamentary elections, 246; question about existence of, 1; as term, 35n76. *See also* Arabs; Christian Arabs; Christians; Israeli-Palestinian conflict; Muslim Arabs; Muslims
Pan-Islamism, 25
Pan-Ottomanism, 25
Pan-Turkism, 25
Paris Disputation of 1240, 208n86
Paris Peace Conference, 242
Paris Sanhedrin of 1807, 62
Paris system, 242–43
Paul the Apostle, 209
Penslar, Derek, 84n157, 88nn166, 167
People of the Book, 72, 224, 225, 226
Petah Tikva, 33
Petrie, W. M. Flinders, *Researches in Sinai*, 169–70
Pharisees, 88n167, 149
Philadelphia Conference of 1869, 62
Philo of Alexandria, 81, 209–10
Pinsker, Leon, *Autoemancipation*, 228n169
Pirkei avot ("Ethics of the Fathers"), 199, 200, 203–4, 205, 206, 207, 210, 212–13, 214–15
Pittsburgh Conference of 1885, 62
Pius X, 237n8
Plato, 209
Poʿalei Ẓiyon (Workers of Zion) Party, 96, 120, 123
ha-Poʿel ha-ẓaʿir, 117, 126–27
Poland, 243
polemic: antisemitic, 228; Arab, 202; against Islam, 118; and Islam, 164; Islam and anti-Jewish, 162; Islamic-Jewish, 43, 70; and M. R. al-Khalidi, 43, 48; and Moyal, 199, 202, 203, 206, 208, 209, 212, 220; Muslim-Christian, 73–74; Muslim-Jewish, 72–73
Powell, Eve Troutt, 28
Protestant missionaries, 171n126
Protestants, 33, 158, 159. *See also* Christians
Protocols of the Elders of Zion, 247
Prussia, 29
Ptolemy II Philadelphus, 212

qāḍī/quḍāh, 32
al-Qassam, ʿIzz ad-Din, 240
qawmiyya, 55n56
al-Quds, 16, 26, 50
Qurʾan, 18, 71, 133; afterlife and divine judgment in, 72–73; and Christianity, 73–74; and Jewish rule in Palestine, 167; and M. R. al-Khalidi, 235; and N. Malul, 224–25; and *al-Manār*, 151, 154, 161, 162; Muslim faithfulness to, 163; revelation in, 77, 78; and Rida, 161, 162, 163, 166, 168; and Salafis, 65

Rabbanites, 225
rabbis, 19, 66, 149; as forbidding Zionism, 60–64; and *hahambaşi*, 19, 36; and M. R. al-Khalidi, 60–63; and Mendelssohn, 60–63; and Moses, 79n141; and Moyal, 199; and Reform Jews, 62–63; and Talmud, 203
race, 235; and ʿAbboud, 236, 238; and Akçura, 25; and antisemitism, 85, 182; in Arabic intellectual journals, 9; and Arabic journals, 26–28; and Arabs, 13;

and Ben-Zvi, 123, 124–25, 237; as category of interpretation, 3–7, 10; and Christian hatred of Jews, 106–7, 114; as common to Jews and Muslims, 106, 107, 114; and Darwinism, 26–28, 139; as distinction and source of intercommunal commonality, 243; and Egypt, 28, 29; and Egypt's relationship to Sudan, 139; in European thought, 30, 139, 140, 146; and European Zionists, 30–31; in Hebrew Zionist press, 9; in *al-Hilāl*, 9, 28; and Israel, 246–47; Jews as, 31, 138, 139–43; as link between Jews and Arabs, 6, 133, 143–50, 240; and Makaryus, 140–41, 173; and N. Malul, 233; in *al-Manār*, 9; and Mandate for Palestine, 237–38, 239, 240, 241–45; in *al-Muqtaṭaf*, 9; and Nahḍa, 26; and nation, 31; and nationalism, 6–7, 13, 237; and Palestinians, 246–47; and Paris Peace Conference, 242; and post-Holocaust Jewish perspectives, 13; and postwar treaties, 242–43; Rida on, 153, 154; rights irrespective of, 241, 243, 244–45; and Russian antisemitism, 85; as source of difference and potential conflict, 243; and Syria, 29; as taboo subject, 13; and toleration vs. persecution of Jews, 159; as tool of inclusion or annexation, 237; Turkish, 25; and Turks in Ottoman Empire, 139; and Young Turk Revolution, 24–26; and J. Zaydan, 28, 141–43; and Zionism, 13, 94, 107, 139n26

Radler-Feldmann, Yehoshua, "Concerning Our Arab Question," 93, 94

Red Slip policy. *See* Ottoman Empire

Reform Jews, 62–63, 66, 229

religion, 235; and ʿAbboud, 236, 238; in *ha-Aḥdut*, 101; and assimilation by western Jews, 87; and Ben-Gurion, 121–22; and Ben-Zvi, 125–26; as category of interpretation, 3–7, 10; and Christian missionaries, 30; and Christians' hatred for Jews, 114–20, 121; essential sameness of all, 222, 224; and government, 165; in Hebrew Zionist press, 8–9; in *ha-Ḥerut*, 98–99, 100, 101–2, 103; and intercommunal commonality, 243; and Israeli-Palestinian conflict, 245–46; and Jewish-Arab racial link, 148; Jews as, 66, 89, 91, 138–39, 142, 155; and M. R. al-Khalidi, 8, 45, 80; and Kremer, 105–6; and N. Malul, 10, 222, 224–28, 233–34; and Mandate for Palestine, 237–40, 241–45; and millet system, 19–20, 238–39; and modernity, 5n6, 8n13; and morality, 224–25; and Moyal, 10, 199, 233; and nationalism, 6–7, 13; and nationality, 138–39; in Ottoman Empire, 19–20; and Ottoman military draft, 22–23; and Palestinians, 245–46; Rida on, 153, 154, 165; rights irrespective of, 241, 243, 244–45; and socialist nationalist ideologues, 95; as source of difference and potential conflict, 243; as taboo subject, 13; and Tanzimat, 20–23; and toleration vs. persecution of Jews, 159; in *ha-Ẓevi* (*ha-Or*; *Hashkafah*), 99–102, 103; and Zionism, 94

Religious Communities Organization Ordinance, 238

Rida, Muhammad Rashid, 134–35, 148–49, 157, 159, 161; and antisemitism, 153–54, 156, 157; and Makaryus, 11, 177–78; and Qurʾan, 163, 166, 168; on religious toleration, 151–54; *Shubuhāt an-naṣārā wa-ḥujaj al-islām*, 74; and Torah, 161, 162, 163–64, 166, 169; and Zionism, 162, 165–69, 178. See also *al-Manār* (The Beacon)

Rire, Le, 180

Rishon Le-Zion, 33

rishon le-ẓiyon, 36

Rohling, August, *Der Talmudjude*, 202

Romaniot, Ashkenazim, Italians, 36

Rome, ancient, 15

Rosh Pina, 33

Rothschild, Alphonse de, 180

Rothschild family, 87, 154–57, 174–75, 183

Rumania, 143
Ruppin, Arthur, 191n28, 192
Russia, 29, 91, 92; antisemitism in, 70, 82–85, 173; de Hirsch's negotiations of 1892 with, 91; Jewish immigration from, 193; Jews in, 82, 183; oppression of Jews in, 83, 143, 165; and representation of non-Muslims in Ottoman lands, 21
Russian Christians, 70
Russian Jews, 21, 193
Russian Revolution, 231
Russkoe znamia, 110
Ryad, Umar, 227n163

Sabbateans, 53, 70
Sadducees, 149
Safed, 33, 53, 97
Ṣahyūn (Zion), 49, 50
as-salaf aṣ-ṣāliḥ (worthy ancestors), 65
Salafis, 65
Samaria, 170
Samaritan Bible, 212
Samaritans, 124
as-Samawʾal, *Silencing the Jews*, 79
Samson, 170
Samuel bin Hofni, 149
Samuel the Prophet, 144
Sanhedrin, 213n103
Sarruf, Yaʿqub, 134
Ṣawt al-ʿuthmāniyya (The Voice of Ottomanism), 197, 218
Schwartz, Shuly Rubin, 42n12
Second Aliyah, 34, 95, 96, 101, 120, 123, 186
Second Aliyah Zionists, 125
sectarianism, 22
secularism, 8, 57; and Ben-Yehuda, 1; in *ha-Ḥerut*, 99; and Israel, 246; and Israeli-Palestinian conflict, 245–46; and M. R. al-Khalidi, 1, 44; and Tanzimat, 21
secularization theory, 13
sefaradi, 36
Sehayik, Shaʾul, 134n9
Selim II, 22n23
Semites, 6, 7, 140–41
Semitic nations, 148
Sephardim, 34, 36, 95, 96, 103, 121, 185; and Agudat ha-Magen, 194; and Arabic, 9, 188–89, 192; and *ascama*, 67; and Ashkenazim, 100, 195; attitude toward Arabs, 126–30; and creation of Arabic newspaper, 197–98; and *ha-Ḥerut*, 97–98; and Islamic religious tolerance, 118–20; and M. R. al-Khalidi, 62; and Zionists' self-conceptions, 94. *See also* Jews
sex, 245n33
shaʿb, 174, 176n146, 218
Shāfiʿī *madhhab* (jurisprudential school), 32
ash-Shahrastani, Abu al-Fath Muhammad ibn ʿAbd al-Karim, 71; *Kitāb al-milal wa-n-niḥal*, 72, 225, 226, 227
El Shakry, Omnia, 28
sharīʿa, 61n80
sharīʿa (Islamic religious) courts, 21
Sharon, Ariel, 246
shaykh al-islām, 32, 44
shemaʿ, 214
Shiites, 25, 32
ha-Shiloaḥ, 231, 233
Shimon bar Yoḥai, 216
ha-Shomer, 123
Simon the Maccabee, 170
Sinai Peninsula, 88
Sixtus V, 158
Smilansky, Moshe, 187–88
Smith, A. D., 8n13
Smolenskin, Peretz, 56n63
Social Darwinism, 139
socialism, 34, 95, 96, 127
Socialist Zionists, 120–26
Society for the Promotion of Christianity among the Jews (SPCJ), 117
Solomon, 49, 168, 172
South African apartheid, 247
Spain, 29; expulsion of Jews from, 53, 150; oppression of Jews in, 165; toleration of Jews in, 158
Spanish Inquisition, 118, 119, 230
State of Israel, 34, 96

Stillman, Norman A., 23n27
Suares, Felix, 146, 148, 176–77
Sudan, 28
Suez, 131
Sunna, 65
Sunni Muslims, 1, 25, 213; estimates of population of, 32; and M. R. al-Khalidi, 63, 64; and millet system, 22
Supreme Muslim Council (al-Majlis al-islāmī al-aʿlā), 239
Syria, 139, 144, 242; as context of Jerusalem, 7; and intellectual and cultural orbit of, 26; Islamic conquest of, 165; Jews in, 156; Ottoman *vilayet* of, 16, 17; and race, 29
Syrian Catholics, 33
Syrian Orthodox, 33
Syrian press, 194
Syrian Protestant College (SPC), 26–27, 171n126
Syrians, 124, 148–49

taʿaṣṣub, 84
at-Tabari, Muhammad ibn Jarir, 152
taḥrīf, 211–13
Talmud, 60, 64, 77, 79n141; and antisemitic polemic, 228; and Arab polemic, 202; Christian attacks on ethics of, 206; and Christianity, 205–10; and hope of return to Holy Land, 70; and human sacrifice, 201, 202, 223, 224; and Islam, 210–16; and M. R. al-Khalidi, 46, 52; and Moyal, 11, 208; as privileging Jews over non-Jews, 204; and ritual murder, 201–3; and J. Zaydan, 11, 203. *See also* Moyal, Shimon: *at-Talmūd*
Tamari, Salim, 37
Tanzimat (Reorganizations of 1839–1876), 20–23, 24, 25
at-tashabbuh, 55n57
Tauber, Eliezer, 217n124
Tavernier, Eugene, 147
Taylor, Charles, 57
Temple, 78, 217; destruction of, 179–80, 225; and M. R. al-Khalidi, 52; Second, 218; of Solomon, 166
Temple Mount, 52n52, 240, 246
Temple of Onias, 208, 210
Tiberias, 33, 97
Tishʿah be-Av, 240
Titus, 180, 225, 229
Torah, 60, 79n141; Babylonian terms in, 164; as corrupted, 164, 166; divinity and antiquity of, 77–80; and Ezra the Scribe, 78, 79; Jews as unfaithful to, 161, 163–64; and M. R. al-Khalidi, 71, 161–62, 235; and Last Day, 162; Makaryus on, 173; and N. Malul, 225; marginal notes in, 164; and Moyal, 206, 206n78, 209; and Muhammad, 164; and Rida, 161, 162, 163–64, 166, 169; and ritual murder, 160; and Septuagint, 212. *See also* Bible, Hebrew
Torquemada, Tomás de, 118
Tosefta, 204
translation, 185–86, 232; of antisemitic works, 228–29; and antisemitism, 233; of antitalmudic texts, 202; of anti-Zionist Arabic press, 191, 192; and attempt to influence Arabic press, 187; and books in Arabic about Judaism, 198; and M. R. al-Khalidi, 46, 48, 68–69; and Nassar, 11; and theories of Venuti, 68–69
Treaty of Sevres, 242, 243
Treaty of Trianon, 242–43
Tripoli, 43, 202
tritheism, 74
Triwaks, A.B.G., "Jesus of Nazareth Never Existed," 115–16
Türk, 25
Turkey, 120–21, 242, 243
Turkish nationalism, 25
Turks, 139

ʿUmar, 124
Umayyads, 156, 230, 231
umma/umam, 63, 174
United Nations General Assembly: Resolution 181, 245n33; Resolution 3379, 246–47
Urabi movement, 220

urban population, 33, 123, 125
Ūrshalīm, 50. *See also* Jerusalem

van den Berg, Emmanuel, 72
Vatican, 33
Venuti, Lawrence, 68–69

Waardenburg, Jacques, 74
Wadi Hawarith, 88
waqf (pl. *awqāf*), 239
Weitz, Eric, 242
Weizmann, Chaim, 240
West Bank, 16
Wolski, Kalixt de, *La Russie Juive*, 228
World Zionist Organization, 172–73

yahūd awlād al-ʿarab, 37
Yathrib (Madina), 144
Yehoshuʿa, Yaʿqub, 193
Yehuda ha-Nasi, 203
Yemen, 144
Yemenite Jews, 114
Yishuv, 34, 35, 96
Yom Kippur, 240
Young Turk Revolution, 23, 24–26, 96, 98, 101, 102, 122, 187; and Jews, 165; and press freedoms, 196; Sehayik on, 134n9
Yusuf, Saadiah bin (Saadiah Gaon), 149
Yuval, Israel, 4n5

Zakka, Iliya, 192–93
Zaydan, Emile, 139, 141; "The Jews and the War," 131–32, 179–84
Zaydan, Jurji (George), 11, 131, 134, 157, 174, 182; "The Jews in the Lands of the Arabs," 143–44; and N. Malul, 227n163; and Moyal, 203, 205, 210; *Ṭabaqāt al-umam aw as-salā ʾil al-bashariyya*, 28, 141–43
ha-Ẓevi (*ha-Or*; *Hashkafah*), 96, 129; "The Arabic Theater," 112–13; Arab-like Jew in, 114; Arabs in, 102–3; "The Arabs in Jaffa," 102; and Ben-Yehuda interview with al-Khalidi, 39; borders of identity in, 111–12; Christian Arabs in, 108–9; "A Christian Muslim Woman," 112; Christians as non-Arabs in, 107–8; Christians in, 99–100; criticism of Ottoman Empire by, 118; and Karaites, 112–13; "Killed," 100–101; and Kremer, 104n37, 105; Muslim Arabs in, 108; Muslims as enemies of Christians in, 109–11; Muslims in, 100–101; "Rabbi for the Jews and Christian Devotee," 118; religion in, 99–102, 103; and Yemenite Jews, 114
Zikhron Yaʿakov, 33
Zion, 49, 75, 80
Zionism: and ʿAbboud, 236–37; apologetics for (*see* apologetics); in Arabic journals, 9, 133; Arabic press opposition to, 9, 106, 127–28, 129, 187, 190, 192, 231–33, 234; and Arab identity and Palestinian nationalism, 75; and Bible, 76, 132; and Christian Arabs, 106, 115; as danger for Palestine, 90; English rabbinic decree against, 90; and Europe, 29; and Faisal Hussein, 240; and fellahin, 125; as form of racism, 247; as Great Danger, 185; and *ha-Ḥerut*, 97, 128–30; and Hirsch, 91; and *ijmāʿ* (consensus), 64; and Islamic tolerance, 115; and Italian Jews, 86; Jewish opponents of, 60–64, 90–91; and Jewish sovereignty, 128–29; and M. R. al-Khalidi, 7–8, 12, 42, 43, 45–92, 162, 166; and Yusuf Diyaʾal-Khalidi, 50–51, 54, 89; lack of Jewish consensus on, 66; language as contested in, 186; and Makaryus, 175–78, 179; and N. Malul, 222, 229, 231; and Mendelssohn, 61; money as central to, 87–89; and Moyal, 199, 217–18; and *al-Muqtaṭaf*, 178–79; and Muslim Arabs, 106; and Nassar, 11, 90, 185, 186, 232; and newspapers, 87; as official organization, 35n74; and Ottoman limits on Jewish migration, 24n32; and Palestinian National Charter, 247; and Pius X, 237n8; rabbis as forbidding, 60–64; and race, 139n26; and racism, 13, 247; and Reform

movement, 229; and religion, 94; and Rida, 162, 165–69, 178; rise of, 18; as secular nationalist movement, 8; Sehayik on, 134n9; as separatist movement, 128–29; translated into Arabic, 69; and UN Resolution 3379, 247; and views of non-Jews, 93–130; and Zakka, 192–93; and E. Zaydan, 132. *See also* anti-Zionism; Jewish nationalism; nationalism
Zionist colonies, 33, 39, 76, 87–88, 92
Zionist Congress, 35n74
Zionist immigrants, 193n37
Zionist Organization, 11, 240; and Makaryus, 175–76; and N. Malul, 229; Palestine Office Press Bureau, 190–91, 192, 196
Zionist Organization of America, 48n32
Zionist press, 8–9
Zionists: and Arabic, 9, 187–90, 233; Arabs as perceived by, 1–2, 93–130; and attempts to influence Arabic press, 11, 186–87, 191–95; attitude toward Arabs, 126–30; and Christianity, 8, 115; and conquest of labor and land, 186–87; creation of Arabic newspaper by, 195–98; and economics, 233–34; and First vs. Second Aliyah, 34; and *ha-Ḥerut*, 97–98; and Islam, 8; and Jewishness as nonreligious, 113; and language and translation, 185, 186; and N. Malul, 233; and Mendelssohn, 61; and money, 192; and nationalism, 33–35; and natives of Palestine, 95; and old vs. new yishuv, 33–34; and race, 107; of Second Aliyah, 125; self-conceptions of, 94; Sephardic, 9, 95, 97–98, 126–30; socialist, 120–26; and urban vs. rural communities, 33; views of non-Jewish neighbors, 93–130
Zohar, 199, 216
Zürcher, Eric-Jan, 23n27

Jews, Christians, and Muslims from the Ancient to the Modern World

Edited by Michael Cook, William Chester Jordan, and Peter Schäfer

Imperialism and Jewish Society, 200 B.C.E. to 640 C.E.
by Seth Schwartz

A Shared World: Christians and Muslims in the Early Modern Mediterranean
by Molly Greene

Beautiful Death: Jewish Poetry and Martyrdom in Medieval France
by Susan L. Einbinder

Power in the Portrayal: Representations of Jews and Muslims in Eleventh- and Twelfth-Century Islamic Spain
by Ross Brann

Mirror of His Beauty: Feminine Images of God from the Bible to the Early Kabbalah
by Peter Schäfer

In the Shadow of the Virgin: Inquisitors, Friars, and Conversos *in Guadalupe, Spain*
by Gretchen D. Starr-LeBeau

The Curse of Ham: Race and Slavery in Early Judaism, Christianity, and Islam
by David M. Goldenberg

Resisting History: Historicism and Its Discontents in German-Jewish Thought
by David N. Myers

Mothers and Children: Jewish Family Life in Medieval Europe
by Elisheva Baumgarten

A Jewish Renaissance in Fifteenth-Century Spain
by Mark D. Meyerson

The Handless Maiden: Moriscos and the Politics of Religion in Early Modern Spain
by Mary Elizabeth Perry

Poverty and Charity in the Jewish Community of Medieval Egypt
by Mark R. Cohen

Reckless Rites: Purim and the Legacy of Jewish Violence
by Elliott Horowitz

Living Together, Living Apart: Rethinking Jewish-Christian Relations in the Middle Ages
by Jonathan Elukin

The Church in the Shadow of the Mosque: Christians and Muslims in the World of Islam
by Sidney H. Griffith

The Religious Enlightenment: Protestants, Catholics, and Jews from London to Vienna
by David Sorkin

American Evangelicals in Egypt: Missionary Encounters in an Age of Empire
by Heather J. Sharkey

Maimonides in His World: Portrait of a Mediterranean Thinker
by Sarah Stroumsa

The Scandal of Kabbalah: Leon Modena, Jewish Mysticism, Early Modern Venice
by Yaacob Dweck

Cultural Exchange: Jews, Christians, and Art in the Medieval Marketplace
by Jacob Shatzmiller

The Bible in Arabic: The Scriptures of the "People of the Book" in the Language of Islam by Sidney H. Griffith

Defining Neighbors: Religion, Race, and the Early Zionist-Arab Encounter
by Jonathan Marc Gribetz

GPSR Authorized Representative: Easy Access System Europe - Mustamäe tee 50, 10621 Tallinn, Estonia, gpsr.requests@easproject.com

www.ingramcontent.com/pod-product-compliance
Ingram Content Group UK Ltd.
Pitfield, Milton Keynes, MK11 3LW, UK
UKHW011645310326
469532UK00003B/154

* 9 7 8 0 6 9 1 1 7 3 4 6 7 *